Preventing Heterosexism and Homophobia

Primary Prevention of Psychopathology

George W. Albee and Justin M. Joffe
General Editors

VOLUMES IN THIS SERIES:

Prevention of Delinquent Behavior, 1987
John D. Burchard and Sara N. Burchard, *Editors*
VOLUME X

Families in Transition, 1988
Lynne A. Bond and Barry M. Wagner, *Editors*
VOLUME XI

Primary Prevention and Promotion in the Schools, 1989
Lynne A. Bond and Bruce E. Compas, *Editors*
VOLUME XII

Primary Prevention of AIDS, 1989
Vickie M. Mays, George W. Albee, and Stanley F. Schneider, *Editors*
VOLUME XIII

Improving Children's Lives, 1992
George W. Albee, Lynne A. Bond, and Toni V. Cook Monsey, *Editors*
VOLUME XIV

The Present and Future of Prevention, 1992
Marc Kessler, Stephen E. Goldston, and Justin M. Joffe, *Editors*
VOLUME XV

Promoting Successful and Productive Aging, 1995
Lynne A. Bond, Stephen J. Cutler, and Armin Grams, *Editors*
VOLUME XVI

Preventing Heterosexism and Homophobia, 1996
Esther D. Rothblum and Lynne A. Bond, *Editors*
VOLUME XVII

Volumes I-IX are available from
University Press of New England
3 Lebanon Street, Hanover, New Hampshire 03755

Preventing Heterosexism and Homophobia

Edited by
Esther D. Rothblum
Lynne A. Bond

Primary Prevention of Psychopathology 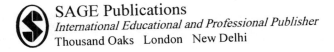 XVII

SAGE Publications
International Educational and Professional Publisher
Thousand Oaks   London   New Delhi

For information address:

SAGE Publications, Inc.
2455 Teller Road
Thousand Oaks, California 91320
E-mail: order@sagepub.com

SAGE Publications Ltd.
6 Bonhill Street
London EC2A 4PU
United Kingdom

SAGE Publications India Pvt. Ltd.
M-32 Market
Greater Kailash I
New Delhi 110 048 India

Printed in the United States of America

Library of Congress Cataloging-in-Publication Data

Main entry under title:

Preventing heterosexism and homophobia / editors, Esther D. Rothblum,
    Lynne A. Bond.
        p. cm. — (Primary prevention of psychopathology; v. 17)
        Based on the 17th Vermont Conference on the Primary Prevention of
    Psychopathology held in June 1995 at the University of Vermont.
        Includes bibliographical references (p.) and index.
        ISBN 0-7619-0022-5 (cloth: acid-free paper). — ISBN
    0-7619-0023-3 (pbk.: acid-free paper)
        1. Heterosexism—United States—Prevention—Congresses.
        2. Homophobia—United States—Prevention—Congresses. 3. Gays—
    United States—Social conditions—Congresses. I. Rothblum, Esther
    D. II. Bond, Lynne A., 1949- . III. Vermont Conference on the
    Primary Prevention of Psychopathology (17th: 1995: University of
    Vermont) IV. Series.
    RC454.P683 vol. 17
    [HQ76.3.U5]
    616.89′05 s—dc20
    [305.9′0664]   96-4511

This book is printed on acid-free paper.

96 97 98 99   10 9 8 7 6 5 4 3 2 1

Contents

Preface

This book grew in large part from the 17th Vermont Conference on the Primary Prevention of Psychopathology (VCPPP) convened in June 1995. This conference and this volume are part of a series of historically annual and more recently biannual meetings and publications developed at the University of Vermont since 1975. Each has drawn together professionals and community leaders from many disciplines—psychology, medicine, social work, education, sociology, biology, among others—to focus upon models, research, and programs of practice for the promotion of competence and the prevention of psychological dysfunction.

In the context of our commitment to address the prevention of heterosexism, we discovered that it was unusually difficult to secure funding for the 1995 meetings—highlighting, no doubt, the continuing hesitancy of public and private organizations to deal with the problem of heterosexism in a serious manner. We are extremely grateful to the array of groups and individuals who extended themselves to support the conference and publication of *Preventing Heterosexism and Homophobia*. We give special acknowledgment to the board of the Vermont Conferences of the Primary Prevention of Psychopathology, housed in the Department of Psychology at the University of Vermont, who not only provided the majority of financial resources necessary to complete this project but also made a commitment to support this effort regardless of the ability to secure additional extramural funds. Their faith in and commitment to the importance of this work were critically important to us.

Very special thanks go to the Wayne Placek Award of the American Psychological Foundation and members of the Placek Award Committee for their very generous support of the conference. This pioneering trust was established to support individual research grants, seminars, conferences, and other activities to advance the goal of increasing the general public's understanding of lesbians and gay men. The extraordinary value of this unique source of support and inspiration became ever more apparent as we worked to assemble resources for the Vermont Conference.

Our sincere thanks are also extended to the Haymarket People's Fund for Popular Struggle, the Society for the Psychological Study of Social Issues, the Haworth Press, and a number of units within the University of Vermont,

viii Preventing Heterosexism and Homophobia

including the Department of Psychology, Women's Studies Program, President's Commission on the Status of Women, Women's Advisory Committee, Division of Student Affairs, Employee Assistance Program, Office of Affirmative Action and Equal Opportunity, Living and Learning Center, Office of the Provost, and Office of the President. Each of these groups made generous contributions of resources to this effort. In particular, we note the extraordinary assistance of the University of Vermont's Division of Continuing Education throughout the planning and hosting of the conference. Their professionalism and expertise contributed significantly to the final product.

We want to acknowledge with special attention the individuals who served on this year's conference planning committee with us: Anna Myers-Parrelli and Melissa Perry played central roles in both planning and coordinating this event; Jacqueline Weinstock served as the instructor for a remarkable course on "Prevention of Heterosexism and Homophobia" that accompanied the conference and involved a number of conference attendees; Larry Rudiger generously assisted with conference publicity; Gisele Lizewski was superb, as always, in guiding us through so many aspects of the conference and speaker arrangements and budget operations.

This book was completed while Esther was a Visiting Scholar at the Institute for Research on Women and Gender at Stanford University. We would like to thank the institute for its resources and support.

We are also grateful to Sage Publications, Inc., for their interest in and support of the Vermont Conference series and their continuing commitment over the past 9 years in helping us in the development and dissemination of scholarly work in Primary Prevention. We continue to be convinced that these efforts are now more important than ever.

Esther D. Rothblum
Lynne A. Bond

Introduction: Approaches to the Prevention of Heterosexism and Homophobia

Esther D. Rothblum and Lynne A. Bond

For almost 20 years, the Vermont Conference on Primary Prevention, Inc., has held an annual or biannual conference in June devoted to some aspect of the prevention of risk factors or pathology and the promotion of competence. The theme for the 1995 conference became *The Prevention of Heterosexism and Homophobia.*

As we began to plan for the conference and this volume, we quickly discovered that few people knew the meaning of the word *heterosexism,* which refers to discrimination based on sexual orientation. In fact, the American Psychological Association guidelines for language free from heterosexual bias (Committee on Lesbian and Gay Concerns, 1991) stated a preference for this term rather than *homophobia,* because the latter individualizes discrimination by its association with a fear or phobia. We found, however, that some people assumed that *the prevention of heterosexism* meant a desire for people not to be heterosexual. Thus, for clarity, we chose to include both terms in the title of this book, recognizing, however, that both the labels *heterosexism* and *homophobia* introduce semantic concerns. Related issues of language will be addressed in greater detail in this volume (see, in particular, Chapter 1).

In the past two decades, there has been an increasing research focus on issues in the lives of lesbians, gay men, and bisexual individuals, such as the coming out process, aging, relationships, social interaction, and parenting. There has been comparatively little research, however, on lesbian, gay, and bisexual mental health, and that which has been done has focused mainly on gay men.

Both areas of research—understanding the lesbian, gay, and bisexual experience as well as lesbian, gay, and bisexual mental health issues—have indicated some domains in which lesbians, gay, and bisexual individuals are at *increased risk* for difficulties (e.g., substance abuse, anti-gay violence, teen suicide) as well as other areas in which they are at *decreased risk* for problems (based, for example, on more egalitarian relationships, shared child rearing, and strong peer supports that are less stratified by age or income). This book will examine both the risks and joys of being gay, lesbian, and bisexual, and how to prevent heterosexism and its effects on the lives of all people, including those of heterosexuals.

Prevention of heterosexism is particularly important for members of the mental health profession. Only recently have they begun to seriously contribute to its prevention; in contrast, through most of history, mental health professionals have contributed to the perpetuation of heterosexism as a pervasive problem. Recognition of this history is acknowledged, for example, by a donor who is seriously considering funding an endowed chair in gay and lesbian studies but who has stipulated that the chair be restricted to individuals outside the discipline of psychology because of the role of psychology in pathologizing homosexuality in the recent past (Linda Garnets, personal communication).

Meanwhile, the resolution of the American Psychological Association to deplore discrimination based on sexual orientation went further than those of other professional organizations by urging psychologists and other mental health professionals to "take the lead in removing the stigma of mental illness that has long been associated with homosexual orientation" (Conger, 1975, p. 633). Consequently, mental health professionals now have the challenge to be leaders in removing the very stigma that they so clearly helped to establish against lesbians, gay men, and bisexual people.

This duality, the shadow of our past and the promise of the future, illustrates health and mental health issues for lesbians and gay men today.

In the current decade, there has been a major shift in public knowledge about lesbians and gay men. The media has written affirmatively about lesbian, gay, and bisexual issues. Consider, for example, *Newsweek*'s June 21, 1993, cover story "Lesbians: Coming Out Strong; What Are the Limits of Tolerance?" that depicted two young, white lesbians embracing, as well as its July 17, 1995, cover story on "Bisexuality: Not gay. Not straight. A New Sexual Identity Emerges." As of the end of 1995, eight states had enacted gay civil rights laws. Surveys have indicated that the number of people in the United States who report "knowing someone gay" has increased from less than 20% to more than 40% in the past 2 years. Increasingly, institutions such as schools, corporations, health care clinics, and even the military have been under pressure to decrease former heterosexist practices.

In view of the national trends to prioritize knowledge about lesbian, gay, and bisexual issues and the currently available research on these topics, this book focuses on the prevention of heterosexism and homophobia. It is organized into three sections: (I) Institutions and Systems; (II) Relationships and Development; and (III) Societal Structures and Social Change.

I. Institutions and Systems

A variety of social, educational, political, and economic institutions and systems provide the context for our daily functioning. We have become more conscious of the dynamic transactional relationship between these systems and our individual and collective thinking, feeling, and behavior—each simultaneously shaping and yet responding to the other. In this way, each institution and system simultaneously reflects as well as contributes to the heterosexist nature of our environment and our assumptions. At the same time, these systems are potentially an extraordinarily powerful resource for resistance and for change—for preventing heterosexism and promoting full expression of human potential. A number of authors in this volume speak of the abuse and potential use of these resources.

We begin the volume with a consideration of language, which, perhaps more than any other system, permeates our lives throughout the life span of individuals and the history of our communities. When members of oppressed groups organize, they call into question the very terminology that has been used to categorize them in the first place. The society at large typically trivializes these efforts to change language (e.g., the efforts of the women's movement to refer to adult females as "women" rather than "girls" or to address women as "Ms." rather than "Mrs." or "Miss"). Meanwhile, the media focus and public outcry about issues of language underscore just how radical these changes are.

Celia Kitzinger has written extensively about the social construction of lesbianism and the language of politics and power in the emerging lesbian movement. In her opening chapter of this volume, "Speaking of Oppression: Psychology, Politics, and the Language of Power," she describes how psychological language has gradually replaced political language. As a result, the values of psychology—the focus on the individual, victim blaming, liberalism, and pervasiveness of therapy as a solution for political problems—have infiltrated the gay and lesbian communities. She examines the political consequences of language in our communities and the power of language in contributing to heterosexism.

The power of our educational system is also widely recognized and, in fact, relied upon by industrialized nations that place such great responsibility in the hands of educational institutions and processes. In many nations around the world, there is a clearly articulated relationship between the priorities, values, and beliefs of communities and those of their educational systems, enacted through the active involvement and control by local and regional school boards and trustees. Thus, in her chapter, Connie Chan discusses strategies to identify and prevent heterosexism in educational settings. She describes ways of addressing heterosexism in the curriculum, in research and scholarship, in the socialization norms that exist in educational settings, in the availability of role models and mentors, in personnel policies, and in overt and covert discrimination against lesbians, gay men, and bisexuals. Her focus is on structural changes in educational institutions and ways to celebrate diversity of sexual orientation.

Given the focus of this volume, mental health systems and institutions are of particular concern. Their role in defining and guiding expressions of health and well-being among those within and outside their formal structures is well established; and lesbians, gay men, and bisexual people are also consumers of all forms of mental health services. For example, Morgan (1992) found that 77.5% of the lesbians she surveyed had been in therapy, compared to 28.9% of the heterosexual women in her study.

Several authors in this volume address various dimensions relevant to the limitations and potential for psychotherapy and counseling to contribute to the prevention of heterosexism. Laura Brown presents an overview of strategies for the prevention of heterosexism in the training of mental health practitioners and in the practice of psychotherapy and counseling. She describes both the invisibility of information on sexual minority persons in the education and training of therapists and the heterosexist bias that still exists in the practice of psychotherapy. She advocates defining heterosexism as an ethical violation, to prevent individual therapists and training programs from ignoring more affirmative practice. She also proposes a model for *anti-domination training* to eliminate oppressive dominant biases.

Beverly Greene pays particular attention to assumptions and omissions that have distorted our understanding and treatment of lesbians and gay men of color. She argues, for example, that we must move beyond the legacy of ethnosexual mythologies in heterosexism if we are to restructure therapy in ways that will truly support *all* lesbians and gay men. Although, historically, most research samples of gay men, lesbians, and bisexual individuals consisted overwhelmingly of people of European descent, the past decade has resulted in an exponential increase in research, writing, and grassroots organizing that reflects the ethnic diversity of our communities. It is no longer possible to speak about lesbians, gay men, and bisexual individuals as ethnically homogeneous groups. The training and practice of mental health workers must reflect and respond to this diversity as well.

In light of the intensity and variety of stressors that our heterosexist society presents to lesbians, gay men, and bisexual individuals, perhaps it is not surprising that two surveys of lesbians found that approximately three-quarters had been in therapy (Bradford, Ryan, & Rothblum, 1994; Morgan, 1992). Meanwhile, in her chapter, Rachel Perkins warns us of the dangers of the overutilization of therapy in our communities. She argues that psychological terminology has replaced political activism in the lesbian communities and that therapy privatizes and individualizes lesbians' lives, weakening their community. At the same time, she notes that there are few resources for lesbians undergoing serious long-term mental health problems. Perkins advocates that lesbian communities organize around sharing resources for long-term caregiving, rather than privatizing and psychologizing pain via individual therapy.

II. Relationships and Development

Relationships provide a critical context for individual development and self-definition. Although the structure, intensity, and influence of various forms of relationships change over time and across the life course, they continue to provide a framework in which we explore, define, and express ourselves—our goals, our values, our potential, and our self-worth.

Most lesbians, gay men, and bisexual individuals develop in two somewhat distinct environments: the heterosexual macrostructure and the lesbian/gay/bisexual communities. Lukes and Land (1990) have described how members of minority groups become bicultural within the majority and minority cultures. They point out that lesbians and gay men differ from members of other minority groups in this process. Most minority groups first become acculturated within their own group and then later are socialized (by schools, the media, the church) within the dominant culture. Lesbians and gay men, however, are first socialized by the dominant culture and later identify with their minority culture.

Although it is true that heterosexual oppression affects everyone, living as a lesbian, gay man, or bisexual individual (whether closeted or out) presents unique challenges. In a society in which everyone is presumed to be heterosexual, the process of redefining the meaning and significance of certain relationships can not only require extraordinary questioning, determination, and strength but also introduce unusual stress, self-doubt, and feelings of isolation. Because the heterosexual macro-society is generally unsupportive of lesbians, gay men, and bisexual people, it becomes very important for lesbians, gay men, and bisexual individuals to have a supportive community. Many people vividly remember the feeling that they were the only lesbian or gay man in their area and the profound isolation they experienced before they came into contact with the gay community (Albro & Tully, 1979). The stress and vulnerability of the coming out process may result in the protective factors of finding (ideally) a supportive community.

Paula Rust considers certain of these issues in her chapter titled "Finding a Sexual Identity and Community." She critiques some of the more linear theories of coming out that fail to consider the possibility of changes in sexual identity over the life span or to conceptualize bisexuality as a mature option. She argues that the process of coming out is complex and can continue to change over time for many individuals. Rust offers strategies for recognizing and avoiding heterosexist, homophobic, and "biphobic" assumptions and behaviors that contribute tensions and difficulties to the ongoing process of identity development.

Life tasks can be especially difficult for lesbian, gay, and bisexual adolescents who rarely have full access to the lesbian and gay communities, which are typically more adult-oriented (Kourany, 1987). Lesbian, gay, and bisexual adolescents may not have access to resources, may be dependent on their school systems or parents for information about lesbian and gay issues, and may be punished or not taken seriously for their sexual orientation.

The U.S. Department of Health and Human Services found suicide to be the leading cause of death among lesbian, gay male, bisexual, and transsexual adolescents (Outright Vermont, 1992). Suicides by members of these groups may compose up to 30% of all completed suicides annually. The isolation of lesbian and gay youths also results in running away from home (or being thrown out of the home) and thus homelessness.

Anthony D'Augelli's chapter focuses on enhancing the development of gay, lesbian, and bisexual youths. As he indicates, there have been significant changes in the experiences of youths in the past decades, so that for some it is possible to come out into contemporary queer culture. At the same time, gay, lesbian, and bisexual youths in the 1990s are still coming out into isolation and invisibility, negative family reactions, and victimization. In addressing these issues, D'Augelli points to the critical and multifaceted strategies that schools, in particular, can pursue in order to support adolescents' transition into adulthood and into healthy gay, lesbian, and bisexual identities.

As individuals become part of a lesbian/gay/bisexual community, they seek to redefine their lives, which were once interpreted in the context of heterosexual norms. Suzanna Rose's chapter focuses on lesbian and gay male sexual relationships in light of the scripts, or pattern of actions, that we use to organize our thinking and actions. In particular, she describes the cultural scripts available for women and for men in the dominant culture, and how these scripts are modified in popular culture aimed at lesbians and gay men, respectively.

Oliva Espín has theorized the ways in which women's sexuality has served a symbolic function for the value systems of immigrant/refugee families. The majority of immigrants and refugees all over the world are women (Cole, Espín, & Rothblum, 1992). Yet there has been little focus on the experiences of female immigrants and refugees, and none on those who are lesbians. Espín's chapter in this volume focuses on immigrant and refugee lesbians. It describes how identity formation as a lesbian differs for women who migrate at early versus later ages and how this affects lesbians' sexual identity, sexual behavior, and the language of sexuality.

The role of parent introduces a complex web of satisfactions and stressors. The presence of young children in the home, in particular, can serve as a major risk factor for stress among heterosexual women who tend to do most of the child rearing in families (e.g., see Rothblum, 1983). Lesbians are less likely than heterosexual women to have children, and lesbians with children are likely to share child care responsibilities more fully with their partners (Peplau, Cochran, Rook, & Padesky, 1978). Thus, from several perspectives, mothering may be less of a risk factor for health and mental health problems among lesbians. On the other hand, lesbians and gay men who do rear children may be at increased risk for such factors as custody battles over competency to rear children, heterosexist/homophobic remarks made to the children, and stressors to children involved in coming out (Hall, 1981). The 1980s appeared to be the start of the lesbian baby boom and the 1990s may well be the start of the gay men's baby boom; thus, the characteristics and dynamics of this parenting factor may well change with these demographic transformations.

In her chapter, Charlotte Patterson considers the increasingly public presence of lesbian parents and points to the contributions of these parents and their children to the prevention of heterosexism. Her own longitudinal research has followed lesbian mothers and their children by birth or adoption. Not only do her results indicate positive adjustment of both the mothers and the children but the social contacts of the mothers and children have also made the larger communities aware of the normative existence of lesbian mothers and their children.

III. Societal Structures and Social Change

Around the world, social and political systems and their institutions are structured in ways that not only perpetuate but also presume heterosexist perspectives and practices. We cannot expect to become free of heterosexism without extraordinary transformations in the structure of our societies.

Michael Ross has examined the ways in which society structures norms regarding sexual orientation. In his chapter, he discusses how heterosexism affects the attitudes and behavior of gay men. Psychologists have measured stress by developing a life events scale; the more life events someone has experienced during a given year (e.g., the death of a family member, a wedding) the more stress they have experienced and the more vulnerable they are to illness and distress. In the context of our social structure and societal reactions, Ross has adapted the life events scale for gay men and examined the effects of gay life events, social supports, and acculturation into the gay communities.

When gay men and lesbians begin to disclose their sexual orientation, they are opening up their lives to public scrutiny and associated negative repercussions, for example, from the workplace, the legal system, and their family of origin (e.g., Gartrell, 1981). Half the sample of lesbians in the National Lesbian Health Care Survey (Bradford et al., 1994) had experienced verbal attacks for being lesbian and 6% had been physically attacked for being lesbian. A survey conducted by a Vermont gay and lesbian newspaper (*Out in the Mountains,* 1987) found that 80% of the respondents had experienced some form of harassment or violence and that 96% had concealed their sexual orientation to avoid intimidation, harassment, or violence. Eighty-nine percent of the sample knew people who were victims of anti-gay violence, 79% feared for their own safety, and 76% expected to be threatened or assaulted at some future point.

Jeanine Cogan's chapter focuses on the prevention of anti-lesbian and anti-gay hate crimes through empowerment and social change. She describes the heterosexist context of hate crimes and their effects on daily life and well-being. She focuses much of her chapter on approaches for conceptualizing and implementing prevention strategies on individual and societal levels to eliminate heterosexism and the anti-gay and anti-lesbian violence that it engenders.

Profound social change has been exhibited in evolving sexual practices since the early 1970s, both shaping and reflecting striking changes in household structure and composition. For example, the number of households headed by a married heterosexual couple decreased dramatically from 71% in 1970 to 55% in 1993, in large part reflecting an increase in households composed of single or nonrelated individuals (from 19% to 29% during the same period; Rawlings, 1994). Just as this social restructuring was gaining momentum, AIDS catapulted into our lives, introducing pressures upon sexual practices with unprecedented power and implications. Meanwhile, the interface of this virus with heterosexism could hardly have been imagined 20 years ago.

In her chapter, "Homo-Phobia, Homo-Ignorance, Homo-Hate: Heterosexism and AIDS," Lynda Ames describes the enormous impact heterosexism has had on how a disease, AIDS, "has been socially understood, scientifically researched, and medically treated." Ames describes how fear, ignorance, and hate have contributed to society's understanding and misunderstanding of gay men and gay male sexuality. Of course, heterosexism has also contributed to the erroneous assumption that lesbians are at high risk for AIDS and at the same time created virtual invisibility for lesbians who do have HIV/AIDS.

This book ends with a chapter by Joy Livingston, who presents a vision of a future free from heterosexism. She emphasizes that heterosexism is so interdependent with other systems of oppression, including sexism, racism, and classism, that a future free from heterosexism may well be imagined as a utopia free of the ills of the world. Meanwhile, Livingston provides some very concrete achievable strategies for battling heterosexism in our current social structure. Focusing on actions on an immediate and individual level as well as more broad-scale political action, she provides a path for accomplishing both short-term and longer-term social change.

It is clear that if we hope to move beyond a heterosexist society, we must pursue a number of strategies for rethinking and restructuring societal assumptions and practices. The authors in this volume point to diverse approaches and with varied levels of optimism about their potential. Although our long history provides reason for doubting the likelihood that we will see rapid advances in combating heterosexism and homophobia, the more recent attention and action on these fronts suggest that continued progress is at least possible. It is clear that for the health and well-being of lesbians, gay men, bisexual individuals, and heterosexual individuals too, we must continue to develop and implement effective prevention and promotion strategies.

Building upon the work of the authors in this volume, and drawing from the broader scholarship and practice, we highlight a few additional related themes that we feel will offer direction for the future:

1. Teaching and Training. Lesbian, gay, and bisexual issues can neither be delegated to writing or lecturing on pathology nor be confined to the context of sexual behavior. Rather, these issues must be discussed throughout the curriculum of social and developmental psychology, the psychology of diverse ethnic populations, social work, aging, obstetrics, public health, and family practice medicine, to mention just a few.

2. Research. A recent APA task force has provided guidelines for conducting nonheterosexist research (Herek, Kimmel, Amaro, & Melton, 1991). The report indicates that research should neither ignore the existence of lesbians, gay men, and bisexual individuals nor stigmatize or stereotype these populations. Further, we would urge researchers to reward and encourage others to conduct research on lesbian, gay male, and bisexual issues instead of expressing caution that it might adversely affect their careers.

3. Practice. The APA Task Force on Bias in Psychotherapy (Garnets, Hancock, Cochran, Goodchilds, & Peplau, 1991) also identified a number of examples of lesbian-, gay-, and bisexual-affirmative practice. These included not only sensitivity in assessment and intervention but also recognition of issues facing lesbians, gay men, and bisexual people in identity development, relationship formation and maintenance, and the importance of practitioner education and expertise.

4. Protective Factors. Factors that protect lesbians, gay men, and bisexual individuals from health and mental health risks should be recognized and serve as models for affirming the lesbian and gay communities. These factors should be cited in the training of health and mental health professionals rather than raised only in the context of a focus on lesbians and gay men under the rubric of pathology or sexual activity.

5. Risk Factors. There is little research on mental health problems that affect lesbians and gay men other than substance use and suicide, and there is practically no mental health research on bisexual people. This is a broad area for development and involves issues related to practice, research, and prevention.

6. Diversity. In the 1970s, the lesbian and gay communities were pictured as predominantly young, European American, middle class, and able-bodied. The past decade has resulted in an exponential increase in research, writing, and grassroots organizing that reflect the diversity of our communities. This diversity must be reflected in all dimensions of the work we do, whether it concerns theory, research, training, or practice.

We have come to realize that there is no simple or unitary goal that we are working toward in the prevention of heterosexism. Instead, our interlocking pathways will form a tightly knit and unique landscape, reflecting the diversity of our experiences. To paraphrase Charles Silverstein (1987, p. 6), may the "love that dare not speak its name" never shut up.

References

Albro, J. C., & Tully, C. (1979). A study of lesbian lifestyles in the homosexual micro-culture and the heterosexual macro-culture. *Journal of Homosexuality, 4,* 331-344.

Bradford, J., Ryan, C., & Rothblum, E. D. (1994). The National Lesbian Mental Health Care Survey: Implications for mental health. *Journal of Consulting and Clinical Psychology, 62,* 228-242.

Cole, E., Espín, O. M., & Rothblum, E. D. (Eds.). (1992). *Shattered societies, shattered lives: Refugee women and their mental health.* New York: Haworth.

Committee on Lesbian and Gay Concerns. (1991). Avoiding heterosexual bias in language. *American Psychologist, 46,* 973-974.

Conger, J. (1975). Proceedings of the American Psychological Association, Inc., for the year 1987: Minutes of the annual meeting of the Council of Representatives. *American Psychologist, 30,* 620-651.

Garnets, L., Hancock, K. A., Cochran, S. D., Goodchilds, J., & Peplau, L. A. (1991). Issues in psychotherapy with lesbians and gay men. *American Psychologist, 46,* 964-972.

Gartrell, N. (1981). The lesbian as a "single" woman. *American Journal of Psychotherapy, 35,* 502-509.

Hall, M. (1981). Lesbian families: Cultural and clinical issues. In E. Howell & M. Bayes (Eds.), *Women and mental health* (pp. 373-384). New York: Basic Books.

Herek, G. M., Kimmel, D. C., Amaro, H., & Melton, G. B. (1991). Avoiding heterosexist bias in psychological research. *American Psychologist, 46,* 957-963.

Kourany, R. F. C. (1987). Suicide among homosexual adolescents. *Journal of Homosexuality, 13,* 111-117.

Lukes, C. A., & Land, H. (1990). Biculturality and homosexuality. *Social Work, 35,* 155-161.

Morgan, K. S. (1992). Caucasian lesbians' use of psychotherapy. *Psychology of Women Quarterly, 16,* 127-130.

Out in the Mountains. (1987, June). VLGR discrimination and violence results, p. 7.

Outright Vermont. (1992, February 20). [Unpublished resource letter.] Burlington, VT.

Peplau, L. A., Cochran, S., Rook, K., & Padesky, C. (1978). Loving women: Attachment and autonomy in lesbian relationships. *Journal of Social Issues, 34,* 2-27.

Rawlings, S. W. (1994). Household and family characteristics: March 1993. *U.S. Bureau of the Census. Current Population Reports, P20-477.* Washington, DC: Government Printing Office.

Rothblum, E. D. (1983). Sex-role stereotypes and depression in women. In V. Franks & E. D. Rothblum (Eds.), *The stereotyping of women: Its effects on mental health* (pp. 83-111). New York: Springer.

Silverstein, C. (Ed.). (1991). *Gays, lesbians, and their therapists.* New York: Norton.

PART I

Institutions and Systems

1

Speaking of Oppression: Psychology, Politics, and the Language of Power

Celia Kitzinger

The North American psychoanalyst Charles Socarides was recently in Britain as the invited guest speaker for a prominent psychoanalytic organization, the Association for Psychoanalytic Psychotherapy in the National Health Service. His view is that homosexuals are sick, compulsively driven by their unnatural urges into abnormal forms of sexual behavior. He has said that homosexuality is "a revision of the basic code and concept of life and biology" and in 1994 he described the 1973 decision by the American Psychiatric Association to remove homosexuality per se from the *Diagnostic and Statistical Manual of Mental Disorders* (*DSM*) as "an encouragement to aberrancy." He continues to recommend conversion therapies to return lesbians and gay men to sexual normality (Rayner, 1995, p. 18).

For the purposes of clinicians concerned with the prevention of psychopathology, it is important to note that Charles Socarides is concerned with the prevention of psychopathology—as he defines it. Historically, the prevention of psychopathology has often meant reinforcing dominant sexual, social, and political values. The prevention of psychopathology has been defined in terms ruthlessly suited to upholding the status quo. By defining certain thoughts or behaviors as pathological, we invalidate them and we justify or legitimate our attempts to change them. Very often, in the history of psychology and psychiatry, the thoughts and behaviors so labeled are those that are socially and politically deviant. This has been seen as the deliberate use of diagnosis as a tool of oppression to punish and control those who fail to conform to the dominant group's expectations of them. Two often quoted prototypical examples of such diseases are "drapetomania" and "dysthesia

AUTHOR'S NOTE: Portions of this chapter are based on material in *The Social Construction of Lesbianism* (Kitzinger, 1987) and *Changing Our Minds: Lesbian Feminism and Psychology* (Kitzinger & Perkins, 1993).

3

aethiopis," both diagnosed by the North American 19th-century physician Cartwright (1981) as diseases peculiar to slaves. The main symptom of drapetomania is running away from the plantations; dysthesia aethiopis (also known as rascality) is caused by idleness and cured by whipping and hard physical labor. Similar inventions include the Victorian diseases of "masturbatory insanity," "moral insanity," and "hysteria," cures for which included compulsory bed rest, bleeding with leeches, incarceration in asylums, hysterectomy, and clitoridectomy (Chesler, 1972). More recently, in the 1970s in the United Kingdom, there was a disease known as "state benefit neurosis," an illness characterized by refusing to take poorly paid employment when more money is available through state benefits (Pearson, 1975).

The authors of the powerful and influential *Diagnostic and Statistical Manual of Mental Disorders* (*DSM*) take upon themselves the right to define who is normal and who is suffering from pathology. One of the diagnostic categories that has caused particular concern is the "self-defeating personality disorder," drawn from the earlier psychoanalytic notion of masochism and disproportionately applied to women, particularly those who apparently "choose" not to leave abusive situations. A leading feminist psychologist (Caplan, 1991) describes this diagnosis as "virulently misogynist," and as "a way to call psychopathological the women who had conformed to societal norms for a 'feminine' woman" (p. 171). Caplan points out that there is no parallel diagnosis that pathologizes men conforming to social norms for "real men"—a sort of John Wayne syndrome or Macho Personality Disorder. This eventually led to her proposal for the inclusion in the *DSM* of the "Delusional Dominating Personality Disorder," which includes criteria such as the delusion of personal entitlement to the services of women; the delusion that women like to suffer and be ordered around; the delusion that physical force is the best method of solving interpersonal problems; and a pathological need for flattery about one's sexual performance, the size of one's genitalia, or both. Like drapetomania and state benefit neurosis, Caplan's new diagnostic category illustrates, albeit from a different perspective, the extent to which social norms are incorporated into diagnostic categories. The explicit justification for *all* these diagnoses is the prevention of psychopathology.

Given this history, it is very important that those psychologists, therapists, and clinicians concerned with the prevention of psychopathology be clear about the social, ethical, and political norms that underlie their definitions of mental health and of mental disease, of psychological well-being and of pathology. In defining homophobia and heterosexism as forms of psychopathology, it is important to think through in some detail just what is meant by these terms, and the political consequences of our various definitions. We cannot assume that this is obvious or nonproblematic, or that psychology necessarily gives us tools adequate for the job we have to do.

Psychology's Heterosexism

One important reason why psychology and its associated mental health disciplines may not offer appropriate tools for challenging or preventing anti-lesbian and anti-gay behavior is because psychology itself is a heterosexist discipline. I am delighted, however, to be able to report that Socarides's message was not well received in the United Kingdom. In addition to the boycotts and demonstrations organized by lesbian and gay groups, his views were widely reported in the media and dismissed as old-fashioned, offensive, or simply ridiculous. Two hundred psychotherapists, including nine professors of psychiatry, signed a letter of concern about the continuing stigmatization of lesbians and gays by the psychoanalytic establishment, which was sent to six academic periodicals, to the Royal College of Psychiatrists, and the Health Secretary (Jones, 1995). The uproar about Socarides's views finally led the Conservative Government Minister, John Bowis, Under-Secretary for Health, to make a public statement condemning prejudice against homosexuality and praising the richness that lesbian and gay people add to our society (Bowcott, 1995).

Does this mean, then, that with the exception of a few diehards whose views are no longer taken seriously, there is no longer a problem of heterosexism within psychology? The evidence suggests otherwise. For example, a survey of 48 undergraduate psychology textbooks found that material on gay men and lesbians was characteristically presented under headings that imply sickness (*sexual deviation* or *sexual dysfunction*), and for every source of accurate information on lesbians and gay men, this textbook survey turned up four sources of misleading information or heterosexual bias (Hall, 1985). Even when male homosexuality merits a passing reference, lesbians are often omitted; only about one quarter of these introductory textbooks mentioned lesbians at all. Even in "psychology of women" textbooks, discussion of lesbianism is typically limited to two or three pages out of several hundred, heterosexuality is depicted as the norm, and all sexuality is assumed to be heterosexual unless otherwise stated (Fontaine, 1982). Although explicit pathologizing of homosexuality per se is now relatively rare, when psychologists are given hypothetical case histories and asked to rate the subjects for severity of problems, likelihood of recovery, and so on, cases are judged as much more severely disturbed when labeled *gay* than if such a label is not present (Hall, 1985). Lesbian and gay psychologists (and their students) continue to suffer discrimination and oppression in the workplace: A recent survey in the United States by D'Augelli (1989) found that three quarters of lesbians and gay men in a university environment had experienced verbal abuse, 26% had been threatened with violence, and 17% had had personal property damaged; a more recent, smaller British study (Wilde, 1995) revealed similar findings. We also confront blatant heterosexism systematically built into conditions of employment and contractual arrangements: Relocation expenses, for example, often apply to the prospective employee plus legally defined "spouse" only, and occupational pension schemes rarely cover a same-sex partner, so there are privileges for people who enter into heterosexual marriages that lesbians and gay men (as well as single people) are prevented from sharing (Kitzinger, 1990, 1991).

Moreover, it is clear that the development of lesbian and gay perspectives in psychology is subject to ridicule, incomprehension, and trivialization. Members of the American Psychological Association rate the work of Division 44 (the Society for the Psychological Study of Lesbian and Gay Issues) *even lower* in importance and interest than that of the Division for the Psychology of Women. In the United Kingdom, there is no formally recognized forum within the British Psychological Society for lesbian and gay psychology because proposals have been turned down by the Society's council on three separate occasions (cf. Comely, Kitzinger, Perkins, & Wilkinson, 1992; Coyle et al., 1995). Very recently, I coauthored (Kitzinger & Coyle, 1995) an article about lesbian and gay relationships for *The Psychologist* (the U.K. national professional journal, roughly equivalent to the North American journal, *American Psychologist*). The following two extracts give an indication of psychologists' responses; they were published under the heading, "Are You Normal?":

> I object to the misleading use in a publication of a scientific society of the innocent-sounding word "gay" when referring to what is the abnormal practice of anal intercourse between males. Secondly, I object to attempts to mislead readers about the epidemiological incidence and prevalence of male and female homosexuality which in statistical-mathematical terms is fortunately still tiny. (Hamilton, 1995, p. 151)

> In their account of lesbian and gay relationships, Drs. Kitzinger and Coyle wrote of it being "usual for heterosexuality to be everywhere flaunted" in the workplace. Do I detect a certain amount of underlying annoyance that at work, as elsewhere, there is, indeed, a normality of life for the vast majority of people? It is certainly not a matter of heterosexuality being flaunted—it is simply the ordinariness of life from which homosexuals and lesbians, however much they may wish it were different, are perforce excluded. (Davis, 1995, pp. 151-152)

Although it is true that these comments provoked a deluge of letters from psychologists protesting against this narrow definition of normality and arguing for the celebration of diversity and difference, it was also significant that those who characterized homosexuality as healthy agreed with those who characterized it as abnormal in opposing the proposal for a formal group (a Section is equivalent to an APA Division) within the British Psychological Society:

> The creation of a Gay and Lesbian Section in the Society would itself be the ultimate in homophobic actions, damaging the very cause it seeks to promote. If it is reasonable to believe that homosexual people are not abnormal, but merely different from heterosexual people in respect of one area of their development, namely their sexuality, what sense can it make to group them together as requiring their own global perspective on psychology? To create such a grouping is surely to stereotype homosexual people and to exaggerate differences between them and heterosexual people beyond the sexual domain. (Seager, 1995, p. 295)

Despite the problems, there have certainly been changes in mental health professionals' approach to homosexuality over the past few decades. During the 1950s and 1960s, the view of homosexuality as psychopathology was commonplace; now that same view is vigorously protested *by psychologists*—the very people who originally endorsed it. Such changes are often incorporated into the mythologized history of a discipline in what has been described (by philosopher of science Richard Rorty, 1980) as the "up-the-mountain" story. Its function is to illustrate the superiority of contemporary research over that of the past. Once upon a time, the story goes, researchers thought that homosexuals were sick and perverted. This was because they were biased by religious prejudices and trapped by the social conventions of their time; their research lacked present-day sophistication and objectivity. Now, in our sexually liberated age, with the benefit of scientific rigor and clear vision, objective up-to-date research demonstrates that lesbians and gay men are just as normal, just as healthy, and just as valuable members of a pluralistic society as are heterosexual people. This story is told in most literature reviews and overviews of research on homosexuality. According to Krieger (1982), all contemporary research discussions of homosexuality reiterate some version of this story.

An alternative to the up-the-mountain story is what one might call the "shifting oppression" story, which is the account of the history of research on lesbianism that I have advanced elsewhere (Kitzinger, 1987). A story of shifting oppression suggests that oppression can take many different forms. One form is prohibition and suppression, the old-fashioned model, in which we were seen as pathological simply by virtue of being lesbian or gay, and psychology's efforts were focused on preventing and eradicating this pathology: That form of oppression was becoming increasingly untenable in the face of lesbian and gay protest. The modern form of psychology's oppression of gays and lesbians is more subtle and more invidious. Instead of simply prohibiting and suppressing homosexuality, psychology shapes and constructs lesbian and gay identities and politics in its own image. As lesbians and gay men, we learn, often through lesbian and gay psychologists, to speak of ourselves and our lives in the language of psychology, thus unwittingly incorporating the value judgments and ideologies on which psychology itself is based—its individualism, its victim blaming, its depoliticizing, its liberalism. Both the pervasiveness of therapy and counseling in lesbian and gay communities and the huge and growing number of popular psychology and self-help books now to be found on lesbian and gay bookshelves contribute to the insistent psychologizing of lesbian and gay experience.

In this chapter, I explore just one way in which this psychologizing manifests itself: through the language used to speak of lesbian and gay oppression. An important aim of this chapter is to encourage us all to reflect on the terms we use to describe the form our oppression takes and how we might struggle against that oppression. As will be obvious from many of the examples, I write from the political position of radical feminism, but the basic argument (that we need to consider the politics implicit in the words and phrases we adopt) is relevant to everyone who speaks of lesbian and gay issues, from whatever political position.

Homophobia

The word *homophobia* (and its "feminine" derivative, *lesbophobia*) has offered an explanation of the hatred, anger, and fear homosexuality arouses in so many people. It has articulated our experience and been useful to us in our struggles as lesbians and gay men. But it is my contention that we have paid heavily for these benefits. Unlike terms such as *sexism* or *heterosexism,* which were developed within the Women's and Gay Liberation Movements and modeled on *political* concepts, the word *homophobia* derives from (and is used within) the academic discipline of psychology: *phobia* comes from the Greek for "fear," as in claustrophobia or agoraphobia, meaning an irrational fear or dread. The notion that some people might have a phobia about gay men and lesbians first began to appear in psychological writing in the late 1960s and early 1970s, and homophobia was defined as "an irrational persistent fear or dread of homosexuals" (MacDonald, 1976, p. 23) or "an irrational fear or intolerance of homosexuality" (Lehne, 1976, p. 89). The word became widely used only after 1973, when a psychoanalyst, Dr. George Weinberg, published a popular book on homosexuality in which he used the word. I want to raise three key concerns about the term *homophobia*.

First, in defining fear of homosexuality as *irrational,* as a phobia, the concept of homophobia is completely at odds with radical lesbian feminist theory. The term *homophobia* assumes a political or ideological position in which homosexuals are basically the same as heterosexuals and do not challenge or threaten society—a political position that is not argued or made explicit but is simply assumed. We cannot think of lesbianism as a challenge to heteropatriarchal structures and values (as radical feminists do) and simultaneously claim that there are no reasonable grounds for heterosexual men (or women) to fear lesbians. We cannot write, as Adrienne Rich (1979) has done, that "a militant and pluralistic lesbian/feminist movement is potentially the greatest force in the world for a complete transformation of society" (p. 226) and simultaneously claim that fear of lesbianism is irrational. The psychological framework within which homophobia is located evades these political implications and presents lesbians as essentially harmless. Fear of lesbianism is just another phobia some people have—thus obscuring the fact that there are good reasons for fearing lesbianism and denying lesbianism its revolutionary potential. Tests designed to measure homophobia include items such as the following—unless you agree with these items you score points toward being homophobic:

> The basic difference between homosexuals and other people is only in their sexual behavior (Dannecker, 1981)
>
> Homosexuals are just like everyone else; they simply chose an alternative lifestyle (Hansen, 1982)
>
> Just as in other species, homosexuality is a natural expression of sexuality in humans (Millham, Miguel, & Kellogg, 1976)
>
> Homosexuality is just as natural as heterosexuality (Millham et al., 1976)

The following statements are reverse scored: that is, unless you disagree with them, you receive homophobia points:

> Homosexuality endangers the institution of the family (Larsen, Reed, & Hoffman, 1980)
>
> If homosexuality is allowed to increase, it will destroy our society (Price, 1982)

According to these tests, the nonhomophobic or unprejudiced person must say that there is no difference between gays and straights, that lesbianism is merely a sexual preference or choice of lifestyle, that it is normal and natural (even the birds and the bees do it), and that it does *not* threaten the nuclear family or society as we know it. The ideas that homosexuality is rooted in nature or biology and that lesbianism poses no threat to a heteropatriarchal society are contested interpretations, however, and cannot simply be incorporated into operational definitions of homophobia as if they represent known truths about the world.

Second, the word *phobia* is a psychological diagnosis; that is, those suffering from homophobia are considered to have something wrong with them psychologically. Although it may be convenient to label one's political enemies as mentally ill, to do so removes the argument from the political arena and relocates it within the domain of psychology, giving more power and prestige to an oppressive institution. The psychological literature on homophobia replaces the "sick" homosexual with the "sick" homophobe. "I would never consider a patient healthy unless he had overcome his prejudice against homosexuality," wrote psychoanalyst George Weinberg (1973, p. 1). Other mental health professionals have described homophobia as "a severe disturbance" (Freedman, 1978, p. 320) and as "a mental health issue of the first magnitude" (Marmor, 1980, p. 1). Psychologists have described homophobes as authoritarian, dogmatic, and sexually rigid individuals who have low levels of ego development and suffer from a whole range of personal problems and difficulties in their relationships (Hudson & Ricketts, 1980; MacDonald & Games, 1974; Weis & Dain, 1979). Not only does this concept reinforce the power of psychology to label people as sick or mentally healthy at will; it also depoliticizes lesbian and gay oppression by suggesting that it comes from the personal inadequacy of particular individuals suffering from a diagnosable phobia. Psychology has systematically replaced *political* explanations (in terms of structural, economic, and institutional oppression) with *personal* explanations (in terms of the dark workings of the psyche, the mysterious functioning of the subconscious). When we use terms like *homophobia* and *lesbophobia,* we are buying into this whole psychological scenario. We are imputing sickness to specific individuals who supposedly deviate from the rest of society in being prejudiced against us. We are borrowing a term from a psychology that has always reserved for itself the right to decide who is and who is not sick, and for which a shift from classifying *homosexuals* as sick to classifying *homophobes* as sick is far less threatening than any attempt to look at the issue in political terms. Moreover, if homophobes are sick, the implication is that they should be treated with compassion. There has already been one court case in which the defense argued that a man who murdered a gay man should be treated leniently because he was suffering from "homosexual panic."

Third, the term *homophobia* is used to attribute psychopathology to lesbians and gay men. Although many of us now no longer believe in the need to go to heterosexual therapists like Socarides to be cured of our homosexuality, we now go to lesbian and gay therapists to be cured of *internalized homophobia.* The focus is yet again shifted away from the oppressor and back onto the victims of oppression: The clients are helped "to see all the ways in which they may maintain a victim attitude or provoke and perpetuate their social isolation" (Decker, 1984, p. 50). Internalized homophobia joins erotophobia, codependency, and merger as forms of pathology especially likely to be suffered by lesbians (cf. Kitzinger & Perkins, 1993).

The term *homophobia* is only one of a whole lexicon of terms that have been invented to talk about our oppression; others include *heterosexism* or *psychological heterosexism, anti-lesbian* and *anti-gay harassment, homo-hatred,* or a specific *hate crime.* Each term draws our attention to some aspect of our oppression but, by the same token, obscures others (see Kitzinger, 1994, for a detailed discussion of this point). So, for example, harassment, derived from a variant of the Old French *harer,* "to set a dog on," suggests a discrete incident or a series of such incidents, directed at the person who is being harassed (name-calling, assault, vandalism). It less obviously refers simply to an offensive milieu, and it still sounds odd, implausible, and extreme for me to claim that I am harassed by having to live and work in a society in which heterosexuality is everywhere flaunted—from the wedding photographs on my colleagues' desks to the heterosexual student couples entwined around each other all over the campus. Harassment primes one to see particular actions rather than the bias of a whole culture—yet no analysis of our oppression can be complete without an understanding both of discrete acts of harassment and of the heterosexist system within which they occur.

Similarly, most of these terms (*homophobia, harassment, homohatred, hate crime*) are interpreted as referring to something that happened. It is quite difficult to read them as meaning silences, absences, evasions. Yet when there is *no* anti-lesbian explosion from your parents, because you have de-dyked your apartment before their visit; when there is *no* queer-bashing after the gay disco, because you anticipated trouble and booked a cab to get home; when you are *not* dismissed from work, because you stayed in the closet; when you are *not* subjected to prurient or disgusted questions, because you talked about your weekend activities in sentences that meticulously avoided the use of any pronouns—when these non-events slip by as part of many gay men and lesbians' daily routine, has *nothing* really happened? Rather, het-erosexism has been functioning in its most effective and most deadly way. In an oppressive society, it is not necessary, most of the time, to beat us up or to murder or torture us to ensure our silence and invisibility. This is because a climate of terror has been created instead in which most gay people *voluntarily* and of our own free will *choose* to stay silent and invisible.

The concept of the hate crime incorporates the important idea that assault can sometimes be understood not as a random, opportunistic, or particularis-tic attack but rather as the targeting of members of specific groups as symbols of that group: The term points to the way in which some actions not only harm their victims but also send a message of intimidation and fear to entire communities. The term also signals the seriousness of anti-lesbian and anti-gay attacks. Like most of the other terms, however, *hate crimes* implies that the major forms of harassment are discrete incidents (thus obscuring the social context) and, more seriously, use of the word *crime* fails to capture the oppression of gay men and lesbians through legal tolerance of, indifference to, or promotion of our oppression.

In sum, then, terms such as *homophobia, heterosexism,* and *anti-lesbian* and *anti-gay harassment* are neither transparent nor unproblematic. We need to notice their political effects and implications and decide whether these are the politics we wish to promote.

Language Matters

Language does much more than simply provide a convenient label or tag for the world. The words we use to talk about lesbian and gay experience reflect and constitute our politics. Lesbian and gay groups have been aware of this for a very long time—certainly since adopting the term *gay* (that "innocent-sounding" little word), going on to argue with each other about the male bias of *gay* and the ethnocentrism of *lesbian,* and appropriating the oppressors' language (dyke, queer, fag) as a badge of pride. To call us lesbians is to make one kind of political statement; to call us gay women, female homosexuals, or queers is to make others, with very different meanings. The power of naming is, as Mary Daly (1978) has shown, to define the quality and value of that which is named and to deny reality to that which is not named.

Psychological language provides us with a particular way of naming our experience and talking about our oppression and, as such, it has political implications. Psychological models reflect and perpetuate certain ways of looking at the world, specific theories of lesbian and gay oppression. These are (almost by definition) profoundly individualistic, privatized, and depoliticized theories. As I showed in my first book, *The Social Construction of Lesbianism* (Kitzinger, 1987), academic psychology, through its rhetorical use of "objectivity," promotes liberal humanistic models of homosexuality that are fundamentally at variance with radical lesbian feminist theories. As I argued in *Changing Our Minds* (Kitzinger & Perkins, 1993), popular psychology (in the form of self-help books, TV talk shows, and the practice of psychotherapy) presents itself as offering what we have sought and often failed to achieve in our political movements—offering us liberation, power, freedom of choice—everything we've always wanted, with personal happiness thrown in as well. In attempting to make these claims plausible, psychology redefines the meanings of these political terms. In their therapeutic reformulations, power, liberation, and freedom of choice refer to individual, internal, psychic phenomena instead of social and political transformation. Words like *choice, power,* and *freedom* can be used in a variety of different contexts to carry all sorts of political freight. In developing our political strategies in and against a heterosexist world, it is important to be aware of the range of ways in which words are used and to understand what is highlighted by these particular uses and what is obscured.

Take the word *power,* for example. Lesbians and feminists have repeatedly demonstrated that men exercise power through their control over women. Male power is vested in the state or in governments that outlaw lesbians, endorse police harassment, refuse public acknowledgment of our relationships, and sack us from our jobs. Male power means domination, oppression, coercion: It is real, concrete, and it affects our daily lives as women and lesbians. Lesbians know that, even under male domination, we are not completely powerless. We have power over those weaker than us; we may have power over other lesbians who are oppressed in ways we are not; we have the power of sabotage, the power to withdraw consent from male versions of reality, and the power to separate ourselves from them. Those are real powers. But we do not have the kind of power men have to the same extent that men have it. Women's power exists only within the framework of male domination and the institution of compulsory heterosexuality. White ruling-class male power makes the rules; lesbians (sometimes) have the power to break, evade, or protest against the rules. Those powers are not symmetrical. Psychology claims to offer us power: real power—but a different, "special" version. This power has nothing to do with governments or states, laws or institutions. It lies inside us. Power, in the psychological reformulation of the term, means getting in touch with our authentic, natural self, the inner child, a free spirit supposedly untouched by social oppression, that can spontaneously generate its own actions and free choices. According to Louise Hay (1984), author of the best-selling *Heal Your Body:*

> No person, no place and no thing has any power over you, for you are the only thinker in your own mind. You are the creative power, and you are the authority in your life. All that is necessary is to get in touch with this inner power.

Psychologist Lynne Namka (1989) describes how to do this:

> Stand and bring your personal power to one place by closing your eyes and breathing deeply. Plant your feet firmly on the ground and feel your connection with the earth. . . . Breathe deeply, knowing you are in touch with the power

of the universe. . . . State the following affirmations as you pull the power of the universe through you by deep breathing. State the following words out loud in your Power Voice. Practice saying them in a loud voice until you really believe from you are saying. I am a woman/man of power. I centre myself drawing on that internal strength from within. I stand tall and proud of my ability to draw from my own inner strength. I am a woman/man of true personal power. (p. 59)

Power, then, is reformulated by psychologists as an awareness, an affirmation, a belief that you already have power. Lesbians and feminists say that we want power. By *power* some of us mean the power to prevent male violence against women and to end the oppression of lesbians, the power to speak and be heard. Psychology redefines power in privatized and individualized terms, as ours already, as waiting to be tapped if only we will stand still, breath deeply, and get in touch with the universe. Power, as it is often used by psychologists, is a sense of personal agency quite unrelated to the objective and material facts of our lives.

In much psychological language, choice, too, is ours for the asking. We have unlimited choices in life and can choose to do or be just whatever we want. Jane Mara (1983), a lesbian/feminist psychotherapist and cofounder of the Women's Growth and Therapy Center Collective in Washington, D.C., says,

We have a choice about our lives. . . . We can choose to live in and collude with the patriarch's creation of reality, thus strengthening and enforcing it, or we can choose to leave it behind and create a reality which nurtures and sustains us as wimmin, as lesbians individually and collectively. In recognizing this choice, we learn that we are utterly responsible for our own lives. (p. 152)

We are utterly responsible for our own lives and can just "choose" to leave patriarchy behind. One of Jane Mara's patients is quoted as saying, "Goodbye patriarchy, hello ME."

When early second-wave feminists fought for a woman's right to choose, this didn't mean women's right to overcome unconscious blocks and to get in touch with their inner needs. It meant actual material changes in the world—free contraception and abortion on demand. As women of color forced white European and North American feminists to become more aware of the oppression of women through compulsory sterilization, the dumping of dangerous contraceptive devices, and enforced abortion, the concept of choice was expanded to mean, again, structural changes in the real world, including challenging drug companies and "population control" policies. Choice was not conceptualized as an individual, private phenomenon, it was public and political. Susan Himmelweit (1988) has addressed the question of what choice means with specific reference to reproductive rights:

> If we question whether the right to choose has been genuinely exercised when a woman chooses to abort a female foetus because of the greater value put on sons, should we not also do so when she aborts a foetus with Downs syndrome because society does not provide sufficient support to make raising a mentally handicapped child a choice she can contemplate? And what about the woman who chooses an abortion because her low woman's wage does not make single parenthood, even with a healthy child, economically feasible? Have any of these women really exercised a right to choose? (pp. 41-42)

Reproductive decisions, like all others, are always made within a material and cultural context. A relentless focus on the individual decision maker and her choice obscures the material and cultural context that constrains and controls these choices. As radical feminists have pointed out, the everyday personal choices made by women in their private lives are irrevocably and inextricably connected to women's powerlessness under male supremacy: "When material conditions eliminate 99% of the options, it is not meaningful to call the 1% of things a woman can do 'choice' " (Douglas, 1987, p. 10). We have no choice about living under heteropatriarchy, and to insist on choice *within* that system, rather than opposing the system itself, disguises the nature of the problem we face—which is not that we don't have choices but that we are systematically oppressed.

Freedom and liberation have also become psychological rather than political phenomena. According to Colette Dowling (1981), the author of a self-help book that purports to deal with "women's secret fear of independence":

> We have only one real shot at "liberation" and that is to liberate ourselves from within. I have learned that freedom and independence can't be wrested from others—from the society at large or from men— but can only be developed, painstakingly, from within. (p. 214)

Finally, I am concerned about the way in which certain words—particularly words relating to ethics and morality—seem increasingly to be frowned upon. Morality is not the exclusive property of the political Right. To say that oppression is *wrong* and that prejudice and discrimination *should* be ended is to make a set of moral judgments. In order to develop both lesbian and gay politics, we need to be able to make explicit moral decisions about what is right and wrong, and we need to be able to talk about what we think we (or indeed others) *should* do. But psychologists tend to be very skeptical of moral terms. The phrase "the tyranny of should" is used by psychoanalyst Karen Horney, and she, like many others, wants us to overcome this tyranny, to drop words like *should* from our vocabulary. Consumers of psychology are asked to put aside moral considerations: The question "Is this right or wrong?" becomes "Is this going to work for me?" "Oughts" and "shoulds" are rejected as intrusive manifestations of coercive authoritarianism. In the self-help book, *In Our Own Hands* (Ernst & Goodison, 1981), "shoulds" and "shouldn'ts" are described as "pressures which have alienated us from our feelings":

> Many of these pressures can be summed up under the word "should." Since childhood we have been told "You should be clean" or "You should work hard" or "You should behave yourself." It is very helpful to become aware of the "shoulds" we have heard during our life because often we are still carrying them round as a voice in our heads. When we are familiar with them we can start to recognise when they affect or inhibit us in the present and begin to lessen their grip on us. (p. 53)

There is no mention here of the potential *benefits* of some of the "shoulds" and "shouldn'ts" we might have learned as children—those imbued with values that we might want to carry through into adulthood rather than "lessen their grip on us." Moreover, there is no mention of the "shoulds" and "shouldn'ts" we may consciously have worked out as adults as part of our developing political theory. This is a commonplace in psychology: We are not supposed to confine ourselves "to the political dogmas of 'shoulds' and 'oughts' " and we are exhorted "for the sake of better mental health, give up the 'shoulds' for others and learn how to change your unrealistic expectations" (Ryan & Trevithic, 1988, p. 106). Louise Hay (1984) is characteristically more authoritarian in her approach:

> Even using the word "should" limits us, and removing it from your vocabulary will make a great difference in your life. . . . Let's take the word "should" and discard it forever, never to be heard of again. "Should" is a word that makes a prisoner of us.

What are the political implications of banning words like *right* and *wrong, should* and *ought* from our vocabulary? In treating these terms as suspect and unauthentic manifestations of personal psychopathology, we dismiss the opinions of those speaking from principled positions. There is even a group therapy exercise, described in *In Our Own Hands* (Ernst & Goodison, 1981), called the "Exercise in Not Judging"—as though the worst thing one can do is make a moral judgment, stigmatized as "being judgmental."

Conclusion

The language of psychology often involves a focus on internal states and personal behaviors. Terms in common use during the conference from which the chapters in this book are based include *ego strength, psychological distress, internalization, negative psychological affect, psychological well-being, denial, projection, defensive behavior, psychological vulnerability, disclosure, role conflict,* and *stress.* Although some of these terms can be conceptualized as relating to external forces, they all refer to fundamentally internal states that are the property of the individual. If our goal is to reduce the psychological distress that results from anti-lesbian and anti-gay hate crimes, do we risk losing sight of the need to stop hate crimes altogether? If our aim is to decrease stress and increase the ego strength of the victim, do we risk forgetting that it is the perpetrator, not the victim, who is the real problem? What political choices are we making when we focus on the problems of the oppressed rather than on the problem of the oppressor? What are the political consequences when, instead of interrogating and challenging heterosexuality (e.g., Wilkinson & Kitzinger, 1993), we concentrate on mopping up the problems heterosexuals cause in the lives of lesbians and gay men.

As people concerned with the prevention of heterosexism, we need to be aware of our politics, to be both self-conscious about the way in which our language reflects or undermines those politics and open to the possibility that there will be political disagreements between us that cannot—and should not—be camouflaged by the dishonest use of words. In a publication titled *Preventing Heterosexism and Homophobia*, we should, at the very least, consider how might we be discussing these issues differently if the title were instead *Challenging Heterosexual Power* or even *Ending the Oppression of Lesbians and Gay Men.*

References

American Psychiatric Association. *Diagnostic and Statistical Manual* (4th ed.). (*DSM-IV*). (1994). Washington, DC: Author.

Bowcott, O. (1995, June 22). Tory minister praises gay "richness." *The Guardian*, p. 15.

Caplan, P. (1991). Delusional dominating personality disorder (DDPD). *Feminism & Psychology, 1*(1), 171-174.

Cartwright, S. A. (1981). Report on the diseases and physical peculiarities of the Negro race. In A. L. Caplan, H. T. Engelhardt, & J. J. McCartney (Eds.), *Concepts of health and disease: Interdisciplinary perspectives* (pp. 305-325). Reading, MA: Addison-Wesley.

Chesler, P. (1972). *Women and madness*. New York: Avon.

Comely, L., Kitzinger, C., Perkins, R., & Wilkinson, S. (1992). Lesbian psychology in Britain: Back into the closet? *Feminism & Psychology, 2*(2), 265-268.

Coyle, A., Kitzinger, C., Flynn, R., Wilkinson, S., Rivers, I., & Perkins, R. (1995, April). [Letter to the editor]. *The Psychologist, 8*(4), 151.

D'Augelli, A. R. (1989). Lesbians' and gay men's experiences of discrimination and harassment in a university community. *American Journal of Community Psychology, 17,* 317-321.

Daly, M. (1978). *Gyn/ecology.* London: Women's Press.

Dannecker, M. (1981). *Theories of homosexuality.* London: Gay Men's Press.

Davis, M. (1995, April). [Letter to the editor]. *The Psychologist, 8*(4), 151-152.

Decker, B. (1984). Counseling gay and lesbian couples. *Journal of Social Work & Human Sexuality, 2*(2/3), 39-52.

Douglas, C. A. (1987, May). Feminism: Beyond "choice." *off our backs,* pp. 9-12.

Dowling, C. (1981). *The Cinderella complex: Women's hidden fear of independence.* London: Fontana.

Ernst, S., & Goodison, L. (1981). *In our own hands.* London: Women's Press.

Fontaine, C. (1982). Teaching the psychology of women: A lesbian feminist perspective. In M. Cruikshank (Ed.), *Lesbian studies: Present and future* (pp. 70-80). Old Westbury, NY: Feminist Press.

Freedman, M. (1978). Towards a gay psychology. In L. Crew (Ed.), *The gay academic* (pp. 315-326). Palm Springs, CA: ETC Publications.

Hall, M. (1985). *The lavender couch.* Boston: Alyson.

Hamilton, V. (1995, April) [Letter to the editor]. *The Psychologist, 8*(4), 151.

Hansen, G. L. (1982). Measuring prejudice against homosexuality (homosexism) among college students: A new scale. *Journal of Social Psychology, 117,* 233-236.

Hay, L. (1984). *Heal your body: The mental causes for physical illness and the metaphysical way to overcome them* [Cassette recording]. London: Eden Grove.

Himmelweit, S. (1988). More than "A woman's right to choose?" *Feminist Review, 29,* 38-56.

Hudson, W. W., & Ricketts, W. A. (1980). A strategy for the measurement of homophobia. *Journal of Homosexuality, 5,* 357-372.

Jones, J. (1995, June 18). Minister to rebuke "anti-gay" disciples of Freud. *The Observer,* p. 21.

Kitzinger, C. (1987). *The social construction of lesbianism.* London: Sage.

Kitzinger, C. (1990). Heterosexism in psychology. *The Psychologist, 3*(9), 391-392.

Kitzinger, C. (1991). Lesbians and gay men in the workplace: Psychosocial issues. In M. J. Davidson & J. Earnshaw (Eds.), *Vulnerable workers: Psychosocial and legal issues* (pp. 223-240). London: John Wiley.

Kitzinger, C. (1994). Anti-lesbian harassment. In Y. L. Too & C. Brant (Eds.), *Cross categories: Rethinking harassment* (pp. 125-147). Boulder, CO: Westview/London: Pluto.

Kitzinger, C., & Coyle, A. (1995). Lesbian and gay couples: Speaking of difference. *The Psychologist, 8*(2), 64-68.

Kitzinger, C., & Perkins, R. (1993). *Changing our minds: Lesbian feminism and psychology.* New York: New York University Press.

Krieger, S. (1982). Lesbian identity and community: Recent social science literature. *Signs, 91,* 91-108.

Larsen, K., Reed, M., & Hoffman, S. (1980). Attitudes of heterosexuals toward homosexuality: A Likert-type scale and construct validity. *Journal of Sex Research, 16*(3), 245-257.

Lehne, G. K. (1976). Homophobia among men. In D. Davis & R. Brannon (Eds.), *The forty-nine percent majority: The male sex role* (pp. 89-104). Reading, MA: Addison-Wesley.

MacDonald, A. P. (1976). Homophobia: Its roots and meanings. *Homosexual Counseling Journal, 3,* 23-33.

MacDonald, A. P., & Games, R. G. (1974). Some characteristics of those who hold positive and negative attitudes toward homosexuals. *Journal of Homosexuality, 1,* 9-27.

Mara, J. (1983). A lesbian perspective. In J. H. Robbins & R. J. Siegel (Eds.), *Women changing therapy: New assessments, values & strategies in feminist therapy* (pp. 145-155). New York: Harrington Park.

Marmor, J. (1980). *Homosexual behavior.* New York: Basic Books.

Millham, J., Miguel, C. L. S., & Kellogg, R. (1976). A factor analytic conceptualisation of attitudes toward male and female homosexuals. *Journal of Homosexuality, 2*(1), 3-10.

Namka, L. (1989). *The doormat syndrome.* Deerfield Beach, FL: Health Communications.

Pearson, G. (1975). *The deviant imagination: Psychiatry, social work, and social change.* London: Macmillan.

Price, J. H. (1982). High school students' attitudes toward homosexuality. *Journal of School Health, 52,* 469-474.

Rayner, J. (1995, April 25). Shrink resistant. *The Guardian,* p. 18.

Rich, A. (1979). The meaning of our love for women is what we have constantly to expand (1977). In A. Rich, *On lies, secrets and silence: Selected prose 1966-1978* (pp. 223-230). New York: Norton.

Rorty, R. (1980). *Philosophy and the mirror of nature.* Oxford, UK: Basil Blackwell.

Ryan, J., & Trevithic, P. (1988). Lesbian workshop. In S. Krzowski & P. Lane (Eds.), *In our own experience: Workshops at the women's therapy centre* (pp. 102-113). London: Women's Press.

Seager, M. (1995, July). Sectioned off? [Letter to the editor]. *The Psychologist, 8*(7), 295.

Weinberg, G. (1973). *Society and the healthy homosexual.* New York: Anchor.

Weiss, C. B., & Dain, R. N. (1979). Ego development and sex attitudes in heterosexual and homosexual men and women. *Archives of Sexual Behavior, 8,* 341-356.

Wilde, J. (1995). *Discrimination against lesbians and gay men in academia.* Unpublished undergraduate dissertation, Loughborough University, Loughborough, England.

Wilkinson, S., & Kitzinger, C. (1993). *Heterosexuality: A "Feminism & Psychology" reader.* London: Sage.

2

Combating Heterosexism in Educational Institutions: Structural Changes and Strategies

Connie S. Chan

Heterosexism, heterocentrism, and homophobia are different forms of discrimination against recognizing homosexuality and bisexuality as normative forms of sexual expression/orientation. There are many ways in which heterosexism and heterocentrism affect education settings, including the following: in the curriculum, in scholarship and research, through socialization norms, having role models or a lack of role models, in personnel policies that include or exclude domestic partner benefits and relationship/family recognition for lesbians and gay men, through covert discrimination, and through slurs and overt hostility against lesbians, gay men, and bisexuals.

This chapter discusses strategies to identify heterosexism in educational settings, with a primary focus on colleges and universities, and suggests ways to work toward the acceptance and celebration of diversity in sexual orientation at these institutions. Identifying, defining, and addressing the heterosexism found in educational settings at all levels involves an analysis of the current situation in regard to policies and practices. The first step is to analyze what structures are currently in place for lesbian/gay/bisexual *affirmative* and anti-discrimination policies and practices. Most schools and institutions have an anti-discrimination statement or policy, which states that they do not discriminate on the basis of race, ethnicity, gender, religion, and national origin. Many schools include sexual orientation in this anti-discrimination statement, found on all official materials and policies. If an institution lists sexual orientation in such a statement, there is a solid foundation to ensure that the actual practices conform to nondiscrimination. However, if the institution does not list sexual orientation as a protected category, then it should be included in the anti-discrimination statement as a matter of principle and practice. The inclusion of sexual orientation indicates an official stand against discrimination against individuals on the basis of their sexual orientation and is a position that all education institutions should adopt. The American Psychological Association, which accredits both schools of psychology and psychology programs, has included sexual orientation in its anti-discrimination policy since 1975 and will generally accredit only schools that follow this anti-discrimination policy. Having an anti-discrimination policy is a necessary beginning, but it in no way means that either the practice of anti-discrimination or the true inclusion of lesbian, gay, and bisexual persons and issues is in place. It is, however, an important principle and statement of intent on the part of the institution's administration to be, in principle, committed to equal treatment of lesbians, gay men, and bisexuals at their institution. The implementation of the policy is what distinguishes between an institution that is truly gay/lesbian/bisexual affirmative and one that is gay/lesbian affirmative in word only and is still heterosexist in its practices.

Curriculum Issues

Adrienne Rich (1986) wrote,

> It is nothing new to say that history is the version of events told by the conqueror, the dominator. Even the dominators acknowledge this. What has been more feelingly and pragmatically been said by people of color, by white women, by lesbians and gay men, by people with roots in the industrial or working class is that without our own history we are unable to imagine a future because we are deprived of the precious resource of knowing where we came from: the valor and the waverings, the visions and defeats of those who went before us. (p. 141)

Beyond knowing our history, *all* of our histories, we have to help our students to imagine a future, to be part of a future where all students, even the 10% to 20% of the population who identifies as lesbian, gay, or bisexual, are able to participate fully in all aspects of our society, a society that acknowledges and values relationships between women and women, men and men, as it currently does that of a man and a woman. Forms of homophobia and forms of heterosexism include the censorship and neglect of gay, lesbian, and bisexual topics in all areas of the curriculum. This neglect may result in an absence of gay/lesbian/bisexual literature about lesbians, gay, and bisexual lives and experiences in all levels of education; little support for scholarship in gay and lesbian studies; an absence of the stories of the contributions and lives of gay men and lesbians in anthologies and on reading lists; in short, what is unnamed and not openly discussed translates to the invisibility and the silencing of a history of a whole group of people's unique experiences.

This silence has profound effects at every level of education. When preschools and elementary schools teach about families led by lesbians and gay men; when they include characters who are openly lesbian, gay, and bisexual in their story selections and plays; and when they have guest speakers who discuss their lives as gay, lesbian, or bisexual individuals in addition to their careers or their avocations and interest, these schools are working against heterosexism, the assumption and acceptance that heterosexual relationships are the only norm and are superior to other types of relationships. Educational settings are learning environments where social norms defining what is and is not appropriate behavior are taught from preschool to advanced graduate studies. Opening up educational institutions and educational materials to include the lives, stories, contributions, and existence of lesbians, gay men, and bisexuals is essential in moving from heterosexism to an open institution of learning at all levels, where one tenth of the population had previously been invisible or underrepresented. Much can be accomplished merely by being *inclusive* even before moving to a gay/lesbian/bisexual affirmative position in an educational setting.

Outright homophobia can take the form of censorship of materials and denial of exposure to gay, lesbian, and bisexual issues. Sometimes this can take the form of not presenting information on sexuality in all its forms. Other times, it means pretending that homosexuality, lesbians, gay men, and bisexuals simply do not exist, at least not in the classroom. More extreme versions of homophobia include censorship of books with gay and lesbian characters. The following example indicates how school boards and community opinion can create homophobic censorship in a school setting.

In 1995, an English teacher, known as an excellent, popular instructor in the Mascenic Regional School District of southern New Hampshire, won a grant from the Respect for All Youth Foundation to lessen homophobia in the high school. The teacher, Penny Culliton, along with her principal and department chair, selected and purchased the following four books to comply with the terms of the grant: *Maurice* by E. M. Forster, *The Education of Harriet Hatfield* by May Sarton, *The Drowning of Stephan Jones* by Bette Green, and *Walt Whitman: The Complete Poems,* for distribution to her students. A month later, some members of the regional school board complained about the pro-lesbian and pro-gay content of the books. The principal required all students to return their books, and the school superintendent, along with the school board, dismissed the English teacher, who had more than 10 years' experience, from her position in September 1995 with a charge of "insubordination," because she did not change her syllabus and obtain approval for these books from her department chair and principal. The board denied that either the content of the books or homophobia was the reason for Ms. Culliton's dismissal, but it was apparent to all that the objection to her syllabus was based on the lesbian and gay characters in some of the books of her syllabus. Ms. Culliton has appealed the dismissal of her position, some students and parents have rallied to her defense, and a final outcome is still pending. However, the censorship of the books has been successful, because the students in the senior English class are no longer reading any of the books that their teacher selected in accordance with the grant to lessen homophobia in the high school.

Most examples of homophobia and heterosexism in the schools do not involve dismissal for inclusion of gay and lesbian themes—often because many instructors do not include gay and lesbian content in the curriculum, texts, syllabi, and materials or during discussions in class. The reasons for their absence stems both from neglect and ignorance. Yet, the inclusion of positive gay, lesbian, and bisexual experiences can make a difference in the attitudes that students learn to hold about themselves and their relationship to others, who may or may not be different from the way they perceive themselves.

Psychological research indicates that it is far easier and more common to hold negative attitudes toward members of a stigmatized group if you do not know or feel connected to someone, if you cannot see their humanity and similarity to yourself. When college or high school or elementary school students are not familiar with lesbian and gay people, either in real life or as characters in books, it is easier to continue to hold negative attitudes toward the "other"—lesbians and gay people.

There are different ways in which attitude change could occur in the context of courses that do have issues of sexual orientation as their focus. In a graduate course on Client Assessment and Counseling Techniques, I assigned Karen Thompson's book, *Why Can't Sharon Kowalski Come Home?* (Thompson & Andrzejewski, 1988), with about Thompson's legal battle to gain contact and legal guardianship of her partner, Kowalski, after she suffered serious brain injury in an automobile accident. The issues addressed in the book, and in the graduate course, were a lack of legal recognition of their relationship, a lack of social recognition of their domestic/financial partnership, and the prevalence of sexist and homophobic attitudes in the courts that initially resulted in granting guardianship to Kowalski's family, which allowed them to prevent her friends, including her partner, Sharon Thompson, from visiting her. Prior to reading this book, students in the course were surveyed on their attitudes toward domestic partnership, and the need for lesbians and gay men to have the ability to establish legal partnership relationships akin to marriage. Only 25% of the students responded that they believed in domestic partnership rights for lesbians and gay men before reading the book, but after reading the book, more than 90% of the class responded that they supported legislative changes to allow lesbians and gay men to have legal sanction for and protection of their rights as currently granted to heterosexual married couples.

The presentation of a case focusing on a lesbian relationship and a legal challenge as an example in the context of several case studies demonstrates the effectiveness of changing heterosexist assumptions in the social sciences and in other disciplines. Not only do students focus on the current heterosexist system in the courts and in our institutions, and begin to question the current definition of *family,* but they also become familiar with gay and lesbian individuals and stories that can change attitudes toward an entire group of previously stigmatized individuals. The attitude change may be even more pronounced when students meet openly lesbian, gay, and bisexual individuals who may serve as role models in their positions of educators, librarians, staff, counselors, administrators, and guest speakers. Cognitive dissonance may occur when students who have never previously known openly gay men and lesbians and bisexuals, and have held negative assumptions about such individuals, know and learn to like or respect openly lesbian, gay, and bisexual people. It is in these situations that attitude change occurs, and that is precisely why some school systems, institutions, and organizations attempt to restrict the exposure of lesbian, gay, and bisexual content, characters, stories, and teachers in the schools—in essence, to perpetuate the valuing of one type of primary relationship between individuals above others.

Curricular change is a slow process in educational institutions, but there has been a national movement toward a curricular transformation that seeks to address the issue that the traditional works of the canon are not inclusive of the experiences of many people's lives. As scholar Elizabeth Minnich said (quoted in Gaard, 1992), " 'you cannot build a scholarship of and for humanity if you take account of only a small part of it' " (p. 30). Gaard continues,

> [it] is the notion that to be truly humane, our humanities curriculum must genuinely reflect the characteristics of the world's population in terms of race, class, and gender. And in this impetus towards transformation, we can no longer afford to overlook a characteristic that crosses the boundaries of all classes, genders, and colors: that is the characteristic of sexual preference. (p. 30)

Although a body of literature and research on gay, lesbian, and bisexual studies does exist within the humanities and in the social sciences, the inclusion of such material within the curriculum and within the canon has been slower to occur. In spite of the increased visibility of lesbian and gay studies programs at institutions such as Yale, City University of New York, City College of San Francisco, Duke, and others (Gaard, 1992), both cutbacks in resources and heterosexism have made it difficult to develop lesbian and gay studies programs. Yet there have been some gains; courses and content focusing on lesbian and gay issues in psychology have increased, partially as a result of some American Psychological Association accreditation teams' requirement of the inclusion of a curriculum of gay, lesbian, and bisexual issues in graduate psychology programs and in the training programs of other mental health professions such as social work and psychiatry. However, structural changes and inclusion of gay, lesbian, and bisexual issues in undergraduate and graduate curriculums will require the commitment of resources such as rewards for the development of courses related to gay and lesbian scholarship; research awards for lesbian and gay studies; resources for symposia, lectures, and films on lesbian and gay issues; and the creation of a lesbian, gay, and bisexual studies program or department, an interdisciplinary research and teaching center that supports faculty scholarship and teaching in this area. This research and teaching center can play a large role in the development of curricular transformation to address issues of diversity and multiculturalism.

Structural Changes in Educational Institutions to Combat Heterosexism

As college and university campuses have focused on the diversity of their student bodies and have begun to address issues of multiculturalism in their curriculum and among their faculty, staff, and students, the issues of race, gender, and class have been the primary issues in the discourse around diversity. The issue of sexual orientation has sometimes been included in this discussion, but there is still greater silence and ignorance about the impact of heterosexism on college and university campuses than other diversity issues. Institutions that have undertaken campus studies about lesbian and gay issues on campus, including Penn State, University of Oregon, Oberlin, Rutgers, UCLA, and UMASS-Amherst, have almost uniformly found that the overall climate for lesbians and gay men, educators and students alike, is "oppressive" and that "invisibility" is the norm around gay and lesbian issues in the curriculum and on campus. A report from the University of Oregon states that "the university environment is neither consistently safe for, nor tolerant of, nor academically inclusive of lesbians, gay men, or bisexuals" (Tierney, 1992a, p. 43). These findings are remarkably consistent across institutional studies and draw attention to the need for awareness, education, and structural changes in addressing the heterosexism and homo-phobia in institutions of higher education. That these findings are so similar and the heterosexism so prevalent in educational settings is even more remarkable, because colleges and universities are ideally the very institutions that strive to be communities of learning, communities of tolerance that celebrate and appreciate diversity among their members. Given the failure of educational institutions to provide a safe and supportive environment for an estimated 10% of their members within the current structures, definitive leadership and structural changes must be developed both to address the heterosexist assumptions and policies and to combat the open homophobia and discrimination faced by lesbian, gay, and bisexual members of the educational communities in which they learn, work, and live.

Defining the Issues of Heterosexism and Homophobia on Campuses

The initial step for addressing issues of heterosexism and homophobia is to identify and define the specific problems on each campus. Often this step is avoided by administrators because of the potential for unearthing unpub-licized problems and creating bad publicity for the institution. However, left unaddressed, the problems will not only not disappear but might increase and cause even greater difficulties. When institutions such as Penn State, UC-Santa Cruz, and UMASS-Amherst sponsored surveys to measure atti-tudes of students and employees toward gay and lesbian issues as well as to describe the current climate for gay men, lesbians, and bisexuals on campus, their findings provided much information for addressing the ways to improve the situation for all involved (Nelson & Baker, 1990; Tierney, 1992b; Yeskel, 1985).

The results of these comprehensive surveys indicate that the campuses do not provide a safe and open environment for lesbians, gay men, and bisexual students, faculty, and staff. As one report states,

> A statement of nondiscrimination that includes the words "sexual orientation" garnered the widest possible support on campus and received the approval of the Board of Trustees . . . however, profound problems beset Penn State. . . . An openly gay faculty member, for example, finds death threats under his office door. A lesbian professor has epithets hurled at her on the street. A young man who someone says "acts gay" awakens in the early morning hours to find that his room has been set on fire by a homophobic student. All but a small cadre of lesbian and gay faculty fear letting their colleagues know about their sexual orientation because they assume that they will be denied promotion and tenure, or will be marginalized in their colleges. (Tierney, 1992b, p. 6)

The UMASS-Amherst survey (Yeskel, 1985) found that "lesbian, gay and bisexual students experience a range of verbal and physical assault which exceeds that of any other group of students" (p. 20). Similar findings of a generally negative climate have been reported in other institutional surveys of lesbian, gay, and bisexual issues (UCLA, Rutgers, Oberlin) in spite of the presence of nondiscrimination clauses for sexual orientation; in spite of lesbian, gay, and bisexual student organizations; in spite of openly lesbian, gay, or bisexual faculty and staff and even the presence of a lesbian/gay studies curriculum. What is happening? Why are the visible safeguards and structures already in place to prevent discrimination ineffective or insufficient to combat heterosexism and homophobia in educational institutions?

Clearly, although the nondiscrimination clauses and the gay/lesbian/bisexual organizations or centers are a necessary beginning, the structures that are currently in place are inadequate to combat heterosexism. There is a climate of intolerance in most educational institutions that does not make it safe for open expression of an individual's lesbian, gay, or bisexual identity. Although a national climate of intolerance against lesbians and gay men has been documented, with increases in reports of anti-gay violence (D'Augelli, 1989; Herek, 1989), colleges and universities were presumed to be *less* intolerant and more accepting of experimentation and diversity within the boundaries of their campuses. The research data demonstrate otherwise: that colleges and universities—while making marked improvements toward diversity in their student bodies, faculty, and staff composition and in their development of multicultural curriculum—have neither the structures nor the positive attitudes in place for the acceptance of gay, lesbian, and bisexual individuals on their campuses.

There are various ways in which the institutional structure at colleges and universities perpetuates heterosexism, both intentionally and unintentionally. The greatest obstacle to combating heterosexism is the invisibility of lesbian, gay, and bisexual issues, individuals, and materials on campuses. How this invisibility has developed is a vicious cycle of sorts. When campus climates are hostile or indifferent to lesbian, gay, and bisexual issues, individuals supporting these issues (both gay and heterosexual) remain closeted and are often invisible. The result is little or no visibility of lesbian, gay, and bisexual issues or individuals, particularly faculty or staff. Given the lack of involvement and publicity around issues of sexual orientation, the hegemonic majority assumes that there are few, if any, lesbians, gay men, or bisexuals on campus, and if there are, that they are satisfied with the situation because they don't see any visible complaints or hear any voices of dissent. The research data indicate that although gay and bisexual faculty and staff often come out to one or two close colleagues, the majority of the faculty and staff do not come into contact with openly gay, lesbian, and bisexual coworkers. In the Penn State survey, 87% of the faculty and staff surveyed replied that they had no friends on campus who were lesbian or gay (Tierney, 1992b); at UMASS-Boston, 85% of the faculty and staff reported that they did not personally know colleagues who were lesbian, gay, or bisexual (Chan, 1993).

If there is so little contact with and knowledge of gay, lesbian, and bisexual colleagues among faculty and staff, how do faculty and staff teach about and work with issues of diversity? Even more remarkable from an educational perspective, how do students, both lesbian, gay, bisexual, and heterosexual, learn about difference and learn from role models who are like or different from themselves? The invisibility and silence of lesbian, gay, and bisexual faculty and staff, the core of the colleges and universities in which we live, make for a structural problem. There have not been supports or benefits from being openly lesbian, gay, or bisexual in our schools. Rather, there has been active discouragement of being open about one's sexual orientation if it is not heterosexual in nature. The consequences for lesbians, gay men, and bisexuals on campus is that either they experience subtle and overt discrimination or they encounter little, if any, positive reinforcement about their own identities. Gay men, lesbians, and bisexuals are excluded in many ways in university and college life, from social situations where bringing one's same-sex lover to a social gathering would be considered scandalous, to a lack of domestic partner benefits granted automatically to heterosexual married employees, to married student/faculty housing opportunities, to downplaying community service to gay/lesbian service organizations in résumés. Yet, because many students, faculty, and staff, particularly those who answer that they don't know any lesbian, gay, or bisexual colleagues, hold such negative attitudes about lesbians, gay men, or bisexuals (Nelson & Baker, 1990; Tierney, 1992b; Yeskel, 1985), the reality is that it is usually easier, safer, and certainly less trouble to remain closeted about one's identity as a gay man, a lesbian, or a bisexual than to risk discrimination in tenure and promotion and hiring—or risk the discomfort that comes from being different and not fitting in. As one gay faculty member was quoted in the Penn State study,

> "I am ambivalent about participating in departmental social gatherings with my partner." A woman continued, "It made me nervous to attend the lectures in the Contemporary Scholarship on Lesbian and Gay Lives series." This individual concluded by saying, "As long as we live in a world that says 'don't flaunt it' [discrimination] will continue." (Tierney, 1992b, p. 12)

Without lesbian, gay, and bisexual individuals becoming visible, their concerns do go unnoticed, and the common assumption that everyone is heterosexual goes unchallenged. This vicious cycle continues. Either attitudes about them are negative or lesbians and gays are ignored. The reality of the life of the university and college community only reinforces the culture of those who are in the mainstream, in the hegemonic group—heterosexuals.

If lesbian, gay, and bisexual people, either individually or as a group, become more vocal and seek the same kinds of benefits, support, and privileges extended to heterosexuals, they may be accused of seeking special treatment or being militant. Structurally, and in reality, what is truly being sought is treatment that is equal to the rest of the academic community.

Given the structural problems that perpetuate heterosexism and homophobia in our educational institutions, only structural solutions will be effective in identifying and combating heterosexism. In generic terms, the problems that colleges and universities face are the following:

1. The college and university communities are either ill-informed or ignorant about lesbian, gay, and bisexual communities and their issues on campuses.
2. The majority of the policies, structures, and actions of the universities and colleges support this climate of ignorance, intolerance, and discrimination even if there are anti-discrimination clauses that include sexual orientation or if there are student lesbian, gay, and bisexual organizations.
3. A consequence of the negative climate is that lesbian, gay, and bisexual people, individually and collectively, feel unsafe in being open about their sexual orientation, their lives, and their work. This invisibility perpetuates a vicious cycle and continues negative consequences for all involved, including the absence of gay, lesbian, and bisexual contributions that would especially benefit a majority culture that is unexposed to this community.

Heterosexism exists in many institutions in our society, but in an academic community devoted to learning, to enrichment of one's experiences, to exposure to difference, and to the development of all individuals' potential, it is especially necessary to seek ways to expose and change the heterosexist assumptions behind our schools.

The current safeguards and services that exist at universities and colleges are ineffective and insufficient to address the issues of heterosexism, homophobia, and discrimination. Even as educational institutions have tried to become more responsive to the needs of not only a far more diverse student body but also their employees, the current services that exist are generally inadequate to meet the needs of lesbian, gay, and bisexual students, faculty, and staff. In a comprehensive survey of gay, lesbian, and bisexual students at UMASS-Amherst (Yeskel, 1985), almost all services on campus were rated as inadequate in meeting their needs, and they believed the majority of staff in these agencies to be either "insensitive to, or discriminatory against lesbian and gay students and/or issues" (Yeskel, 1985, p. 20). Other studies confirm that primary sources of anguish for lesbian, gay, and bisexual students are harassment by other students, including verbal and physical abuse, particularly in residence halls; academic life (including prejudicial comments from faculty in classes); or ignorance of the realities of being different in sexual orientation (students report that faculty tend to be extremely heterosexist both in their assumptions around class material and about students' lives and experiences). These surveys point out that established sources of support for students, such as the counseling center, deans' offices, academic affairs offices, and the like, may not be available to students who have problems with insensitivity and prejudice on lesbian, gay, and bisexual issues, whether in the classroom or in social situations on campus.

Using College and University Structures to Identify Issues and to Change the Climate on Campus

Initially, the leadership of the educational institution, starting with senior administrators (president, deans, faculty leaders), should take a stand on making the school a safe, supportive environment in which lesbians, gay men, and bisexuals can work and learn. Because the climate has previously been one where heterosexism has been tacitly accepted on campus, and staff have commonly responded to anti-gay violence or discrimination on a case-by-case basis to cope with the problems, the steps that must be taken to make a difference within the institution must be *proactive* rather than reactive.

A commission or committee on lesbian, gay, and bisexual issues should be appointed or selected and should include members from the various constituencies across the institution—students, faculty, staff, and administrators—a mix of openly gay, bisexual, and heterosexual members. This should be a senior-level commission whose charge is to identify the various issues and concerns of lesbian, gay, and bisexual individuals on campus and to make specific recommendations concerning structural changes that need to occur. This commission could ensure that the words *sexual orientation* be included in the nondiscrimination clause of the institution, giving it an official policy of nondiscrimination against lesbians, gay men, and bisexuals. The inclusion of sexual orientation is an important first step, but the implementation of such a clause is the key to changing heterosexism at the institution.

A commission might begin its work by examining institutional policies to determine where lesbian, gay, and bisexual individuals are treated differently from heterosexuals. The most obvious policies are the employee benefit packages, which provide married employees (and often students) with a variety of "spousal" and "family" benefits such as insurance, housing, library privileges, bereavement leave, tuition waivers, and so on, but which lesbian and gay employees and students do not have available to them in their relationships with same-sex partners. These domestic partner benefits—providing spousal equivalent benefits to lesbians and gay men—are beginning to be offered at many institutions, which demonstrates a commitment both to recognition of the primary relationships of lesbians and gay men and to being fair or equitable in providing lesbian and gay employees with the same benefits that have always been offered to married employees. Other policy issues that need to be examined, beyond equity of employee benefits, may include student benefits in the areas of housing and similar spousal equivalent benefits.

Second, although a senior-level commission with representation from all sectors of the institution can define and examine the issues and make recommendations, there still must be implementation on an ongoing basis of the recommendations and of the nondiscrimination clause. An officially funded and staffed office or center for lesbian, gay, and bisexual concerns needs to be established to carry out the functions of implementation, program development, education, and outreach programs for all members of the campus community. This office would serve a number of functions, including outreach and advocacy for lesbian, gay, and bisexual individuals on campus; providing information on issues of sexual orientation; conducting workshops, training, and increasing awareness of lesbian, bisexual, and gay issues on campus; holding programs and social events; and serving as a clearinghouse for matters relating to lesbian, gay, and bisexual issues in other spheres of the institution.

A comprehensive program of training on heterosexism and homophobia and the ways in which the assumptions of heterosexism affect the functioning of all staff or faculty members at the institution would ideally be held. Although it would require some initial time and resources to educate all current staff and faculty, once that phase had been completed, then new faculty and staff orientation would include comprehensive coverage of not only heterosexism but also lesbian, gay, and bisexual issues and how these issues can be integrated into their work at the school.

Student services and the residential life departments can play a major role in breaking down heterosexism through education, outreach, and training. With a new turnover of students every year, and freshman orientation programs that are designed to introduce and set expectations for all incoming students, there is great potential for establishing nonheterosexist norms. Much as the standards around diversity are set initially with incoming students, expectations of positive gay/bisexual affirmative behavior can be conveyed through visible lesbian, gay, and bisexual role models at all levels, from student leaders to faculty and administrators; through official college publications that picture lesbian and gay couples and document participation in lesbian/gay/bisexual social and political events; and by holding panels and open discussions of sexuality and alliances between gay/bisexual and heterosexual individuals and groups during orientation and consistently throughout the school year. Student surveys have reported that there is little communication and interaction between lesbian/gay/bisexual students and heterosexual students.

Because the development of sexual identity and explorations of sexuality are primary tasks for college-age students, this issue is often very charged in the classrooms, on the playing fields, and in the dining halls of educational institutions. For students who are exploring or claiming a lesbian, gay, or bisexual identity, the task can be very stressful. When a homophobic or blatantly heterosexist bias exists at a school, the forms it takes can include a lack of physical protection on campus, insensitivity from various areas of student and academic services, and an openly anti-gay atmosphere in many residence halls. This can create "a climate producing anxiety and depression for many students, particularly those whose self-image may suffer from the negative attributes assigned to lesbian, gay, and bisexual people by historical societal prejudice" (Yeskel, 1985, p. 21). At UMASS-Amherst, students reported that the climate in the residential halls is so hostile to lesbian and gay students that many students feel forced out of campus housing and must find alternative housing off-campus. Because a great deal of learning in the collegiate experience occurs out of the classroom and in the residences, residential service departments need to focus specifically on the issue of sexual orientation. Systematic in-service training on issues of inclusiveness and civility for all residents, particularly in regard to sexuality and sexual orientation, is essential to developing reasonable expectations for student and staff attitudes and behaviors. Campus housing options that foster a comfortable and sensitive atmosphere for lesbian, gay, and bisexual students, faculty, and staff can be developed and made available. These inclusive and integrative measures serve not only to decrease the alienation experienced by lesbian, gay, and bisexual members of the community but also to provide a model of a learning environment that accepts, accommodates, and even celebrates true diversity.

Two other areas of college and university life that are visible and important to the general public, but that have been less active in accommodating diversity of culture and lifestyle, are alumni affiliations and networks, and athletics. These are the two aspects of college and university life with which graduates have the most continuing contact with the institution after completion of their degrees. They are also among the most heterosexist and homophobic organizations in educational institutions. They also have great potential for attitude change if educational and outreach efforts are under-taken. Colleges and university alumni offices that have been able to create an alumni organization or network of their lesbian, gay, and bisexual gradu-ates have reported success in attracting donations and alumni participants who heretofore have been disenfranchised or alienated from their institu-tions. These organizations often sponsor programs that highlight gay and lesbian graduates and their work, bringing both honor and recognition not only to the individuals but also to their institutions. If a college or university is truly committed to lifelong learning, there is good potential for educating graduates about lesbian, gay, and bisexual classmates and the changes they have experienced over the years since college as well as potential for learning about current issues of sexual orientation on campuses today.

In athletics, homophobia and heterosexism are major issues on college and university campuses. Even the NCAA has taken notice of this issue, working on a seminar program to help athletics departments deal with issues of diversity, including sexual orientation, for both male and female athletes. This awareness developed after several incidents involving NCAA teams. Several years ago, an unsigned letter was circulated among female basketball recruits, containing a list on which it claimed were college basketball coaches who were lesbians, a kind of blackballing and a form of negative recruiting. With few openly gay women in sports and few people in athletics willing to confront issues relating to sexuality, homosexuality remains a hidden and often taboo subject; yet the issue is surfacing more and more. Several years ago, the Penn State women's basketball coach, Rene Portland, told a news-paper reporter that she did not allow lesbians on her team, and a large protest ensued, resulting in workshops on homophobia and policy changes of non-discrimination for the athletic department. Even at the same institution (Penn State), Sue Rankin, the head women's softball coach since 1981, possibly the only female head coach at a major university who is openly gay, remarked,

"Coming out is the single most important thing a person can do to improve the campus climate and the climate in general for women's sports. It's a very personal decision and one that can affect your job, your personal life, every-thing. But it would go a long way toward breaking harmful stereotypes." (quoted in Blum, 1994, p. A38)

Rankin, like many educators, stresses the importance of being openly gay, lesbian, or bisexual as role models for students. As historian John D'Emilio stated,

"The ideals of our profession demand that we come out. The teachers that we all remember best and cherish most are the ones who were models of integrity in the classroom and in their lives, the ones for whom the search for justice and truth did not represent empty words. If we decline to take up this challenge, we will be failing our students and ourselves." (quoted in Gaard, 1992).

The burden, and the challenge, of working to expose heterosexism and going toward a truly acceptable diversity of sexual orientation no longer need fall only on lesbian, gay, and bisexual educators in our schools. Students are increasingly doing their part. As stated in an article about homophobia in women's sports in the *Chronicle of Higher Education* in 1994,

> as issues of sexual orientation creep into the public forum, many observers say that it may be the young, female athletes who provide the greatest impetus for change. As girls grow up in a society that is slowly becoming more tolerant of diversity, they say, the athletes—many of whom will one day be coaches and administrators—may be more likely to be open about their own sexuality and to demand respect and fairness. A former athlete at the University of Maryland at College Park last year sued the institution's field hockey coach, claiming she had been forced to conceal her homosexuality. . . . "Women's sports needs these kinds of silence-breaking events," says Don Sabo, a professor of social science at D'Youville College. "People are starting to talk about lesbianism and even say the word, the L-word. That's a healthy situation, because homophobia is only able to thrive in silence." (Blum, 1994, p. A36)

One goal of educators—and one goal of educational institutions—is not only to help students break silences but also to educate students about diverse life experiences that may be the same or different from their own. Fighting heterosexism in schools falls within these goals and is a challenge for educators, students, and staff alike. However, it should no longer be a battle fought individually, even for the college basketball player at the University of Maryland, or Penny Culliton teaching in New Hampshire. Although we as individual educators can do what we are able within our own spheres of influence, we must also work toward institutionalizing structural policy and procedural changes at our schools, colleges, and universities. As the Committee on Lesbian and Gay Concerns at Penn State University wrote in its report to the University, in 1992:

> We are arguing that for the University to promote a climate that enhances diversity, structural changes must occur. Such changes will create systematic arenas for action on lesbian, gay, and bisexual issues so that activity no longer takes place merely on an ad-hoc basis or because of the desire of a particular individual. The suggestion we are making is in keeping with any number of other initiatives that the University undertakes. When the University wanted to raise money for a capital campaign, we enlarged the development office.

When the University wanted to enhance student learning through programs abroad, we created a University Office of International Programs. Similarly, if the University wants to overcome the ignorance and bigotry of our community, then, of necessity, we must create a structural solution.

We are not suggesting that everyone is bigoted or ignorant. Some individuals have been remarkably supportive, yet, the University also have raised funds without additional staff in a development office. Some students would have found their way to other countries without a University Office of International Programs. The University, however, set specific goals so that fund-raising, student awareness of other cultures, and innumerable other activities were not left to serendipity. The same kinds of initiatives must occur to overcome the discrimination and harassment that confront Penn State's gay, lesbian, and bisexual communities. (Tierney, 1992b, p. 13)

References

Blum, D. E. (1994, March 9). College sports' L-word. *The Chronicle of Higher Education, 40*(27), A35-A36.

Chan, C. S. (1993). *Lesbian, gay and bisexual concerns at the University of Massachusetts, Boston: Survey results.* Unpublished report.

D'Augelli, A. R. (1989). Lesbians' and gay men's experiences of discrimination and harassment in a university community. *American Journal of Community Psychology, 17,* 317-321.

Gaard, G. (1992). Opening up the canon: The importance of teaching lesbian and gay literatures. *Feminist Teacher, 6*(2), 30-33.

Herek, G. M. (1989). Hate crimes against lesbians and gay men: Issues for research of social policy. *American Psychologist, 44,* 948-955.

Nelson, R., & Baker, H. (1990). *The educational climate for gay, lesbian, and bisexual students at the University of California at Santa Cruz.* Unpublished report from the Gay, Lesbian, Bisexual Community Concerns Advisory Committee, UCSC.

Rich, A. (1986). Resisting amnesia: History and personal life. In *Blood, bread and poetry: Selected prose, 1979-1985* (pp. 136-155). New York: Norton.

Thompson, K., & Andrzejewski, J. (1988). *Why can't Sharon Kowalski come home?* Duluth, MN: Spinsters Ink.

Tierney, W. G. (1992a). Building academe communities of difference. *Change, 24*(2), 40-46.

Tierney, W. G. (1992b). *Enhancing diversity: Toward a better campus climate.* Report of the Committee on Lesbian and Gay Concerns. University Park: Pennsylvania State University.

Yeskel, F. (1985). *The consequences of being gay.* Unpublished report from the program for Gay, Lesbian, and Bisexual Concerns. Amherst: University of Massachusetts at Amherst.

3

Preventing Heterosexism and Bias in Psychotherapy and Counseling

Laura S. Brown

Sexual minority persons—gay men, lesbians, bisexual men and women, and transgendered people—are estimated to constitute somewhere between 1% and 10% of the adolescent and adult populations, depending on the manner in which this identity is defined and sampled by research. This robust presence in the general population means that the modal psychotherapist will see at least one identified sexual minority client during her or his career (Garnets, Hancock, Cochran, Goodchilds, & Peplau, 1991). Caucasian lesbians in the United States are particularly active consumers of psychotherapy services (Ryan & Bradford, 1993), and anecdotal evidence suggests that Caucasian gay men have similar high rates of utilization. Several commentators (Brown, 1989; Gonsiorek, 1982) have noted that in Caucasian sexual minority communities, the therapist has fulfilled the role of a secular priesthood, helping to address one of the most common aspects of heterosexist stigma, the inference of mental illness to sexual minority persons, and providing support for coping with the mental health consequences of exposure to bias and violence. (Evidence regarding therapist utilization in sexual minority communities of color is unavailable.) It is not simply because this is a conference in the field of psychology that we are addressing the question of heterosexism in psychotherapy today; it is because psychotherapy, whatever its actual merits (Kitzinger & Perkins, 1993), is a commonplace in the lives of many sexual minority persons. Nonsexual minority friends and relatives of sexual minority persons who may themselves be negatively affected by heterosexist bias may also seek the care of psychotherapists or counselors for support in dealing with these concerns. Consequently, the presence of heterosexist and anti-sexual minority bias in the delivery of psychotherapy services is meaningful and problematic, something deserving of attention and change.

36

Mental health professionals in general have attempted to challenge and change biases about minority groups so as to more accurately and ethically offer services to members of those groups. Yet, a variety of factors continue to converge in the training and experiences of most mental health professionals that lead to ignorance, bias, or both, in regard to the treatment of the sexual minority client and to general failures to integrate accurate information into the usual training curriculum. These factors can lead to practices that are potentially harmful to sexual minority clients and, consequently, to the credibility of mental health professionals (Garnets et al., 1991). Because the mental health disciplines in North America, particularly organized psychiatry and psychology, have a history of being actively involved at the institutional level in the persecution and oppression of sexual minority persons in the period between World War II and the early 1970s (Duberman, 1991) and have institutional amends to make to the sexual minority communities as a result, the lingering presence of heterosexist and anti-sexual minority bias among mental health professionals is especially egregious and fraught with the potential for harm. It also remains ironic that in 1995, as this chapter is being written, sexual minority status is still worthy of comment as a problematic issue in mental health service delivery and continues to be actively targeted for prejudice and violence; more ironic still that after two decades of a movement for social change, overt bias-based violence appears to be on the upsurge, as changes in the general culture have highlighted and reinforced biases against sexual minority people at a new level of fervor little seen since the emergence of lesbian and gay liberation movements a quarter century in the past. Attention to this issue in the mental health professions is thus of increased urgency.

Preventing heterosexism and anti-sexual minority bias in the practice of psychotherapy and counseling is a function of several interventions. It is unclear, given the present state of cultural attitudes, whether *primary* prevention, in the sense of stopping the problem before it begins, is truly possible as regards psychotherapy. To a large degree, we still find ourselves at the level of more secondary interventions, because trainees enter the process of becoming mental health professionals with many heterosexist attitudes already firmly ensconced in their conscious and nonconscious databases. But a variety of interventions are possible that could have as their long-term goal the elimination of those preexisting biases prior to the point where the person begins to practice. These include interventions at the curricular and practicum levels, in the early training of mental health professionals; the development of scholarly data that can be integrated into basic course work at the undergraduate level; the creation of models that would assist clinicians in assessing and changing affective and nonconscious bias; the provision of continuing professional education to inculcate knowledge in already practicing clinicians; and the development of clear standards of care to which clinicians can be held to account when other interventions have not yet accomplished the goal of eliminating bias.

This chapter will address several topics. First, it will explore the roots of heterosexism and anti-sexual minority bias in the training and practice of psychotherapists and counselors, as a precursor to understanding what may be necessary for prevention. Second, it will explore manifestations of heterosexism and anti-sexual minority bias in the actual attitudes and practices of mental health professionals to illustrate those practices that have escaped prevention but may respond to remediation. The ethical and professional competency implications of these biased behaviors will be addressed, with an eye toward institutionalizing nonheterosexist practice as the only ethical practice for mental health professionals. Finally, we will analyze how such bias might be both prevented at various stages of the training process and remediated when it has been allowed to go unchecked at early periods in professional development.

Bias and Invisibility in Education and Training

The coverage of unbiased information or, indeed, of any information on sexual minority persons in the undergraduate curriculum appears to be sparse. Except when a textbook author has a known commitment to the inclusion of this sort of material, most general undergraduate texts continue to describe some kinds of sexual minority status as a version of deviant psychology, thereby reinforcing the stereotype of sexual minority status as a sort of sickness. Or, there may be coverage of AIDS-related issues, which, although important to include in the undergraduate psychology curriculum, are not in any way synonymous with adequate exploration of sexual minority topics. Courses on human diversity do not routinely integrate materials on sexual minority persons; those on identity development rarely include questions about the development of a sexual minority identity. Exposure to the general benefits of a liberal undergraduate education seems to make little dent in attitudes toward sexual minority persons, because a number of studies using undergraduate student research participants have identified high levels of prejudice against sexual minorities, particularly gay men.

The lacunae in undergraduate education on sexual minority topics provide a fertile breeding ground for the perpetuation of ignorance and stereotypy in mental health professionals, even those whose stated desire is to be supportive of sexual minority persons. Many clinicians assert, erroneously, that they do not need to have information about sexual minority persons because they will never treat them. Others believe that their knowledge base is adequate until faced with circumstances that make clear that matters are otherwise. A personal anecdote illustrates how this can function. This story underscores my earlier comment that the largest problem in prevention of heterosexism and bias in the mental health professions is that prevention of these problems in the general culture has not taken place.

I have been out as a lesbian and a writer on lesbian issues in the profession of psychology for many years, with the result that for many colleagues I am the sexual minority person with whom they are most familiar, even when the acquaintanceship is somewhat distant. At a time somewhere in the past, I was approached by a colleague, whom I like and admire and who had always appeared to be comfortable with the fact of my being lesbian (e.g., inquiring about the well-being of my partner in the same manner that similar inquiries were made about the spouses of heterosexual colleagues). One of this colleague's adult offspring was a sexual minority person. My colleague shared with me, in a loving and touching manner, concerns about what would happen to this beloved child who was a member of my minority group. Would the offspring be able to find a partner, have a satisfying relationship? Would that person be discriminated against in the profession to which that person belonged? It was a pleasure to encounter a loving and concerned parent of a sexual minority person among my colleagues and to be able offer reassurances that sexual minority persons lead happy and fulfilling lives, and so on.

But my colleague's own unconscious bias (i.e., that sexual minority persons might not be able to have satisfying and happy lives), which was apparently fed by a simple lack of information, was evident in the questions, even thought though their intent was simply one of genuine love and concern. The questions were surprising to me because this individual does not hold overt negative biases against sexual minority persons. If this "good colleague," a senior psychotherapist and the parent of a sexual minority adult, was so lacking in information, what did this tell me about the general database and attitudes of mental health professionals and the need for training? I would argue that it is illustrative of the common state of affairs in the best of circumstances; that is, the most usual outcome of professional training in the mental health fields is profound ignorance and unchallenged stereotypes about persons of sexual minority status.

Formal training for mental health professionals on topics related to sexual minority persons appears to be sparse at all levels of mental health education (Buhrke & Douce, 1991; Greene, 1994; Markowitz, 1991). In one of the few empirical studies of this problem, Buhrke (1989) found that almost 30% of a group of female counseling psychology graduate students had had no exposure to sexual minority issues in their training, and most of the research participants gleaned their information from informal sources such as friends. Because counseling psychology is a mental health subdiscipline viewed from without as especially friendly to sexual minority issues (and quite well populated by openly sexual minority colleagues), the omission of this subject area from graduate training is particularly striking and troubling.

Although graduate trainiong fails to include a number of topics that would appear important to the practicing clinician (for instance, childhood sexual abuse [Pope & Feldman-Summers, 1992] or domestic violence [Goodman et al., 1994]), there are reasons particular to the status of sexual minority persons that make this an especially risky omission. First, as noted above, there is the heritage of the mental health disciplines vis-à-vis homosexuality. Organized psychiatry and psychology played a leading role in the post-World War II pathologizing of gay men and lesbians, and the attitudes and beliefs that fueled those overtly biased activities continue to be present and active in the various mental health disciplines through such organizations as the National Association for Research and Treatment of Homosexuality (NARTH), which promotes the use of dangerous conversion therapies and whose president, Charles Socarides, has taken leadership in identifying sexual minority persons as severely disturbed (although he is himself the father of a sexual minority person).

Second, as too many commentators than can be cited have noted, heterosexism and anti-sexual minority bias are pervasive in North American cultures. Sexual minority persons of color face such bias within their own ethnic groups; Jewish and Muslim sexual minority persons encounter it within their religious minority communities. Most sexual minority persons are invisible to those around them, out of concern for becoming the targets of bias or simply because they do not adhere in their manners to common stereotypes about sexual minority individuals. This large-scale invisibility is, however, a factor in the perpetuation of bias and ignorance of a sort that is somewhat less common and overt today as regards members of racial and ethnic minorities.

The probability that new graduate students will have solid and unbiased information about the range of sexual minority lives parallel to the similar amount of data available regarding heterosexual experience is about equal to the likelihood that they are at that moment prepared to write their dissertations; in other words, absent exceptional circumstances, slight. As noted above, the undergraduate curriculum is likely to be very short on this sort of data. This may be true even when the student is a member of a sexual minority group, because individual experiences are idiosyncratic and may provide incomplete, skewed, or even dangerously wrong information. Sexual minority individuals, like other members of stigmatized groups, may also harbor self-hatred and have biases against their own group, based on the interaction of personal negative experiences with preexisting prejudice acquired while growing up in a heterosexist and biased society. In addition, it is not unheard of for a person's sexual minority identity to develop during the course of graduate training (in one program of which I am aware, a class began with only one lesbian in it, and had only one woman who identified as heterosexual by the beginning of the fourth year of training). Much research on attitudes toward homosexuality (which are presumed for the purposes of this chapter to have some relationship to attitudes toward bisexuality and transgender, the other sexual minority groups) points to the value of knowledge as a means of transforming heterosexist and anti-homosexual biases. When this knowledge is absent, as it is likely to be, bias can flourish if only by default.

When coursework is offered, it is rarely required and may appear on the schedule only infrequently. For the busy and overwhelmed graduate student already struggling to keep up with what is required, the choice to take a class that is not mandatory may be difficult. Instructors of such classes thus may find themselves "preaching to the choir," addressing students who already have a commitment to knowledge beyond that of the average mental health professional in training, but students with more apparent heterosexist or anti-sexual minority biases can emerge from training untouched even by this sort of infrequent offering. The implicit or explicit assumption is that not every clinician is likely to see sexual minority clients and, consequently, only those with a special interest in working with this population need to opt for such a course. The presence of tenured sexual minority faculty at a program is not a guarantee of having this sort of course work offered, either; not all sexual minorities in psychology have this as a field of study, and they may be no more—or even somewhat less—qualified to teach such a course than a well-informed and bias-free member of the majority group. Often, when there is a sexual minority student present in a training cohort, she or he is given the burden of being expert and educator not only for peers but also for faculty (akin to what happens to members of other minority groups). Because not all sexual minority students are knowledgeable about matters important to training, this can have the effect not only of placing undue responsibility on the student at a vulnerable stage of professional development but also of creating an information base that appears to be informed but in fact contains inaccurate or distorted information.

In an example of the latter, a lesbian graduate student was frequently called on in her classes to share information about the lesbian experience of parenting, couple relationships, coping with families of origin, and so on. However, she found that she was then told by faculty that she was "overly involved" in lesbian issues, and she was discouraged from pursuing her research interest in lesbian adolescents. Because she was in their classes, her faculty felt a false sense of security that they had adequately addressed sexual minority concerns, all the while using her expertise as a tool to punish and silence her and to prevent her from developing scholarship that might have contributed to the knowledge base and facilitated future training.

Something that I have identified as "liberal" heterosexist biases are of particular concern with respect to the absence of sexual minority topics in the formal training curriculum of mental health professionals. Many mental health graduate students are willing to endorse positive or at least neutral attitudes toward sexual minority persons. But like my concerned colleague, they may have large gaps in their knowledge or may lack awareness about the manner in which they take for granted the privilege ascribed to heterosexual status. They may have good intentions but be misinformed or uninformed about how best to implement those intentions as a clinician in a professional role and this misinformation may be crystallized by those who train them. Such persons may see themselves as tolerant or accepting, ignoring the subtexts of either stance, both of which imply a power differential in which the heterosexual person maintains the right to socially construct the sexual minority individual as acceptable or tolerable, or not, should certain unspoken rules be violated.

Thus, the liberal heterosexist person may inquire humanistically why it is so important that sexual minority persons label themselves, insisting that because we are all human, what we do sexually should be of no consequence to identity. Such persons fail to note that people are given the presumptive label of *heterosexual* by those around them in the absence of any other data and are consequently subjected to treatment that runs the gamut from simply insensitive to potentially dangerous. As Woolley (1991) noted in an article aptly titled "Beware the Well-Intentioned Therapist,"

> My experience as a therapy client was valuable. . . . But not one of them (prior therapists) was prepared or brave enough to ask me the one question that might have saved me—and two ex-wives—a lot of pain . . . do you think you might be gay? (p. 30)

The liberal person with heterosexist attitudes may disapprove of overt bias and prejudice, but may be uncomfortable with overt displays of affection between same-gender persons, or with the ambiguity of the transgendered individual. Or they may downplay the reality of discrimination and violence faced by sexual minority persons. In the last category, we may find the health psychologist who counseled a closeted Karen Thompson to come out to the parents of her severely head-injured lover, Sharon Kowalski, without first assessing what the risks of this might be to Karen and Sharon, precipitating many years of separation and court battles for the pair (Thompson & Andrzejewski, 1988). However, the liberal person, unlike the person whose bias is ego-syntonic and overt, usually has an interest and investment in becoming less biased, and so is likely to obtain positive results from being offered adequate information to challenge ignorance or stereotype.

Buhrke's research on counseling psychology students also noted that less than half had had the opportunity to work with a sexual minority client at any stage of their practicum or internship training. Although such exposure cannot per se alleviate the bias held by a trainee (and under some unfortunate circumstances might actually, in the absence of appropriate supervision, reinforce some biases and stereotypes, because in the absence of knowledge of nonclient sexual minority persons, it will be relatively simple for a therapist to conclude that all of the sexual minority people in the world are, like clients, in a state of psychological distress), an encounter with a sexual minority client frequently provides the necessary stimulus for an otherwise uninterested student to obtain information and supervision that might have a salutary effect on the reduction of bias. Again, given the research participant pool, this is an especially troubling statistic, because many counseling psychology students do practicum and internship placements in college counseling centers where the number of clients with these concerns is likely to be high, given the development stages encompassed by the college experience. How much less likely might it be that graduate students in clinical psychology, social work, or psychiatry, being trained in settings less obviously conducive to encounters with sexual minority clients, will have this sort of potentially useful training experience?

Anecdotal evidence from discussions with graduate students and observations of training programs in various settings also indicates that it is rare for students to have access to a sexual minority affirmative and nonheterosexist psychotherapy supervisor. As I have suggested elsewhere (Brown, 1989), a supervisor with such a perspective can be of value in helping students to examine heterosexist assumptions, not simply with their sexual minority clients but also with their heterosexual ones, and can potentially expand the trainee's skills at analysis by offering challenges to deeply embedded assumptions about gender and sexuality that are contained in heterosexist bias.

These absences send a message to trainees that can itself compound bias. This message is that knowledge about sexual minority persons and the exploration of biases about them and, by implication, such persons themselves, are unimportant; certainly, less important than statistics and research methodology, for instance, which is a required part of psychology graduate training. This neglect of the topic of sexual minority issues thus lays the foundation for heterosexist and anti-sexual minority biases in practice.

Heterosexism and Bias in Psychotherapy Practice:
A Chilling Picture

I would like to begin with two case examples. Two Caucasian, middle-class professional women have lived together as partners for their entire adult lives since meeting when both were in professional training. The relationship was initially sexual but after a few years, not unlike many female pairs, the sexual component of the relationship became inactive (Rothblum & Brehony, 1993). However, the women slept in the same bed, owned a home and vacation property together, had wills and powers of attorney in one another's favor, and in general continued to see one another as their spouse. The couple was highly closeted because of the perception that one woman's job would be put at risk; they socialized with no other lesbians. During one woman's middle fifties, she became depressed and sought the services of a psychotherapist. The therapist, after taking a history from her client, informed her that she was not a lesbian and that this was not a relationship; rather, the client was experiencing a delayed adolescence. The client had her depression framed to her as grief over lost heterosexual opportunities. The therapist's stated reason for declaring this woman not a lesbian and her relationship not a true adult pairing was the absence of sexual activity, even though some data suggests that this is normative for many lesbian couples. The other partner in turn became struck by grief as her spouse of many years, under the tutelage of the therapist, began to date men and distance herself from the relationship.

A second case example concerns a Caucasian woman in her early twenties who sought treatment for sexual dysfunction. She reported a history that included one episode of sexual abuse by an uncle while she was in early adolescence, some "OK" experiences of heterosexual intercourse with a boyfriend and her fiancé, and an absence of sexual desire for her husband since marriage. She had consulted a number of therapists and tried a variety of sex therapy techniques, all to no avail. However, at intake, she was asked, for what was later determined to be the first time, about feelings for or experiences with women. This yielded a history of a number of sexually very positive relationships that this woman had had with female peers since early adolescence, which she had failed to reveal to past therapists out of fear of stigma. The client, who was raised in a fundamentalist religious family, reported having a good deal of negative stereotypes about homosexuality, worrying that her uncle's actions had "made me a lesbian," and an active and conscious strategy of engaging in heterosexual activities in an attempt to erase her same-sex desires. Had the therapist not inquired, however, the client had not intended to volunteer any of this information.

Each of these case examples illustrates the possible problems and pitfalls inherent in the perpetuation of heterosexist and anti-sexual minority biases in the delivery of psychotherapy services. In each case, damage was done because a therapist held ignorant beliefs that were founded in biased perceptions. For example, the first therapist expressed the nonconscious prejudice that lesbian (and by inference, gay male) relationships are primarily defined by the presence or absence of overt sexual contact in the couple, and thus presumed to declare her client's relationship "not real" and her client probably heterosexual, although it would be rare for a similar and parallel set of assumptions to be made about a heterosexually identified person with a similar history. This last assertion is illustrated by the second case example, in which a person with a history indicating a possible bisexual or lesbian orientation but with a public heterosexual identity, had been presumed to be a sexually dysfunctional heterosexual person, not a lesbian manqué, and whose marriage, despite the complete absence of sexual contact, had never been questioned as to legitimacy. In her case, the possibility of same-sex feelings and desires had been ignored through three different courses of treatment.

The American Psychological Association (APA) Committee on Lesbian and Gay Concerns (1990), in publishing the report of its Task Force on Bias in Psychotherapy with lesbian and gay men, identified no fewer than 29 separate themes by which such bias could be defined and coded. The report, based on research in which participants, themselves psychotherapists, reported critical incidents of problematic or exemplary practice with sexual minority clients and were also queried regarding their own attitudes and values, is one of the best sources of empirical evidence about the persistence of this bias, 20 years after the APA resolved to take leadership toward "removing the stigma of mental illness long associated with homosexual orientation" (Conger, 1975, p. 633), because it provides concrete information about the state of practice with sexual minority clients.

Some of the bias evinced by the findings of this report was overt, of the extremely negative sort to which Isay (1989) has referred as a form of undigested countertransference regarding homosexuality. One respondent commented,

> "I'm convinced that homosexuality is a genuine personality disorder and not merely a different way of life. Everyone that I have known socially or as a client has been a complete mess psychologically. I think they are simply narcissistic personality disorders—see the description in the DSM III[1]— that's what they have looked and acted like—all of them." (quoted in Committee on Gay and Lesbian Concerns, 1990, p. 15)

Another respondent noted,

> "I have found homosexuals to be disturbed by their homosexuality and distressed by the consequences of that orientation. I state my own bias that homosexuality is abnormally atypical, that is results in excessive emphasis on the sexual aspects of life, and is ultimately self-defeating." (quoted in Committee on Gay and Lesbian Concerns, 1990, p. 15)

Given the demand characteristics of the research itself (e.g., conducted by a sexual-minority-affirmative committee within a group known for its overt support of sexual minority rights), it is likely that a number of therapists with similar attitudes and values simply did not respond to the survey. Such commentary, and other critical incidents of problematic practice reported in this research, indicates that heterosexist and anti-sexual minority bias is pervasive in psychotherapy practice. Common themes of such problematic practice included not simply the sort of overt bias expressed by the two quotes above, but also, as illustrated in the two case examples, other more buried and consequently potentially more pernicious biases. Many sexual minority clients can easily avoid being in treatment with a therapist who expresses overt prejudice. Haldeman (1991) has reviewed the literature on the sort of "sexual orientation conversion" therapies propounded by organizations such as NARTH and has found that they are singularly inefficacious. Few sexual minority persons seek out these treatments, although they represent a continuing presence of problematic overt bias in the mental health disciplines.

But because they are more subtle, what are potentially more problematic than the overtly and intentionally biased therapies and create more risk for clients are the attitudes held by liberal heterosexist therapists who see themselves as friendly to sexual minority persons. For instance, in the first case example cited above, the therapist listed herself in a referral service for lesbians and prided herself on being open to lesbian clients. But like many other therapists affected by heterosexist bias, she viewed sexual minority identity status as hinging entirely on overt sexual behavior and was not able to conceptualize such persons as the celibate lesbian or gay man, or a genuine same-sex couple in which rates of overt sexual activity were low. It is not infrequent for therapists, otherwise well-meaning, to make similar errors that are fundamentally rooted in bias and stereotype that, in turn, have never been challenged by any aspect of training. Common categories of such errors include assuming that an adolescent cannot have a sexual minority identity, assuming that sexual minority feelings are a passing phase or an acting-out behavior, interpreting the normative questioning and distress of sexual minority identity development as evidence of the pathological nature of a person's sexual minority status, or informing clients that they are not "really" sexual minorities because they fail to meet some arbitrary criterion set by the therapist (e.g., gender role nonconformity, or no history of any hetero-sexual feelings or behavior).

There are manifold ways in which unspoken biases that are not identified as such by the therapist can interact with a client's own presenting problems and distress, creating problems for both the client and the therapy process. Incorrect diagnoses are often made and appropriate treatment strategies are not engaged, creating frustration for therapists, who often use these as examples of the greater pathology of sexual minority persons (as per the quote above). Such mistakes also create distress for clients, who feel more hopeless about achieving well-being and perhaps more discounted with respect to their sexual minority status. In the second case example above, a woman came to perceive herself as having a resistant form of sexual dys-function, when perhaps the treatment issue was not sexual dysfunction per se but problems of sexual orientation and identity. The bias of her previous therapists—that everyone who appears heterosexual (i.e., married) must be so—contributed to her feelings of hopelessness about herself as a sexual person and did nothing for her opportunities to explore the meanings of her well-functioning same-sex relationships.

In a case example not previously discussed, an African American man presented to treatment with complaints of social inadequacy, fears of being badly treated, and intrusive images of being harmed. His therapist diagnosed him as having obsessive-compulsive disorder and a possible inadequate personality. She discounted her concerns that the client's problems might have their root in fears of being the target of anti-gay bias, because she discounted these feelings as "irrational in our modern age when homosexu-ality is so accepted." The interaction of the client's shyness and the therapist's certainty that this was not an issue in which his gayness mattered were the genesis of a treatment failure in which the client's self-esteem was even further damaged by his supposed "failure" to respond to either the cognitive-behavioral interventions or the medication prescribed by the therapist. The therapist's failure (in fact, active resistance) to take into account the very real meanings of discrimination and violence in the client's life led to a perpet-uation of his distress. Moreover, it may have contributed to a possible mis-diagnosis, because the presence of frequent insidious trauma (Root, 1992) in the client's life may have warranted a diagnosis of posttraumatic stress disorder (PTSD) instead.

Bisexual and transgendered clients can be especially at risk from this liberal form of heterosexism. The ambiguities presented by either group challenge the therapist's capacity to contain uncertainty, and rather than being taken seriously and respectfully as a real sexual orientation or identity, the behaviors and feelings associated with either status can become the foundation for stigmatizing misdiagnosis. Given prejudices within the lesbian and gay communities, such bias can also be found among lesbian and gay therapists, who may also have more dichotomous and concrete perceptions of human sexuality and sexual identity than are required for respectful treatment of people who fit badly into neat boxes. In another case example, a Caucasian bisexual woman described feeling pressured by a previous therapist to "make up her mind" about her "real" sexual orientation, with the implied message that bisexuality did not meet the criteria for "realness."

Can This Be an Ethical Issue?

I have recently suggested that one way to conceptualize these problems in practice with sexual minority clients is as ethical dilemmas involving competency, both intellectual and emotional (Brown, 1996), parallel to a previous framing of racism in psychotherapy as an ethical issue (Brown, 1991). In this paradigm, *intellectual competency* refers to possessing the requisite training and data to be able to practice safely with a vulnerable population group. *Emotional competency* refers to the awareness of attitudes and feelings that might impair both the therapist's capacity to effectively and compassionately offer services and her or his ability to assess emotional readiness to practice. Both components of competency are equally necessary for ethical practice. Ethical dilemmas arise when either form of competency is deficient or absent. In addition, those practices that contribute to or enable societal oppression of a stigmatized group may be defined as ethically problematic, potentially failing to rise to the standard of ethical practice. Arguably, mental health professionals might see the problem of heterosexism in psychotherapy as a more serious and general concern if linked to the overarching issue of ethical treatment.

There is no clear standard of care in the treatment of sexual minority persons, including no standard that would expressly forbid overtly biased and inefficacious treatments. Many professional organizations have shrunk from identifying a specific standard in this area, because of a variety of expressed rationales about anti-trust considerations and the wish not to alienate members who continue to believe that it is helpful to offer people treatment to change sexual orientation. But in addition to being a possible ethical issue, failures of competency with sexual minority clients may also represent a failure to meet general standards of care.

Prevention Strategies

As is evident from the review above of the current state of practice, much remains to be done to ensure that the mental health professions are free from heterosexist and anti-sexual minority bias. In this section of the chapter, I will outline a variety of strategies for personal, institutional, and discipline-wide changes that would, taken together, result in the eventual prevention of such bias in psychotherapy and counseling.

Making It an Ethical Issue

I would argue that the most effective way to ensure that the prevention, remediation, and elimination of heterosexism and anti-sexual minority bias take place in the mental health professions is to clearly and unequivocally define this as a matter of ethics in psychotherapy. This constitutes a discipline-wide strategy that would have sweeping effects. That is, the expression of such bias in the context of mental health practice must be defined as a gross deviation from the norms of good care, not simply a matter of personal beliefs; failure to demonstrate either or both forms of competency, either intellectual or emotional, regarding sexual minority persons would be failure to meet a consensus standard of care. In fact, this proposition is not a radical change from the current state of affairs. Most extant ethics codes already imply that ethical practice with any vulnerable minority group requires specialized knowledge and careful self-assessment for bias. But one of the ironic effects of anti-sexual minority bias has been to allow exceptions to this rule where sexual minority persons are concerned. The therapist who would refer to a more knowledgeable colleague in a heartbeat when the client has an unfamiliar diagnosis still feels quite comfortable taking on the client about whose identity development and community of reference equally little is known, because one effect of heterosexist bias is to create the impression that human beings are generically heterosexual and thus can be completely comprehended from a heterosexual model.

This explicit enunciation of the ethical framework would require those mental health professionals who persisted in holding biased views to cease their treatment of sexual minority clients or face ethical charges. This would preclude the further development of groups such as NARTH. It would also serve to spur those therapists who hold the liberal position to become more aware and precise in their understanding of sexual minority persons, and their own possible biases, out of a desire to practice ethically in a direction toward which they were already favorably disposed. Because training programs are strongly invested in the creation of ethical and well-regarded practitioners, this would be an incentive to integrate necessary knowledge into the curriculum so that graduates of a training setting would be prepared to practice ethically. Accreditation standards imposed on training programs by the various mental health disciplines would consequently also reflect this norm. Currently, for instance, a program may receive accreditation from the American Psychological Association even if it overtly teaches heterosexist or anti-sexual minority bias, if it claims exemption from normal standards about diversity under a religious freedom clause. However, clear definition of such bias as an ethical violation would preclude this sort of exemption and would require training programs to align themselves firmly with mental health ethics should accreditation be desired.

Anti-Domination Training

In a previous piece of writing, I identified a personal strategy for approaching the problem of racism in psychotherapy that I believe also transfers well to the discussion of preventing heterosexist and anti-sexual minority bias and is conceptually interactive with the construction of bias as an ethical violation. This is the concept of *anti-domination training* (Brown, 1993) as a paradigm for individual awareness and change on variables of oppression and domination. Several premises underlie this model. First, that in a society pervaded by an oppressive bias, all members of that society, including those from the targeted group, will be affected, both cognitively and emotionally, by that bias. This premise challenges one of the core notions of liberal heterosexism, that is, the notion that the absence of overt hostile prejudice is equivalent to the absence of bias. It instead asserts that all both dominant and target group members carry some degree of bias due to membership in a biased culture. The second premise is that members of the dominant group (in this case, the nonsexual minorities) will, even with goodwill, make assumptions and take actions that assert the supremacy of their group over the minority, and that members of the minority group may have learned how to collude in their own oppression through similar sets of actions and attitudes. A third premise is that challenging such bias is a constant and evolving process; no persons can consider themselves to be "done" but only to be advancing to more complex and sophisticated levels of awareness. Fourth is the premise that such biases are created both intellectually and affectively, and as such must be addressed on both levels and at the point of interaction to most effectively eliminate the oppressive dominant biases. The final premise is that unchecked dominant biases interfere with the effective and competent delivery of services, with the corollary that remediation of such bias is necessary for effective treatment.

Thus, anti-domination training requires exposure to cognitively based data to fill in gaps and clarify errors in information about sexual minority identity and experience. In addition, it requires both personal encounters with the reality of sexual minority lives and personal challenge by the clinician to the meanings and value attached to heterosexist biases. For the dominant group clinician, this means exploring the privileges attached to the presumption of heterosexuality and an analysis of how one has participated in making sexual minority persons marginal or invisible. For sexual minority clinicians, this process evokes the manner in which collusion with biases has occurred and the ways in which one may have attempted to disown or minimize sexual minority status so as to aspire to assimilation into the dominant majority.

Personal commitment to the prevention of heterosexist and anti-sexual minority bias requires such a stance of anti-domination. When such a stance pervades the work of a clinician, prevention and remediation of such bias will be ongoing. It is not possible to take the position that one is "not prejudiced" or to affirm that one is unlikely to work with sexual minority clients because one is a neuropsychologist, or a child psychologist, or a health psychologist, or a social worker for refugees, or a psychiatrist who only prescribes medication. The first position is belied by the core assumptions of an anti-domination model, which includes everyone, including members of the minority group, as potentially and probably affected by the bias in question. The second position is challenged both by the general principle inherent in an anti-domination stance, that of willingness to pursue the end of bias for nonutilitarian means, and by the awareness, engendered by participation in the cognitive, information-gathering aspect of anti-domination training, that such statements of "I don't work with" simply cannot be truthfully made. Instead, growing awareness of heterosexism allows a mental health professional to observe the assumptions embedded in such statements; that is, that the generic client of many clinicians is erroneously assumed to be heterosexual.

Institutional Strategies

Institutions for the training and delivery of mental health services are among the most effective places for the propagation of change. As described above, most programs in the mental health disciplines, including internship and residency programs, seek accreditation from their respective professional organizations. The adoption of discipline-wide standards prohibiting biased training and services on ethical grounds would doubtless be an incentive for change in many training programs. However, absent such a large-scale, top-down maneuver, a number of other rationales can be advanced for the inclusion of training materials and experiences that would serve to reduce, remediate, and eventually prevent heterosexist bias.

At a minimum, course material on topics related to sexual minorities needs to be mainstreamed into the entire mental health curriculum at both undergraduate and graduate levels. I personally find the creation of special topics courses to be somewhat problematic. These "word ghettos" tend to be occupied by the few, and to separate out sexual minority concerns from the rest of the training curriculum implies a certain negative uniqueness that runs contrary to the goal of what Baron (1991) has called "making homosexuality boring," that is, normative and integrated into the mainstream of knowledge without the loss of integrity that would come from outright assimilation. Thus, coursework on developmental psychology would include sexual minority identity development among the topics; social psychology courses would study the social organization of lesbian or gay communities and explore the psychology of anti-sexual minority prejudice; psychology of the family would embrace sexual minority families; deviant development or abnormal psychology would study the pathology of prejudice against sexual minorities and the interactive effects of oppression with other forms of psychological distress; and so on. Ethics classes at the graduate level would address the question of competency and standard of care to practice with populations at risk for exploitation or oppression by psychotherapists, including the sexual minority population. Course materials would include information on the special strengths and resilience that derive from sexual minority experience and would consider how the *sexual minority paradigm* (Brown, 1989) might better inform understandings of heterosexual individuals and institutions. Sexual minority students, although respected as any person might be for the information they could bring to a shared learning experience, would not be given the burden of having to teach and train peers and faculty, but rather faculty, including heterosexual faculty, would identify these topics as their responsibility, of interest and value to them.

This last requirement would create some interesting challenges to bias, because implicit assumptions are commonly made about the sexual orientations of faculty with interests in sexual minority concerns. One would hope that all faculty in this position would respond as did a colleague, Cynthia Villis, now the Dean of Students at the University of San Diego, who, while working at a university counseling center in Lubbock, Texas, served as the faculty sponsor of the student lesbian and gay group. When informed several years later that most of the students had assumed that Dr. Villis, a heterosexually identified person, was a lesbian, because "who else would take the risk to sponsor this group in Lubbock?" (to paraphrase my informant, who had been a psychology doctoral student there at the time), she replied that she was delighted that people had come to that conclusion but was afraid she was going to have to disappoint them. In other words, Dr. Villis accepted the ascription of possible sexual minority status as a compliment reflecting the feelings of respect and inclusion emanating from the student group to her; her acceptance also reflected her willingness to be so identified and to not be concerned about "setting the record straight." A similar experience was had by Arnold Kahn, now a professor of psychology at James Madison University, and formerly the APA staff person responsible for working with the Committee on Lesbian and Gay Concerns. For many years, Dr. Kahn was assumed to be gay simply because of his work with and consequent advocacy for lesbian and gay issues in psychology. He has responded to this in a manner similar to Dr. Villis's. Although initially faculty in training programs need to be prepared that they may be assumed to be sexual minority once they take an interest in these matters, one salutary effect of making this topic everyone's responsibility is that working or teaching on topics related to sexual minority issues will not imply anything about one's sexual orientation.

Ideally, students would be exposed to practicum, internship, and supervision experiences that would aid them in becoming aware of heterosexist and anti-sexual minority bias. Supervisors would be screened by training programs for evidence that they were actively participating in their own anti-domination work on this topic; internship and practicum settings would be designed to maximize the possibility that all students, no matter what their interests, will have some opportunities to work with sexual minority clients, or members of their families and support systems, or both. Available evidence suggest that this sort of exposure would tend to greatly reduce heterosexist biases in students so trained.

The provision of specific training in sexual minority affirmative models of treatment would also be an important aspect of preventing bias. Such models integrate into their paradigms for normal development and their understandings of what constitutes pathology the normative life experiences and developmental concerns of sexual minority individuals (Gonsiorek, 1982; Hancock, 1995). Although these models have been designed primarily with lesbians and gay men in mind, they are potentially applicable both to other sexual minority clients and to an enhanced understanding of heterosexual clients who may in some other manner not conform to mainstream cultural norms and values. In essence, sexual minority affirmative models for treatment constitute paradigms for positively valuing resistance, a reframing of deviance into a nonpathological and potentially resilient response pattern. The inclusion of training in such models would greatly enhance prevention of heterosexism but would also likely aid in reducing other forms of nonconscious adherence by trainees to oppressive dominant norms on other dimensions.

Heterosexism and Effective Outcomes: At Odds

Recently, the psychotherapy professions have been challenged from within and without to demonstrate effectiveness and to reduce clients' dependency on therapists. Pressures from without arise from the managed care industry, which favors payment for short-term, solution-focused therapy and has been systematically winnowing out those therapists who cannot demonstrate effectiveness in this model. Internally, particularly within psychology, there has been a movement for a more empirically based approach to treatment in which students are taught only those methods whose effectiveness has been proven in a research context. Although both of these perspectives are not without controversy (the former for prescribing one-size-fits-all models of treatment, the latter for biases against noncognitive-behavioral models of intervention), they represent very important concerns to many academics who are involved in the training of mental health professionals.

Arguably, heterosexist and anti-sexual minority bias impedes treatment effectiveness. Consequently, a commitment to treatment effectiveness would entail the prevention or remediation of such bias. Referring back to the case example of the client with the social discomfort and intrusive thoughts of being discriminated against, it would appear that treatment would have been far more effective had the issue of his fears of bias-based violence been directly addressed rather than discounted by the therapist. A cognitive constructivist model for cognitive therapy, which has proven treatment effectiveness and can potentially be conducted within a relatively short time frame, would take into account the fact that for this client such fears are not irrational but instead are reflective of social realities. When both client and therapist are struggling past the barriers created by heterosexist belief and assumptions, therapy will not progress as planned.

Taken together, a number of different rationales can be embraced for inclusion of topics on sexual minority issues into the graduate training curriculum. It is important that training faculties cease to define this as a political issue and instead realize that this is a matter of ethics, standard of care, and psychotherapy effectiveness, all broad general principles that are universally embraced by those training mental health professionals. The clear linkage of such principles to the elimination of heterosexist bias would strongly increase the likelihood of prevention in training programs.

Postprofessional Education

But what of the many already practicing mental health professionals who are currently working with their heterosexist biases already in place? This may be a more difficult population to reach, and in this case we are clearly speaking of secondary and tertiary intervention strategies rather than primary prevention of the pathology of the heterosexist and biased psychotherapist. However, several possible interventions have been shown to be helpful in reaching currently practicing clinicians.

The institution of continuing education requirements for all mental health professions, and the specific targeting of a requirement for further education on the topic of sexual minorities, is one such possible strategy. Several states that require continuing education already earmark certain portions of it for specific topics; for example, Washington State requires 7 hours of AIDS education for psychologists and psychiatrists and 4 hours for other mental health professionals; California requires a specific number of hours of training in both human sexuality and child abuse. Training on sexual minority issues can be integrated into extant continuing education requirements. This would have the secondary effect of increasing the status and value ascribed to the topic and to those expert and capable in the field of sexual minority issues, because the topic would no longer be marginalized.

The development and enforcement of clear standards of care for the treatment of sexual minority clients would be another strategy for reaching the practicing clinician. This could parallel such documents as the *Standards for Delivery of Services to Culturally Diverse Populations* currently published by the APA, which establishes a standard of care for the entire range of psychological services with racial and ethnic minority populations. Such documents would require careful formulation both to be inclusive of a variety of theoretical orientations and to avoid possible anti-trust exclusions; however, it is clearly possible to achieve such a goal. Thorough dissemination of such a document and a willingness to enforce the standards contained therein would also motivate clinicians to remediate gaps in their knowledge base and thus become aware of potential sources of nonconscious bias in their work.

Consumer Education

The world of psychotherapy practice has become ever more clearly a marketplace in which therapists are required to sell themselves and their work to increasingly skeptical and demanding consumers. If sexual minority clients, who are high-end users of psychotherapy services, began to demand care that was free of bias, this would likely go far toward its prevention and elimination. Currently, many sexual minority persons who seek treatment are inadequately informed as to their rights as psychotherapy consumers and unaware that they can demand bias-free care from their psychotherapists. A parallel can be drawn with trends in the treatment of women over the past two decades. Since Chesler (1972) first drew public attention to the presence of sexist biases in psychotherapy, women, both heterosexual and sexual minority, have been demanding nonsexist treatment and specialized knowledge about women's lives from their mental health providers. Although the project of eliminating sexism from psychotherapy is far from being accomplished, nonetheless it is striking to note how many psychotherapists advertise themselves as knowledgeable about "women's issues." Consumer pressure has made the acquisition of such expertise a valuable tool in the marketplace.

Similarly, the acquisition of special skills and knowledge regarding sexual minority concerns should be seen as a consumer selling point. Anecdotally, it would appear that even in the age of managed mental health care, clinicians who serve a largely sexual minority population report little diminution in their incomes or client populations. Although this market advantage might be diminished somewhat by an increase in clinicians who could offer clients bias-free therapy, it is my belief that this would continue to be a valuable aspect of what a clinician would offer consumers.

Promotion and strengthening of a consumer rights movement in sexual minority communities would thus be likely to have a strong impact on the remediation and prevention of heterosexist bias. In addition, such a movement might help to raise questions about the overuse of therapy in sexual minority communities and work to provide alternatives that are more peer-based and equal than is psychotherapy.

Conclusion

Ultimately, all of our efforts to reduce and prevent heterosexist and anti-sexual minority bias in psychotherapy must reflect the political realities of the social and cultural milieu in which psychotherapy and the training for its practice take place. The ultimate strategy for eliminating bias in psychotherapy is to eliminate it in the culture at large; much of the work that must be done in the training of clinicians is about detection and engagement with the cognitive and affective artifacts of growing up in a biased culture. Thus, the mental health provider with a commitment to preventing bias in psychotherapy must also be engaged in combating bias in the broader community, either specifically as a mental health professional or simply as a concerned citizen. As long as bias and violence flourish, the goals of primary prevention will not be met.

Specific strategies that can be engaged by mental health professionals include offering of expert testimony at hearings on civil rights legislation, preparing amicus curiae briefs in court cases involving sexual minority civil rights, developing public education campaigns to raise awareness and information and to combat prejudice, and developing curricula at a variety of educational levels. In addition, mental health professionals can continue to ensure that our respective professional organizations take the lead in combating heterosexist biases on a society level in addition to making it an important aspect of mental health education and training.

Preventing heterosexist and anti-sexual minority bias in psychotherapy should be a simple matter of ethical, effective practice. This goal will be accomplished when the equation of the two is taken for granted by all mental health professionals and by those who educate and train them.

Note

1. See American Psychiatric Association (1987).

References

American Psychiatric Association. (1987). *Diagnostic and statistical manual of mental disorder* (3rd ed., rev.). Washington, DC: Author.

Baron, A. (1991). The challenge: To make homosexuality boring. *The Counseling Psychologist, 19*, 239-244.

Brown, L. S. (1989). New voices, new visions: Towards a lesbian/gay paradigm for psychology. *Psychology of Women Quarterly, 13*, 445-458.

Brown, L. S. (1991). Anti-racism as a ethical imperative: An example from feminist therapy. *Ethics and Behavior, 1*, 113-127.

Brown, L. S. (1993). Anti-domination training as a central component of diversity in clinical psychology education. *The Clinical Psychologist, 46*, 83-87.

Brown, L. S. (1996). Ethical issues in mental health treatment with sexual minorities. In T. Stein & R. Cabaj (Eds.), *Textbook of homosexuality and mental health* (pp. 897-916). Washington, DC: American Psychiatric Press.

Buhrke, R. A. (1989). Female student perspectives on training in lesbian and gay issues. *The Counseling Psychologist, 17*, 629-636.

Buhrke, R. A., & Douce, L. A. (1991). Training issues for counseling psychologists in working with lesbian women and gay men. *The Counseling Psychologist, 19*, 216-234.

Chesler, P. (1972). *Women and madness.* New York: Doubleday.

Committee on Lesbian and Gay Concerns. (1990). *Final report of the Task Force on Bias in Psychotherapy with lesbians and gay men.* Washington, DC: Author.

Conger, J. (1975). Proceedings of the American Psychological Association, Inc., for the year 1987: Minutes of the annual meeting of the council of representatives. *American Psychologist, 30*, 620-651.

Duberman, M. (1991). *Cures: A gay man's odyssey.* New York: Dutton.

Garnets, L., Hancock, K. A., Cochran, S. D., Goodchilds, J., & Peplau, L. A. (1991). Issues in psychotherapy with lesbians and gay men: A survey of psychologists. *American Psychologist, 46*, 964-972.

Goodman, L., Koss, M., Russo, N. F., Fitzgerald, L., Browne, A., & Keita, G. P. (1994). *No safe haven*. Washington, DC: American Psychological Association.

Gonsiorek, J. (Ed.). (1982). *Homosexuality and psychotherapy: A practitioner's handbook*. New York: Haworth.

Greene, B. (1994). Lesbian and gay sexual orientation: Implications for clinical training, practice and research. In B. Greene & G. Herek (Eds.), *Lesbian and gay psychology* (pp. 1-24). Thousand Oaks, CA: Sage.

Haldeman, D. (1991). Sexual orientation conversion therapy for gay men and lesbians: A scientific examination. In J. Gonsiorek & J. Weinrich (Eds.), *Homosexuality: Research implications for public policy* (pp. 149-160). Newbury Park, CA: Sage.

Hancock, K. (1995). Psychotherapy with lesbians and gay men. In A. R. D'Augelli & C. J. Patterson (Eds.), *Lesbian, gay and bisexual identities over the lifespan* (pp. 398-432). New York: Oxford University Press.

Isay, R. (1989). *Being homosexual: Gay men and their development*. New York: Giroux.

Kitzinger, C., & Perkins, R. (1993). *Changing our minds: Lesbian feminism and psychology*. New York: New York University Press.

Markowitz, L. M. (1991, January-February). Homosexuality: Are we still in the dark? *The Family Therapy Networker*, pp. 26-29, 31-35.

Pope, K. S., & Feldman-Summers, S. (1992). National survey of psychologists' sexual and physical abuse history and their evaluation of training and competence in these areas. *Professional Psychology: Research and Practice, 23,* 353-361.

Root, M. P. P. (1992). Reconstructing the impact of trauma on personality. In L. S. Brown & M. Ballou (Eds.), *Personality and psychopathology: Feminist reappraisals* (pp. 229-266). New York: Guilford.

Rothblum, E. D., & Brehony, K. (Eds.). (1993). *Boston marriages: Romantic but asexual relationships among contemporary lesbians*. Amherst: University of Massachusetts Press.

Ryan, C., & Bradford, J. (1993). The national lesbian health care survey: An overview. In L. Garnets & D. K. Kimmel (Eds.), *Psychological perspectives on lesbian and gay male experiences* (pp. 541-556). New York: Columbia University Press.

Thompson, K., & Andrzejewski, J. (1988). *Why can't Sharon Kowalski come home?* San Francisco: Spinsters/Aunt Lute.

Wooley, G. (1991, Jan./Feb.). Beware the well-intentioned therapist. *The Family Therapy Networker*, p. 30.

4

Lesbians and Gay Men of Color: The Legacy of Ethnosexual Mythologies in Heterosexism

Beverly Greene

Racism, sexism, and heterosexism are all embedded pervasively in our society and in our socialization. These varied types of oppression assume both personal and institutional designs. Furthermore, the discriminatory practices that accompany them create a unique range of psychological demands and stressors that victims of oppression must learn to manage in addition to the routine range of developmental tasks and life stressors that everyone else faces. Clinical training must include an understanding of the salient factors that must be considered in human development in the context of discriminatory systems and institutions, and in ways that are sensitive to the complex psychological and cultural realities of oppressed group members. In the context of heterosexism, its varied incarnations and the different ways that it is experienced must be explored and better understood for a wider range of lesbians and gay men. Failing to consider these variables in the delivery of mental health services and in the theoretical perspectives underlying practice may serve only to perpetuate our ignorance and ultimately contribute to rather than mitigate social ills.

There has been a significant growth in the psychological literature that finally explores gay and lesbian sexual orientations from affirmative perspectives (see Garnets & Kimmel, 1991, for an overview). Similarly, there has been a parallel increase in the study of the role of culture, ethnicity, and racial discrimination on psychological development. Discussions of the relevant effects of membership in institutionally oppressed groups and of the development of psychological resilience as well as vulnerability are gradually gaining visibility. This is reflected in a rapidly expanding literature that explores these areas from a wide range of perspectives. The degree to which racism, sexism, and heterosexism are embedded in theoretical paradigms and research in mental health, and their subsequent effects on practice have also

59

been an appropriate focus of attention in the psychological literature (Espín & Gawelek, 1992). Relevant questions have been raised about the effects of negative stereotypes about people of color and lesbians and gay men on the thinking of practitioners and theoreticians and the subsequent role of such thinking in perpetuating those negative stereotypes. Rarely, however, do these inquiries examine the complexity of issues when a person is a member of both groups. In this context, the process of psychological assessment and treatment must incorporate an understanding of these phenomena and their effects on the delivery of psychological services (Chan, 1989; Greene, 1994b, 1994c; Mays & Cochran, 1988). Lesbians and gay men who are members of ethnic minority groups, however, find themselves and their concerns as invisible in scholarly research in these areas as they often find themselves in the faces of their respective communities. Failing to understand their plight will limit our understanding of heterosexism, because it is not a singular or isolated experience for lesbians and gay men who are members of visible ethnic minority groups.

Most of the empirical research on or with lesbians and gay men is conducted with overwhelmingly white middle-class participants (Chan, 1989; Greene, 1994b, 1994c; Morales, 1992). Similarly, research conducted with people of color rarely acknowledges that not all of a group's members are heterosexual. Hence, the complex interaction between sexual orientation and ethnic identity development remains largely unexplored. Similarly, the realistic social tasks and stressors that are a component of gay and lesbian identity formation for visible ethnic minority group members are not well understood or studied. The vicissitudes of racism, ethnic similarities, and ethnic differences in same-gender couples and the effect of these variables on their relationships are also neglected both in the narrow focus on heterosexual couples found in the literature on ethnic minority clients and in the equally narrow focus on predominantly white couples in the gay and lesbian literature.

Furthermore, the sampling biases found in the research in this area are rarely discussed explicitly either in titles of papers or in statements warning readers of the limited generalizability of their findings. This may not only reflect but in fact reinforce the invisibility of lesbians and gay men of color. It can facilitate the tendency for ethnic minority families and communities to deny the existence and appropriate visible inclusion of their gay and lesbian members. Also, it may allow the lesbian and gay communities to avoid examining the diversity, ethnocentrism, and racism within their own ranks.

An exclusive focus on heterosexism as the primary locus of oppression for all lesbians and gay men presumes that it is experienced in the same way for all group members and that it has the same meaning for them. The core of this assumption is not uncommon either in the psychological literature or in practice. Human identity is often understood as something that consists of isolated parts that can be observed and experienced wholly separate from one another, rather than as an integrated whole. The tendency to partition identity into hierarchies leads us to assume that we can view oppressions hierarchically as well. These assumptions make it more difficult for us to understand more complex experiences. For example, feminist psychology has been appropriately assailed for its tendency to put forth an analysis of issues deemed relevant to all women when in fact the analysis has been created and articulated primarily by white middle- and upper-class women and based on their experiences. Although those experiences and the assumptions that follow certainly have some validity for those who articulate them, they cannot be considered generalizable to all women. Such an analysis does not reflect the wide range of diversity among women nor has it, traditionally, seriously considered the interlocking and complex nature of racial and gender oppression for women of color (Espín & Gawelek, 1992). Essentially, we need to better understand how racial oppression transforms the meaning or affects the salience of gender oppression for women of color and how gender affects racial oppression. Similarly, lesbian and gay psychology has failed to reflect the diversity among lesbians and gay men and, in doing so, it leaves us with an incomplete view of the range of dilemmas confronting lesbians and gay men as a group. As in the former example, we are not given any solid appreciation of the way in which not only racial and ethnic oppression but also ethnic and cultural derivatives transform or color the meaning and experience of heterosexism. Without some discussion of social and cultural context, we are left with a limited view of what is involved in sexual orientation identity development; indeed, we may even question whether, in certain cultures, there is an equivalent concept. Another more serious consequence of such omissions is that when doing clinical work with lesbians and gay men of color, practitioners are left ill equipped to address their clients' clinical needs in ways that are culturally literate and competent.

In both the psychology and the politics of oppression, we acknowledge that those who have the power to define experience also have the power to confer or deny legitimacy to experience. Celia Kitzinger (1995; see Chapter 1, this volume) eloquently notes that an exclusive focus on the most explicit, blatant, or outrageous incidents of heterosexism fails to capture the oppressiveness of omission. She aptly characterizes these omissions as silences, absences, and evasions. In his work on the silencing of African American men, Anderson Franklin (in press) refers to the collective effect of these phenomena as the *invisibility syndrome*. Maya Angelou (1989) uses Jules Feiffer's term, the *little murders,* with her own term, *the petty humiliations,* to refer to the violent and oppressive effect of silencing. She notes that although the most blatant incidents of oppression, which she refers to as the *grand executions,* are obviously deadly, the petty humiliations have a grinding, wearing-down effect as they accumulate over time, just as oppressive and just as deadly. Therefore, the effects of chronic, lifelong stressors associated with multiple identities and complex solutions must be more carefully addressed.

The very act of defining the experiences of all lesbians and gay men by the characteristics of the most privileged and powerful members of that group is an act of oppression. It does not ultimately undermine heterosexism, because heterosexism has an interlocking relationship to other forms of oppression. On the contrary, it facilitates it. It does so by tolerating the invisibility and thus the silencing of group members who are not members of the dominant group. The silence and absence of lesbians and gay men of color in all considerations regarding lesbian and gay persons, often reflected in the failure to speak about them or their needs, and the tendency to represent the needs of the dominant group as if it represents the full spectrum of lesbians and gay men, permit this sinister evasion. This tendency permits majority lesbians and gay men to identify themselves simply as victims of heterosexism and to use that status as a victim to ignore, at the very least, and to perpetuate, at the worst, racial hierarchy and oppression. It also permits them to avoid a realistic confrontation with their own racism.

In psychotherapy with lesbians and gay men of color, a range of factors should be considered in determining the impact of ethnic or racial identity and its ongoing, dynamic interaction with sexual orientation or any other aspect of a client's life. An exclusive focus on sexual orientation development and heterosexism will not be helpful. Heterocentric thinking leads to a range of inaccurate but commonly held assumptions about gay men and lesbians that are believed to varying degrees among people of color as they are in the dominant culture. One of the most commonly accepted of these false beliefs is that to be gay or lesbian is to want to be a member of the other gender, which is socially constructed as if it were the opposite gender. This is also presumed to be direct evidence of one's defect. Men are expected to be sexually attracted to women only, and women to men only. Sexual attraction to the other gender is believed to be an explicit and essential component of being a "normal" man or woman. Quite simply, reproductive sexuality is presumed to be the only form of sexuality that is psychologically normal and morally correct, deeming lesbians and gay men defective (Greene, 1994b; Kite, 1994). Another insidious assumption is that there is a linear connection between sexual orientation and people's conformity or failure to conform to traditional gender stereotypes of roles and physical appearance (Kite, 1994). The questionable conclusion in this scheme is that men and women who do not conform to traditional gender role stereotypes must be gay or lesbian. An equally mistaken assumption is that those who do conform to such stereotypes must be heterosexual. Hence, to understand the meaning and the reality of being a lesbian or gay man of color requires a careful exploration and understanding of the importance of cultural gender roles, the nature of the culture's traditional gender role stereotypes, the relative fluidity or rigidity of those roles, their range, and their place in the family hierarchy.

For members of some oppressed groups, specifically African Americans and Native Americans, reproductive sexuality is viewed as the only real way of continuing the group's presence in the world. Hence, birth control or sexuality that is not reproductive may be viewed by group members as part of the dominant culture's deliberate scheme to limit the numbers of these groups or eliminate them entirely. Kanuha (1990) refers to such beliefs as *fears of extinction* and suggests that although these fears themselves are legitimate, they are being used to support the scapegoating of lesbians and gay men of color as if they were responsible for threats to the group's survival. The expression of such fears conveniently ignores the reality that a lesbian or gay sexual orientation and parenthood are not mutually exclusive, particularly among lesbians of color. Fears of extinction are not a result of paranoia. Furthermore, there are realistic threats to the survival of people of color. However, it is the institutional racism of the dominant culture that places the survival of people of color at risk—not lesbians, gay men, or heterosexuals who choose not to reproduce. Nonetheless, the internalization of this view, especially if lesbians or gay men of color believe that they are disappointing parents or family or failing to live up to their responsibility to "uplift and preserve the race," can make it more difficult for them to affirmatively accept their sexual orientation. It may also increase the difficulty of maintaining ties to both the family of origin and the ethnic peer community.

Within the family context, the role and expectations of parents in the lives of adult children are important to consider. For example, what is the extent to which the parents or family of origin may control or influence adult family members? The answer to this question and the importance of the family as a source of tangible and emotional support warrant understanding. Other factors to consider include the importance of procreation and the continuation of the family line, continuation of the racial or ethnic group, the degree and intensity of religious values as well as the presence of religiosity in the family, the importance of ties to the ethnic community, the degree of acculturation or assimilation of the individual, and the history of discrimination or oppression the particular group has experienced from members of the dominant culture. When the history of discrimination of the ethnic group is examined, it is imperative that group members' understanding of their oppression and their strategies for coping with it be an explicit part of any analysis.

Another important dimension is that of sexuality. Sexuality and its meaning are contextual. Therefore, what it means to be a gay man or lesbian will be related to the meaning assigned to sexuality in the culture (Chan, 1989; Greene, 1994a, 1994b; Mays & Cochran, 1988; Morales, 1992). It is important to explore the range of sexuality that is sanctioned, regardless of whether or to what degree sexuality may be expressed or to what degree it must be repressed. It is also important to explore whether it may be expressed or acknowledged directly or indirectly and whether such injunctions are gender coded. Women in some cultures may be expected to notice but appear oblivious to sexual attention or desire. If so, how does this affect the lesbians or gay men in that culture in their relationships? Finally, what are the repercussions for those who deviate from these cultural norms, and what are the rewards for conforming?

In the treatment of lesbians and gay men of color, gross descriptions of cultural imperatives of a specific ethnic minority group cannot be presumed to represent uniformly all of the group's members. Although there is much diversity between ethnic groups and the dominant culture that makes them different, there is great diversity within them as well. The clinician should always start with a framework or outline from which to begin looking at lesbians and gay men of color from a more diverse perspective. This diverse perspective begins with a familiarity with the cultural norms and practices of the client's ethnic group. Clinicians then need to explore every client's individual background from that person's unique experience of that background and its importance to him or her. This information can help sensitize practitioners to cultural factors bearing significantly on the ways that individuals understand the world, their dilemma, and their range of options.

Ethnosexual Mythology and Heterosexism

It is important to determine both the ethnosexual mythology that applies to any person of color and the relationship of this mythology to the understanding of a gay or lesbian sexual orientation (Greene, 1994a, 1994c). Ethnosexual mythology may be defined as the sexual myths the dominant culture has generated and maintains about men and women of color. Such myths and stereotypes often represent a complex combination of racial and sexual stereotypes originally designed to objectify men and women of color, set them apart from their idealized, white counterparts, and facilitate their sexual exploitation, exploitation of their labor, and ultimately their control (Collins, 1990). Their meaning and interaction with stereotypes held about lesbians and gay men are important areas of inquiry. I will offer a brief analysis with African Americans as an example.

For African Americans, families involve an often large and extended group of people or kin who might not be blood related, that exists in complex networks of obligation and support and tends to be more tribal and group-oriented than the Western model of rugged individualism (Boyd-Franklin, 1990). For many African Americans, the people in the communities that they grew up in are experienced as family; hence, the loss of family or rejection by it can go beyond the loss of nuclear family and can have a profound effect on the person's sense of connectedness or belonging. This has many important implications for African American lesbians and gay men (Greene & Boyd-Franklin, 1996).

Ethnosexual stereotypes about African Americans have their roots in images created by a white society struggling to reconcile a range of contradictions. Examples include the use of female slaves for breeding purposes with other slaves, the practice of forced sexual relationships with slave masters in what we understand was essentially rape, and perhaps the existence of slavery itself, conducted openly and with legitimacy, in a society purporting to base its values on the principles of democracy and the Christian faith (Fox-Genovese, 1988). The successful reconciliation of these blatant contradictions was accomplished in part by brute force, by discriminatory legal civil practices, and by reconfiguring the identities of African Americans (Carraway, 1991; Collins, 1990). They were depicted as not only less than human but also as sexually bestial, sexually aggressive, and victims of their own natural propensities (propensities deemed unnatural for the dominant group but viewed as representing normative behavior for African Americans), rather than as victims of a system in which they were allowed no control over their destinies for centuries (Greene, 1994a).

One of many of the mechanisms used for maintaining the distortions of African Americans is described by bell hooks (1981). She proposes that the image of women as castrating was promulgated by psychoanalysis of the 1950s to stigmatize any woman who wanted to work outside the home or cross the gender role stereotypes of a patriarchal culture. Although not specifically created for the purpose of stigmatizing African American women per se, the effect of this view on their already distorted identities will become obvious. Historically, the status of slave superseded the status of female. Because racism had not historically deferred to African American and Caribbean women's femininity, these women already worked outside the home in larger numbers than their white counterparts (Collins, 1990; Greene, 1994a). Popular images of these women of color as castrating were created in the interest of maintaining the arrangement of social power in which African American men and women were subordinate to whites, and women were subordinate to men. The African American woman was once routinely depicted in popular television programs as the strong, shrewish, nagging wife of a simpering, lazy black man. Hence, today's stereotypes, the descendants of these images, are riddled with a legacy of ethnosexual myths that depict African American women both as not sufficiently subordinate to African American men and as being inherently sexually promiscuous, morally loose, independent, strong, assertive, matriarchal, castrating, and masculinized when compared to their white counterparts. African American women clearly did not fit the traditional stereotypes of women as fragile, weak, and dependent. Economic conditions precluded this, even for those who would have gladly adopted such roles. They came to be defined as all the things that normal women were not supposed to be. These images of what so-called normal women should be are connected to heterosexism.

Negative stereotypes of lesbians as masculinized females poignantly intersect with stereotypes of African American women in this regard. Both are negatively depicted with similar characteristics as if they are defective women who want to be or act like men and are sexually preoccupied predators. It is important to understand the link between these negative images of lesbians and the history of institutional racism, particularly the significant role institutional racism has held in the development of a legacy of confounded myths and distortions regarding the sexuality of women of color. Lesbians of color may be more vulnerable in these arrangements. First, they are women of color and deemed inferior to their white counterparts. Second, they are women and deemed inferior to men. Third, as lesbians they are deemed failures as women, defective women, because they are not exclusively attracted to men.

Racism, sexism, and heterosexism converge in the attempts to present African American women as the cause of failure of their family structures— reflected in the matriarchy theories (Moynihan, 1965). Thus emerged an assertion that is still held by some members of the African American community, and the dominant culture as well, that male dominance and female subordination are the real keys to liberating people of African descent. The use of gender hierarchies to minimize the pernicious role of racism in the lives of African Americans is implicated in the stigmatization of African American lesbians. Men in the culture are encouraged to believe that not racist institutions but strong women are responsible for their oppression. Remember, for African American communities just as for the dominant culture, sexual attraction to the other gender is embedded in what it means to be a normal man or woman (Gomez & Smith, 1990). Gay men and lesbians are presumed, because they are attracted to members of the same gender, to *want* to be members of the other gender, and they are deemed defective. Hence, women who are not subordinate to men may be seen as deserving to be controlled by men who, if they are "real men," want to dominate them. Of course, this includes sexual domination. Therefore, even the heterosexual man who is not interested in dominating women becomes suspect. Is he a "real man" or is he a defective man?

The history of role flexibility in African American families was both an important cultural derivative and an adaptive response to racism (Boyd-Franklin, 1990). Rigid gender role stratification was never practically suited to their economic survival. Despite the adaptive value of this practice, the threat of being labeled gay or lesbian and perceived as having a gender defect, regardless of whether one is, may be used to maintain rigid gender roles. These rigid gender roles, in turn, reinforce gender hierarchies of sexism and, in the ways I have described, reinforce heterosexism. A link is established between the coveted achievement of manhood for African American men and the subordination of women. Women who fail to adhere to gender role stereotypes or subordination are deemed defective, and lesbians are seen as defective women.

Many African American women and men have internalized these myths. When internalized, these myths, distortions, and stereotypic depictions of African Americans' sexuality as depraved can intensify the negative psychological effects on African American lesbians and gay men in ways that are obvious. This can further compromise their ability to obtain support from their families and their ethnic communities.

Popular ethnosexual myths and images are relevant to the way that lesbians and gay men of color are viewed and certainly the way that many of them view themselves. Similarly, this legacy of sexual racism plays a role in the response of many people of color to lesbians and gay men either in their families or as visible members of their communities. It is therefore important to determine the ethnosexual mythology that applies to any person of color and its relationship to that person's understanding of sexual orientation.

Ethnosexual mythology may be defined as the sexual myths the dominant culture has generated and holds about persons of color. Such myths and stereotypes often represent a complex combination of racial and sexual stereotypes, whose original purpose was to disguise the social reality of racial oppression for large numbers of people by simply objectifying them and devaluing them while simultaneously idealizing their white counterparts, all in the interest of facilitating their sexual exploitation and control. Hazel Carby (1987) reminds us that the purpose of stereotypes is not to accurately reflect reality but to disguise a social reality, one that those in power benefit from and do not want exposed. Their meaning and interaction with stereotypes held about lesbians and gay men are important areas of inquiry.

In this context, there is the potential for negative effects on the health and psychological well-being of lesbians and gay men of color. Mental health practitioners must make themselves aware of the distinct combinations of stressors and psychological demands impinging on members of these groups, particularly the potential for isolation, anger, and frustration. Aside from being culturally literate and competent, the practitioner must develop a sense of the unique experience of the client with respect to the importance of ethnic identity, gender, and sexual orientation, and the need to establish priorities in an often confusing and painful maze of loyalties and estrangements. Effective work with African Americans or members of any visible ethnic minority group must first acknowledge the significance of multiple, overlapping, and conflicting realities and identities that constitute the complexity of their being. Furthermore, we are challenged to develop a broader understanding of both the complex nature of human beings and the role of varied ethnic, sexual orientation, and other identities as reflections of a healthy range of human diversity.

Summary

The focus of this volume reflects our attempts to better understand heterosexism and to place it in as many contexts as possible, with the hope that our greater understandings will assist us in preventing its occurrence. We are reminded, however, that when we seek to understand and prevent heterosexism in the life of an individual or group, we must place this phenomenon in the context of the culture of the person or persons whose dilemma we seek to address. For lesbians and gay men of color, heterosexism is complicated and affected by the history of cultural imperatives of the group and the history of discriminatory practices against that group by the dominant culture in the United States.

Race, gender, and sexual orientation are at once visible and invisible, important characteristics of a person's identity. Racial minority status, gender roles, and gay and lesbian sexual orientations are dimensions that create intense feelings and opinions in most people socialized in the United States. Psychologists are no exception. Therefore, it is important that psychologists learn to explore and understand these issues appropriately, first in themselves and then in their clients. Few topics, however, are more scrupulously avoided in the formal training of clinicians. Just as ethnic minority group members have been harmed by a legacy of racially stigmatizing psychological folklore, gay and lesbian clients are also harmed by the negative heterosexist bias that pervades psychotherapy literature and practice. Just as ethnic minority clients can be harmed by the unexamined racism in the therapist, gay and lesbian clients can be harmed by the unexamined heterosexist bias in their therapists. The ethnic minority gay or lesbian client in therapy is doubly and triply vulnerable to the vicissitudes of the therapist's ignorance of the important ways in which routine life stressors may be intensified, and catastrophic stressors made unmanageable, for individuals who are actively discriminated against by the dominant culture and may find few safe havens on any side. Unraveling the conundrum of heterosexism requires explicit attention and exploration of the variables discussed in this chapter.

References

Angelou, M. (1989, June 2). In D. DiMaio (Exec. Prod.), *The Oprah Winfrey Show: Between Friends*. Chicago: American Broadcasting Company.

Boyd-Franklin, N. (1990). *Black families in therapy: A multisystems approach*. New York: Guilford.

Carby, H. (1987). *Reconstructing womanhood: The emergence of the African American woman novelist*. New York: Oxford University Press.

Carraway, N. (1991). *Segregated sisterhood: Racism and the politics of American feminism*. Knoxville: University of Tennessee Press.

Chan, C. (1989). Issues of identity development among Asian American lesbians and gay men. *Journal of Counseling and Development, 68*(1), 16-20.

Collins, P. H. (1990). Homophobia and black lesbians. In P. H. Collins (Ed.), *Black feminist thought: Knowledge, consciousness, and the politics of empowerment* (pp. 192-196). Boston: Unwin Hyman.

Espín, O., & Gawelek, M. A. (1992). Women's diversity: Ethnicity, race, class, and gender in theories of feminist psychology. In L. Brown & M. Ballou (Eds.), *Personality and psychopathology: Feminist reappraisals* (pp. 88-107). New York: Guilford.

Fox-Genovese, E. (1988). *Within the plantation household: Black and white women of the old South*. Chapel Hill: University of North Carolina Press.

Franklin, A. J. (in press). *The invisibility syndrome*. San Francisco: Jossey-Bass.

Garnets, L., & Kimmel, D. (1991). Lesbian and gay male dimensions in the psychological study of human diversity. In J. Goodchilds (Ed.), *Psychological perspectives on human diversity in America* (pp. 137-192). Washington, DC: American Psychological Association.

Gomez, J., & Smith, B. (1990). Taking the home out of homophobia: Black lesbian health. In Evelyn C. White (Ed.), *The black women's health book: Speaking for ourselves* (pp. 198-213). Seattle, WA: Seal.

Greene, B. (1994a). African American women. In L. Comas-Diaz & B. Greene (Eds.), *Women of color: Integrating ethnic and gender identities in psychotherapy* (pp. 10-29). New York: Guilford.

Greene, B. (1994b). Ethnic minority lesbians and gay men: Mental health and treatment issues. *Journal of Consulting and Clinical Psychology, 62,* 243-251.

Greene, B. (1994c). Lesbian women of color. In L. Comas-Diaz & B. Greene, (Eds.), *Women of color: Integrating ethnic and gender identities in psychotherapy* (pp. 389-427). New York: Guilford.

Greene, B., & Boyd-Franklin, N. (1996). African American lesbians: Issues in couples therapy. In J. Laird & R. J. Green (Eds.), *Lesbian and gay men in families: A handbook for therapists*. San Francisco: Jossey-Bass.

hooks, b. (1981). *Black women and feminism.* Boston: South End.

Kanuha, V. (1990). Compounding the triple jeopardy: Battering in lesbian of color relationships. *Women & Therapy, 9,* 169-183.

Kite, M. (1994). When perceptions meet reality: Individual differences in reactions to lesbians and gay men. In B. Greene & G. Herek (Eds.), *Lesbian and gay psychology: Theory, research and clinical applications* (pp. 25-53). Thousand Oaks, CA: Sage.

Kitzinger, C. (1995, June). *Speaking of oppression: Psychology, politics, and the language of power.* Keynote address presented at the Vermont Conference on the Primary Prevention of Psychopathology, Burlington, VT.

Mays, V., & Cochran, S. (1988). The black women's relationship project: A national survey of black lesbians. In M. Shernoff & W. Scott (Eds.), *The sourcebook on lesbian/gay health care* (2nd ed., pp. 54-62). Washington, DC: National Lesbian and Gay Health Foundation, Inc.

Morales, E. (1992). Latino gays and Latina lesbians. In S. Dworkin & F. Gutierrez, (Eds.), *Counseling gay men and lesbians: Journey to the end of the rainbow* (pp. 125-139). Alexandria, VA: American Association for Counseling and Development.

Moynihan, D. P. (1965). *The Negro family: The case for national action.* Washington, DC: U.S. Department of Labor.

5

Rejecting Therapy: Using Our Communities

Rachel E. Perkins

Most lesbian discussions of therapy are predicated on the assumption that lesbian therapy is "a good thing," and attention has focused on providing the best possible therapy to as many lesbians as possible. As a result, concern has revolved around the relative merits of different types of therapy. Many lesbians and feminists have published critiques of particular kinds of therapy: cognitive therapy (Perkins, 1991), Rogerian therapy (Waterhouse, 1993), 12-step programs (Tallen, 1990b), codependency treatments (Brown, 1990; Gomberg, 1989; Tallen, 1990a). Alternatively, there has been consideration of the extent to which different therapies are available to all lesbians rather than to limited groups (for example, via sliding scales and specific consideration of accessibility for lesbians of all racial and ethnic origins and disabled lesbians; Laws, 1991; O'Sullivan, 1984) and ethical guidelines (see Brown, 1985; Brown, 1989) designed to minimize the various abuses that can occur within therapeutic settings (see Caplan, 1992; Silveira, 1985). Issues such as the type of furniture that should be used and whether certificates should be hung on the wall have also been addressed (Brown, 1985).

It is undoubtedly the case that much of feminist therapy is implicitly anti-lesbian, and that much lesbian feminist therapy can be, and has been, criticized for its commitment to a white, middle-class view of the world. Some lesbian therapists do abuse their clients. There are, and will continue to be, debates about the relative merits of different therapies and therapists. However, such debates detract attention from the problems inherent in therapy as a whole: what might be wrong with the very idea of therapy itself. In this chapter, the assumptions underlying all psychological therapies will be addressed. It will be argued that therapy, albeit of a lesbian or feminist variety, is a very *bad thing* for lesbian/feminist politics and lesbian communities.

AUTHOR'S NOTE: Certain of the arguments presented in this chapter are based on those presented in *Changing Our Minds: Lesbian Feminism and Psychology* (Kitzinger & Perkins, 1993).

71

In criticizing the very idea of lesbian feminist therapy, people who have been very critical of each other have been lumped together. Of course it matters *how* therapy is done—the perspective or model adopted—but it also matters *whether* therapy is done and the implications of doing it. My intention here is to address therapy not as a specific set of clinical techniques and approaches but rather as a cultural phenomenon that has invaded lesbian communities.

This chapter will not address heteropatriarchal therapy. The oppressive nature of white, heterosexual, male psychology is well documented and these arguments will not be repeated here (see Chesler, 1972; Hanisch, 1971; Leon, 1970; Weisstein, 1971). I will focus attention, instead, on lesbian feminist therapies—therapies that claim to be, or are widely accepted as being, lesbian, or feminist, or both. It is these therapies that have been widely influential in lesbian feminist communities.

At the outset, it is also important to emphasize that, in criticizing lesbian therapy, I am *not* arguing that lesbians do not suffer or that the therapists who attempt to alleviate that suffering are bad people. The oppression of lesbians causes suffering, sometimes great suffering. For us as lesbians and as feminists, the question is how best both to prevent and to alleviate this suffering and to challenge the oppression that lies at its root. It will be argued here that therapy—albeit lesbian feminist therapy—is not the answer.

The Pervasiveness of Therapy

Over the past two decades, there has been an upsurge in therapy among the Western middle classes and leftist liberal communities, but this upsurge has probably been most prominent among lesbians. As Loulan (1990) says, "Nowhere did therapy become so universal as in the lesbian community" (p. 73). A national survey in the United States revealed that three out of every four lesbians had been in therapy at some point in their lives (Bradford, Ryan, & Rothblum, 1994). Lesbian therapy is a booming industry, and therapy now pervades lesbian communities. More and more lesbians are in individual therapy, attend therapy workshops, read psychological self-help manuals, and are training to be therapists.

Most lesbians go to therapy as a consequence of the ordinary miseries of everyday life. One lesbian health group (O'Donnell, Loeffler, Kater, & Saunders, 1979) recommends going into therapy when one feels lonely, isolated, alienated, overburdened with responsibilities, filled with ongoing unhappiness, constantly exhausted, anxious, numb, out of touch with one's feelings, or wanting to become more assertive or to show softness and gentleness. Basically, they say you should go into therapy when you want to make a change in your life and would like someone to be there with you, to really listen to you in a focused way, and to act as your guide.

Anti-lesbianism causes pain and suffering, and many other problems are exacerbated by anti-lesbianism. Anti-lesbianism can mean losing our jobs and our children and being mocked, ridiculed, and physically assaulted. Invisibility and the assumptions of heterosexuality mean that our lives and existence are continually denied, marginalized, and minimized. These experiences cause distress. Most lesbians, at some time, feel angry, hurt, rejected, lonely, frustrated, or confused because we do not fit into a heterosexually defined society, and sometimes this leads to our hating ourselves and other lesbians. Some very serious problems are caused, in one way or another, by anti-lesbianism. Self-starvation, drug and alcohol abuse, depression, and severe anxiety attacks, as well as the trauma of physical assault and rape, memories of childhood rape, and anguish over the death of those we love can all have their roots in the lesbian-hating world we inhabit.

When lesbians take these problems to therapy, we are taking our difficulties out of our communities and into a private, special relationship with a therapist.

Many lesbians do suffer and many have experienced therapy as lifesaving. Many lesbians have described how therapy enabled them to leave abusive relationships, deal with fears and anxieties, stop problems with drugs and alcohol. Many say that through therapy they felt stronger, happier, better able to cope with the demands of day-to-day life, better able to fight the oppression they experience. Anything that saves lesbians' lives must be good, must be feminist, mustn't it?

Well, no.

First, it is possible to patch lesbians up and make changes in their lives without ever addressing the underlying political issues that caused their problems in the first place. Therapy and feminism offer different explanations for lesbian lives and experience. Feminism tells us that our problems are caused by oppression; psychology tells us that they are in our minds. Even if psychology tells us that it was oppression that caused the problems in our minds—problems such as internalized homophobia—then it seeks solutions in our minds rather than in oppressive social and political structures (Kitzinger & Perkins, 1993).

Second, although it is clear that many lesbians find in therapy a source of support that they lack elsewhere, this does not make that therapy feminist. Tallen (1990b) describes how many women have sought refuge in institutions such as the Catholic Church and the military, but this does not mean that such institutions should be fully embraced by feminists, let alone lesbians. As Anna Lee (1986) says,

Many wimmin have been strengthened by many things which we would probably not consider intrinsically good. It does not matter if one womon is helped, unless it helps wimmin free ourselves from the institutions which hold us down and keep us weak. . . . In the black community, the availability of alcohol and heroin increases as black people increase our struggle against racism. Those who survive these addictions often become incredibly strong. . . . I believe few would argue that alcohol or heroin are intrinsically good. Therapy must stand on some intrinsic good, instead of parading a token womon who has become strong to prove its value. (p. 34)

Third, it is also necessary to consider what it is about therapy that lesbians find helpful. Often, it is having someone who will listen, who will not dismiss your feelings, who will attend to you and bear witness to your experiences. The fact that lesbians in distress have nowhere to turn but therapy for a consistent source of support does not mean that therapy is good or feminist; it is an indictment of lesbian communities.

Fourth, in a similar vein, it is necessary to ask what is meant by therapy "working." What is achieved and how is it achieved? For example, it could be argued that nuclear power stations "work" in the sense that they produce electricity, or chemical fertilizers "work" in that they produce more food, but many would want to balance such effectiveness against the costs of this working in terms of toxic waste and destruction of the earth's resources. It may well be argued that, despite the short-term benefits of electricity and increased food production, the costs are too high and there may be other ways of generating at least some of the electricity and food that are needed. In the same way, therapy may work to help individual lesbians survive, but there are costs in this working to lesbian communities, and there are other ways of helping their individual members.

Thinking about the costs of something that may make us feel good is not easy, but it is important. There is a high price to be paid by all lesbians, including those who have never been in therapy, for acceptance of therapy as a way of life in our communities.

Therapy and the Privatization of Pain

Pain and misery are part of life. When lesbians take these things to therapy, we are taking them outside everyday life. They become something "wrong" that we have to "get rid of"—"cure." It is becoming difficult for lesbians to imagine misery and unhappiness as just an ordinary part of life. Instead, such feelings are seen as symptoms that there is something wrong with them that can and should be put right. Misery becomes a problem for which a "special" lesbian—a therapist—is needed to help us "heal" and "grow." A version of the North American dream: everyone's right to the pursuit of happiness through therapeutic intervention.

Ordinary emotions like fear, frustration, despair, grief, and anxiety have become "psychological problems" in need of psychological treatment in the form of therapy. Within a therapeutic framework, emotions like these are made to appear not only undesirable but also unnecessary—curable—and therapy has become a way of life. Suffering is increasingly equated with poor mental health, and we seem to have given up the right to be both mentally healthy and desperately unhappy at the same time.

This transformation of misery into a remediable problem has actually created psychopathology from something that is ordinary. The translation of the effects of anti-lesbianism into individual, private problems that can be cured by therapy is in no one's interests but our oppressors'. Such a translation involves moving from a position where one has to change the world to a position where the oppressed individuals within that world have to be changed so that they are better able to cope with their oppression.

One of the great insights of second-wave feminism was that "the personal is political" (Hanisch, 1971, p. 152). This means that the personal, day-to-day details of our lives and our feelings have political meaning. They are both shaped by and influential in the social context in which they were formed. They cannot be understood outside this context. This does not mean that everyone should abandon therapy and go on marches. A feminist understanding of politics means moving away from male definitions of politics as something exclusively external—to do with governments and banner waving—and moving toward an understanding of politics as central to our very beings: our thoughts, our feelings, our daily lives.

There is much lesbian/feminist therapy that overtly replaces political explanations with psychological ones. The psychological concept of *internalized homophobia* is one such example (see Kitzinger, 1987). Many lesbian therapists acknowledge the extent and importance of anti-lesbianism, but then go on to reformulate it in individual psychological terms. Structural oppression ceases to be the target and is replaced by internal psychological problems. Therapists talk about how "the major source of distress is usually the individual's internalized homophobia" (Sophie, 1987, p. 53) and the task is one of "identifying and treating the oppressor within" (Margolies, Becker, & Jackson-Brewer, 1987, p. 229).

Some lesbians actively try to promote political explanations for personal distress. Brown (1992), for example, explicitly tries to encourage her clients to see their difficulties in political terms. Indeed, she describes lesbian therapy as "a potentially powerful means for *un*adjusting ourselves to patriarchal realities" (Brown, 1992, p. 252). Therapy could be seen as a means of helping a lesbian understand her difficulties in political terms: as one lesbian persuading another that her own perspective is the correct one. Obviously, there is nothing wrong with political debate, nothing wrong with lesbians trying to persuade each other that their perspective is correct. However, this should be an *open* political debate about what is right and what is wrong—of different values (Kitzinger & Perkins, 1993; Perkins, 1991). Therapy is not political debate.

The therapeutic relationship is a special, privileged, and asymmetrical one. As Brown (1989) says,

> Lesbian therapists occupy a special position in the social structure of lesbian communities. . . . We are leaders, teachers, oracles. In much the same way that the clergy, who healed the wounds in the Black community, are leaders there, so we, the perceived healers of the wounds of sexism, misogyny, and homophobia, have become leaders among white lesbians. The power available to any therapist is potentially magnified for lesbian therapists because of this special position in our culture. (p. 15)

Within therapy, a powerful lesbian (the therapist) helps another in distress (the client) to understand her experience in the therapist's "expert" terms. Raymond (1986) describes how lesbians come to believe that what really counts in their lives is their "psychology," and because they do not really know what their psychology means, they go to another who purports to know—a therapist. As Brown (1985) says, therapists are "practitioners of a healing art that is neither intuitive nor naturally present in all women" (p. 298).

Therapists, even lesbian therapists, have no special training or expertise in lesbian politics. Their "healing art" comes from a training in how to interpret experience within therapeutic theoretical frameworks. They are experts in reframing and reinterpreting beliefs, thoughts, and feelings *not* in political terms of reference but within the psychological frameworks that their profession has invented (Perkins, 1991). When a therapist helps a client explore her feelings, she is helping her client frame and understand her problems within the therapist's framework.

Even if, as Brown (1992) suggests, therapy is a way of helping lesbians understand their distress in political terms, *no one* enters therapy to have their politics changed. Therapy is, therefore, essentially a form of covert political reeducation, whether this reeducation takes the form of replacing political explanations with psychological ones (as in the case of concepts like homophobia) or reframing personal distress in political terms. Regardless of whether we like the politics dispensed, therapy is an underhanded method of political conversion that makes open political analysis impossible (Kitzinger & Perkins, 1993; Perkins, 1991).

Therapy and Community

Most of all, therapy deprives our lesbian friendships and lesbian communities. Because therapy defines ordinary, everyday emotions like misery, despair, fear, and frustration as indications that something is "wrong" with a person that must be put right via therapy, a situation is rapidly being approached in which all the bad things that happen to lesbians are taken out of lesbian communities and put into therapy. Even if lesbian therapists are considered to be part of lesbian communities, it is still the case that lesbian distress becomes the preserve of a few—those with the proper training.

In embracing therapy, there is a very real risk of destroying the capacity for genuine lesbian friendship and community. With the institutionalizing of therapy, lesbians cease to expect to deal with each other's distress. The pain of those we love and care about is simply not safe in our untrained hands; it should be left to the experts. This deprives lesbian communities of a whole realm of experience. It strips lesbians of our strength and ability to support each other and prevents us from understanding the context and meaning of our distress. Misery and emotional crises are part of life—they are ordinary emotions, common to all—they do not belong in the specialist preserve of therapy. Therapy privatizes pain and severs connections between lesbians, replacing friendship and community with the private therapist-client relationship.

This becomes a vicious circle. The more that distress is seen as a special and private affair, the more we see ourselves and our friends as unable to cope with our distress. Lesbian friendships and communities become arid places to which we cannot bring our anguish and our pain and in which we cannot rely on other lesbians to accept our suffering and help us survive it. As Lee (1986) says,

> We bring the most intimate parts of ourselves to paid friends [therapists], while offering the most superficial parts to non-paid friends. The excuse is that burdening our friends with our pain or anger or sorrow is unacceptable. But if we can only bring our joy to our friends how can we value them? When we exclude our most intimate selves from our friends, we weaken the bonds between wimmin that are necessary to fuel a social movement. (p. 36)

As lesbians, we should be looking for ways of supporting and helping each other, of dealing with our distress collectively and politically. Nowhere is this more essential than among those whom lesbian therapy does not serve: those lesbians who are seriously disabled by the severe cognitive and emotional problems that have been accorded such labels as *schizophrenia* and *manic-depressive illness*. Lesbians who experience such difficulties have often been marginalized and excluded both by lesbian therapy and by lesbian communities.

The vast majority of therapists advertising in the lesbian and feminist press do not aim to help those who are seriously disabled by ongoing mental health problems. They hope to attract "ordinary" lesbians who need help to get over a crisis or who want to explore and develop themselves. Some lesbian and feminist therapists, in both the United Kingdom and the United States, state explicitly that their workshops or therapy programs are not suitable for severely disturbed lesbians. Therapy is rarely accessible for those who are seriously disabled. They may be unable to get to the therapy session unaided, unable to remain there for the expected "50-minute hour," and unable to engage in a manner that is considered appropriate (Perkins, 1992; Perkins & Dilks, 1992; Perkins & Repper, 1996). Those whose disabilities are such that they are unable to work are unlikely to be able to afford therapy, no matter how sliding the scale (Laws, 1991; Perkins & Repper, 1996).

Lesbians who are seriously disabled by ongoing mental health problems often find themselves excluded by lesbian communities in a variety of ways. Some are simply asked to leave activities and venues because of their behavior. Others are disbelieved and have their experiences dismissed: "She's crazy. She doesn't know what she is talking about. You don't have to listen to her." In a more subtle manner, others may create the appearance of listening but then ignore or disregard what is said. A further form of marginalization comes under the guise of inclusiveness: "I know what you mean. I feel like that sometimes," when the listener, in fact, has no idea what it is like to believe that your nose controls the weather or that thoughts are quite literally being removed from your head. Several seriously disabled lesbians have written about their marginalization and exclusion from lesbian communities.

Nancy, quoted by Chamberlin (1977/1988), said,

Women in the women's movement, in the lesbian movement, women I had known for a long time and worked with, started treating me differently after I had been in hospital. . . . They had been my friends, but now they would look at me as if I was crazy. (p. 75)

Elizabeth (1982) described how

women pretend that my depression doesn't exist. So they never ask me about it and somehow communicate that it's not the sort of thing they're interested in talking about. (p. 15)

Jenny, quoted by O'Hagan (1991), commented that " 'The women's movement has not been terribly receptive to ex-patients; there are an awful lot of
therapists in the women's movement' " (p. 37).

If someone behaves in unusual and disruptive ways, or expresses strange
beliefs that no one else shares, then it is often very difficult for that person
to be accepted as a lesbian. An old school friend of mine believes that she
became a lesbian when a golf ball broke her little finger; all too often, her
lesbianism is doubted along with her account of how she came to be this way.

Severely distressed and disabled lesbians do not need a psychiatry or a
lesbian therapy that individualizes and privatizes their problems and attempts
to enable them to "fit in" to an able-minded world. Their difficulties are not
individual problems, they are the responsibility of all lesbians (Cook, 1985).
Seriously disabled lesbians need friends and allies, practical help, and, at
times, asylum from the demands of everyday life within (not apart from)
lesbian communities. Most of all, it is necessary to find ways to render our
communities accessible and to accommodate lesbians with problems such as
these. In the words of Chamberlin (1977/1988), "We must begin to turn
toward the people we now isolate—the troubled (and troubling) relatives and
friends we both love and fear" (p. 239).

Chamberlin describes how therapy is actively destructive of our communities' abilities to accommodate disability: "Rather than caring for one
another, we turn to remote authority figures and experts, reinforcing the
notion that one needs professional degrees and credentials to avoid doing
irreparable harm to troubled people . . . " (p. 238). If lesbian communities
do not accommodate that which is increasingly excluded and consigned to
therapy—both the distress that many lesbians experience and the serious
disabilities of a smaller number—then lesbian communities will be weaker
and the bonds between lesbians will be weaker. We all need all of us.

Of course, lesbian communities and friendships are not perfect. Lesbians
let each other down and are not always there when we need one another. The
fact that lesbians in distress have nowhere to turn but therapy is an indictment
of our communities. Winterson (1989) argues that it is "a condemnation of
the broken structures of our society that so few of us, particularly women,
have a group of strong, dependable friends whom we can trust" (p. 35).
However, it is important to remember that therapists let lesbians down as
well, and recourse to therapy actively militates against the development of
lesbian communities that can accommodate all lesbians.

Therapy costs.

An awful lot of lesbian time and energy has been devoted to the giving
and receiving of therapy. It is probably true to say that lesbians have put a
great deal more energy into therapy than into building lesbian communities.

It is essential that this balance be redressed, but there are many serious issues that must be considered.

First, accommodating distress and disability within lesbian communities will not be easy. The distress of others is not pleasant. It is often easier to consign to therapy and psychiatry those in distress, those who are difficult to understand, and those who behave in ways that others find unacceptable. The task of helping someone is often greater than any lesbian can manage alone. Therefore, it is important to think collectively and politically about how effective support networks can be created within lesbian communities— networks that will simultaneously accommodate and help lesbians survive their distress and celebrate lesbian strength and competency.

In work with people who experience serious long-term mental health problems, there has long been a focus on defining people in terms of their strengths and abilities and maximizing these, rather than dwelling on problems and disabilities (see Bachrach, 1989). Such an emphasis is important for all lesbians, disabled or not. Most lesbians are, for most of the time, strong and able to cope, and on those occasions when we are not able to manage on our own, we must work out ways of supporting and taking care of one another. Lesbians' strengths are increasingly denied by psychological and therapeutic endeavors that encourage us to define ourselves in terms of an ever multiplying list of wounds. It is, of course, possible for lesbians to continue to refine the psychological vocabulary for describing distress. Defining ourselves in terms of our wounds, however, weakens individual lesbians and lesbian communities alike in a way that can only be in the interests of our oppressors.

Calls for more supportive communities have often involved the mass education of lesbians in therapeutic models: the wholesale translation of feminist goals into psychological goals that Raymond (1986, p. 159) calls the "therapeutising of friendship." Lesbians do not need therapy training in how to be friends with each other and support each other. Friendship between lesbians is not a psychological technique, and the therapist/client relationship is not a good model for lesbian relationships. Instead, lesbian communities must become able to accept misery, distress, and anguish (as well as joy, delight, and happiness) as normal, ordinary experience—part of the rich fabric of lesbian lives. Dealing with these emotions in ourselves and others should be part of going about our normal everyday lives. Lesbian communities must become able to include those severely disturbed and disabled lesbians, whom we currently marginalize, as part of the rich diversity of lesbian experience. We need a politics of madness to parallel that which we have begun to construct around physical disability.

Second, we have to ask, "Who are our communities?" On the one hand, the understandable rifts and differences in lesbian politics have often led to an ever greater fragmentation of communities, to the point where many lesbians see their community as comprised of a few best friends with whom they agree. It is a mistake to assume that the only relationships that matter are those with lovers and friends. Lesbians will always disagree with each other and lesbian communities are bound to be fraught with differences; however, these differences are important relationships too (Penelope, 1990). Frye (1990) describes how lesbians in her community don't agree about anything, from the importance of recycling jars and paper to whether it's okay to go to weddings, but they survive in droves.

On the other hand, there are also "all-inclusive" tendencies to think about lesbian communities as including gay men, those who are bisexual, lesbians who live with and have sex with men, transsexuals, and just about anyone else who does not fall into the traditional heterosexual mold. The political debates around these issues are enormous and will not be addressed here. Suffice it to say that there are many political questions to be addressed in any definition of community.

Third, it is important to consider what it is about therapy that is thought to be so valuable and to ask whether all the psychological superstructure is needed to provide it. Therapy affords

- someone who will take us seriously,
- someone who is prepared to understand and sympathize with our distress,
- someone who will be there when we need them,
- someone who will really listen to what we have to say,
- someone whom we can rely on,
- someone who does not get fed up when we go over the same ground again and again,
- someone who is not scared by our pain,
- someone who doesn't give up when we remain miserable,
- someone who will treat what we say as confidential,
- someone who is outside our immediate life and social network and can provide a much needed anonymity.

These are all things that lesbians say they have valued in therapy, but none requires a therapeutic framework. Is it really so impossible to imagine that lesbian communities could provide these things within a feminist framework?

Many lesbians and feminists have embraced therapeutic understandings of themselves and the world. In part, this is a consequence of the growth and popularity of these types of models in Western cultures more generally. Lesbians have learned to frame ourselves and our distress in therapeutic terms, because these are some of the dominant culturally available frameworks for understanding experience. Furthermore, women historically have been excluded from the public world and expected to be more concerned with so-called personal issues, generally getting more support and sympathy if problems are framed in psychological rather than political terms.

The popularity of therapy is probably also a reflection of perceived deficits in lesbian communities. It provides a kind of prosthetic friendship for lonely and unhappy lesbians when real friendship and community are lacking (Kitzinger & Perkins, 1993). Lesbians can feel isolated and overwhelmed by problems, and therapy appears to offer answers. In an increasingly right-wing political climate where real change and revolution seem a long way off, it is tempting to turn away from political change toward the individual and private solutions of therapy. But the cost in terms of our lesbian communities and lesbian politics is high.

It is possible to address those issues that therapy claims collectively and politically. Most lesbians are adequate human beings most of the time, and if we put even part of the energy now devoted to therapy into our communities instead, we could support one another when we are unable to cope. Lesbians could build communities that could not only celebrate and foster our joys and competencies but also accommodate and ameliorate our distress and disability. Instead of distress, misery, and disability being privatized and pathologized, they could be embraced as part of everyday lesbian lives and communities.

References

Bachrach, L. L. (1989). The legacy of model programs. *Hospital & Community Psychiatry, 40,* 234-235.

Bradford, J., Ryan, C., & Rothblum, E. D. (1994). National Lesbian Health Care Survey: Implications for mental health care. *Journal of Consulting and Clinical Psychology, 62,* 228-242.

Brown, L. S. (1985). Ethics and business practice in feminist therapy. In L. B. Rosewater & L. E. A. Walker (Eds.), *Handbook of feminist therapy: Women's issues in psychotherapy* (pp. 290-312). New York: Springer.

Brown, L. S. (1989). Beyond thou shalt not: Thinking about ethics in the lesbian community. *Women & Therapy, 8,* 13-25.

Brown, L. S. (1990). What's addiction got to do with it? A feminist critique of codependence. *Psychology of Women: Newsletter of Division 35, 17*(1), 1-4.

Brown, L. S. (1992). While waiting for the revolution: The case for a lesbian feminist psychotherapy. *Feminism & Psychology, 2,* 239-253.

Caplan, P. (1992). Driving us crazy: How oppression damages women's mental health and what we can do about it. *Women & Therapy, 12,* 5-28.

Chamberlin, J. (1988). *On our own* (Rev. ed.). London: MIND Publications. (Original work published 1977)

Chesler, P. (1972). *Women and madness*. New York: Avon.

Cook, G. (1985). Psychiatry as male violence. In D. Rhodes & S. McNeill (Eds.), *Women against violence against women* (pp. 102-105). London: Onlywomen.

Elizabeth, R. (1982). Deprivatising pain. *Catcall, 14*, 15-16.

Frye, M. (1990). The possibility of lesbian community. *Lesbian Ethics, 4*, 84-87.

Gomberg, E. S. L. (1989). On terms used and abused: The concept of "codependency." *Drugs and Society, 3*, 113-132.

Hanisch, C. (1971). The personal is political. In J. Agel (Ed.), *The radical therapist* (pp. 152-157). New York: Ballantine.

Kitzinger, C. (1987). Heteropatriarchal language: The case against homophobia. *Gossip: A Journal of Lesbian Feminist Ethics, 5*, 15-20.

Kitzinger, C., & Perkins, R. E. (1993). *Changing our minds: Lesbian feminism and psychology*. New York: New York University Press.

Laws, S. (1991). Women on the verge. *Trouble & Strife, 20*, 8-12.

Lee, A. (1986). Therapy: The evil within. *Trivia, 9*, 34-44.

Leon, B. (1970, August). Brainwashing and women: The psychological attack. *It Ain't Me Babe*, pp. 10-12.

Loulan, J. (1990). *The lesbian erotic dance*. San Francisco: Spinsters Ink.

Margolies, L., Becker, M., & Jackson-Brewer, K. (1987). Internalized homophobia: Identifying and treating the oppressor within. In Boston Lesbian Psychologies Collective (Ed.), *Lesbian psychologies* (pp. 229-241). Urbana: University of Illinois Press.

O'Donnell, M., Loeffler, V., Kater, P., & Saunders, Z. (1979). *Lesbian health matters*. Santa Cruz, CA: Santa Cruz Women's Health Collective.

O'Hagan, M. (1991). *Stopovers on my way home from Mars*. Aukland, NZ: New Moon Productions.

O'Sullivan, S. (1984). Patients and power. *Trouble and Strife, 3*, 50-53.

Penelope, J. (1990). The lesbian perspective. In J. Allen (Ed.), *Lesbian philosophies and cultures* (pp. 89-108). New York: State University of New York Press.

Perkins, R. E. (1991). Therapy for lesbians? The case against. *Feminism & Psychology, 1*, 325-338.

Perkins, R. E. (1992). Working with socially disabled clients: A feminist perspective. In J. Ussher & P. Nicholson (Eds.), *Gender issues in clinical psychology* (pp. 171-193). London: Routledge & Kegan Paul.

Perkins, R. E., & Dilks, S. (1992). Worlds apart: Working with severely socially disabled people. *Journal of Mental Health, 1*, 3-17.

Perkins R. E., & Repper, J. M. (1996). *Allies: Working with people who have serious mental health problems*. London: Chapman Hall.

Raymond, J. (1986). *A passion for friends: Toward a philosophy of female friendship*. London: Women's Press.

Silveira, J. (1985). Lesbian feminist therapy: A report of some thoughts. *Lesbian Ethics, 1*, 22-27.

Sophie, J. (1987). Internalized homophobia and lesbian identity. *Journal of Homosexuality, 14*, 53-65.

Tallen, B. S. (1990a). Co-dependency: A feminist critique. *Sojourner, 15*, 20-21.

Tallen, B. S. (1990b). Twelve step programs: A lesbian feminist critique. *National Women's Studies Association Journal, 2*, 390-407.

Waterhouse, R. (1993). "Wild women don't have the blues": A feminist critique of "person centred" counselling and therapy. *Feminism & Psychology, 3*, 54-71.

Weisstein, N. (1971). Psychology constructs the female. In V. Gornick & B. K. Moran (Eds.), *Woman in sexist society: Studies in power and powerlessness* (pp. 207-224). New York: Basic Books.

Winterson, J. (1989, Jan. 27). Mind your head. *The Guardian*, p. 46.

PART II
Relationships and Development

6

Finding a Sexual Identity and Community: Therapeutic Implications and Cultural Assumptions in Scientific Models of Coming Out

Paula C. Rust

Coming out, as the term is commonly used, is the process by which individuals come to recognize that they have romantic or sexual feelings toward members of their own gender, adopt lesbian or gay (or bisexual) identities, and then share these identities with others. Coming out is made necessary by a heterosexist culture in which individuals are presumed heterosexual unless there is evidence to the contrary. Because of this heterosexual presumption, most lesbians, gay men, and bisexuals grow up with heterosexual parents who expect them to be heterosexual and socialize them as heterosexual. Thus, they are raised with default heterosexual identities. Coming out as lesbian, gay, or bisexual involves replacing that default identity—one so taken for granted that it is rarely recognized as an identity—with a new lesbian, gay, or bisexual identity that is not at all taken for granted but rather is stigmatized.

Because identity is the link connecting the individual to the social world, this change in sexual identity usually leads to changes in the individual's relationships with others and with society as a whole. As a newly self-identified lesbian, gay, or bisexual person, one holds a very different position in society than one held as a presumed heterosexual. This refers to more than the fact that one is now socially marginalized and potentially rejected by friends and family—the very people most of us turn to for help in hard times—it also means that one has a different relationship to social institutions. For example, heterosexuals and LesBiGays[1] have very different positions vis-à-vis the institution of marriage. Heterosexuals are expected to marry and usually expect themselves to marry, whereas lesbian, gay, and bisexual individuals are denied the right to marry their same-gender partners and are therefore excluded from this institution and deprived of the social and legal privileges that married couples enjoy.[2] Lesbian, gay, and bisexual people also discover that the culture they grew up in is, to a great extent, irrelevant to their needs because the norms, values, and traditions of that culture assume and facilitate heterosexuality. For example, same-gender friendships are predicated on the assumption that these friendships lack romantic potential, as evidenced by the discomfort sometimes displayed by individuals who discover that a same-gender friend is lesbian or gay and fear that this friend might be attracted to them. Conversely, on the presumption that they are heterosexual, young people learn to initiate and participate in a heterosexual romance; they don't learn how to establish a romantic same-gender relationship or even how to find another person who would be open to such a relationship. They have abundant role models for heterosexual relationships but they don't know the norms, values, and traditions of gay culture. So, coming out means not only adopting a lesbian, gay, or bisexual identity but also losing familiar social and cultural connections, finding a new community of people with similar sexual identities, and becoming resocialized to the norms, values, and traditions of that community.

Because coming out often involves extensive psychological and social changes, and because during these changes individuals might be unable to rely on their usual sources of support, it can be a period of psychological vulnerability during which lay and professional support is needed. It is, therefore, important for counselors to understand the process of coming out and the issues that arise for individuals going through this process. Much of the research on the coming out process was done in the 1970s, when, in the aftermath of the removal of *homosexuality* per se from the *Diagnostic and Statistical Manual* (*DSM*) of the American Psychiatric Association, researchers turned their attention away from etiological questions and toward issues of concern to lesbians and gay men. Researchers asked lesbian and gay male subjects about their coming out experiences, and subjects typically described coming out as a linear developmental process of self-discovery in which they had replaced a false, socially imposed heterosexual identity with a lesbian or gay identity that reflected their true, essential selves. They told about the milestone events that marked turning points or progress in their coming out experiences, including their first experience of feeling same-gender attraction, their first same-gender sexual experience, the first time they labeled themselves homosexual or gay, the first time they told another person about their homosexuality, and their first encounter with a gay community. Based on these accounts, scientists proposed linear developmental models of coming out that closely mirrored the coming out stories told by lesbians and gay men.

These models are both useful and dangerous when applied to therapeutic settings. They are useful because they accurately describe the way some individuals experience the process of coming out, and for these individuals they pinpoint the issues that arise at each stage of the process and suggest ways in which a counselor or friend can help. But they can also be dangerous because they make assumptions about the nature and development of sexual identity that are not true for all individuals—assumptions that are borrowed from popular sexual ideology. Thus, they can also obscure or invalidate issues that arise for certain types of individuals. In particular, these models assume that coming out is a linear goal-oriented process, a conception that more accurately reflects the way individuals view their coming out in retrospect than the way they actually experienced it; they are based on Euro-American concepts of sexuality that are not necessarily meaningful to individuals from a variety of cultural backgrounds; and they are based on a dichotomous understanding of sexuality that does not validate the possibility of bisexual identity as a mature outcome.

This chapter is divided into two sections. In the first section, I discuss linear developmental models of coming out and the useful suggestions these models hold for counselors whose clients are questioning their sexuality. In the second section, I point out the assumptions made by these models and show how these assumptions can lead to a misunderstanding of the issues faced by some clients. The arguments I make in this latter section draw partially on the findings of two research studies that I did in 1986 and 1993–1996. The first was a study of lesbian- and bisexual-identified women's identities, sexual experiences, and attitudes toward bisexuality. The second is an ongoing international study of the construction of bisexual identities, communities, and politics. For methodological details and sample descriptions, see Rust (1992) for the first study, and Rust (1996b) for the second study.

Linear Models of Coming Out—What They Reveal

Typical examples of linear models of coming out are those proposed by Cass (1979), Coleman (1982), and McDonald (1982). Each of these models consists of a series of stages or steps, with the last stage constructed as a "goal" toward which movement through the other stages is directed. Cass's model centers on the individual's psychological development. In this model, each stage of coming out is characterized by a psychological inconsistency that causes tension, pushing the individual toward a resolution and propelling her or him into the next stage. The models by Coleman and McDonald center on particular events that occur as an individual comes out, although both

Coleman and McDonald also discuss the psychological issues that surround each event. None of these authors discussed the therapeutic applications of the coming out models, but each model highlights different issues that arise for their individual who is coming out, and I will use the models as a starting point for discussing the role counselors and friends can play in supporting individuals who are coming out.

In Cass's (1979) model, the goal of coming out is "to acquire an identity of 'homosexual' fully integrated within the individual's overall concept of self" (p. 220). Psychological integration is characterized by consistency between one's perceptions of one's own behavior and one's self, and between one's private and public identities. The model consists of six stages: Identity Confusion, Identity Comparison, Identity Tolerance, Identity Acceptance, Identity Pride, and Identity Synthesis.

Individuals in the *Identity Confusion* stage begin to perceive that their behavior might be called homosexual, a perception that contrasts with their heterosexual identity, and they begin to wonder if they are homosexual. Cass argues that the individual reacts to this dilemma either by seeking information about homosexuality to resolve the identity question or by denial. Denial can involve inhibiting the behavior that could be called homosexual or it can involve reinterpretation of the behavior as nonhomosexual by attributing it to, for example, experimentation or drunkenness, or by considering it a means to another end such as money.

Individuals at the Identity Confusion stage of development usually have not yet sought counseling, so there is little a counselor can do within the traditional context of counseling practice. But today, nearly two decades after Cass described this stage, there is a great deal that can be done to ensure that individuals experiencing Identity Confusion have access to positive, accurate information that will decrease the chances of a denial reaction and lead to a healthy resolution of the identity question. Denial can be both physically and psychologically damaging, because it might include denial of the risks involved in unsafe sexual practices. Positive LesBiGay images reduce the chances of a denial reaction by reducing internalized homophobia. Individuals at this stage gather information from the mainstream media, including television, libraries, and the classroom; therefore, it is important that these media present positive and accurate images of lesbian, gay, and bisexual people.

Unfortunately, efforts to include positive LesBiGay images in the media are often frustrated by the counterefforts of people who believe, usually on the basis of religious teachings, that sexuality should only be expressed within the context of heterosexual marriage and who wish to impose this belief on others via the control of information. Schools and libraries that want to make positive LesBiGay materials available to students and the public are sometimes forced by political pressure to eliminate these materials or make them less accessible; the controversy over the Rainbow Curriculum in New York City schools is a case in point. Therefore, efforts to make positive LesBiGay images available as positive heterosexual images need the support of all interested community members, especially members of the helping professions. Go to your local public library to find out what young people in your area would find if they looked up *homosexuality*. Is there any information at all, and will this information be helpful or harmful? Ask your local school how the curriculum is taking the needs of lesbian, bisexual, and gay students into account and how the school is teaching students to respect sexual diversity. Write letters supporting television shows that include positive LesBiGay characters; the producers of and advertisers on these shows receive many letters calling for the elimination of such characters.

In Cass's second stage, *Identity Comparison,* individuals begin to think that they might be homosexual while continuing to present a heterosexual identity to others. During this stage, individuals might confide in trusted friends or counselors, making it possible for these confidants to provide them with one-on-one support. Cass described this stage as an opportunity for individuals to consider the implications of identifying as homosexual, that is, to "try on" the identity themselves before presenting it to others and risking negative reactions. De Monteflores and Schultz (1978) noted that individuals usually have to cognitively transform the category *homosexual* to dispel the negative meanings ascribed to homosexuality before they can place themselves in that category. Other issues that arise at this stage include social alienation stemming from the difference between how one views oneself and how others view one, and from the sense of being different from others; the realization that norms, ideals, and expectations based on the presumption of heterosexuality are no longer applicable; and the stress involved in utilizing passing strategies that involve concealment, deception, avoidance, and role distancing. Cass also noted that, at this stage, individuals lose a sense of continuity between the past, present, and future, because they are no longer the persons they thought they were; this constitutes a psychological break with the past.

An issue that Cass did not discuss is the fact that at this stage individuals have to try out the gay identity in their mind's eye not only to see what the social implications of that identity would be but also to see what the psychological implications of adopting a gay identity would be for the rest of their self-concept. One's sexual identity is intertwined with one's gender, racial/ethnic, religious, and other identities; a change in one implies changes in others. For example, a man who thinks he might be gay but thinks gays are effeminate might wonder what kind of man he could be if he were gay. A Latina, for whom part of being a woman is being heterosexual, getting married, and becoming a mother, might wonder what kind of woman she is. African Americans who are told that gayness is a "white disease," or Vietnamese Americans whose ethnic communities believe that Vietnamese become gay only when they are seduced by whites, might wonder how they could maintain their ethnic identities if they came out as lesbians or gay men. An African American respondent in the author's recent survey wrote, "When I came out, it was made clear to me that my being queer was in some sense a betrayal of my 'blackness'. . . . I spent a lot of years thinking that I could not be me and be 'really' black too." A Mexican American woman in the same study wrote that she has "felt like . . . a traitor to my race when I acknowledge my love of women. I have felt like I've bought into the White 'disease' of lesbianism." The phenomenon of homosexuality being perceived as a "white" thing among particular racial and ethnic groups is discussed by Carrier, Nguyen, and Su (1992), Chan (1989), Espín (1987), H. (1989), Icard (1986), Matteson (1994), Morales (1989, 1990), Tremble, Schneider, and Appathurai (1989), and Wooden, Kawasaki, and Mayeda (1983).

Individuals at this stage of coming out can be facilitated in the process of trying out their new sexual identities. Even though actual social relationships have not yet been lost, the individual can mentally rebuild these relationships and establish new relationships that are consistent with their developing LesBiGay identities. Friends and counselors can help the individual envision herself or himself as a LesBiGay person relating to others by asking questions such as, "If you came out, how would your mother/father/best friend/girl- or boyfriend/wife or husband/children/religious leader/employer react and how would you respond? Do you have any friends who you think would be supportive? How would you handle a situation in which peers expected you to take a date of the other gender to the prom/to the company holiday party? What would be the implications for your marriage and how would you feel about that?" Envisioning themselves with this identity can help individuals realistically assess whether LesBiGay identity—and its attendant social position—is a "good fit," and reduce the sense of social alienation by helping individuals reestablish in their own minds the social connections that are threatened by the switch from heterosexual to LesBiGay identity. For those individuals who do proceed to adopt a LesBiGay identity, the next step of revealing that identity to others will feel less like jumping off a cliff if they have been able to imagine that they will still be able to relate socially to others as LesBiGay people.

As heterosexual identity is replaced by LesBiGay identity, and social relationships are psychologically lost and rebuilt, individuals are also realizing that heterosexual norms, ideals, and expectations no longer apply. They might need time to grieve the loss of heterosexual identity and social relationships as well as the previously taken-for-granted sense of belonging to mainstream society and culture. But some things that they assume are lost might not really be lost. For example, they might mourn the family they expected to have; this expectation needs to be readjusted, not relinquished, via reassurance that LesBiGays can have lifetime partners and children. Although individuals in the Identity Comparison stage might not be ready to seek out gay social scenes, at this point they might appreciate knowing that a community exists in which being LesBiGay is normal and in which the norms and expectations are suited to LesBiGays, not to heterosexuals.

Because coming out as LesBiGay can disrupt one's sense of continuity between the past, present, and future, individuals who are coming out often look back at their pasts to find early signs of their LesBiGayness so as to reestablish a sense of continuity. De Monteflores and Schultz (1978) call this process "recasting the past." To recast the past, individuals might need to reinterpret early (same-gender) experiences; for example, a kiss with a girlfriend that was previously interpreted as "experimentation" might be reinterpreted as an early expression of same-gender attraction. Recasting the past also involves a reexamination of previous heterosexual experiences. Some individuals might feel that they can't be lesbian or gay because they have had pleasurable heterosexual experiences; individuals struggling to reconcile these other-gender experiences with a developing lesbian or gay identity can be reassured that many lesbians and gay men have had hetero-sexual experiences and, in fact, remain attracted to the other gender even after coming out. For example, in my earlier study, I found that 91% of lesbian-identified women had had heterosexual relationships at some point in their lives; this figure is similar to findings obtained by other researchers, such as Chapman and Brannock (1987), Hedblom (1973), and Saghir and Robins (1973). I also found that 43% of lesbian-identified women had had a heterosexual romantic or sexual relationship *since* coming out as a lesbian, and only one third reported that they were 100% attracted to women; two thirds reported that 5% to 50% of their feelings of sexual attraction were toward men (Rust, 1992).

Despite the ubiquity of other-gender experience among lesbians and gay men, or perhaps because of it, once individuals come into contact with a lesbian or gay community, they will probably be encouraged to construct their other-gender experiences as irrelevant to their true sexuality (Rust, 1995). For example, they might be told that their heterosexual experiences were the result of social pressure toward heterosexuality and not authentic feelings on their part. They can be reassured that if these experiences were meaningful to them at the time, they needn't discredit them in order to adopt a *lesbian* or *gay* identity. You can also suggest that *bisexual* might be a better way to describe their sexuality than lesbian or gay; if they have both same-gender and other-gender feelings, they needn't invalidate one or the other in the process of deciding whether they are heterosexual or lesbian/gay. Although they might not take the suggestion immediately, it provides them with the option of identifying as bisexual after they become comfortable enough with their sexuality to adopt an identity—bisexual—that has even less social support than lesbian and gay identities do.

Integrating one's sexual identity with the rest of one's self-concept requires challenging stereotypes, for example, the stereotypes that gay men are effeminate or that there are no black gays. Role models can also help; a counselor should be aware of any organizations in the local area for Les-BiGays, including groups specifically for LesBiGays of color or Jewish LesBiGays. Bear in mind that the mainstream LesBiGay community is predominantly Euro-American. Because of racism—the same racism that permeates heterosexual culture—LesBiGays of color often don't receive the same psychological support from this community as Euro-American Les-BiGays do. Moreover, the norms, expectations, and identities available in the Euro-American LesBiGay community might not suffice as a replacement for the heterosexual but ethnically relevant norms, expectations, and identities that the person of color risks losing by coming out (Greene, 1994; Icard, 1986; Rust, 1996a). Therefore, it is particularly important to provide Les-BiGays of color with ethnically relevant resources.

The written word can be an excellent resource, especially if local groups for LesBiGays of color do not exist. There are a number of books written by and for Asian American, African American, Latin, and Native American LesBiGays. These include *Living the Spirit* (Roscoe, 1988) and *The Spirit and the Flesh* (Williams, 1986) for Native Americans; *Sister/Outsider* (Lorde, 1984), *In the Life* (Beam, 1986), and *Brother to Brother* (Hemphill, 1991) for African Americans; *Loving in the War Years* (Moraga, 1983) and *Chicana Lesbians* (Trujillo, 1991) for Latinas; *The Very Inside* (Lim-Hing, 1994) and *A Lotus of Another Color* (Ratti, 1993) for Asian Americans; *The Great Mirror of Male Love* (Saikaku, 1990) and *Passions of the Cut Sleeve* (Hinsch, 1990) about homosexuality in Japanese and Chinese history, respectively; and *Talking Black* (Mason-John, 1995) for lesbians of Asian and African descent, and *Piece of My Heart: A Lesbian of Colour Anthology* (Silvera, 1991). Some of the anthologies published by and for bisexuals in recent years include essays by bisexuals of color, for example, *Closer to Home* (Weise, 1992) and *Bi Any Other Name* (Hutchins & Kaahumanu, 1991).

Counselors should also be aware that different norms for the expression of sexuality exist in different cultures and that the coming out process, including the potential for integration of a sexual identity with an ethnic identity, therefore differs cross-culturally. For discussions of ways in which counselors can help LesBiGay people integrate their sexual identities with their racial or ethnic identities, and the particular issues that arise for LesBiGays of color, see Chan (1989, 1992), Comas-Díaz and Greene (1994), Espín (1987), Greene (1994, this volume), Gutiérrez and Dworkin (1992), Loiacano (1989), Morales (1992), Rust (1996a), Tafoya and Rowell (1988), Tremble et al. (1989), and Wooden et al. (1983).

The third stage, *Identity Tolerance,* is characterized by greater commitment to gay identity. In Cass's model, the individual is still passing as heterosexual to others. Today, however, tolerance of gayness has increased and the concept of gay pride is more widespread. It is likely that individuals today come out to others earlier, relative to their own degree of commitment to LesBiGay identity, because the risks of coming out before one's LesBiGay identity is firmly established have lessened somewhat and, conversely, the likelihood that by coming out one will find support for the process of LesBiGay identity development has increased. It is in this stage that the individual is likely to seek out a LesBiGay community. In past decades, LesBiGays often found their way into the LesBiGay community through the gay bar, because it was, as Hooker (1967) characterized it, the "tip of the iceberg," that is, the publicly visible corner of a much larger underground gay community. In the 1990s, however, there are gay community centers, political groups, recreational groups, student groups, coffeehouses, bookstores, and a variety of other publicly visible social contexts in which a person can meet other LesBiGays and find the LesBiGay community. Local LesBiGay organizations can often be found in the telephone book under *gay* or *lambda.*

In the *Identity Acceptance* stage, individuals increase their contact with other LesBiGays and accept LesBiGayness as normal and valid. By now, individuals have begun disclosing their identities to other people to reduce the inconsistency between their perceptions of themselves and others' perceptions of them. Reduction of this inconsistency leads to another inconsistency: that between one's concept of one's LesBiGay self as completely acceptable and others' intolerance of that self. Resolution of this inconsistency is the task of the *Identity Pride* stage, during which one might devalue heterosexuals' opinions, or become politically active in the struggle against heterosexism, or both. One issue that confronts individuals at this stage is the conflict between their desire to be completely out and the reality that it is difficult to be out in some situations.

Cass argued that individuals finally reach the *Identity Synthesis* stage, in which the distinction between "us" (accepting LesBiGays) and "them" (intolerant heterosexuals) is muted and individuals experience consistency between their perceptions of self and others' perceptions of them.

Whereas Cass's model of coming out focuses on intrapsychic changes, Coleman's (1982) model focuses on the process of coming out to other people. Coleman notes that telling others is an important step in achieving self-acceptance via external validation. Others' reactions are critical, because those reactions are the mirror in which the LesBiGay individual sees her or his LesBiGay identity reflected and they influence the form that the Les- BiGay identity takes. The impact of these reactions depends on the impor- tance of the other person; the reactions of one's parents or best friend, for example, will have greater impact than the reaction of a stranger. Friends and counselors can help an individual who is coming out predict others' re- sponses and make healthy choices about when and to whom to come out during the vulnerable period when one's LesBiGay identity can still be profoundly affected by others' reactions and when one might not have the skills and self-confidence to defend oneself against psychologically abusive reactions.

Coleman suggests that it might be wise to build up positive responses from others before telling family members, such as parents, who might react negatively. In my experience, however, a growing number of young people want to tell their parents early in the process. They suspect that their parents would otherwise be upset, feeling insufficiently trusted to be informed sooner. But, despite increases in social tolerance of LesBiGayness, some people do react violently to the news that a friend or family member is LesBiGay. Parents do sometimes physically attack their children, throw them out of the house, disown them, or cut off financial support. For a minor child or a young adult in college, dependent on parents' tuition payments, this withdrawal of support can be very serious. If an individual thinks her or his parents might have such a reaction, the possibility of coming out to them should be considered very carefully indeed.

There are a number of books and other resources available for people who are coming out, and for their parents. For example, *Coming Out to Parents* (Borhek, 1983) is written for gay daughters and sons, and *Now That You Know* (Fairchild & Hayward, 1979) addresses itself to their parents. Rafkin's *Different Daughters: A Book by Mothers of Lesbians* (1987) can be useful for both mothers and daughters. Sometimes, parents need to come out to their children; a book like *Different Mothers: Sons and Daughters of Lesbians Talk About Their Lives* (Rafkin, 1990) could be helpful. Parents and Friends of Lesbians and Gays (P-FLAG) is an organization dedicated to increasing understanding between LesBiGay individuals and their families; it offers support to all family members during the adjustment process. P-FLAG is not just for parents and friends, as its name implies; many LesBiGay individuals join to find support in their struggles with their parents. Meeting the accept- ing parents of other LesBiGays can offer individuals hope for their own parents, strategies for dealing with their parents, and even parental substi- tutes who will listen to them when their own parents won't.

Because there are cross-cultural differences in the ways families function, coming out to one's family raises different issues for individuals belonging to different racial/ethnic groups. In some strong family-centered cultures, for example, part of being a woman or man is fulfilling one's family role by marrying and parenting children (Chan, 1989, 1992; Sue, Schneider, & Appathurai, 1981; Tremble et al. 1989). Because the family is the cornerstone of ethnic culture, fulfilling one's family role is also an ethnic obligation and an important aspect of one's ethnic identity. Individuals belonging to such cultures might find that their parents interpret their coming out as LesBiGay as a rejection of the family and of their ethnicity; parental pressure toward heterosexuality must therefore be understood as partially motivated by a desire to preserve ethnic identity (Rust, 1996a). Although individuals in such cultures often experience greater familial control over their sexual expression and identity because the interests of the family supersede those of the individual, they usually also experience greater security in the knowledge that they will not be rejected by their family or deprived of family support (e.g., Carballo-Diéguez, 1989). Facilitating the coming out process of such an individual requires knowledge of that individual's culture to understand both the unique issues that face that individual and the particular cultural resources—such as family ties that do not break—available to the individual to confront these issues.

Two steps in Coleman's coming out model are *Exploration* and *First Relationship*. Exploration is the stage in which LesBiGays begin sexual and social activities with other LesBiGay people. It is a period of sexual discovery and resocialization to gay subculture, including the development of interpersonal skills necessary to socialize with others in the LesBiGay community. But processes of identity formation, sexual discovery, and sociosexual socialization are processes that people typically go through during adolescence; if the LesBiGay person is coming out as an adult, the experience of feeling like an adolescent again can be disconcerting. The experience of a first relationship can also be difficult; although first relationships are usually learning experiences, the fact that there are few role models and a lack of social support for same-gender relationships—not to mention social and legal pressures *against* same-gender relationships—makes it even more difficult for individuals to build workable same-gender relationships. Therefore, an individual who is experiencing her or his first same-gender relationship or who is confronting adolescent developmental tasks again as an adult, might need extra support and encouragement.

In summary, traditional linear models of coming out do shed light on the issues faced by many lesbians, gay men, and bisexual people during coming out. The models reflect the ways in which many people understand their own coming out experiences—as developmental processes consisting of steps toward an end stage or goal—and therefore provide a starting point for understanding and supporting the individual who is coming out. But, like all models, linear models of coming out highlight some aspects of the process by concealing others. They direct our attention toward those issues that are predicted by the model and cause us to overlook other issues or other ways of understanding coming out. The next section of this chapter discusses the biases that linear models of coming out introduce into our understanding of the coming out process and thereby into our perception of people who are coming out and their needs.

A Critique of Coming Out Models—What They Conceal

Although models are developed to *describe* psychological and social phenomena, when they are used in efforts to predict or facilitate the processes they describe, they become *prescriptive*. This is especially true of linear or developmental models, in which the observation that many people have followed a particular path of change through time, ending in a particular state of being, becomes transformed into the expectation that other people will follow the same path and reach the same state of being. Within the context of such an expectation, people who do not follow the process as described come to be seen as deviating from a "normal" path, and people who do not achieve the expected end state—or who achieve other states of being—are perceived as not finishing the process. When the process being described is a sociopsychological one, the end state is generally conceptualized as a state of "maturity," with the implication that people who do not finish or have not yet finished the process are still in a state of immaturity and those who have finished the process are mature and will not change further. The transformation from description to prescription makes the model a moral one; movement toward the end state is defined as progress, whereas movement in the other direction is defined as regression.

So it is with linear developmental models of the coming out process. In all such models presented in the literature, homosexual or gay—and sometimes lesbian—identity is posited as the end stage of the coming out process. The implication is that other outcomes, such as bisexual identity or a refusal to adopt a sexual identity, reflect immaturity. An individual who remains bisexual-identified or nonidentified for any length of time is suspected of having underlying psychopathological issues, such as internalized homophobia, that are preventing her or him from completing the coming out process. Cass (1979), for example, acknowledges the existence of bisexuality and casts it as the "ambisexual strategy" used by some people during the Identity Comparison stage to cope with feelings of alienation, because it allows them to perceive themselves as *potentially* heterosexual. Schäfer (1976) and Chapman and Brannock (1987) characterize bisexuality as a stepping-stone on the way to homosexual identity, used by people who are not yet ready to acknowledge their true lesbian or gay identity. Coleman (1992) did suggest that "many individuals are not exclusively heterosexual or homosexual" (p. 40), thereby implying that bisexual identity could be a legitimate final step in the coming out process; but the last stage in the model he presents is nevertheless "positive gay identity."

Scientific descriptions of bisexuality as a phase some people go through while coming out reflect popular understandings of bisexuality in the lesbian and gay communities. For example, within the lesbian community, bisexual identity is considered a normal phase in the process of coming out as a lesbian. Women who identify themselves as bisexual are assumed to be "really lesbians," and if they persist in identifying as bisexual for lengthy periods of time, they are criticized for not having the courage to acknowledge their "true" lesbian identity. They are also accused of being political cowards or fence-sitters who reap the benefits of lesbian community while keeping a foot in the door of the privileged heterosexual world and shirking their responsibility for fighting lesbian oppression (Blumstein & Schwartz, 1974; Bode, 1976; MacDonald, 1981; Ponse, 1978, 1980; Rust, 1993b, 1995). Many bisexual-identified individuals report that they are confused by their bisexuality because they are constantly trying to figure out which they "really" are—straight or gay.

Contrary to these characterizations of bisexual identity as a sign of psychological immaturity or denial, for many individuals a bisexual identity is psychologically healthy. Numerous studies demonstrate that a substantial proportion of the U.S. population has experienced feelings of attraction to both women and men or has had sexual experiences with both women and men. In fact, this proportion is larger than the proportion of the population that is exclusively same-gender oriented.[3] Why should individuals have to dismiss their feelings for one gender or the other to fit themselves into either the heterosexual or the lesbian/gay categories that are socially available? If an individual feels authentically attracted to both women and men, then bisexual identity might be the most psychologically healthy identity for that individual, because it does not deny the authenticity of either same-gender or other-gender inclinations. Whereas such individuals are often socially pressured into identifying as lesbian or gay by peers who perceive their bisexual identity as a symptom of internalized homophobia, politically minded bisexual-identified individuals are reconstructing this social pressure as an example of *biphobia*.

The fact that linear coming out models have invariably cast bisexuality as a state of immaturity does not mean that they must necessarily do so. Linear models could easily be modified to include the possibility of bisexual identity as a legitimate end stage. In fact, in recent years, preliminary attempts have been made to describe the process of coming out as bisexual (e.g., Fox, 1991). But simply multiplying the number of identities that can serve as coming out goals does not address the assumption that coming out is fundamentally a linear process in which there is an end state and movement toward that end state is morally desirable.

Most theorists who proposed linear developmental models of coming out recognized this assumption and attempted to address it by acknowledging that not everyone goes through all the steps they described, nor does everyone go through the steps in the same order or achieve the end stage—nevertheless, they constructed these variations as deviations from an underlying linear path of development rather than reconceptualizing coming out as a nonlinear process (Rust, 1993a). Coleman (1982) furthermore recognized the danger that his descriptive model might be used as a prescription and cautioned against it. But it is difficult not to measure one's progress against a model produced via scientific research, especially when that model coincides with our "commonsense" understanding of the coming out process. For example, imagine a man who is married to a woman, identifies as heterosexual, and engages in secretive sex with men on the side. Most LesBiGay-positive people would look at this man and say that he is denying the implications of his same-gender behavior; if he is not denying these implications, then he must be experiencing tension because his sexual identity is inconsistent with his behavior. We empathize with his difficulty; if he comes out, he might anger and lose his wife, but everything else being equal, wouldn't he be happier and healthier if he could openly admit his same-gender attraction and come out? This is, in fact, the implication of coming out models whose end stage is identity integration, that is, that one cannot be psychologically mature until one reveals one's LesBiGay identity to others. To achieve maturity, therefore, the man in question needs to confront the internalized homophobia that is presumably preventing him from identifying as gay or bisexual and share this knowledge with his wife and other people who are significant in his life.

The fact that, for some men, this is an accurate interpretation of the situation does not change the fact that for others it contains inappropriate assumptions. These assumptions are especially problematic if we try to apply them cross-culturally. Different cultures construct sexuality differently; what is considered homosexuality in contemporary Euro-American culture is not necessarily considered homosexuality in, for example, Mexican or Chicano culture. What might appear to be incongruence between an individual's sexual identity—in this case, heterosexual—and her or his sexual behavior—in this case, same-gender—might reflect not internalized homophobia but merely a different way of understanding sexuality. In Euro-American culture, sexual orientation is defined in terms of the genders of the people to whom one is romantically or sexually attracted. In contrast, the Chicano who identifies himself as heterosexual might do so because he takes the insertive or *activo* role with his partners, be they men or women; in Mexican culture the homosexual is the man who plays the receptive, or *pasivo,* role.[4] Or it might reflect the fact that sexuality is not a basis for identity; in some cultures, people derive personal identity from their roles in the family, not from the sexual encounters they might have outside the family. Individuals who resist adopting a sexual identity, like those who adopt bisexual identities or identities that appear inconsistent with their behavior, should not be assumed a priori to have unresolved psychological issues anymore than individuals who readily adopt lesbian, gay, or heterosexual identities would be so assumed.

Most of us would agree that for reasons of physical health, if nothing else, the heterosexually married man who engages in same-gender activity should at least practice safe sex and be honest with his wife about his extramarital affairs. Men who identify as heterosexual but have secretive, anonymous sex with other men are perceived to be at increased risk of becoming infected with HIV and transmitting it to their sexual partners. The standard explanation for the presumed increased risk of these men is twofold. First, it is argued that they identify as heterosexual because internalized biphobia or homophobia prevents them from developing a positive bisexual or gay identity, and this same self-loathing underlies their willingness to engage in risky sex. Second, it is argued that safer sex messages aimed at "gay men" or, more recently, at "gay and bisexual men," fail to reach these men, because they do not identify themselves as bisexual or gay. Both explanations imply that these men would be more likely to practice safer sex if they could be encouraged to develop positive bisexual or gay identities. This implication is not applicable cross-culturally, however. For example, the Latino who identifies as heterosexual probably does so because the Latin concept of masculine heterosexuality can accommodate *activo* same-gender activity; such a man's heterosexual identity does not necessarily reflect internalized homophobia or biphobia or any other form of self-loathing that would predispose him to take health risks. If, because he identifies as heterosexual, he is not receptive to safer sex messages aimed at gay and bisexual men, then it seems more appropriate to design safer sex messages that will speak to his situation rather than ask him to alter his identity so that ethnocentric Euro American messages will be meaningful to him.

This discussion of cross-cultural differences reveals another bias inherent in linear models of coming out, that is, that they do not adequately account for the role of social constructs in shaping sexuality. Social constructs limit the possible outcomes of coming out by limiting the interpretations we are able to give our experiences and the self-labels available to us. But linear developmental models describe coming out as a journey experienced by an individual person; at best, they describe it as a journey in which that person interacts with others (e.g., Richardson & Hart, 1981). They therefore focus our attention on the individual and on how that individual can manage her or his interactions with others to facilitate the coming out process. Although they recognize that some identities are socially encouraged whereas others are socially discouraged, they focus on how both external and internalized social pressures (e.g., homophobia) inhibit an individual's journey toward recognition of her or his true essence. They fail to encourage us to look at the broader social forces that map out the terrain across which this journey takes place. For example, they fail to recognize that today, lesbian and gay identities usually signify more than sexual orientation; these identities also have political meanings. Sometimes, as I will discuss below, individuals adopt sexual identities to represent their political commitments, not their sexual feelings or behaviors.

McDonald (1982) began to recognize that same-gender identities have political meanings by asserting that a *gay* identity reflects a more advanced stage of identity development than a *homosexual* identity does, but he failed to recognize the role of social constructive processes in shaping the concept of *gay,* such that a gay identity can signify a more positive self-concept. The fact is that the terms available for the description of sexual identity change over time and hold different meanings for different people. Some men reject the label *gay,* not because they feel any shame over their same-gender inclinations but because the term is political and they do not share these politics. They prefer to describe themselves as homosexual because it is an accurate description of their feelings and behaviors. For them, *homosexual* is an accurate and affectively neutral term, whereas *gay* is a negative one—they are not necessarily any less psychologically mature than men with gay identities. To conclude, from the observation that men with gay identities use the term *gay* because they find it to be a more positive term than *homosexual,* that men who identify themselves as homosexual therefore feel less positively about their sexuality is to privilege one political interpretation of these terms over another.

Similarly, since the 1970s, many women have rejected a *gay* identity in favor of a *lesbian* identity because they find that when most people say or hear the word *gay,* they think of gay *men.* They use *lesbian* to make themselves visible as women. Therefore, for these women, *lesbian* is a more positive identity than *gay.* More recently, in the mid-1980s, the growth of Queer Nation stimulated many LesBiGays to reclaim the word *queer,* and many women and men now find *queer* identity more positive and affirming than either *lesbian* or *gay* identities. *Queer* is a decidedly political term that, for many people, symbolizes a challenge to traditional category boundaries. Any person with same-gender desires can be queer because they challenge traditional heterosexual notions of gendered sexuality. Likewise, a lesbian and a gay man who are attracted to each other might call themselves queer because they challenge more recent notions of what it means to be lesbian or gay, and transgendered people might identify as queer because they challenge the gender categories upon which traditional notions of heterosexuality and homosexuality are based. For many people who adopt queer identity, it symbolizes not only their sexuality but also the challenge their sexuality poses to socially constructed sexuality, gender, or both. Yet, for other people, the term *queer* retains its pejorative connotations; for these people, a queer identity would not reflect a positive self-image.

With the growth of the bisexual and queer political movements, the number of socially available sexual identities has exploded. Many of the newer identities are still only socially available within queer community, because members of mainstream heterosexual society have not yet become aware of the great variety and political nuances that exist within queer community. It is therefore worth noting some of these newer identities. In my current research study, the most common sexual identities among women, after bisexual and queer, are *lesbian-identified bisexual* and *bisexual lesbian*. Similar identities are *bi dyke* and *byke*. These identities are often used by women for whom lesbian and bisexual identities each accurately reflect some aspects of their sexuality but do not completely describe their sexuality. Most commonly, these identities are used by women who feel attracted to both women and men but who, for political reasons often related to feminism or personal reasons involving their emotional feelings about women and men, choose to express these feelings only toward women. Other women use these identities because they previously identified as lesbian and retain the lesbian identity as a reflection of their political commitment to women or to the lesbian community. For them, the term *bisexual* is a more sexual and apolitical term than *lesbian,* so bisexual identity alone would not suffice to express the political meaning of their sexuality. But they feel attracted to both women and men and might be open to or actively engaged in either same-gender or other-gender activity, so they also use the term *bisexual* to express their sexual "essence." As the bisexual movement grows, the term *bisexual* is taking on political meaning, and some women drop the lesbian aspect of their identities because it is no longer needed to politicize their identities.

Another identity that will probably become less common as bisexual identity becomes more socially available and political is the *lesbian who has sex with men* identity. One woman who uses this identity explained, "Sexual identity has more to do with self-perception than actual sexual activity." For her, the fact that she has sex with men does not contradict her lesbian identity. She *is* a lesbian—who also happens to have sex with men. She does not think of herself as bisexual and, like many other lesbians, might believe that bisexuality does not exist as an authentic sexual orientation (Rust, 1995).

Other increasingly common identities are *gay bisexual* among men, and *bisensual, polysexual, polyamorous,* and *polyfidelitous* among both women and men. *Bisensual* is used by people who dislike the cultural privileging of genital sex and the sharp distinction drawn between sexuality and other forms of human relating, and who feel that *sensuality* better describes the range of feelings that they want to express via identity. *Polysexual* and *polyamorous* are used by people who recognize that the term *bi*sexual reifies the gender dichotomy that underlies the distinction between heterosexuality and homosexuality, implying that bisexuality is nothing more than a hybrid combination of these two gendered sexualities, and who wish to define their sexuality independently of these gender and sexual dichotomies. As one polysexual respondent put it, "I dislike the dualistic dichotomy of 'bi'. . . . My sexuality is diffuse." *Polyfidelity* is the practice of fidelity within a group of three or more people, in contrast to monogamy, which involves fidelity between only two people. In short, the point is that the meanings ascribed to sexuality and the language available to express these meanings change over time, and therefore no particular sexual identity should be identified as more mature or morally desirable than any other sexual identity. Instead, the emphasis should be on encouraging each individual to choose or create an identity that feels satisfactory to her or him at a given point in time and within a given social and political context.

Another criticism of linear models is that they fail to acknowledge that coming out is a continuous, lifetime process. Within the context of traditional linear models of coming out, identity change is an indication that one has not yet completed the coming out process, and achievement of the end stage—in which identity accurately reflects essence, and the individual therefore has no further motivation to change—is characterized by identity stasis. The existence of an end stage implies that the process can be "finished." But coming out is never a process that is finished, for two reasons. The first is apparent from the foregoing discussion of historical changes in sexual politics; when we take into account the social factors that shape the terrain across which one's coming out journey takes place, we see that this terrain continues to change even after a given individual has "completed" the coming out process. Therefore, even after they develop an identity that they find comfortable and that they feel reflects their sexuality accurately, individuals might find that they have to go through other identity change processes as the available identity terms change in meaning.

The second reason that coming out is a lifetime process is that whenever LesBiGays enter new situations, they have to decide whether to come out in that situation. Regardless of how out an individual is in other contexts of her or his life, every time she or he encounters a new person (outside specifically LesBiGay settings), that other person will assume that the individual is heterosexual, and the LesBiGay person will have to decide once again whether to correct the assumption and deal with whatever reaction the other person might have or to let the assumption persist and thereby present her- or himself as heterosexual in that encounter.

Coming out, then, is not a singular process with an attainable end stage, but rather an ongoing process of attempting to maintain an accurate self-description of one's sexuality in a world of sexual meanings that vary over time and across context. Maturity is not synonymous with stasis, and change is not an indication of immaturity. Rust (1993a) presents a nonlinear model of coming out that incorporates this understanding of identity change.

Similarly, linear models of coming out do not allow for the possibility of multiple changes in sexual orientation. Linear models lead people to expect that once they come out as LesBiGay, they have discovered their "true" sexuality, and it therefore won't change again. This expectation is subculturally reinforced for lesbians and gay men, who are encouraged by peers to perceive their early heterosexual experiences as merely responses to socialization or social pressure, and their current lesbian or gay identity as the *true* identity that they finally discovered, in spite of all the odds, through hard work. Many people do experience changes in their sexual feelings and behaviors during their lives, however. Less than 4% of respondents in my current study report that they have been at the same point on an 11-point scale of sexual attraction all their lives. Fifty-eight percent have moved 5 scale points or more; a change of 5 points reflects movement from exclusive attraction to one gender to 50:50 attraction to both genders, or from predominant attraction to one gender (e.g., 70:30 in favor of women) to predominant attraction to the other gender (e.g., 20:80 in favor of men). Numerous researchers provide other evidence that sexual orientation can change over the life course (e.g., Blumstein & Schwartz, 1977; Dixon, 1984).

Such changes can be very confusing to people who think they have already finished the coming out process. For example, lesbian- or gay-identified persons who experience renewed heterosexual attraction might wonder whether they came to the wrong conclusion the first time they came out. This potentially undermines the work they did to come out, throwing it all into question. This new change might thereby lead them to invalidate their lesbian/gay feelings, just as their first coming out as lesbian or gay might have led them to invalidate the heterosexual feelings they had previously. In this way, the second identity change experience becomes an entirely new coming out that potentially invalidates another whole section of these individuals' lives, rather than a further evolution of their sexual identities that can build on the lessons learned from their first coming out experience.

Individuals who are experiencing changes in their sexual feelings or behaviors can be encouraged to think of these changes as part of an ongoing process of sexual discovery and can be reassured that many people change their sexual identities more than once over the course of their lives. In my current study of people who have experienced attraction to both women and men, 20% of women and men identified themselves as heterosexual again after coming out as lesbian, gay, or bisexual. Of those who came out initially as lesbian, gay, or homosexual, 91% of women and 68% of men later called themselves bisexual, and of those who came out as bisexual, 39% of women and 35% of men later identified as lesbian or gay. Individuals who are coming out for the first time can be informed that sexuality often changes during the life course, so that they will not be taken by surprise and find their sexual sense of self undermined if they do experience such changes later.

Scientific models have methodological implications; scientists' perceptions of a phenomenon have direct bearing on how they choose to study it. The findings produced by their methodologies, in turn, tend to reinforce the models that generated them. Linear models of coming out encourage scientists to calculate *average ages* at which individuals achieve each of a series of milestone events. For example, McDonald (1982) determined that men first identified themselves as homosexual at an average age of 19 years and became involved in their first homosexual relationship at an average age of 21 years. A problem arises, however, when these data are interpreted as suggesting that individuals necessarily experience these milestone events in a particular order—in the case of McDonald's data, that individuals self-identify as homosexual 2 years before their first involvement in a homosexual relationship. Such simplistic application of aggregate statistics to individuals introduces two errors into our thinking about individual experiences.

First, the average age at which a number of individuals experience a certain event might bear no relationship to the age at which any of those individuals actually experienced that event. To take an extreme example for the purpose of illustration, if half a sample first experienced same-gender attraction at age 12, and the other half first experienced same-gender attraction at age 34, then the average would be 23, an age that bears no resemblance to the actual experience of any one individual. Figures 6.1 through 6.4 show the range and distribution of ages at which the women and men in my current survey experienced each of four milestone events. These figures show that there are modal ages at which these events are experienced; for example,

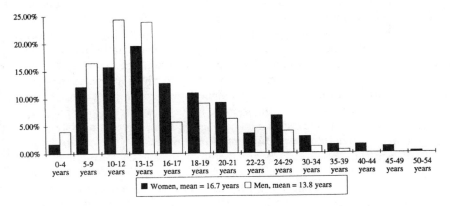

Figure 6.1. Ages at Which Women and Men First Experienced Same-Gender Attraction

women and men are more likely to first experience same-gender attraction between the ages of 10 and 15 than at any other age (Figure 6.1) and they are more likely to realize that they are not heterosexual in their mid- to late teens than at any other age (Figure 6.2). But the most striking feature of each figure is the breadth of the range of ages at which individuals have experienced a given event. Individuals report having experienced same-gender

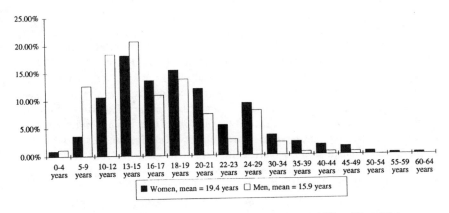

Figure 6.2. Ages at Which Women and Men First Realized They Were Not Heterosexual

attraction for the first time at ages as young as the beginning of childhood memory and as old as age 52. If the sample had included a larger number of elderly people, we would probably find people experiencing same-gender attraction for the first time at even older ages. Note also that the *average* age at which women in this sample first experienced same-gender attraction is 16.7 years, an age that is outside the modal range in which individual women were actually most likely to first experience same-gender attraction. This is because, relative to the mode, the average is biased upward by the fact that women continue to come out throughout the life span. Average ages conceal a great deal of individual variation and do not necessarily reflect any individual's actual experience. They are, therefore, poor bases for predicting or evaluating the experiences of someone who is in the process of coming out.

Second, the fact that one average age is lower than another does not mean that any given individual experiences one event before another. As noted by McDonald (1982), individuals experience milestone events in varying orders. For example, linear models of coming out typically lead to the finding that the average age at which individuals first experience same-gender attraction is lower than the average age at which they adopt a lesbian or gay identity. This makes sense superficially; one would expect people to label themselves lesbian or gay only after they have had the experience of same-gender attraction to which the lesbian or gay label presumably refers. But it is not always true. In my earlier study, I discovered that one fourth of lesbian-identified respondents had identified themselves as lesbians *before* ever feeling attracted to women (Rust, 1993a). Probably, these women adopted a lesbian identity for political reasons, as an expression of a feminist commitment to women and a belief that a lesbian identity is more consistent with feminism than a heterosexual identity is; they are the *political lesbians* of the 1970s and early 1980s.

The coming out process experienced by these women is misrepresented by descriptions of coming out based on average ages, and none of the linear models of coming out that exist in the literature could have predicted the issues they faced while coming out. For example, some of these women felt the anxiety of wanting desperately to experience an attraction to women that would validate their desired and already adopted lesbian identities; such an issue cannot be predicted by a model that assumes that the normal course is for an individual to experience same-gender attraction and then label it. *Political lesbians* also faced criticism and distrust from *real lesbians*— that is, those whose lesbian identities were based on same-gender attractions—who, ironically, were the very same lesbian feminists who had only a little while earlier exhorted them to identify as lesbians in expression of their feminist commitment to women. This issue also could not have been predicted by linear developmental models that focus on individual self-

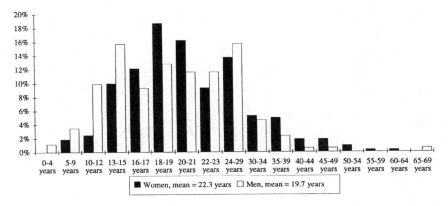

Figure 6.3. Ages at Which Women and Men Adopted First Nonheterosexual Identity

discovery while failing to consider the social and political context within which this "discovery" is taking place.

Researchers calculating average ages based on a linear understanding of coming out also have "determined" that some groups of people tend to come out at different ages and different speeds than other groups of people. For example, their calculations suggest that women come out at later ages, and more slowly, than men do; that is, women experience given events at higher average ages and have longer time lags between successive milestone events (Bell, Weinberg, & Hammersmith, 1981; Cronin, 1974; De Monteflores & Schultz, 1978; Riddle & Morin, 1977). One study that included bisexuals suggested that bisexual-identified individuals come out more slowly than lesbian- or gay-identified individuals (Kooden et al., 1979). Figures 6.1 through 6.4 confirm that women experience each milestone event at a higher average age than men do but they show that there is also considerable overlap in the ages at which women and men experience each event. For example, there is a 2.9-year difference in the average ages at which women and men first experience same-gender attraction, but there is approximately a 35-year overlap in the range of ages at which women and men can have this experience; both women and men can first experience same-gender attraction as early as the beginning of childhood memory and both can experience it at least as late as their mid-30s (Figure 6.1). Thus, in terms of understanding a particular individual's experiences of coming out, the similarities between women and men are greater than the differences.

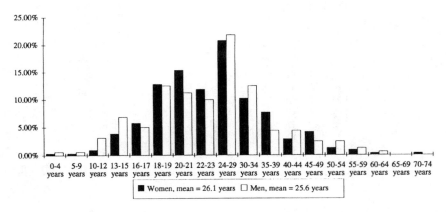

Figure 6.4. Ages at Which Women and Men Adopted Their Current Sexual Identities

Besides highlighting difference at the expense of similarity, the use of average ages to compare groups of people with one another can produce findings that actually are empirically false. My previous research demonstrates that the apparent finding that bisexual women come out more slowly than lesbians reflects the failure to recognize that women experience events in varying orders. If we exclude from the analysis women who questioned their heterosexuality and identified themselves as lesbians *before* feeling attracted to women, the findings change dramatically. A comparison of lesbians who experienced same-gender attraction before questioning their heterosexuality with bisexuals who had these experiences in the same order reveals that bisexual women actually question their heterosexuality *sooner* after their first experience of same-gender attraction than lesbians do, not later (Rust, 1993a). Thus, the earlier finding is a statistical artifact produced by statistical procedures chosen based on linear understandings of coming out.

Specific Comments on Bisexuality

Because bisexuality has been neglected in the literature on coming out, as it has been neglected generally in the literature on sexual difference, a discussion of issues particular to bisexuals is in order. The first issue confronting individuals who have both same-gender and other-gender feelings or sexual experiences is the problem of finding an identity that suffices to represent their sexuality. Because the dominant conceptualization of sexuality in northwestern European and North American societies is a dichotomous one that authenticates only heterosexuality and homosexuality, individuals with both same-gender and other-gender feelings or experiences often attempt to fit themselves into one of these socially available categories. They might discredit same-gender feelings and experiences to maintain a heterosexual identity or they might discredit other-gender feelings and experiences and come out as lesbian or gay. For some people, this is a satisfactory resolution; many people with same-gender experience happily remain heterosexually identified, and many lesbian- and gay-identified people report extensive other-gender experience. But other people find that both their same-gender and their other-gender feelings and experiences are important and ego-syntonic. These individuals cannot or do not want, and should not be encouraged, to deny any part of their sexuality in order to fit into either a heterosexual or a lesbian/gay identity.

Oftentimes, the difficulties for these individuals are compounded because their emotional feelings for women and men differ from their sexual feelings. For example, one might feel emotionally closer to women and more capable of forming lasting romantic attachments with them but more sexually attracted to men. Someone trying to fit into either a lesbian/gay or a heterosexual category might wonder whether she or he should give greater weight to emotional or sexual feelings. Such individuals can benefit from reassurance not only that it is possible and common for individuals to feel attracted to both women and men but also that there are many dimensions to sexuality and that these dimensions vary independently of each other. The Klein Sexual Orientation Grid (KSOG), for example, includes seven dimensions, including sexual attraction, sexual behavior, sexual fantasies, emotional preference, social preference, self-identity, and lifestyle (Klein, Sepekoff, & Wolf, 1985). Each dimension is represented by a 7-point scale, ranging from "other sex only" to "same sex only." A given individual can be at different positions on each of these seven dimensions. For example, a woman might feel sexually attracted equally to women and men but emotionally closer to women than men while fantasizing mostly about men, having sex only with women, identifying as bisexual, and socializing within a lesbian community. Moreover, an individual's position on these dimensions can change over the life course. Knowing that sexuality is multidimensional gives individuals the validation necessary to recognize the complexity of their feelings, eliminating the need to figure out which feelings are real and which are not to fit themselves into preestablished categories. Of course, the number of dimensions is limited only by one's imagination; once individuals free themselves from conceptualizing sexuality as dichotomous or unidimensional, they will probably discover additional dimensions that contribute to their own senses of sexuality or sensuality.

Although multidimensional scalar models of sexuality can give individuals the freedom to recognize the complexity of their sexuality, these models are usually not satisfactory bases for sexual identity. Because sexuality is considered a basis for identity in contemporary northwestern European and dominant North American cultures, most individuals will feel a need to develop a particular sexual identity. Imagine, however, trying to form an identity around the concept of oneself as a "sexual 2.0, an emotional 5.4, and a behavioral 3.1." For many individuals, bisexual identity can encompass the range of their various feelings for and experiences with women and men.

But the lack of social recognition given to bisexual identity makes it difficult to develop and sustain a bisexual identity. Because others retain dichotomous conceptualizations of sexuality, they are likely to believe either that bisexuality does not exist at all or that it exists as a hybrid form of sexuality, combining heterosexual and homosexual elements. Others' beliefs that bisexuality does not exist have obvious implications for the formation of bisexual identity, given the importance of others' reactions to the development of sexual identity. Individuals who are repeatedly told that they can't be bisexual because there is no such thing, or that they are really lesbian or gay and should overcome their internalized homophobia and finish coming out, might have difficulty maintaining a bisexual identity. These individuals need reassurance that bisexuality is, indeed, an authentic sexual orientation.

The implications of conceptualizing bisexuality as a hybrid are more subtle. Some people believe that bisexuality has to consist of exactly equal parts of heterosexuality and homosexuality; that is, that a person has to be a "perfect hybrid" to qualify as bisexual. In this view, anyone who feels more strongly about one gender or the other should identify as lesbian/gay or heterosexual accordingly. But sexual attraction is difficult, if not impossible, to gauge: How is one to determine if one's feelings for women and men are equal in strength, especially if one's sexual and emotional feelings differ? Such a definition of bisexuality, although appearing to acknowledge bisexuality as an authentic orientation, effectively makes it impossible for any individual to find a secure sense of self in bisexual identity. Figure 6.5 shows that most bisexuals reject this narrow definition of bisexuality; women and men who identify themselves as bisexual cover almost the entire spectrum of sexual feeling, ranging from those who feel 100% attracted to women to those who feel 90% attracted to men. In fact, less than one in four reports feeling equally attracted to women and men.

Another implication of the hybrid concept of bisexuality concerns the relationship between homosexuality and heterosexuality. As a combination of homosexuality and heterosexuality, bisexuality is a combination of attractions to women and men. But women and men are constructed as cultural

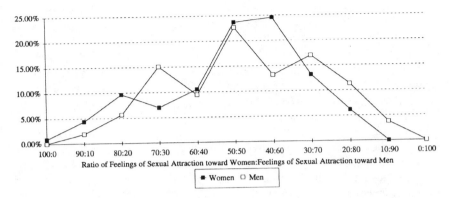

Figure 6.5. Range of Feelings of Attraction Toward Women and Men Among Bisexuals of Both Genders

opposites—as in "the opposite sex"—therefore, attractions to women and men are typically thought of as opposite, and even contradictory, attractions. Scalar models of sexual orientation, such as the KSOG, illustrate this. On most such scalar models, attraction to women and attraction to men occupy two ends of the same scale, implying that as one becomes more attracted to women, one must become less attracted to men and vice versa. Bisexuality, then, consists of two forms of sexuality that are diametrically opposed to one another. If it were possible to combine them at all, the result would be conflict between these two opposing desires. Therefore, bisexuality is stereotyped as an unstable form of sexuality, one that is most likely a transitional phase during coming out. Others expect bisexuals either to flip-flop between heterosexuality and homosexuality or settle into either heterosexuality or homosexuality but not to remain consistently bisexual. These expectations are tautologically confirmed as soon as the bisexual becomes romantically involved with another person, because that person is usually either a woman or a man. This relationship, therefore, is either same-gendered or other-gendered, and the bisexual is then said to have revealed her or his true sexuality, which is either lesbian/gay or heterosexual. Because it can be difficult and exhausting to explain to others that one has not *become* lesbian/gay or heterosexual just because one's current partner is of a particular gender, and because some bisexuals—who, after all, exist in the same sexual culture as do lesbians/gays and heterosexuals—also consider themselves either lesbian/gay or heterosexual whenever they are involved with a person of a particular gender, many bisexuals identify themselves as either lesbian/gay or heterosexual while they are romantically involved. Blumstein and Schwartz (1976) observed that there are people who maintain a bisexual identity only during periods in which they are romantically uninvolved.

If conceptualizing bisexuality as a hybrid form of sexuality is problematic because it undermines the potential for a stable bisexual identity, what is the alternative? Many bisexual-identified people prefer to conceptualize bisexuality as the ability to be attracted to people *regardless* of gender or to be attracted to people on the basis of a number of criteria, only one of which might be gender. Bisexuals, in this view, are not attracted to women *and* men but to *people,* whose gender might or might not be relevant to the attraction. Thus, bisexuality is not a hybrid combination of two gender-exclusive sexualities but a holistic sexuality that is not gender-exclusive. When such a bisexual becomes involved with another person, this involvement is always an expression of bisexuality, not an expression of either "homosexuality" or "heterosexuality" just because the other person happens to have a particular gender. Unfortunately, the word *bi*sexual tends to promote the concept of bisexuality as a hybrid form of sexuality, hence the proliferation of alternative identities such as polysexual.

Although bisexual identity still does not have the cultural legitimacy accorded heterosexual and lesbian/gay identities, it is receiving increasing recognition for two reasons. One reason is the recent rapid growth of the bisexual political movement, which has bisexual visibility as a primary goal. The other reason is that the AIDS epidemic has dramatically demonstrated the inadequacy of dichotomous models of sexuality in which behavior is assumed to be consistent with identity. Heterosexuals, fearing that bisexuals would be the gateway through which HIV would spread from gay men to the heterosexual population, became very aware of the existence of bisexuality during the 1980s. Indeed, bisexuality has become a hot topic in the media, particularly on talk shows. Unfortunately, the media usually choose to sensationalize bisexuality. Besides portraying bisexuals as people who spread HIV, the media promote images of bisexuals as men who cheat on their wives with other men and as people who have simultaneous female and male lovers. The problem is not that these images are available—they are accurate portrayals of some bisexuals—but that they overshadow all other images of bisexuality. The message conveyed is that bisexuality consists of having sexual relations with *both* women and men, a message rooted squarely in the concept of bisexuality as a hybrid form of sexuality.

These media images have negative effects on individuals who are coming out as bisexual. First of all, negative portrayals of bisexuals as cheating disease carriers can make it difficult to form a positive bisexual identity. Second, they promote a concept of bisexuality defined in terms of behavior; that is, a bisexual is one who *behaves* bisexually by having simultaneous sexual relationships with both women and men. People who are coming to grips with the fact that they are attracted to both women and men have limited role models for being bisexual and might conclude, on the basis of the evidence at hand, that they are doomed to a life of shallow relationships, cheating, or, at best, serial monogamy. Sometimes, people who identify as bisexual feel as if they haven't fully come out until they have had sexual relationships with people of both genders, which creates pressure on them to find people of both genders to have sex with just to validate their sexual identity. This is dangerous because it encourages people to have sex simply to conform to an image they have applied to themselves, a situation not conducive to making psychologically or physically healthy choices about sexual behavior.

Individuals who are struggling with feelings for both women and men or who are coming out as bisexual need to know that having sexual feelings does not mean that these feelings must be acted on. They need to know that bisexuality need not be defined in terms of behavior, but that being bisexual can also mean being attracted to members of both genders or to people regardless of gender. A person does not have to have sex with both women and men either to "prove" she or he is bisexual or to validate those feelings. The feelings are valid in themselves.

Bisexuals often encounter rejection in both heterosexual society and lesbian/gay communities. The fact that bisexuals experience rejection from lesbians and gay men comes as a surprise to many heterosexuals, who lump bisexuals together with lesbians and gay men, in a process analogous to the racist "one drop" rule of racial classification, and therefore assume that bisexuals, lesbians, and gay men similarly lump themselves together. Although there are efforts to create unity among lesbians, gay men, bisexuals, and trangenderists within queer community, there are also intensely emotional divisions between these different groups. Bisexuals within the lesbian community are sometimes accused of being traitors or of wanting to hang on to heterosexual privilege. They are told to stop hiding behind the relatively "safe" bisexual identity, to come out as lesbians and shoulder their share of the burden of being part of an oppressed group. My earlier research documented lesbians' attitudes toward bisexual women. It showed, for example, that 75% of lesbian respondents believed that bisexual identity was a transitional identity, 60% believed that bisexuals are not as committed to other women as lesbians are, and the vast majority avoided dating bisexual women (Rust, 1993b, 1995). Not all lesbians have negative opinions of and feelings toward bisexual women, but enough do to create an unwelcoming environment in some lesbian groups. In recent years, controversies have erupted over the inclusion of the word *bisexual* in the names of lesbian and gay community centers and pride marches, either because some lesbians and gay men do not recognize bisexuality as a distinct sexual orientation or because they do not want bisexuals included in lesbian and gay community. Examples are the controversies over the names of the Northampton Pride March and the 1993 March on Washington.

The kinds of issues that exclusion from lesbian and gay communities raise for people coming out as bisexual depend on whether they are coming out from a heterosexual identity or from a lesbian or gay identity. People who are coming out as bisexual from a heterosexual identity might expect to be accepted by lesbians and gay men. They probably will be accepted for a time, because lesbians and gay men will expect them to finish coming out and adopt a lesbian or gay identity eventually. But if they persist in identifying as bisexual, they are likely to find this acceptance replaced by criticism. They then face the choice of either adopting a lesbian or gay identity or being marginalized within a community from which they had expected and temporarily received acceptance. People who are coming out from a lesbian or gay identity, on the other hand, are familiar with the politics surrounding bisexual identity in the lesbian and gay communities. Knowing these politics, many conceal their emerging other-gender feelings from their lesbian and gay friends. Bisexual activist Robyn Ochs speaks of being the "bisexual confessor" for countless lesbian-identified women, who tell her about their attractions to men while professing a lesbian identity to others. For anyone coming out as bisexual, *Bi Any Other Name: Bisexual People Speak Out* (Hutchins & Kaahumanu, 1991) can be an important source of validation, and for women coming out as bisexual from a lesbian identity, *Closer to Home: Bisexuality & Feminism* (Weise, 1992) will have particular relevance.

The bisexual community is much smaller and less politically powerful than the lesbian and gay communities. Although the bisexual political movement grew at an astonishing rate during the late 1980s and early 1990s and is remarkably well organized, it has limited resources and numbers. Many bisexuals living outside large cities have no access to bisexual support groups, let alone bisexual political organizations or cultural institutions. Some rely on electronic mail to communicate with other bisexuals or see other bisexuals only when they attend conferences sponsored by national or regional bisexual organizations. Some eagerly await the arrival of their favorite bisexual magazine or newsletter, such as *Anything That Moves: Beyond the Myths of Bisexuality,* published by the Bay Area Bisexual Network; *Bi Women,* published by the Boston Bisexual Women's Network; or *North Bi Northwest,* published by the Seattle Bisexual Women's Network. Others seek support within the lesbian and gay communities. Because bisexual organizations often do not have dedicated phone lines, they can be more difficult to locate than lesbian or gay organizations. One way to find bisexual organizations is through the *Bisexual Resource Guide* (Ochs, 1995), which is updated regularly and lists not only bisexual and bisexual-inclusive organizations around the world but also bi-related books and films.[5] BiNet USA is a national bisexual network that publishes *BiNet Newsletter* and holds national and regional conferences. These resources can provide individuals coming out as bisexual with positive bisexual role models and validation for their emerging bisexual identities.

The Importance of Prevention: Easing the Coming Out Process by Eliminating Heterosexism

Coming out can be an exciting, but difficult, process. Individuals going through this process face many psychological and social issues, and they often face these issues without adequate support from others. Ironically, at a time when they most need support, many people are afraid to ask for it for fear of receiving rejection instead of support. Although social attitudes toward lesbians and gay men are becoming more positive, and lesbians and gay men themselves are becoming more visible, homophobia and heterosexism still pervade both our culture and our social, legal, and political systems. Moreover, despite the increasing visibility of lesbians and gay men, bisexuals still remain largely invisible.

Therefore, individuals who are coming out are often in need of supportive friends and counselors who understand the process of coming out. Linear models of coming out, both those codified in scientific literature and the popular versions on which these scientific models are based, provide insight into coming out as it is experienced by some individuals. But they also lend a moral quality to the process of coming out by casting it as a developmental process leading toward certain forms of sexual identity, thereby privileging these sexual identities over others. In so doing, they blind us to the legitimacy of other sexual identities, to the possibility that refusing to adopt a sexual identity might be a healthy choice, and to the reality that for many people coming out is a lifelong process of recurrent self-creation and self-discovery, not a singular goal-oriented process of self-classification. Moreover, because most research on coming out was done using Euro-American subjects, this research sheds little light on coming out as it is experienced by members of other cultural groups. Views of sexuality, and of the relationships between sexuality, gender, and the family, differ cross-culturally, causing profound differences in the issues faced by members of different cultural groups during coming out.

But the entire process of coming out is made necessary by the fact of heterosexism, in particular, the usually unspoken assumption that individuals are heterosexual. Although it is necessary to provide support for individuals who are coming out in a heterosexist society, it is perhaps even more important to attack the problem at its root by dismantling heterosexism. This work needs to be done at all levels, including the individual, social, and legal levels. Individually, each of us should work on eliminating our own heterosexual assumptions. For example, instead of asking a new acquaintance "Are you married?" which, in a country in which same-gender relationships are not legally sanctioned as marriages, assumes heterosexuality, ask "Do you have a partner?" If you are heterosexual, recognize your heterosexual privilege and use it to undermine the heterosexism that gave you that privilege. For example, notice that you can casually mention your other-gender spouse or partner without other people noticing that you have just revealed your heterosexuality—this is because they already assumed that you were heterosexual. In contrast, a lesbian or gay person cannot casually mention a same-gender partner, because such a mention constitutes an announcement of that person's sexuality. Try disrupting others' heterosexual assumptions by referring to your partner in gender-neutral terms.

Socially, we need to work on making lesbianism, gayness, and bisexuality as visible as heterosexuality. Besides the obvious visibility provided heterosexuality by the disproportionate media attention given to it, heterosexuality is made visible through subtle means that are taken for granted by heterosexuals but appear blatant to lesbians, gay men, and bisexuals. For example, the wearing of gold wedding bands, heterosexual personal classified ads, and the announcement of engagements in the local paper all celebrate and normalize other-gender relationships in ways that same-gender relationships are rarely celebrated or normalized. Bisexuality, in particular, is rendered invisible because even those of us who are cognizant of the existence of same-gender relationships tend to deduce a person's sexual orientation from the gender of her or his partner. For example, both individuals in an other-gender couple are assumed to be heterosexual and both individuals in a same-gender couple are assumed to be lesbian or gay; rarely do we consider the possibility that either or both members of the couple might be bisexual. Work on avoiding assumptions about any individual's sexuality, and when others make such assumptions, point it out to them.

Lesbians, gay men, and bisexuals do not enjoy the same legal rights as heterosexuals do, and partners in same-gender relationships do not receive the same legal rights as partners in other-gender marriages do, for example, next-of-kin rights, certain property rights, and the right to joint custody of children. Even individuals who are comfortable with their own lesbianism, gayness, or bisexuality often hesitate to come out to others because of fear that they will lose their jobs or apartments because of discrimination; most states and cities offer no protection from discrimination based on sexual orientation. Ironically, legislators often want proof that sexual orientation discrimination occurs before they will support legislation to outlaw it; such proof can be difficult to provide, because the victims of this discrimination fear suffering discrimination again if they come out publicly. Use your voice to educate others about sexual orientation discrimination and to convince legislators that it should be illegal. Support organizations such as the Lambda Legal Defense and Education Fund or the Human Rights Campaign Fund, whose purposes are to acquire legal and political equality for lesbians, gay men, and bisexuals. Educate yourself about the laws affecting lesbians, gay men, and bisexuals in your city and state and, whether you are heterosexual, lesbian, gay, or bisexual, consider it your responsibility to help end heterosexism at the legal level as much as at the individual and social levels. If we succeed in eliminating heterosexism at all levels, the difficult process of coming out will be no more necessary for the lesbians, gay men, and bisexuals of the future than it is for the heterosexuals of today, and we will have faced as a society the most difficult coming out issue of all.

Notes

1. *LesBiGay* refers to *lesbian, bisexual, and gay* or *lesbian, bisexual, or gay.*

2. As of this writing, the *Baehr v. Lewin* case in Hawaii might lead to the extension of marriage rights to same-gender couples. If it does, other states would theoretically be obliged to recognize these same-gender marriages because of the *full faith and credit* clause of the Constitution. In some states, however, radical religious right groups are attempting to pass laws that would preempt this recognition.

3. For statistics on the incidence of homosexual and bisexual behavior, see Diamond (1993); Hunt (1974); Janus and Janus (1993); Kinsey, Pomeroy, and Martin (1948); Kinsey, Pomeroy, Martin, and Gebhard (1953); Laumann, Gagnon, Michael, and Michaels (1994); and Rogers and Turner (1991).

4. For information about the construction of sexuality in Latin cultures, see Almaguer (1993); Alonso and Koreck (1993); Carballo-Diéguez (1989); Carrier (1976, 1985); and Magaña and Carrier (1991).

5. *The Bisexual Resource Guide* is available from The Bisexual Resource Center, P.O. Box 639, Cambridge, MA 02140.

References

Almaguer, T. (1993). Chicano men: A cartography of homosexual identity and behavior. In H. Abelove, M. A. Barale, & D. M. Halperin (Eds.), *The lesbian and gay studies reader* (pp. 255-273). New York: Routledge & Kegan Paul.

Alonso, A. M., & Koreck, M. T. (1993). Silences: "Hispanics," AIDS, and sexual practices. In H. Abelove, M. A. Barale, & D. M. Halperin (Eds.), *The lesbian and gay studies reader* (pp. 110-126). New York: Routledge & Kegan Paul.

Beam, J. (Ed.). (1986). *In the life: A black gay anthology.* Boston: Alyson.

Bell, A. P., Weinberg, M. S., & Hammersmith, S. K. (1981). *Sexual preference: Its development in men and women*. Bloomington: Indiana University Press.

Blumstein, P., & Schwartz, P. (1974). Lesbianism and bisexuality. In E. Goode & R. R. Troiden (Eds.), *Sexual deviance and sexual deviants* (pp. 278-295). New York: William Morrow.

Blumstein, P., & Schwartz, P. (1976). Bisexuality in men. *Urban Life, 5*(3), 339-358.

Blumstein, P., & Schwartz, P. (1977). Bisexuality: Some social psychological issues. *Journal of Social Issues, 33,* 30-45.

Bode, J. (1976). *View from another closet: Exploring bisexuality in women.* New York: Hawthorn.

Borhek, M. V. (1983). *Coming out to parents: A two-way survival guide for lesbian and gay men and their parents.* New York: Pilgrim Press.

Carballo-Diéguez, A. (1989). Hispanic culture, gay male culture, and AIDS: Counseling implications. *Journal of Counseling and Development, 68*(1), 26-30.

Carrier, J., Nguyen, B., & Su, S. (1992). Vietnamese American sexual behaviors and HIV infection. *The Journal of Sex Research, 29*(4), 547-560.

Carrier, J. M. (1976). Cultural factors affecting urban Mexican male homosexual behavior. *Archives of Sexual Behavior, 5*(2), 103-124.

Carrier, J. M. (1985). Mexican male bisexuality. In F. Klein & T. J. Wolf (Eds.), *Two lives to lead: Bisexuality in men and women* (pp. 75-85). New York: Harrington Park.

Cass, V. C. (1979). Homosexual identity formation: A theoretical model. *Journal of Homosexuality, 4,* 219-235.

Chan, C. S. (1989). Issues of identity development among Asian-American lesbians and gay men. *Journal of Counseling and Development, 68*(1), 16-21.

Chan, C. S. (1992). Cultural considerations in counseling Asian American lesbians and gay men. In S. Dworkin & F. Gutiérrez (Eds.), *Counseling gay men and lesbians: Journey to the end of the rainbow* (pp. 115-124). Alexandria, VA: American Association for Counseling and Development.

Chapman, B. E., & Brannock, J. C. (1987). Proposed model of lesbian identity development: An empirical examination. *Journal of Homosexuality, 14,* 69-80.

Coleman, E. (1982). Developmental stages of the coming out process. *Journal of Homosexuality, 7,* 31-43.

Comas-Díaz, L., & Greene, B. (Eds.). (1994). *Women of color: Integrating ethnic and gender identities in psychotherapy.* New York: Guilford.

Cronin, D. M. (1974). Coming out among lesbians. In E. Goode & R. R. Troiden (Eds.), *Sexual deviance and sexual deviants* (pp. 268-277). New York: William Morrow.

De Monteflores, C., & Schultz, S. J. (1978). Coming out: Similarities and differences for lesbians and gay men. *Journal of Homosexuality, 34,* 59-72.

Diamond, M. (1993). Homosexuality and bisexuality in different populations. *Archives of Sexual Behavior, 22*(4), 291-310.

Dixon, J. K. (1984). The commencement of bisexual activity in swinging married women over age thirty. *The Journal of Sex Research, 20*(1), 71-90.

Espín, O. (1987). Issues of identity in the psychology of Latina lesbians. In Boston Lesbian Psychologies Collective (Eds.), *Lesbian psychologies: Explorations and challenges* (pp. 35-51). Urbana: University of Illinois Press.

Fairchild, B., & Hayward, N. (1979). *Now that you know: What every parent should know about homosexuality.* New York: Harcourt Brace Jovanovich.

Fox, A. (1991). Development of a bisexual identity: Understanding the process. In L. Hutchins & L. Kaahumanu (Eds.), *Bi any other name: Bisexual people speak out* (pp. 29-36). Boston: Alyson.

Greene, B. (1994). Ethnic-minority lesbians and gay men: Mental health and treatment issues. *Journal of Consulting and Clinical Psychology, 62*(2), 243-251.

Gutiérrez, F. J., & Dworkin, S. H. (1992). Gay, lesbian, and African American: Managing the integration of identities. In S. H. Dworkin & F. Gutiérrez (Eds.), *Counseling gay men and lesbians: Journey to the end of the rainbow* (pp. 141-155). Alexandria, VA: American Association for Counseling and Development.

H., P. (1989). Asian American lesbians: An emerging voice in the Asian American community. In Asian Women United of California (Eds.), *Making waves: An anthology of writings by and about Asian American women* (pp. 282-290). Boston: Beacon.

Hedblom, J. H. (1973). Dimensions of lesbian sexual experience. *Archives of Sexual Behavior,* 2, 329-341.

Hemphill, E. (Eds.). (1991). *Brother to brother: New writings by black gay men.* Boston: Alyson.

Hinsch, B. (1990). *Passions of the cut sleeve: The male homosexual tradition in China.* Berkeley: University of California Press.

Hooker, E. (1967). The homosexual community. In J. H. Gagnon & W. Simon (Eds.), *Sexual deviance* (pp. 167-184). New York: Harper & Row.

Hunt, M. (1974). *Sexual behavior in the 1970's.* Chicago: Playboy Press.

Hutchins, L., & Kaahumanu, L. (Eds.). (1991). *Bi any other name: Bisexual people speak out.* Boston: Alyson.

Icard, L. (1986). Black gay men and conflicting social identities: Sexual orientation versus racial identity. *Journal of Social Work and Human Sexuality, 4*(1/2), 83-92.

Janus, S. S., & Janus, C. L. (1993). *The Janus report on sexual behavior.* New York: John Wiley.

Kinsey, A. C., Pomeroy, W. B., & Martin, C. E. (1948). *Sexual behavior in the human male.* Philadelphia: W. B. Saunders.

Kinsey, A. C., Pomeroy, W. B., Martin, C. E., & Gebhard, P. H. (1953). *Sexual behavior in the human female.* Philadelphia: W. B. Saunders.

Klein, F., Sepekoff, B., & Wolf, T. J. (1985). Sexual orientation: A multi-variable dynamic process. *Journal of Homosexuality, 11*(1/2), 35-49.

Kooden, H. D., Morin, S. F., Riddle, D. I., Rogers, M., Sang, B. E., & Strassburger, F. (1979). *Removing the stigma: Final report of the Board of Social and Ethical Responsibility for Psychology's Task Force on the Status of Lesbian and Gay Male Psychologists.* Washington, DC: American Psychological Association.

Laumann, E. O., Gagnon, J. H., Michael, R. T., & Michaels, S. (1994). *The social organization of sexuality: Sexual practices in the United States.* Chicago: University of Chicago Press.

Lim-Hing, S. (Ed.). (1994). *The very inside: An anthology of writing by Asian and Pacific Islander lesbian and bisexual women.* Toronto: Sister Vision.

Loiacano, D. K. (1989). Gay identity issues among black Americans: Racism, homophobia, and the need for validation. *Journal of Counseling and Development, 68*(1), 21-25.

Lorde, A. (1984). *Sister/outsider.* Freedom, CA: Crossing Press.

MacDonald, A. P., Jr. (1981). Bisexuality: Some comments on research and theory. *Journal of Homosexuality, 6,* 21-35.

Magaña, J. R., & Carrier, J. M. (1991). Mexican and Mexican American male sexual behavior and spread of AIDS in California. *The Journal of Sex Research, 28*(3), 425-441.

Mason-John, V. (Ed.). (1995). *Talking black: Lesbians of African and Asian descent speak out.* New York: Cassell.

Matteson, D. R. (1994). *Bisexual behavior and AIDS risk among some Asian-American men.* Unpublished manuscript.

McDonald, G. J. (1982). Individual differences in the coming out process for gay men: Implications for theoretical models. *Journal of Homosexuality, 8,* 47-60.

Moraga, C. (1983). *Loving in the war years: Lo que nunca pasó por sus labios.* Boston: South End.

Morales, E. S. (1989). Ethnic minority families and minority gays and lesbians. *Marriage and Family Review, 14*(3/4), 217-239.

Morales, E. S. (1990). HIV infection and Hispanic gay and bisexual men. *Hispanic Journal of Behavioral Sciences, 12*(2), 212-222.

Morales, E. S. (1992). Counseling Latino gays and Latina lesbians. In S. H. Dworkin & F. Gutiérrez (Eds.), *Counseling gay men and lesbians: Journey to the end of the rainbow* (pp. 125-139). Alexandria, VA: American Association for Counseling and Development.

Ochs, R. (Ed.). (1995). *The bisexual resource guide.* Cambridge, MA: The Bisexual Resource Center.

Ponse, B. (1978). *Identities in the lesbian world: The social construction of self.* Westport, CT: Greenwood.

Ponse, B. (1980). Finding self in the lesbian community. In M. Kirkpatrick (Ed.), *Women's sexual development: Explorations of inner space* (pp. 181-200). New York: Plenum.

Rafkin, L. (Ed.). (1987). *Different daughters: A book by mothers of lesbians.* San Francisco: Cleis.

Rafkin, L. (Ed.). (1990). *Different mothers: Sons and daughters of lesbians talk about their lives.* San Francisco: Cleis.

Ratti, R. (Ed.). (1993). *A lotus of another color: An unfolding of the South Asian gay and lesbian experience.* Boston: Alyson.

Richardson, D., & Hart, J. (1981). The development and maintenance of a homosexual identity. In J. Hart & D. Richardson (Eds.), *The theory and practice of homosexuality.* London: Routledge & Kegan Paul.

Riddle, D., & Morin S. (1977, November). Removing the stigma: Data from institutions. *APA Monitor,* pp. 16-28.

Rogers, S. M., & Turner, C. R. (1991). Male-male sexual contact in the U.S.A.: Findings from five sample surveys, 1970-1990. *The Journal of Sex Research, 28*(4), 491-519.

Roscoe, W. (Ed.). (1988). *Living the spirit: A gay American Indian anthology.* New York: St. Martin's.

Rust, P. C. (1992). The politics of sexual identity: Sexual attraction and behavior among lesbian and bisexual women. *Social Problems, 39*(4), 366-386.

Rust, P. C. (1993a). "Coming out" in the age of social constructionism: Sexual identity formation among lesbian and bisexual women. *Gender & Society, 7*(1), 50-77.

Rust, P. C. (1993b). Neutralizing the political threat of the marginal woman: Lesbians' beliefs about bisexual women. *The Journal of Sex Research, 30*(3), 214-228.

Rust, P. C. (1995). *Bisexuality and the challenge to lesbian politics: Sex, loyalty, and revolution.* New York: New York University Press.

Rust, P. C. (1996a). Managing multiple identities: Diversity among bisexual women and men. In B. Firestein (Ed.), *Bisexuality: The psychology and politics of an invisible minority* (pp. 53-83). Thousand Oaks, CA: Sage.

Rust, P. C. (1996b). Monogamy and polyamory: Relationship issues for bisexuals. In B. Firestein (Ed.), *Bisexuality: The psychology and politics of an invisible minority* (pp. 127-148). Thousand Oaks, CA: Sage.

Saghir, M. T., & Robins, E. (1973). *Male and female homosexuality.* Baltimore: Williams and Wilkins.

Saikaku, I. (1990). *The great mirror of male love.* Stanford, CA: Stanford University Press.

Schäfer, S. (1976). Sexual and social problems of lesbians. *The Journal of Sex Research, 12,* 50-69.

Silvera, M. (Ed.). (1991). *Piece of my heart: A lesbian of colour anthology.* Toronto: Sister Vision.

Sue, D. W. (Ed.). (1981). *Counseling the culturally different: Theory and practice.* New York: John Wiley.

Tafoya, T., & Rowell, R. (1988). Counseling gay and lesbian Native Americans. In M. Shernoff & W. A. Scott (Eds.), *The sourcebook on lesbian/gay health care.* Washington, DC: National Lesbian/Gay Health Foundation.

Tremble, B., Schneider, M., & Appathurai, C. (1989). Growing up gay or lesbian in a multi-cultural context. *Journal of Homosexuality, 17*(1-4), 253-267.

Trujillo, C. (Ed.). (1991). *Chicana lesbians: The girls our mothers warned us about.* Berkeley, CA: Third Woman.

Weise, E. R. (Ed.). (1992). *Closer to home: Bisexuality & feminism.* Seattle: Seal.

Williams, W. L. (1986). *The spirit and the flesh: Sexual diversity in American Indian culture.* Boston: Beacon.

Wooden, W. S., Kawasaki, H., & Mayeda, R. (1983). Lifestyles and identity maintenance among gay Japanese-American males. *Alternative Lifestyles, 5*(4), 236-243.

7

Enhancing the Development of Lesbian, Gay, and Bisexual Youths

Anthony R. D'Augelli

The "homosexual adolescent" was discovered by empirical social science in 1972, with the appearance of a research paper titled "Youthful Male Homosexuality: Homosexual Experience and the Process of Developing Homosexual Identity in Males Aged 16 to 22 Years" (Roesler & Deisher, 1972). Based on interviews with 60 males who "had engaged in homosexual acts to orgasm," the paper conceptualizes sexual orientation as a developmental process that accelerates after puberty. More important, the authors describe substantial stressors related to homoerotic identity consolidation, which they relate to social and cultural censure. Echoing later research, Roesler and Deisher found evidence of mental health problems; 48% of the youths had visited a psychiatrist at least once, and 31% had made a suicide attempt. Eschewing the psychodynamic interpretations of homosexuality current at the time, the researchers simply presented their observations among their conclusions that

- same-sex sexual behavior and self-identification as gay were synchronized but did not occur at the same time;
- self-labeling as gay typically followed actual same-sex sexual experience;
- most homosexual experiences occurred with friends, not strangers;
- many youths (60%) had also had heterosexual intercourse;
- 73% had come out, defined as "the event or time of introducing a person to the homosexual subculture as a potential member" (p. 1019); and
- 73% felt it improbable that they would become heterosexual.

Roesler and Deisher describe the socialization of the *youthful male homosexual,* especially the critical nature of the gay bar in the urban male homosexual culture of that time and the inability of adolescents to enter such settings. They note the consequence of the lack of an appropriate social setting for youth development. The youths in their study needed to learn about their sexual identity in "places where adolescents are free to go"—parks, theaters, beaches, and public restrooms. Their interviews revealed that those coming out earlier more often frequented parks and theaters known to be homosexual meeting places. The physical risks associated with such socialization requirements are unstated in the report, as are the consequences to personal identity for youths to develop in such milieus. The portrait of adolescents struggling with self-definition only to emerge in dangerous social settings is a prescient one. Both the general description of the developmental processes experienced by homoerotically oriented youths and the substantial risks they face would be corroborated by the studies completed two decades later. Fortunately, there are now more settings for lesbian, gay, and bisexual (lgb) youth development.

Although there is a refreshing avoidance of the kind of pathologizing found in the literature at the time, the image created by the report is of alien boys who are on their way to the so-called homosexual subculture. Without families, without relationships, without a social context, the youthful male homosexual is a very different creature from an urban heterosexual male teen. This image may have been accurate. Given the cultural ethos of that time, a gay male adolescent would need to be exceedingly unusual to come out in the way the authors describe. How many gay males now in their early 40s, the approximate current age of the males in the report, took the risks required to come out in the late 1960s or early 1970s? Not only was homosexuality—not just sexual behavior—illegal in many states at that time (Rivera, 1991), but it was also de facto evidence of mental disorder, despite the research Hooker (1957) had conducted. Legal protection from discrimination in employment and housing, still not guaranteed in most locales, was unheard of at that point in history. Given the circumstances, a teenager's openness about being attracted to other males was rare; those who were willing to take the risks or who were unable to hide their feelings would enter the psychosocial "sexual outlaw" role and its corresponding social settings. Those from more conventional backgrounds—those with more to lose—would enact heterosexual expectations with varying degrees of success (see Trillin, 1993, for an example). They, too, might come out, but later in life, having been encouraged to seek a number of "cures" (Duberman, 1991). An understanding of the experience of the average young gay male in 1970 cannot be based on a group of 60 highly unusual youths who came to the attention of two researchers.

More than 20 years after the appearance of this early paper, significant conceptual and empirical advances have occurred in the study of youths—preadolescents, teenagers, and young adults—who experience and acknowledge homoerotic desire, defining themselves as lesbian, gay, or bisexual (lgb) or, using the current argot, queer. (See Rhoads, 1994; Schulman, 1994; and

Signorile, 1993, for analyses of contemporary queer culture.) Fortunately, contemporary research is based on increasingly large and more diverse samples than the first report. The research reflects the gradual diminution of explicit cultural prejudices against lgb people, especially the removal of homosexuality from the psychiatric nomenclature in 1973 (Bayer, 1987). The research has also been facilitated by increased protection against discrimination. The HIV epidemic has also encouraged empirical investigations of lgb people, including lgb youths, a group at special risk for HIV infection. These and cultural trends, too numerous to detail here, have led to lgb people becoming more accessible to research. As more lgb adults come out at younger ages, we can learn more about their earlier years with less time transpiring. Also, more and more lgb youths are acknowledging their sexual identity in an open way, at a time in their own development when it is age appropriate. Indeed, some have argued that contemporary youths have redefined the process of lgb identity development in a profound way (Herdt, 1989). The cohort that has come of age during the HIV epidemic—youths born in 1980—will experience the transition to adulthood in a dramatically different way from youths born in 1960. Just as Roesler and Deisher framed their interviewees from within their own cultural parameters, however, so are contemporary researchers inherently bound by their own conventions. Thus, we may be little closer to an accurate view of the typical lesbian, gay, bisexual, or queer youth than our predecessors. Heterosexism remains a powerful cultural force; among its many consequences is the near impossibility of generating a representative sample of youths aged 10 through 20 who acknowledge same-sex erotic feelings. This chapter will explore some of these issues by reviewing available empirical information about lgb youths and the social contexts of their lives—their families, their peers, their schools, and their communities. Implications of these findings for the development of preventive interventions will be presented. For descriptive and conceptual analyses of lgb youths, the reader is referred to the several excellent anthologies now available (DeCrescenzo, 1994; Evans & Wall, 1991; Herdt, 1989; Unks, 1995).

Current Research on Lesbian, Gay, and Bisexual Youths

It would not be until the late 1980s that additional empirical reports on gay male youths would appear. Even as of this writing, only a handful of published reports of any kind include lesbian youths (see Schneider, 1989). No study has focused exclusively on youths who consider themselves bisexual, although reports on lesbian and gay youths demonstrate that many have engaged in heterosexual as well as homosexual sexual experiences.

Because our assessments of sexual expression often omit description of change over time (probably because we presume that sexual orientation is fixed), few reports consider patterns of change in gender of preferred sexual object (see Fox, 1995, for an excellent analysis of bisexual identity). Finally, there are no empirical reports of youths who identify themselves as trans-gendered, a label that signifies nonconformity to bipolarized gender norms (see Bornstein, 1994).

Between the early 1970s and now, interest in lgb youths has gradually increased, with most of the earlier work occurring in the form of observations by clinicians and counselors, who, like Roesler and Deisher (1972), no doubt encountered youths who were different from the many who never come to the attention of professionals. Nonetheless, these insights have had an enormous impact in delineating the psychosocial issues confronted by any young person faced with the emergence of same-sex eroticism. For instance, the landmark analysis by Malyon (1981) provided a foundation for a psychosocial model for the adolescent years, arguing that adolescent same-sex sexual orientation is not simply a transition to heterosexuality. Malyon was also among the first to elaborate on what he called "the special problems of the adolescent homosexual," integrating the routine developmental tasks of puberty and young adulthood with the challenges unique to gay males. Malyon noted the long-term consequences of less than optimal adaptation for the gay male adolescent who represses or attempts to suppress his feelings. He also emphasized the crucial importance of disclosure of sexual orientation in a supportive context, one that was much less available to the gay male adolescent in the early 1980s than it is now.

Others would continue in this tradition of explication of issues facing lesbian and gay teenagers. Martin (1982) titled his overview of the core psychological dilemmas facing lesbian and gay youths "Learning to Hide." With Hetrick, Martin contributed several crucial reviews of the social stigmatization of lesbian and gay teenagers (e.g., Martin & Hetrick, 1988). Their observations were derived from their roles as cofounders of what was then called the Institute for the Protection of Lesbian and Gay Youth, under whose auspices the alternative Harvey Milk High School developed. Similar observations about Canadian youths were made by Schneider in Toronto as a result of her involvement with the influential Sexual Orientation and Youth Project (SOYP), which was established in 1983 to provide social services to lesbian and gay youths (Schneider, 1988, 1991). Explication of school problems of lesbian and gay teens was provided by Hunter and Schaecher (1987); they highlighted social isolation, harassment, and violence as the most serious problems. It would not be long before the crucial role of the schools in the adjustment of lgb youths was articulated. Schools are the primary institutional context in which adolescents are housed; messages about homoerotic development can be conveyed explicitly and implicitly by administrators, teachers, counselors, coaches, and so on. Schools are also the site for the enactment of peer cultural norms, which are deeply heterosexist in adolescence. Thus, lgb youths are highly vulnerable in school settings, a conclusion that led Ross-Reynolds and Hardy (1985) to urge school psychologists to reach out to lgb youths in schools. This was followed by Slater's (1988) important paper, which, among other things, pointed to the threat posed by the HIV epidemic. Slater's arguments were also directed to professionals, especially those in the schools, encouraging them to acknowledge the presence of lgb youths and advocate on their behalf.

It is worth noting that relatively little early work focused on the ways families dealt with lgb youths. Perhaps this reflected the absence of a focus on family relationships in research on adult gay men, many of whom left their families of origin to pursue an identity that was highly stigmatized at that time (see D'Augelli & Hart, 1987, for an analysis of this issue among rural lesbians and gay men). Indeed, it is not surprising in this regard that so little research has examined the relationship of adult lgb people to their families. Furthermore, many of the youths described in early reports had been rejected by their families, and more pressing survival needs were most salient to the professionals who worked with them. Nonetheless, as more youths come out earlier and tell their families while still at home, more attention will need to be addressed to the role of parents, siblings, and extended family (Laird, 1993). It is certain that a young lesbian who has told every member of her family and who has received praise from each (a highly improbable outcome) will develop in a very different manner from a lesbian teen who has told no one at all (perhaps the most common pattern), or a lesbian teen who tells only carefully selected friends because she expects abuse at the hands of her family during the years she must live at home (a common phenomenon).

Just as some of the earlier observations emerged from direct experience with youths who sought out clinical services or who were referred to special programs like the Harvey Milk School, most recent empirical research on lgb youths is based on small samples of convenience with unknown representativeness. Remafedi's two studies of gay males (Remafedi, 1987a, 1987b; Remafedi, Farrow, & Deisher, 1991) contained 29 males aged 15 to 19 and 137 males aged 14 to 21; Schneider, Farberow, and Kruks's (1989) study contained 108 men aged 16 to 24; and Savin-Williams's survey (1990) of 14- to 23-year-olds contained 317 respondents. The Chicago Horizons Youth Project (Herdt & Boxer, 1993) included about 200 youths attending programs at an lgb-identified social services agency. Rotheram-Borus's research on ethnic minority gay male youths is based on a sample of 59 clients aged 14 to 18 at the Hetrick-Martin Institute in New York City

(Rotheram-Borus & Koopman, 1991; Rotheram-Borus et al., 1992). Her most recently published research adds other youths (including white youths) from Hetrick-Martin, creating a final sample of about 130 who range in age from 14 to 19 (Rotheram-Borus, Hunter, & Rosario, 1994; Rotheram-Borus, Reid, & Rosario, 1994; Rotheram-Borus, Rosario, Meyer-Bahlburg, et al., 1994; Rotheram-Borus, Rosario, Van Rossem, Reid, & Gillis, 1995). Remafedi's more recent research (1994a, 1994b) is based on 239 gay male youths aged 13 to 21 from Minnesota. My own study (D'Augelli & Hershberger, 1993) included 194 youths involved in lgb-identified support and recreational groups in 14 different metropolitan areas. The study with the largest sample of young gay and bisexual males to date investigated HIV seroprevalence and HIV risk-related behaviors in 425 males aged 17 to 22, interviewed in public settings in San Francisco (Lemp et al., 1994). Despite sophisticated sampling techniques, Lemp et al. acknowledge the problem of generalizing to all gay male youths; they are also forthright in noting that their findings (e.g., a seropositivity rate of 10%; one third reporting unprotected anal intercourse in the 6 months prior to the study) are relevant for young gay males similar to those in their study. That their concerns about external validity are worth heeding is shown when their results are contrasted with those of Osmond et al. (1994), who used a different sampling strategy to study young males, also in San Francisco. (They found a seropositivity rate of 5% for the men aged 18 to 23.)

The problem of limited information derived from nonrepresentative samples cannot be dealt with until mainstream psychological research includes questions about sexual orientation as routine sociodemographic information. This process will take time, judging by the very near absence of lgb youths from the recent *American Psychologist* issue on adolescence (Takanishi, 1993). Furthermore, even if developmental psychologists could be coaxed into including sexual orientation on self-report instruments, there will remain the problem of acknowledgment. The recently publicized surveys of homosexual activity among men (e.g., Billy, Tanfer, Grady, & Klepinger, 1993), which found that only 2% of 20- to 39-year-old sexually active men acknowledge in a personal interview that they had homosexual contact within a 10-year period, point out the problems with collection of data about homoeroticism. This study has a high school counterpart. Remafedi, Resnick, Blum, and Harris (1992) found 1.1% of 35,000 Minnesota teens surveyed admitted being lesbian, gay, or bisexual, although 11% of the overall sample said they were unsure of their sexual orientation. The Minnesota study was conducted in classrooms and it is safe to assume that underreporting occurred, although routine confidentiality and anonymity assurances were given. Even assuming a reasonable error rate, imagine the expense of a procedure that would generate a random sample of Minnesota lgb high school students who are *not* uncertain about their sexual orientation. Herek (1995) has noted that a national survey commissioned by the *San Francisco Examiner* in 1989 required 27,000 telephone calls to obtain 400 self-identifying lesbian and gay *adult* respondents to compare to 400 hetero-sexual respondents. In addition, once these rare lgb people willing to be counted are found, can it not be assumed that they are substantially different from those who are *really* unsure and from those who are too afraid to tell the truth on an official survey from a prestigious research university that guarantees that "no one will know"? The sampling problem will not be overcome in the near future and it is an enduring problem that researchers will face. We are fundamentally constrained to samples of convenience. We must build a literature on a piecemeal basis, because we are unable to follow standard sampling procedures and generate random, representative samples and we lack longitudinal studies of lgb youths. Research such as Meyer's (1995) longitudinal study, which documents the linkage between discrimi-nation and health problems in adult gay males, needs to be extended to young lgb people. The information that we do have, however, suggests the need for professional attention to the needs of lgb youths. Not acting because of the many methodological weaknesses of current studies poses its own problems, especially ethical ones.

Developmental Processes

A developmental approach to sexual orientation takes into account the individual's developmental status. This means that same-sex eroticism will be experienced, thought about, and expressed not only in different ways at different ages but also in ways that reflect the individual's physical, cogni-tive, emotional, and social development at a particular point in her or his life (D'Augelli, 1994). Although no research based on representative samples has explicitly focused on sexual orientation prior to puberty, the conclusion of the most recent studies is that personal awareness of same-sex erotic feelings generally predates puberty and becomes increasingly crystallized at puberty. There are suggestions of developmental uniqueness during child-hood, at least for males who later identify themselves as gay. Research indicates that many males who self-identify as gay at some point later in life report traditional gender-nonconforming behavior in early childhood (see Bailey & Zucker, 1995, for a review). As many as three quarters of highly stereotypically "feminine" boys identify as gay in adulthood. It is entirely possible that same-sex orientation follows the same developmental pattern as gender development, but its expression in early childhood results in such severe sanctions that further development of such feelings is inhibited, and they are suppressed until they reemerge at puberty. Such speculation is also consistent with a biological component of sexual orientation development. Evidence supporting a hypothesis of a biological contribution to adult male homoerotic orientation has been found (Hamer, Hu, Magnuson, Hu, & Pattatucci, 1993; Levay, 1991), but it has also been challenged (Byne & Parsons, 1993). It is entirely possible that other early indications of lgb identity will be discovered if researchers begin to study children's developing sexuality, an area that has been greatly neglected.

The biological processes of puberty accelerate the expression of same-sex orientation while the social pressures of adolescence provide powerful barriers to its expression. The hegemony of heterosexuality evidences its most powerful influence as youths are establishing sociosexual roles that they will presumably carry into adulthood and family life. The tension between the eruption of physiological maturity (which propels the externalization of eroticism toward social objects) and the rigid channelization of this eroticism into heterosexual social scripts (which delimit the choice of objects for externalizing) makes early adolescence, the teenage years, and early adulthood crucial developmental periods for lgb people. During this second decade of life, the expression of homoerotic desire is deeply conflictual. Most lesbian, gay, or bisexual adults report knowing the heterosexual imperative as soon as they violate it. For some, the violation occurs early in life with gender-nonconforming behavior as children; for others, the violation occurs in adolescence if they express their homoeroticism directly and are assaulted. For most lgb youths, the lesson is learned vicariously as they observe—whether consciously or peripherally—the penalties that such violations draw for openly lgb peers. It is a common reflection of young adults who are lesbian or gay that they maintained total secrecy in high school, because they knew what would happen to someone who came out in their school or in their community. Self-acknowledgment often represents the beginning of the process of identity exploration and consolidation; this is sometimes called coming out to oneself. Such personal acknowledgment precedes disclosure to someone else. Ordinarily, telling another person for the first time is experienced as extremely difficult. The first disclosure to another may follow self-awareness and self-labeling by many years. There are multiple, overlapping processes involved in the core lesbian/gay/bisexual developmental task of coming out, such as telling family (parents, siblings, extended family), friends (ranging from casual acquaintances to close friends), and the important others in one's social network (such as coworkers, religious leaders, and teachers). These disclosure processes facilitate an exiting from heterosexual identity and its social expectations. The more people who know, the more complete is the person's repositioning to develop a lesbian, gay, or bisexual identity. This exit from heterosexuality, however, is stressful both for the person, who has been socialized within a heterosexual model, and for her or his social network, whose expectations have been violated. Coming out to others sets up new problems associated with public knowledge of homoerotic interests. Past thinking about these dilemmas has not focused on chronological age at disclosure as a crucial dimension of individual difference. Yet, coming to terms with one's sexual orientation and the many personal and social dilemmas involved in coming out are considerably different for a 14-year-old than a 24-year-old. We have only begun the systematic process of understanding identity development for lgb youths; we are surely conditioned by an "adultocentric" model wherein ways in which adult lgb people have developed are presumed to be relevant for people many years younger who occupy a rapidly changing cultural space.

Major Stressors in the Lives of
Lesbian, Gay, and Bisexual Youths

Lgb adolescents have few opportunities to explore their developing identities without severe risk. Cultural sanctions against the expression of lgb identity have diminished since the first male homosexuals were described; however, there remain enormous risks. Given the stressors still associated with lgb identity formation in contemporary society, it is not surprising that the earliest phenomenological experience of a young lgb person is a profound sense of difference. This sense of otherness results both from isolation from those with similar feelings and from messages that homoerotic feelings are shameworthy. A cyclical pattern emerges: Feeling different (and often not being able to understand the feeling), the youth withdraws from others, may distort his or her life, or may try to act straight, with varying degrees of success. This widens the gap between core identity and public identity. The process also intensifies social vigilance, lest others figure out one's true identity. A recent study of sexual harassment in high school found that being called gay by others was deemed the most psychologically upsetting form of verbal harassment (American Association of University Women, 1993). As a result of discerning others' views, lgb youths may experience increased tension and loneliness as they become increasingly aware of the nature of their difference. During the initial period of recognition and labeling of homoerotic feelings, lgb youths have few, if any, helping resources to aid them in understanding their concerns. Lesbian/gay-affirming written materials may be inaccessible, or the youth may feel embarrassed to buy them in his or her local community. Casual discussions with family and friends are risky, so concerns cannot be expressed. Talking with counseling personnel in schools is hampered by fear of counselors' disclosure to others and by fear of judgment (Rofes, 1989; Ross-Reynolds & Hardy, 1985). Lgb youths in urban areas can seek services from agencies, support groups, and informal networks devoted to their distinct concerns. In some urban areas, youths can access telephone help/counseling systems anonymously, if they are aware of these systems and can overcome their fears. Increasingly, youths learn of on-line computer resources; they can use these resources both to obtain accurate current information and to communicate anonymously with other youths. In many areas, few resources exist and the sense of isolation and lack of support can be profound. Sadly, even when there are excellent helping resources available, only a slight percentage of lgb youths seek help.

The development of a supportive friendship network occurs very slowly for lgb youths. Fear of rejection by heterosexual peers is commonplace. A recent national survey of male adolescents 15 to 19 years of age found that only 12% felt they could have a gay friend; most (89%) considered sex between males to be "disgusting" (Marsiglio, 1993). Many youths thus become dependent on small networks of friends whom they have told about themselves; disruptions in these friendships can be exceedingly stressful. Having a small network of knowing friends while hiding one's sexuality from everyone else (including parents and siblings) reinforces a sense of being deviant. Without the opportunity to discuss their feelings, lgb youths further internalize the negative views of society. The developmental costs of this process are high. All available research points to higher than expected problem behavior among lgb youths. Savin-Williams (1994) summarizes the literature on problems of lgb youths as follows: (a) many lgb youths experience problems at school because of harassment from other students, leading to excessive absences, poor academic performance, and dropping out; (b) many lgb youths run away from home, and some end up homeless; (c) many gay and bisexual male youths engage in conduct problems that bring them in contact with the law; (d) lgb youths abuse alcohol, drugs, and other substances at rates that are unusually high, reflecting such factors as coping with high stress, and despair about having to face the future as a member of a stigmatized group.

Family Problems

Many of these problems are caused by a lack of family support, a critical component of normative adolescent development. Research on parental reactions to disclosure of sexual orientation reveals considerable upset among parents, many of whom respond negatively at first (Strommen, 1989). Remafedi (1987b) found that 43% of a sample of gay male adolescents reported strong negative reactions from parents about their sexual orientation; 41% reported negative reactions from friends. Rotheram-Borus,

Hunter, and Rosario (1994) found that the most common gay-related stressors were experienced by youths coming out to parents and siblings, being discovered as gay by parents or siblings, telling friends or being discovered by friends, and being ridiculed for being gay. Using an adult gay male sample, Cramer and Roach (1988) found that 55% of the men's mothers and 42% of their fathers had an initially negative response. Robinson, Walters, and Skeen (1989) sampled parents of lesbian and gay adults through a national support group for parents and found that most reported initial sadness (74%), regret (58%), depression (49%), and fear for their child's well-being (74%). Boxer, Cook, and Herdt (1991) studied youths 21 and younger and a sample of these youths' parents. More youths had disclosed to their mothers than their fathers. Of the lesbian youths, 63% had disclosed to mothers and 37% to fathers; of the males, 54% to mothers and 28% to fathers. Parents reported a period of considerable family disruption after disclosure. Herdt and Boxer (1993) found that most youths first disclose their orientation to friends, with more males finding this difficult than females. Only a small group of youths perceived their family's response to be supportive. D'Augelli and Hershberger (1993) found that only 11% of a sample of lesbian, gay, and bisexual youths received a positive response from parents upon disclosure. Indeed, 20% of mothers and 28% of fathers who were aware of their offsprings' identity were either intolerant or rejecting.

HIV/AIDS

Issues related to HIV and AIDS are also major stressors in the lives of lgb youths. Male youths who have sex with other males (especially receptive anal intercourse without a condom) are at particular risk for HIV infection regardless of their self-identification. The deleterious effect of the epidemic on youths transcends particular sexual behaviors, however. It is beyond the scope of this chapter to review the history of HIV/AIDS and its impact on young bisexual and gay males or on young lesbians (see Cranston, 1991). Historically, many gay and bisexual men became infected with HIV as many as 10 years prior to the emergence of any symptoms; surely this occurred for some when they were teenagers or in their early 20s. In contrast to the generation who became adults (20+) in 1980, the generation now approaching 20 years of age was less than 10 years old when the first cases of AIDS were reported in 1981. They became teenagers and young adults during the HIV/AIDS epidemic; for many, coming to an awareness of their own identity occurred during enormous cultural controversy about the relationship of homoeroticism to HIV infection. Their adolescence was also lived at a time when gays were more visible than ever before, and they were instructed about the existence of gay men within the context of AIDS education in high schools. The psychological impact of growing up in the second decade of the HIV epidemic remains uncertain. The possibility of becoming infected with a fatal virus in the course of expressing one's sexual identity has had a profound effect on normative development for gay and bisexual youths and their significant others, including their families, people with whom they create relationships of varying durations, and their communities.

Several studies have shown that gay and bisexual male youths engage in risky sexual behaviors. Remafedi (1994b) found that 63% of a sample of Minnesota youths had unprotected anal intercourse or used intravenous drugs. Silvestre et al. (1993) studied Pittsburgh men who were 22 years old or less. About 7% were HIV-seropositive; of those engaging in receptive anal intercourse, only 12% consistently used condoms and 39% did not use condoms regularly despite having multiple sexual partners. Stall et al. (1992) studied San Francisco gay men in 1989 and found that the youngest group (18 to 29 years of age) was at the highest risk. About 10% engaged in unprotected anal sex with multiple partners. Lemp et al. (1994) found that 4% of the 17- to 19-year-olds and 12% of the 20- to 22-year-olds in their San Francisco sample were HIV-positive and one third had engaged in unprotected anal intercourse during the prior 6 months. Unsafe sexual contact was associated with not only the lack of peer support for safe sex but also a history of forced sex. Most (70%) HIV-positive men did not know their HIV status, despite prior HIV testing. Lifetime injection drug use was reported by 17% of the men. Rotheram-Borus, Rosario, Meyer-Bahlburg, et al.'s (1994) New York study revealed that 40% of those engaging in anal sex (about half of the sample) did not use condoms in the 3 months before the research. Dean and Meyer (1995) studied 18- to 24-year-old gay men in New York and found that 37% had engaged in unprotected receptive anal intercourse over a 2-year period. Continuing research will surely delineate these matters more precisely, but it is clear that HIV poses a major threat to the lives of these youths, far more so than it threatens adult gay and bisexual men who have both considerable peer support for safer sex and the social skills to negotiate sexual encounters. The rates of risky sexual activity and HIV-positive seroprevalence among urban gay and bisexual male youths will produce many future cases of AIDS in the absence of concerted preventive efforts.

Victimization and Its Consequences

Research suggests that young lesbians and gay males are often the victims of assaults (D'Augelli & Dark, 1995; Dean, Wu, & Martin, 1992). Gross, Aurand, and Adessa (1988) found that 50% of a sample of gay men reported victimization in junior high school and 59% in high school; of lesbians sampled, 12% were victimized in junior high school and 21% in high school. In a study of New York City lesbian, gay, and bisexual youths, 41% had suffered from physical attacks; nearly half of these attacks were specifically provoked by the youths' sexual orientation (Hunter, 1990). There is evidence of family victimization of lesbian and gay adolescents. Lesbians and gay males are more likely survivors of childhood physical or sexual abuse than are heterosexual youths. In national surveys of victimization, between 19% and 41% of adult lesbians and gay males report family verbal abuse and between 4% and 7% report family physical abuse (Berrill, 1990). Pilkington and D'Augelli (1995) found that more than one third of their lgb youth sample had been verbally insulted by a family member and 10% were assaulted by a family member because of their sexual orientation. Bradford, Ryan, and Rothblum (1994) reported that 24% of a sample of 1,925 lesbians had been harshly beaten or physically abused while growing up; 21% reported rape or sexual molestation in childhood; and 19% reported childhood incest. Of 1,001 adult gay and bisexual males attending sexually transmitted disease clinics, Doll et al. (1992) found that 37% said they had been encouraged or forced to have sexual contact (mostly with older men) before age 19. Using the same sample, Bartholow et al. (1994) reported a significant association between earlier sexual abuse and current depression, suicidality, risky sexual behavior, and HIV-positive serostatus. Harry (1989a) found that gay males were more likely to be physically abused during adolescence than heterosexual males, especially if they had a history of childhood femininity and poor relationships with their fathers. In comparison to the rates of victimization found in lesbian or gay samples, prevalence estimates in general survey findings are much lower (Finkelhor & Dziuba-Leatherman, 1994).

In addition to parental conflicts and violence, lgb youths who are open about their sexual orientation face verbal harassment and physical attacks at school and in their local communities. Between 33% and 49% of those responding to community surveys report being victimized in school, presumably in high school (Berrill, 1990). Remafedi's (1987a) gay male youths' reports were similar, with more than half (55%) noting peer verbal abuse and nearly one third (30%) reporting physical assaults. Nearly 40% of the male youths in the Remafedi et al. (1991) study said they experienced physical violence. In the Bradford et al. (1994) study, 52% of the total said they had been verbally attacked and 6% said they had been physically attacked. Pilkington and D'Augelli (1995) found that 80% of the lgb youths in their study reported verbal abuse specifically based on sexual orientation; 48% reported such abuse occurred more than twice. Gay male youths reported significantly more verbal abuse. Of the total group, 44% had been threatened with physical violence (19% more than twice); 23% had personal property damaged; 33% had objects thrown at them; 30% had been chased (16% more than once); 13% had been spat upon. As to more serious attacks, 17% had been assaulted (punched, kicked, or beaten); 10% had been assaulted with a weapon; and 22% reported sexual assault. Many reported fear of verbal (22%) or physical (7%) abuse at home; more reported fear of verbal (31%) or physical (26%) abuse at school. Harassment and violence directed at open lesbian and gay male college and university students have been documented as well (Comstock, 1991; D'Augelli, 1992).

Critical Mental Health Issues

Lgb youths have been found to be at unusual risk for mental health problems. In the Bradford et al. (1994) survey of mental health problems among lesbians, such problems were common among the 17- to 24-year-old women. When asked how often they were so worried that they "couldn't do necessary things," 13% said they often felt this way, 29% sometimes felt this way, and 43% said rarely. Only 15% of these young lesbians responded that they never felt overwhelmed. Nearly two thirds (62%) had received counseling. The most frequently occurring problems taken to counselors were family problems (46%), depression (40%), problems in relationships (29%), and anxiety (26%). Remafedi (1987a) found that nearly three quarters of a sample of adolescent gay males had received mental health services for emotional problems. A study of young gay males in college (D'Augelli, 1991a) revealed many personal and emotional problems: The most frequent concerns were dealing with parents about sexual orientation (93% reported it to be a concern), relationship problems (93%), worry about AIDS (92%), anxiety (77%), and depression (63%). In D'Augelli and Hershberger's (1993) report, 63% of the youths said they were so worried or nervous in the past year that they could not function, 61% reported feeling nervous and tense at the time of the study (21% very much so), and 73% said they were depressed (38% very much so). In addition, 33% reported excessive alcohol use and 23% reported illegal drug use.

The available evidence also suggests a disproportionately high incidence of suicide attempts among lgb youths. The early study of gay male youths noted in the beginning of this chapter found that 31% had made a suicide attempt (Roesler & Deisher, 1972). The first Kinsey report devoted exclusively to homosexuality (Bell & Weinberg, 1978) found that 20% of the gay men studied reported a suicide attempt prior to age 20. A decade later, Martin and Hetrick (1988) found that 21% of their clients at a social service agency for troubled youths had made a suicide attempt. Gibson (1989) concluded that most suicide attempts by lesbians and gay males occurred in their youth; that lesbian, gay, and bisexual youths are two to three times more likely to commit suicide than their heterosexual peers; and that suicides of lesbians, gay males, and bisexuals may constitute up to 30% of all completed youth suicides. Gibson estimated that from 20% to 35% of lesbian, gay, and bisexual youths have made suicide attempts. Harry (1989b) concluded that lesbians and gay men were more likely to make suicide attempts at times of conflicts about sexual orientation, especially in adolescence. Unfortunately, Gibson's and Harry's conclusions were based on very limited empirical data; meanwhile, these figures are considerably higher than current estimates of high school suicide attempts (Garland & Zigler, 1993).

Recent empirical studies have come to similar conclusions about a high risk for suicide among lesbian, gay, and bisexual youths. Remafedi (1987a) found that 34% of his gay male adolescent sample had attempted suicide. In a later study with a larger sample, Remafedi et al. (1991) found that 30% had made a suicide attempt. Those who had attempted suicide were younger, had more feminine gender role concepts, and were more likely to report drug and alcohol abuse. Another study of gay male youths found that 23% had attempted suicide at least once and that 59% evidenced serious suicidal thinking (Schneider et al., 1989). Of the young women in the National Lesbian Health Care survey (Bradford et al., 1994), only 41% said they had never contemplated suicide and about one quarter had made an attempt. D'Augelli and Hershberger (1993) found that 42% of a sample of lesbian, gay, and bisexual youths drawn from 14 metropolitan areas had made a suicide attempt. Only 40% of the youths in the study had never considered suicide. Herdt and Boxer (1993) found that 29% of lesbian, gay, and bisexual youths in a Chicago youth support group program had made a suicide attempt. More than half (53%) of the lesbian youths reported suicide attempts, compared to 20% of the gay male youths. Remafedi et al. (1991) found that nearly half (44%) of the gay male youths studied reported that their suicide attempts were precipitated by family problems. Schneider et al. (1989) found that those attempting suicide had not yet established a stable sexual identity; attempts occurred most often before youths acknowledged their sexual identities to others. They also found that early awareness of their sexual orientation was associated with suicide attempts. D'Augelli and Hershberger (1993) found that youths attempting suicide were more open with others about their sexual orientation than youths who made no attempts, and had lost more friends because of their sexual orientation. It will likely turn out that a complex interplay of sexual identity-related factors and other factors such as victimization history work together to produce suicide attempts in this population (Hershberger & D'Augelli, 1995).

The Development of Intervention Strategies

The development of approaches that would diminish the common life stressors experienced by lgb youths must be consonant with the core paradox of lgb identity development: that candidness about sexual orientation leads to crucial benefits as well as serious risks. Telling parents, siblings, extended family members, peers, teachers, and so on is difficult in its many practical details *even for adults with supportive resources to call upon.* The most effective strategy for preventing mental health problems in this population emphasizes changes in *others'* attitudes and reactions. Effective approaches must target heterosexism, homophobia, and harassment in the social ecologies of lgb youths. A comprehensive approach to the prevention of heterosexism must operate at several levels; it must address current problems of youths and forestall further deterioration (tertiary prevention); it must specify which lgb youths may be at special risk and address their particular circumstances (secondary prevention); and, finally, it must be poised to create circumstances that prevent the development of heterosexism in the first place (primary prevention). Primary prevention of heterosexism should be the ultimate goal.

I have argued elsewhere that the prevention of mental health problems in lgb youths calls for four strategies: affirmative services development, the development of safe settings, curriculum integration in educational settings, and policy review (D'Augelli, 1993). The implementation of these general strategies will be discussed below.

Affirmative Services Development

Counseling and mental health services are crucial resources for lesbian, gay, and bisexual youths, given the developmental challenges they face and the years of confusion and conflict they experience. Many of their situations call for professional attention and cannot be adequately addressed by reliance on peer support. Many metropolitan areas have lgb human services centers that provide professional help, but schools and other mental health/counseling systems must also be prepared to assist lgb youths and their families. To be effective, services must be perceived by the informal community of lgb youths as accessible and helpful. The reputation of an unresponsive system spreads very quickly. Assurance that staff do not display outright homophobia or heterosexism is a necessary but insufficient step. Services must be affirmative; the presence of open lgb staff is evidence of institutional commitment. Just adding an open staff member will not be sufficient, however; it is necessary that all staff participate in training experiences to expose them to contemporary views of sexual orientation, to affirmative modes of helping, and to local lgb youth culture. Although professional staff may feel capable of seeing lgb youths in their work, training is required for heterosexually oriented staff (Garnets, Hancock, Cochran, Goodchilds, & Peplau, 1991; Graham, Rawlings, Halpern, & Hermes, 1984; Holahan & Gibson, 1994).

In addition to providing unbiased and affirmative counseling, schools (both secondary schools and colleges and universities) should take the initiative in outreach to the lgb youth population. The subpopulations within this large group of young people need specialized programs. For those who are closeted or uncertain of their sexual orientation, general public lectures on human sexuality and sexual orientation are an important method for outreach. Closeted youths are the largest group; they are the neediest and the hardest to reach. An option for such youths is a telephone help line, which can assure anonymity. Another enormous group are those who have taken some steps to come out to others; this questioning group might not consider themselves lgb. For this group, the most useful approach is a support/discussion group with other youths who are clear about their sexual orientation and those who are exploring. Schools and community centers should have semester-long coming out support groups, given the complex nature of the processes involved. Lgb youths can be trained as facilitators and should be supervised by staff. Peer facilitation is most effective; over time, the center can develop a cadre of trained facilitators to meet an increasing need. Finally, a whole array of specialized support groups and educational workshops must be developed. The highest priority should be given to coping with disclosure to family and others, dating and intimacy, and avoiding HIV infection, but attention to vocational development is also crucial. Clearly, the scope of issues involved is considerable, and the need for liaison to the local lgb communities obvious. Because of the demands involved, it is recommended that a staff coordinator of lgb youth services be appointed at local lgb community centers. Within schools, it is useful to assign a professional staff member the responsibility for lgb youth program development.

The Development of Safe Settings

The accumulated evidence of the impact of heterosexism and homophobia provides a strong case for the need to assure "safe spaces" for lgb youths. Much harassment and victimization takes place in schools, and it may be unrealistic for schools to guarantee privacy and safety. Nonetheless, it is important to enhance the school climate for lgb youths. School policies about intolerance and harassment must be inclusive of sexual orientation. Teachers and other staff must not only be trained in issues related to sexual orientation but also be made aware of their special role in creating a social climate in which expression of anti-lesbian and anti-gay views is unacceptable. Lgb youths must be assured that their living spaces are free of harassment and victimization. The critical need for safety led to the development of Project 10 (Uribe & Harbeck, 1991), a high school-based program that provides discussion, support, and advocacy. However important, school-based programs may be too visible for many lgb youths to seek out. Programs in community settings, which may be less intimidating, need to be expanded (see Gerstel, Feraios, & Herdt, 1989; Greeley, 1994; Singerline, 1994).

Other safe spaces are needed as well. Most college and university campuses have a student organization for lgb students. Historically, these groups alone have addressed the needs of lgb students, because counseling centers and campus housing personnel paid little attention to the problems of lesbian and gay students until very recently. Lgb student organizations play a pivotal role in preventing mental health problems, because they will likely be the only organized groups that most students will access. Much informal counseling and crisis intervention occurs in these organizations. Because of their critical role in mental health prevention, it is important that the lgb student organizations be supported. The administration should provide resources for programs and adequate meeting space. A large, comfortable office, for instance, is particularly important, because many closeted students will take their first "baby step" out of the closet by stopping by or calling the office of a student organization. This safe space literally represents a lifeline for many youths, so it is important that it be accessible. More campuses are supplementing the operations of student organizations with professionally staffed centers for lgb students, units that can engage in a wide variety of support and educational functions both for lgb students and for others on campus. Given the many years of isolation that lgb youths experience, such a center can be a powerful preventive intervention. Such centers can spearhead the enormous task of addressing the climate for heterosexism on campuses, a role that is legitimately fulfilled by administrative staff, not students. A center can also advocate for administrative and policy changes that can indirectly prevent heterosexism.

Curriculum Integration

Lesbian, gay, and bisexual people are a hidden population in the curriculum, even in colleges and universities (D'Augelli, 1991b). In secondary schools, little material about lesbians and gay men is included in classes, even if it is relevant. For example, few history classes address the gay/lesbian rights movement. Few literature classes mention the sexual orientation of many of the authors covered, so they are presumed to be heterosexual. The only explicit mention of gay men occurs in AIDS education programs, and the message may be a destructive one for lgb youths and a seriously misleading one for heterosexual students. Indeed, this situation may perpetrate the stereotypes that provide the foundation for biases and victimization. Considerable impact on school climate can be affected if teachers include informative discussions of sexual orientation in relevant courses. Such efforts not only help the many lgb youths in these classes (who, perhaps for the first time, find their lives addressed) but also educate heterosexually identified students and help them modify heterosexist assumptions. These events also provide an opportunity for teachers and others to communicate to all students that heterosexism is unacceptable. As more and more schools strive to address issues of diversity, it is crucial that sexual orientation be included (Jennings, 1994; Lipkin, 1994). It should be remembered that such inclusiveness will be highly controversial for some segments of the local community.

Policy Review

Educational settings contribute to the way lgb youths are perceived by the nature of their formal policies, especially those that define harassment or intolerance and those that prohibit discrimination in employment and access to services. By including sexual orientation in policy statements, institutions break the pattern of denying that lgb people exist. Statements that neither harassment nor discrimination based on sexual orientation will be tolerated convey the idea that lgb people are part of the community at large. Such statements demand institutional mechanisms for implementation, resulting in direct prevention of victimization and its consequences. In addition to policies about harassment, the overall institutional policy concerning discrimination must include sexual orientation. Without formal protection, lgb faculty or staff can be removed from their jobs without cause. Many of the other suggestions made earlier depend on actions that could be compromised if simple protection from discrimination for employees is not provided. Counseling staff, for example, might hesitate to suggest programs for lgb youths because they fear reprisals. Staff in athletic programs might be hesitant to be *too* supportive not only because this could bring suspicions on them but also because they might risk career advancement. This aspect of human diversity is least protected by federal, state, and local law. Few institutions include sexual orientation among protected classes in prohibiting discrimination. Without formal protection in policy, efforts to develop programs to prevent problems among this population will be jeopardized by fear and hesitancy, much of which might be justifiable. The efforts suggested above cannot be undertaken if professionals are unable to assume leadership roles without fear. Disinhibiting professionals with responsibilities for youth development from helping lgb youths is a crucial step in breaking the cycle of invisibility.

An illustration of a comprehensive plan that operationalizes these strategies with specific initiatives to prevent heterosexism is shown in Table 7.1. This model borrows from a framework used in another report (D'Augelli, 1989), in which levels of operation for social interventions suggested by Rappaport (1977) and intervention goals articulated by Thomas (1984, pp. 30-31) are crossed. Thomas suggests these goals for intervention:

Remediation: Intervention directed toward altering a problem that is a source of difficulty for the client.

Enhancement: Intervention directed toward improving functioning above an already satisfactory level.

Competence: Intervention directed toward strengthening the client's ability to handle not only an existing difficulty but also a variety of difficulties in a given area, including those that may arise in that area in the future.

Education: The presentation of information to facilitate understanding in an area of intervention.

Prevention: Intervention directed toward eliminating potential difficulties before they arise or become sufficiently problematic to require remediation.

Advocacy: Speaking up for and taking other action on behalf of the client to protect the client's rights and to pursue client interests.

Resource provision: Provision of such resources as food, clothing, shelter, money, or medicine.

Social control: Interventions directed toward protecting client or society or both.

Conclusions

Based on a reading of the available research literature, some general predictions are possible regarding the future needs of lesbian, gay, and bisexual youths. There will be more youths disclosing their sexual orientation

TABLE 7.1 Preventive Interventions for Lesbian, Gay, and Bisexual Youths

	Level of Operations[a]			
Objectives[b]	*Individual*	*Small Group*	*Organizational*	*Institutional/ Community*
Remediation	Affirmative counseling	Groups on coping with parental rejection	Alternative protective programs for high-risk youths	Community-coalitions for service development
Enhancement	Life goals groups	Programs on dating skills	Awareness programs in schools	Cultural events related to lgb youths
Competence	Assertiveness training	Problem-solving skills for relationship building	Methods for reporting discrimination	Sexual health promotion
Education	Brochures on stress management, etc.	Pamphlets for parents, siblings, teachers, etc.	Information on anti-discrimination/violence in policies	Information about local and national sources of help
Prevention	Coping skills training groups for coming out	Discussion groups for families with newly disclosed youths	Publication of procedures for discrimination/ violence management	Safer sex campaigns for lgb youths
Advocacy	Case management; testimony in judicial hearings, etc.	Work for inclusion of same-sex dating and partnerships in classes	Advocacy for explicit equal protection clauses in educational settings	Advocacy for protective legislation and funds for services
Resource Provision	Telephone help lines; Internet materials	Mentor and buddy systems for youths	Funding youth outreach programs in human service settings	Help for homeless, poor, HIV+, and victimized youths
Social Protection and Control	Education on legal rights of lgb youths	Seminar on partnership legal issues	Assurance of confidentiality of youth counseling	Protective legislation; penalties for violence and discrimination

a. From Rappaport (1977).
b. From Thomas (1984).

to others, and at earlier ages. As youths self-label at earlier ages, they will experience greater stress and will be at higher risk unless given accessible helping resources. The increased cultural visibility of lesbians, gay males, and bisexuals will escalate negative reactions, causing greater conflicts among lgb youths. As more and more conflict is experienced, more will seek counseling and mental health services. Some will seek help as a result of the psychological consequences of persistent verbal harassment, and some will need help in recovering from assaults. More youths will self-identify as lgb during their college years as this is the first time that parental scrutiny is systematically diminished. These disclosed youths, given access to helping resources such as peer support and affirming professional helping resources, will do well in meeting the challenges of developing into well functioning lesbians, gay men, and bisexual people. This cohort of lgb bisexual youths has benefited from the accomplishments of earlier generations, which have led to a greater sense of collective self-esteem. For lgb youths in the 1990s, sexual orientation issues are highly psychologically salient. They have been more aware of their sexual identity at earlier ages than previous generations. Greater social acceptance makes denial increasingly difficult to sustain for youths who acknowledge their own feelings. In addition, the ideology of queer affirmation provides an invigorating model for confronting dilemmas that earlier generations avoided until they were self-sufficient adults. It is crucial to avoid stereotyping lgb youths as victims; they have indeed provided a challenge to older lgb people to assert their presence and demand fair treatment in society. Yet, young lesbian, gay, and bisexual people have many problems and remain the most poorly served group in educational settings as far as health and mental health services are concerned.

The challenges unique to lgb youths are caused by cultural and institutional factors, and any preventive approach must eliminate these factors. We must not revictimize lgb youths by setting our sights on self-contained, modest educational programs that ignore the pervasive heterosexism of the community and of the contexts in which these youths spend many crucial years of their development. Considerable psychological tension occurs during adolescence and young adulthood in the management of lgb issues with families, neighbors, peers, teachers, and coworkers. After the initial disclosure and with the building of a social network of lgb people and supportive heterosexual people who know, increasingly complex issues in identity management arise in the lives of lgb youths as they move toward adulthood. The building of a social identity progresses simultaneously with increased consolidation of personal confidence. Personal and social identities can develop appropriately in supportive social contexts. Serious interference in the processes of identity development can occur in heterosexist environments. In such environments, fear and social hesitancy replace self-esteem and social interaction. For alarmingly high numbers of lgb youths, diminished self-esteem and loneliness lead to despair and self-destruction. Professionals must provide leadership in creating a more supportive climate so that lgb youths can survive to meet the challenges of adulthood. The need for concerted preventive interventions directed toward this population is intense and urgent. Such interventions themselves cannot develop in an atmosphere of heterosexism. Making a public commitment to helping lgb youths is a coming out experience for institutions because this problem entails risks, but it also provides an opportunity to make an enormous difference in the lives of a highly vulnerable group of young people.

References

American Association of University Women. (1993). *Hostile hallways: The AAUW survey on sexual harassment in America's schools.* Washington, DC: Author.

Bailey, J. M., & Zucker, K. J. (1995). Childhood sex-typed behavior and sexual orientation: A conceptual analysis and quantitative review. *Developmental Psychology, 31,* 43-55.

Bartholow, B. N., Doll, L. S., Joy, D., Douglas, J. M., Bolan, G., Harrison, J. S., Moss, P. M., & McKirnan, D. (1994). Emotional, behavioral, and HIV risks associated with sexual abuse among homosexual and bisexual men. *Child Abuse and Neglect, 18,* 753-767.

Bayer, R. (1987). *Homosexuality and American psychiatry: The politics of diagnosis.* Princeton, NJ: Princeton University Press.

Bell, A. P., & Weinberg, M. S. (1978). *Homosexualities: A study of diversity among men and women.* New York: Simon & Schuster.

Berrill, K. T. (1990). Anti-gay violence and victimization in the United States: An overview. *Journal of Interpersonal Violence, 5,* 274-294.

Billy, J. O. G., Tanfer, K., Grady, W. R., & Klepinger, D. H. (1993). The sexual behavior of men in the United States. *Family Planning Perspectives, 25,* 52-60.

Bornstein, K. (1994). *Gender outlaw: On men, women, and the rest of us.* New York: Routledge & Kegan Paul.

Boxer, A. M., Cook, J. A., & Herdt, G. (1991). Double jeopardy: Identity transitions and parent-child relations among gay and lesbian youth. In K. Pillemer & K. McCartney (Eds.), *Parent-child relations throughout life* (pp. 59-92). Hillsdale, NJ: Lawrence Erlbaum.

Bradford, J., Ryan, C., & Rothblum, E. D. (1994). National Lesbian Health Care Survey: Implications for mental health care. *Journal of Consulting and Clinical Psychology, 62,* 228-242.

Byne, W., & Parsons, B. (1993). Human sexual orientation: The biological theories reappraised. *Archives of General Psychiatry, 50*(3), 228-239.

Comstock, G. D. (1991). *Violence against lesbians and gay men.* New York: Columbia University Press.

Cramer, D. W., & Roach, A. J. (1988). Coming out to mom and dad: A study of gay males and their relationships with their parents. *Journal of Homosexuality, 15,* 79-92.

Cranston, K. (1991). HIV education for gay, lesbian, and bisexual youth: Personal risk, personal power, and the community of conscience. *Journal of Homosexuality, 22*(3/4), 247-259.

D'Augelli, A. R. (1989). The development of a helping community for lesbians and gay men: A case study in community psychology. *Journal of Community Psychology, 17,* 18-29.

D'Augelli, A. R. (1991a). Gay men in college: Identity processes and adaptations. *Journal of College Student Development, 32,* 140-146.

D'Augelli, A. R. (1991b). Teaching lesbian and gay development: A pedagogy of the oppressed. In W. G. Tierney (Ed.), *Culture and ideology in higher education: Advancing a critical agenda* (pp. 213-233). New York: Praeger.

D'Augelli, A. R. (1992). Lesbian and gay male undergraduates' experiences of harassment and fear on campus. *Journal of Interpersonal Violence, 7,* 383-395.

D'Augelli, A. R. (1993). Preventing mental health problems among lesbian and gay college students. *Journal of Primary Prevention, 13*(4), 1-17.

D'Augelli, A. R. (1994). Identity development and sexual orientation: Toward a model of lesbian, gay, and bisexual development. In E. J. Trickett, R. J. Watts, & D. Birman (Eds.), *Human diversity: Perspectives on people in context* (pp. 312-333). San Francisco: Jossey-Bass.

D'Augelli, A. R., & Dark, L. J. (1995). Vulnerable populations: Lesbian, gay, and bisexual youth. In L. D. Eron, J. H. Gentry, & P. Schlegel (Eds.), *Reason to hope: A psychosocial perspective on violence and youth* (pp. 177-196). Washington, DC: American Psychological Association.

D'Augelli, A. R., & Hart, M. M. (1987). Gay women, men, and families in rural communities: Toward the development of helping communities. *American Journal of Community Psychology, 13,* 79-93.

D'Augelli, A. R., & Hershberger, S. L. (1993). Lesbian, gay, and bisexual youth in community settings: Personal challenges and mental health problems. *American Journal of Community Psychology, 21,* 421-448.

Dean, L., & Meyer, I. (1995). HIV prevalence and sexual behavior in a cohort of New York City gay men (aged 18-24). *Journal of Acquired Immune Deficiency Syndrome and Human Retrovirology, 8,* 208-211.

Dean, L., Wu, S., & Martin, J. L. (1992). Trends in violence and discrimination against gay men in New York City: 1984 to 1990. In G. M. Herek & K. T. Berrill (Eds.), *Hate crimes: Confronting violence against lesbians and gay men* (pp. 46-64). Newbury Park, CA: Sage.

DeCrescenzo, T. (Ed.). (1994). *Helping gay and lesbian youth: New policies, new programs, new practice.* Binghamton, NY: Haworth.

Doll, L. S., Joy, D., Bartholow, B. N., Harrison, J. S., Bolan, G., Douglas, J. M., Saltzman, L. E., Moss, P. M., & Delgado, W. (1992). Self-reported childhood and adolescent sexual abuse among adult homosexual and bisexual men. *Child Abuse and Neglect, 16,* 855-864.

Duberman, M. (1991). *Cures: A gay man's odyssey.* New York: Dutton.

Evans, N. J., & Wall, V. A. (Eds.). (1991). *Beyond tolerance: Gays, lesbians, and bisexuals on campus.* Alexandria, VA: American College Personnel Association.

Finkelhor, D., & Dziuba-Leatherman, J. (1994). Victimization of children. *American Psychologist, 49,* 173-183.

Fox, R. C. (1995). Bisexual identities. In A. R. D'Augelli & C. J. Patterson (Eds.), *Lesbian, gay, and bisexual identities over the lifespan: Psychological perspectives* (pp. 48-86). New York: Oxford University Press.

Garland, A. F., & Zigler, E. (1993). Adolescent suicide prevention: Current research and social policy implications. *American Psychologist, 48,* 169-182.

Garnets, L., Hancock, K. A., Cochran, S. D., Goodchilds, J., & Peplau, L. A. (1991). Issues in psychotherapy with lesbians and gay men: A survey of psychologists. *American Psychologist, 46,* 964-972.

Gerstel, C. J., Feraios, A. J., & Herdt, G. (1989). Widening circles: An ethnographic profile of a youth group. *Journal of Homosexuality, 17,* 75-92.

Gibson, P. (1989). Gay male and lesbian youth suicide. In ADAMHA, *Report of the Secretary's Task Force on Youth Suicide, Vol. 3* (pp. 110-142) (DHHS Publication No. ADM 89-1623). Washington, DC: Government Printing Office.

Graham, D. L. R., Rawlings, E. I., Halpern, H. S., & Hermes, J. (1984). Therapists' needs for training in counseling lesbians and gay men. *Professional Psychology, 15,* 482-496.

Greeley, G. (1994). Service organizations for gay and lesbian youth. *Journal of Gay and Lesbian Social Services, 1*(3/4), 111-130.

Gross, L., Aurand, S., & Adessa, R. (1988). *Violence and discrimination against lesbian and gay people in Philadelphia and the Commonwealth of Pennsylvania.* Philadelphia: Philadelphia Lesbian and Gay Task Force.

Hamer, D., Hu, S., Magnuson, V., Hu, N., & Pattatucci, A. (1993). A linkage between DNA markers on the X chromosome and male sexual orientation. *Science, 261,* 321-327.

Harry, J. (1989a). Parental physical abuse and sexual orientation. *Archives of Sexual Behavior, 18,* 251-261.

Harry, J. (1989b). Sexual identity issues. In ADAMHA, *Report of the Secretary's Task Force on Youth Suicide, Vol. 2* (pp. 131-142) (DHHS Publication No. ADM 89-1622). Washington, DC: Government Printing Office.

Herdt, G. (Ed.). (1989). *Gay and lesbian youth.* New York: Harrington Park.

Herdt, G. H., & Boxer, A. M. (1993). *Children of Horizons: How gay and lesbian teens are leading a new way out of the closet.* Boston: Beacon.

Herek, G. M. (1995). Psychological heterosexism in the United States. In A. R. D'Augelli & C. J. Patterson (Eds.), *Lesbian, gay, and bisexual identities across the lifespan* (pp. 321-346). New York: Oxford University Press.

Hershberger, S. L., & D'Augelli, A. R. (1995). The consequences of victimization on the mental health and suicidality of lesbian, gay, and bisexual youth. *Developmental Psychology, 31,* 65-74.

Hooker, E. (1957). The adjustment of the male overt homosexual. *Journal of Projective Techniques, 21,* 18-31.

Holahan, W., & Gibson, S. A. (1994). Heterosexual therapists leading lesbian and gay therapy groups: Therapeutic and political realities. *Journal of Counseling and Development, 72,* 591-594.

Hunter, J. (1990). Violence against lesbian and gay male youths. *Journal of Interpersonal Violence, 5,* 95-300.

Hunter, J., & Schaecher, R. (1987). Stresses on lesbian and gay adolescents in schools. *Social Work in Education, 9*(3), 180-190.

Jennings, K. (Ed.). (1994). *Becoming visible: A reader in gay and lesbian history for high school and college students.* Boston: Alyson.

Laird, J. (1993). Lesbian and gay families. In F. Walsh (Ed.), *Normal family processes* (pp. 282-328). New York: Guilford.

Lemp, G. F., Hirozawa, A. M., Givertz, D., Nieri, G. N., Anderson, L., Lindegren, M. L., Janssen, R. S., & Katz, M. (1994). Seroprevalence of HIV and risk behaviors among young homosexual and bisexual men. *Journal of the American Medical Association, 272,* 449-454.

LeVay, S. (1991). A difference in hypothalamic structure between heterosexual and homosexual men. *Science, 253,* 1034-1037.

Lipkin, A. (1994). The case for a gay and lesbian curriculum. *The High School Journal, 77,* 95-107.

Malyon, A. K. (1981). The homosexual adolescent: Development issues and social bias. *Child Welfare, 60,* 321-330.

Marsiglio, W. (1993). Attitudes toward homosexual activity and gays as friends: A national survey of heterosexual 15- to 19-year-old males. *Journal of Sex Research, 30,* 12-17.

Martin, A. D. (1982). Learning to hide: Socialization of the gay adolescent. *Adolescent Psychiatry, 10,* 52-65.

Martin, A. D., & Hetrick, E. S. (1988). The stigmatization of the gay and lesbian adolescent. *Journal of Homosexuality, 15,* 163-184.

Meyer, I. H. (1995). Minority stress and mental health in gay men. *Journal of Health and Social Behavior, 36,* 38-56.

Osmond, D. H., Page, K., Wiley, J., Garrett, K., Sheppard, H. W., Moss, A. R., Schrager, L., & Winkelstein, W. (1994). HIV infection in homosexual and bisexual men 18-29 years of age—The San Francisco Young Men's Health Study. *American Journal of Public Health, 84,* 1933-1937.

Pilkington, N. W., & D'Augelli, A. R. (1995). Victimization of lesbian, gay, and bisexual youth in community settings. *Journal of Community Psychology, 23,* 33-56.

Rappaport, J. (1977). *Community psychology.* New York: Holt, Rinehart & Winston.

Remafedi, G. (1987a). Adolescent homosexuality: Psychosocial and medical implications. *Pediatrics, 79,* 331-337.

Remafedi, G. (1987b). Male homosexuality: The adolescent's perspective. *Pediatrics, 79,* 326-330.

Remafedi, G. (1994a). Cognitive and behavioral adaptations to HIV/AIDS among gay and bisexual adolescents. *Journal of Adolescent Health, 15,* 142-148.

Remafedi, G. (1994b). Predictors of unprotected intercourse among gay and bisexual youth: Knowledge, beliefs, and behavior. *Pediatrics, 94,* 163-168.

Remafedi, G., Farrow, J. A., & Deisher, R. W. (1991). Risk factors for attempted suicide in gay and bisexual youth. *Pediatrics, 87,* 869-875.

Remafedi, G., Resnick, M., Blum, R., & Harris, L. (1992). Demography of sexual orientation in adolescents. *Pediatrics, 89,* 714-721.

Rhoads, R. A. (1994). *Coming out in college: The struggle for a queer identity.* Westport, CT: Bergin & Garvey.

Rivera, R. R. (1991). Sexual orientation and the law. In J. C. Gonsiorek & J. D. Weinrich (Eds.), *Homosexuality: Research implications of public policy* (pp. 81-100). Newbury Park, CA: Sage.

Robinson, B. E., Walters, L. H., & Skeen, P. (1989). Response of parents to learning that their child is homosexual and concern over AIDS: A national survey. *Journal of Homosexuality, 18,* (Suppl. 1/2), 59-80.

Roesler, T., & Deisher, R. (1972). Youthful male homosexuality. *Journal of the American Medical Association, 219,* 1018-1023.

Rofes, E. E. (1989). Opening up the classroom closet: Responding to the educational needs of gay and lesbian youth. *Harvard Education Review, 59,* 444-453.

Ross-Reynolds, G., & Hardy, B. S. (1985). Crisis counseling for disparate adolescent sexual dilemmas: Pregnancy and homosexuality. *School Psychology Review, 14,* 300-312.

Rotheram-Borus, M. J., Hunter, J., & Rosario, M. (1994). Suicidal behavior and gay-related stress among gay and bisexual male adolescents. *Journal of Adolescent Research, 9,* 498-508.

Rotheram-Borus, M. J., & Koopman, C. (1991). Sexual risk behavior, AIDS knowledge, and beliefs about AIDS among predominantly minority gay and bisexual male adolescents. *AIDS Education and Prevention, 3,* 305-312.

Rotheram-Borus, M. J., Meyer-Bahlburg, H. F. L., Rosario, M., Koopman, C., Haignere, C. S., Exner, T. M., Matthieu, M., Henderson, R., & Gruen, R. S. (1992). Lifetime sexual behaviors among predominantly minority male runaways and gay/bisexual adolescents in New York City. *AIDS Education and Prevention, Supplement,* 34-42.

Rotheram-Borus, M. J., Reid, H., & Rosario, M. (1994). Factors mediating changes in sexual HIV risk behaviors among gay and bisexual male adolescents. *American Journal of Public Health, 84*(12), 1938-1946.

Rotheram-Borus, M. J., Rosario, M., Meyer-Bahlburg, H. F. L., Koopman, C., Dopkins, S. C., & Davies, M. (1994). Sexual and substance use acts of gay and bisexual male adolescents in New York City. *Journal of Sex Research, 31*(1), 47-57.

Rotheram-Borus, M. J., Rosario, M., Van Rossem, R., Reid, H., & Gillis, R. (1995). Prevalence, course, and predictors of multiple problem behaviors among gay and bisexual male adolescents. *Developmental Psychology, 31,* 75-85.

Savin-Williams, R. C. (1990). *Gay and lesbian youth: Expressions of identity.* New York: Hemisphere.

Savin-Williams, R. C. (1994). Verbal and physical abuse as stressors in the lives of lesbian, gay male and bisexual youths: Associations with school problems, running away, substance abuse, prostitution and suicide. *Journal of Consulting and Clinical Psychology, 62,* 261-269.

Schneider, M. (1989). Sappho was a right-on adolescent: Growing up lesbian. *Journal of Homosexuality, 17,* 111-130.

Schneider, M. (1991). Developing services for lesbian and gay adolescents. *Canadian Journal of Community Mental Health, 10,* 133-151.

Schneider, M. S. (1988). *Often invisible: Counseling gay and lesbian youth.* Toronto: Central Toronto Youth Services.

Schneider, S. G., Farberow, N. L., & Kruks, G. N. (1989). Suicidal behavior in adolescent and young adult gay men. *Suicide and Life-Threatening Behavior, 19,* 381-394.

Schulman, S. (1994). *My American history: Lesbian and gay life during the Reagan/Bush years.* New York: Routledge & Kegan Paul.

Signorile, M. (1993). *Queer in America: Sex, the media, and the closets of power.* New York: Random House.

Silvestre, A. J., Kingsley, L. A., Wehman, P., Dappen, R., Ho, M., & Rinaldo, C. R. (1993). Changes in HIV rates and sexual behavior among homosexual men, 1984 to 1988. *American Journal of Public Health, 83*(4), 578-580.

Singerline, H. (1994). Outright: Reflections on an out-of-school gay youth group. *High School Journal, 77,* 133-137.

Slater, B. R. (1988). Essential issues in working with lesbian and gay male youths. *Professional Psychology: Research and Practice, 19,* 226-235.

Stall, R., Barrett, D., Bye, L., Catania, J., Frutchey, C., Hennessey, J., Lemp, G., & Paul, J. (1992). A comparison of younger and older gay men's HIV risk-taking behaviors: The Communication Technology 1989 Cross-Sectional Survey. *Journal of Acquired Immune Deficiency Syndrome, 5,* 682-687.

Strommen, E. F. (1989). Hidden branches and growing pains: Homosexuality and the family tree. *Marriage and Family Review, 14,* 9-34.

Takanishi, R. (Ed.). (1993). Adolescence [Special issue]. *American Psychologist, 48,* 85-201.

Thomas, E. M. (1984). *Designing interventions for the helping professions.* Beverly Hills, CA: Sage.

Trillin, C. (1993). *Remembering Denny.* New York: Farrar, Straus & Giroux.

Unks, G. (Ed.). (1995). *The gay teen.* New York: Routledge & Kegan Paul.

Uribe, V., & Harbeck, K. M. (1991). Addressing the needs of lesbian, gay, and bisexual youth: The origins of Project 10 and school-based intervention. *Journal of Homosexuality, 22,* 9-28.

8

Lesbian and Gay Love Scripts

Suzanna Rose

Cultural scripts for lesbian and gay love relationships are emerging rapidly as lesbians and gay men seek to define relationships on their own terms rather than subscribe to heterosexual norms. In the past, heterosexist assumptions were used to evaluate lesbian and gay relationships as less stable, less serious, and less loving (Peplau, 1993). However, current attitudes and research on lesbian and gay couples portray a much more positive picture (e.g., Kurdek, 1994). A greater appreciation of lesbian and gay culture has both resulted from and led to a more objective assessment of same-sex relationships. Established and emerging love scripts now are being viewed and developed from a lesbian and gay affirmative standpoint.

Script refers to a cognitive schema, or set of stereotypical actions, that is used to organize our interpersonal worlds and guide behavior (Abelson, 1981; Ginsburg, 1988). It represents shared understandings of what typically happens in specific situations. Sexual scripts pertain to the schemas used in sexual contexts not only to decide how to act and feel but also to predict others' behaviors (Gagnon, 1977). For instance, how relationship initiation is affected by the interaction of gender and sexual orientation has been captured brilliantly by comedians Lea DeLaria and Emmett Foster for lesbians and gay men, respectively, in the routines described in Table 8.1. DeLaria's response to the question, "How do I approach a woman I like?" describes one script that reflects the anxiety and indecision many lesbians feel when initiating love relationships. Foster's script focuses on issues gay men confront when physical attractiveness and sexuality are valued more than intimacy in relationships.

Scripts occur on three distinct levels: cultural, interpersonal, and intrapsychic (Simon & Gagnon, 1986). Cultural scripts are schemas that exist at the level of collective life and are sometimes institutionalized. The wedding script is one example of a cultural sexual script. Tradition as well as legal and religious institutions provides guidelines for people concerning what behaviors and emotions are appropriate for the specific roles of bride, groom, mother of the bride, and so on. The sequence of events also is defined clearly.

151

TABLE 8.1 Two Comic Views of Lesbian and Gay Relationship Initiation Scripts

Lesbian Relationship Initiation

Q: I've seen this woman I really like, but I have no idea how to approach her.
A: This is THE perfect lesbian question. Lesbians have no idea how to approach each other. If lesbians had to procreate, there would be no people in this world.

This is what lesbians do. You see this woman you like and you say to yourself, "Ooh, ooh, I really like her, I mean I REALLY like her. I like her. I like her. You know what? I like her! You know what I'm gonna do? I'm gonna get up. I'm gonna go over there and I'm gonna ask that woman to dance 'cause I like her. Yes I do, I like her. I like her. I like her. I like her. I REALLY like her. . . . So I'm gonna get up . . . I'm gonna go over there and I'm gonna ask that girl to dance 'cause I like her. Yes I do, I like her. I like the way she looks, the way she's sitting over there in her little miniskirt sipping her martini. So I'm gonna get up, go over there and ask that girl to dance. Maybe we'll have two dances, three dances, four, dances, maybe she'll tell me her name. We could go out on a date, this could be a relationship. . . . THIS COULD BE A RELATIONSHIP! And all I have to do is GET UP, go over there and ask that girl to dance, so that's what I'm gonna do. Get up and go over and ask her to dance."
Then you go home and write about it in your journal . . .

Lea DeLaria (1995, pp. 64-65)

Gay Men's Relationship Initiation

In this routine, a gay man who is staffing the Community Center Hot Line has a telephone conversation with his friend, Jeff, about how empty his life feels:

(*To Jeff*) I mean, I socialize, go dancing on the weekends, and do the bars occasionally. . . . Dating?! What's that?! They have these dating workshops here but I would never, I mean, I know HOW to date: you ask someone out, you squint over candlelight, you suffer through subtitles, and then go home and mess up my comforter. I just never could get the order of these things right. I'm too rambunctious. I always fuck first, then if they're really good, I say maybe we should go to a movie sometime . . .
Oh, I think "slut" is such an ugly word. Hold on . . .
Hi, that was Kelly . . .
What am I looking for? What do you mean?
No. No, I don't think I'm too picky.
Well, someone who has a really sexy body but doesn't go to the gym too much. Someone who I'll never get tired of having hot sex with, it'll just keep getting better and better. Someone who loves my personality and is tickled by everything I say and do. Someone who has his own life, so I won't feel smothered by him. And someone who has his own money, so I won't wonder if he's after mine; my grandfather worked hard for my money and I'm tired of throwing it away on ingrates. But most of all, someone who will really support me in getting my cabaret act off the ground.

Foster (1995, pp. 71-73)

For example, the bachelor party is supposed to take place before the wedding, not after it. Interpersonal scripts represent the individual's use of cultural scripts in a specific situation. For instance, the wedding script may be modified by an individual to conform to personal values (e.g., the removal of *obey* from the vows) or by past experience (e.g., the inclusion of a prenuptial agreement). Private wishes and desires are embodied at the third, or intrapsychic, level. Included here might be the wish for a private legal ceremony versus a large public celebration.

The first goal in this chapter is to identify what cultural scripts are available to lesbians and gay men concerning love relationships, including the extent to which they have been shaped by heterosexism. The scripts will be drawn from popular culture, as represented in fiction and comedy. The analysis will identify elements contained in the most dominant cultural scripts, including the following: (a) the stage(s) of the relationship addressed, (b) the contribution of gender roles, (c) the extent to which sexual motives are present, (d) the impact of sexual orientation, and (e) the significance of relationships in life. A second goal is to explore the impact scripts may have on behavior by identifying issues of concern in actual relationships, as expressed through self-help books. Last, alternatives scripts available to and emerging from lesbian and gay communities will be discussed.

Heterosexual Love Scripts

The love scripts most widely available to lesbians and gay men are ones based on heterosexual relations. Heterosexual scripts are likely to be the first—and perhaps only—love scripts that are learned in childhood, even for those who have *always known* they were lesbian or gay. Two specific heterosexual scripts analyzed previously by Rose (1985) include a *romance script* for women and an *adventure script* for men. The romance script is exemplified in a host of entertainment aimed at girls and women, including fairy tales and contemporary romance novels. For boys and men, relationships occur in the context of an adventure script found in action comic books, adventure novels, and pornography.

In heterosexual love scripts, the socially sanctioned purpose of sexual love is to establish a long-term relationship (Laws & Schwartz, 1977). Thus, once the courtship period has ended, the relationship is assumed to be permanent; further scripting is therefore unnecessary. The story typically ends with the couple living happily ever after. As Simon and Gagnon (1986) have pointed out, the courtship script is drawn almost exclusively from the requirements of (heterosexual) adolescence and young adulthood.

According to script theory, scripts guide both behavior and affect. Gender is a key determinant of how each is expressed in heterosexual scripts. The female role is defined as reactive. Women are to be the objects of desire, that is, to be seductive, to surrender, and to be desirable. The male role is active, dictating that men should take possession of the object of desire, including seducing, conquering, and desiring it or her (Simon & Gagnon, 1986). Sexual behaviors parallel this dichotomy, with heterosexual men being designated as the initiators of sexual interaction and as preferring coital/genital activities in relationships more than women do (e.g., Purnine, Carey, & Jorgensen, 1994).

The gender roles described above are embedded in the romance and adventure scripts. In the romance script, four major script elements guide girls and women concerning what to expect during courtship (Rose, 1985). The first two convey that the woman is to be both beautiful and passive. For instance, in *Snow White, Sleeping Beauty, Cinderella,* and *Rapunzel,* it is the woman's beauty that makes her worthy of love (as well as a threat to other women). In both *Snow White* and *Sleeping Beauty,* the heroine's passivity is symbolized by her unconscious state; in *Cinderella* and *Rapunzel,* it is expressed by *being* rather than *doing,* that is, by waiting patiently for the man to find her. A third element suggests that obstacles to love are inevitable. Obstacles include evil older women who cast spells on or imprison the beautiful young competitor, and contests that must be won. A fourth element indicates that a male rescuer will overcome these obstacles and reward the beautiful passive woman with his attention. A bit of confusion is sometimes added to the last element when, occasionally, the male rescuer appears to be an actual beast or has "beastlike" qualities (e.g., hostility, indifference) that must be tamed in the service of love. This obstacle of mistaken identity requires that the women be ever vigilant not to overlook any beast/man as being a potential rescuer.

The adventure script contains four key elements that instruct boys and men concerning how to establish relationships (Rose, 1985). The first element focuses on independent achievement. Male protagonists are thrust into the world and have to provide for themselves in fiction ranging from *Jack and the Beanstalk* to *Tarzan* to *Conan the Barbarian.* The plot reassures boys that although it is terrifying to leave friends and family, doing so will lead to success, parental acceptance, and female admiration. Seeking fame and fortune prepares males to overcome the obstacles to love comprised in the second script element. They scale the tower, hack through the thorns, slay the dragon or giant, or search for the treasure. The agentic role assigned to males reinforces the idea that they are the proper initiators of relationships. The third element, a beautiful, defenseless female, operates as both a motive and a reward. However, very little contact occurs between the woman and man in the typical adventure script; thus, no basis for a conversation is developed, much less a relationship. Perhaps this is why a fourth element often is present: ambivalence about intimacy. The male-as-beast theme suggests that men may not be too well suited for intimate relations. Comic books often utilize a hero/beast persona as the main character. For example, the *Hulk* alternates between being mild-mannered Bruce Banner and his hulk alter ego, a violent green behemoth.

Sexual elements in the romance and adventure script are also gender-specific. In the romance script, they are largely covert. The woman's sexual innocence fuels the man's passion; she is desired, not desiring. It is his privilege and responsibility to awaken her to sexual pleasure. The adventure script has more overtly sexual elements. Phallic sexual imagery permeates descriptions of heroes, who are "hard," "taut," "rigid," and "stand erect" (Snitow, 1979). Adult male literature contains even more explicit images of male sexual potency, women with desirable sexual attributes, and graphic descriptions of sexual acts.

Script theory also details how affect is gender-typed into two sets of affects culturally defined as representing an *inferior female* set of affects (enjoyment, fear, distress, shame) and a *superior male* set (excitement, surprise, anger, disgust) (Mosher & MacIan, 1994). What matters to an individual within a particular sexual script will be guided by the affects associated with it. For instance, the gender socialization of females will focus their attention on script elements that elicit enjoyment rather than the masculine affect of excitement. Such elements might include having a familiar and loved sexual partner or a safe, private place to have sex. Conversely, male socialization will focus men's attention on script elements that elicit excitement, such as the sexual attractiveness of the partner or the novelty of the sexual activity.

Gender-typed affects are a strong component of the romance and adventure scripts. The romance features distress, fear, shame, and joy. The heroine responds to crisis and adversity not with anger and disgust (male affects) but with fear and distress. Sexual shame or embarrassment also often are present. When the woman inadvertently exposes her body to the man (e.g., is seen bathing or has to change clothes after being caught in a downpour), her appropriate response is an embarrassed modesty, not sexual pride. Last, she is free to express joy when she is rescued by and joined with the man. In contrast, masculine affects dominate in the adventure script. The man is excited by the woman's beauty, by competition and conquest, and by male camaraderie. He also is expected to express anger, surprise, and disgust during combat rather than shame, fear, or distress. Script actions that enhance these emotions are emphasized, including chase scenes, the cruelty of the villains, the shaming or loss of buddies, and the woman's physical attributes.

The importance of relationships in life also is differentiated by gender within heterosexual scripts. Although both scripts also often embed a coming-of-age story within or alongside the courtship, with the youthful female or male stepping into adulthood, the romance script presents the establishment of a relationship as the singular most important life event for women. Marriage is the road to maturity. Other life achievements are usually absent and relations with friends and family are rarely developed. In contrast, the adventure script identifies achievement as the route to adulthood. For men, life's true adventures involve bonding or competing with other males; love relationships are expected to complement these activities, not supersede them.

In summary, gender roles underlie every aspect of heterosexual love scripts, including the content of script elements, their associated affect, and the meaning attributed by individuals to relationships. The complementarity of the romance-adventure script pairing shapes and reinforces a heterosexual sexual orientation. The interdependency of the romance and adventure scripts make other script pairings less likely and less compatible. The courtship plot does not easily move forward for romance-romance or adventure-adventure pairings, should they occur. Nevertheless, heterosexual love scripts set the stage for how relationships are to be conducted and are likely to be incorporated in some fashion into lesbians' and gay men's love scripts.

Lesbian and Gay Love Scripts

Lesbians and gay men are likely to be affected by the heterosexual love scripts described above in two significant ways. First, the emphasis on the courtship phase is likely to be carried over due to the lack of alternative relationship scripts. Second, enculturation into gender roles also probably will shape the scripts of many lesbians and gay men. Thus, a romance script is likely to be in strong evidence in fiction and comedy aimed at lesbians, whereas an adventure script should be reflected in gay men's entertainment. However, the nonnormative status of same-sex relationships will require some alteration of heterosexual scripts. The stigma associated with homosexuality has several potential consequences for lesbian and gay love scripts. First, because feelings for someone of the same sex are deemed inferior, according to heterosexist standards, same-sex attractions may initially be labeled or encoded as friendship rather than love or attraction. Further relationship development may then follow a friendship script. Second, acknowledging the feelings as sexual requires the individual to begin the process of accepting a stigmatized identity. The universality of this experience for lesbians and gay men requires that a coming out script be added to whatever original relationship script is followed. Last, the stigma of homosexuality as abnormal may affect specific script elements, such as how public the courtship is or what role family and friends play in the script.

Examples will be used below to illustrate the prototypic romance and adventure script as they are expressed in novels and comedy aimed at lesbians and gay men. Concepts to be explored include the phase of the relationship addressed, specific script elements, the role of sexuality, types of affect expressed, and the importance of relationships in life.

Lesbian Romance Script

Numerous classic and contemporary lesbian novels rely on the romance script. Quite parallel to the heterosexual romance, the lesbian romance script has been described by Rose, Zand, and Cini (1993) as having the following four primary characteristics: a high level of emotional intimacy, an emphasis on sexual attraction rather than sexual activity, a relatively direct relationship initiation phase, and a quick progression to a commitment. The genre of the lesbian romance is exemplified in *The Price of Salt* (written by mystery writer Patricia Highsmith under the pseudonym Claire Morgan, 1952/1984), reputed to be the first gay novel in the United States to have a happy ending.

The Price of Salt describes the courtship between Therese, an aspiring 19-year-old stage designer, and Carol, a wealthy, about-to-divorce woman in her early thirties. The courtship is set within the context of a coming out story; it is the first lesbian relationship for Therese and the first serious same-sex one for Carol. The women are physically attracted to each other immediately when they meet at the department store where Therese works as a clerk and Carol is a customer:

> Their eyes met at the same instant, Therese glancing up from a box she was opening, and the woman just turning her head so she looked directly at Therese. She was tall and fair, her long figure graceful in the loose fur coat. . . . Her eyes were gray, colorless, yet dominant as light or fire, and caught by them, Therese could not look away . . . [she] stood there mute. The woman was looking at Therese, too . . . [she] felt sure the woman would come to her. Then Therese saw her walk slowly toward the counter . . . . (p. 31)

Therese and Carol approach each other tentatively. Neither is sure about the other's motives; therefore, direct sexual intent is not emphasized. Specific sexual content also is not present, perhaps reflecting what was permissible in terms of publishing in the 1950s but also in keeping with the valuation of emotional intimacy over sexuality. In fact, it is not clear that the relationship has become sexual until the plot indicates that a detective hired by Carol's ex-husband has made an incriminating tape of their activities in a hotel room.

The obstacle to love in this novel is the ex-husband, who uses the tape and a love letter to gain full custody of their daughter and demand that Carol quit seeing Therese if she wants any visitation privileges. The obstacle to love is overcome when Carol ultimately gives up her parental rights and reunites with Therese. The story ends with the intimation that theirs will be a long-term commitment. The final lines describe Therese, unobserved, watching Carol across a room:

> Carol raised her hand slowly and brushed her hair back, once on either side, and Therese smiled because the gesture was Carol, and it was Carol she loved and would always love. . . . It would be Carol, in a thousand cities, a thousand houses, in foreign lands where they would go together, in heaven and in hell. (Morgan, 1952/1984, p. 276)

Other popular lesbian romances such as *Patience and Sarah* (Miller, 1969/1973), *Desert of the Heart* (Rule, 1964), and *Choices* (Toder, 1980/1991) and numerous more recent releases (e.g., Kaplan, 1995; McDaniel, 1991) also describe a courtship between two women that leads to a supposedly permanent union. Greatly similar to the heterosexual romance, the plot commonly focuses on the sweet anticipation of the two joining together as a couple. *Choices* (Toder, 1980/1991) and *Devotion* (Kaplan, 1995) provide examples of a common recent variation on the girl meets girl, loses girl, and gets girl back script. Both stories set the drama within an already established relationship that has become estranged or is threatened and both end with the couple's romantic reunion.

Other parallels between the lesbian and heterosexual romance scripts are found in terms of how sexuality is represented, what affects are emphasized, and the importance of relationships in life. In terms of sexuality, one or both of the women are portrayed as "innocent," but the innocence is more emotional than a lack of actual sexual experience. The sexual awakening occurs within the context of responding to another woman's love. Thus, the emotional element heightens sexual desire more than specific or explicit sexual acts (few of which are mentioned). Traditionally feminine affects also are strongly in evidence in the lesbian romance, including fear and distress over being separated or discovered, shame at being publicly embarrassed, and enjoyment at being united. The lesbian heroine typically does not aggressively pursue the object of her desire, lash out at her enemies, or relish their defeat.

Finally, although a coming out and coming-of-age script often are incorporated within the lesbian romance, they usually converge on the establishment of a permanent relationship as the route to happiness and maturity. For example, in *Patience and Sarah* (Miller, 1969/1973), a story about a lesbian couple based on the life of Mary Ann Willson, an American primitive painter of the early 1800s, the lovers realize they have "found their mate" after the first kiss.

Comedy reiterates the themes present in fiction; the romance script is a cornerstone of what is considered to be funny by contemporary lesbians. First, lesbians' desire for intimacy and commitment has been lampooned by many humorists. For example, Lea DeLaria (1995) advises lesbians,

> Keep your sense of humor, especially when dealing with women because we are a pain in the ass. Believe me, sometimes I wish I was straight. You screw a guy, he falls asleep. That's it. None of this "What are you thinking?" (p. 65)

The quick merger that results from high levels of intimacy also has been described by Gail Sausser (1990) as leading to some strange courtship rituals:

> Women go places together in small impenetrable groups. If you talk to a strange woman she's liable to think you are coming on to her. That is why in order to meet lesbians, you have to pretend you have no intention of picking them up. You get to know women on committees or in activities and then get so attracted to one another you end up kissing, and then she moves in with you. (p. 21)

Sexual inhibition and loss of desire in long-term relationships are a second target for lesbian humor. For example, a lesbian comedy team called Planet Q (1995) describes the phenomenon of Lesbian Bed Death. In the routine, a commentator enters the bedroom of a lesbian couple who have just decided not to have sex because they are too tired. She announces,

> What you have just witnessed is the beginning of the end of a three-year lesbian relationship. Although Kathy and Elaine may not be ready to admit it, their sex lives are being slowly, yet painlessly eaten away by a silent killer that is creeping into bedrooms from Northampton to Santa Cruz. Normally healthy, sexually active lesbians are going to bed . . . and going to sleep. (p. 131)

The commentator goes on to explain that Lesbian Bed Death (LBD) is one of the most deadly but little known killers that "sends approximately 60% of lesbians into couples' counseling at one or more times during a relationship." However, she reassures them that, although no single cause of LBD has been found, "working round the clock on a cure are doctors, psychic herbalists, and folk singers" (Planet Q, 1995, p. 132).

Stereotypically, lesbians opt for monogamous rather than nonmonog-amous solutions to the loss of passion. Comic Sarah Cytron has described one of her own as follows:

> Relationships are not easy. Harriett and I have been together over 8 years, and by this time the sex life isn't what it was. So I keep trying to jazz it up. Sometimes when we're making love, I'll put on an accent so she'll think she's with somebody new. But she complains. She says, "Look, I'm just not attracted to your grandmother." (Cytron & Malinowitz, 1995, p. 33)

A last theme that is more thoroughly developed in lesbian comedy than in romance fiction is the concept that beauty is only skin deep. This concept appears to be translated by lesbians into a lack of concern about physical beauty that, in turn, has provided a foil for many jokes (e.g., "The term *lesbian fashion* is an oxymoron"). Similarly, comic Kate Clinton's routine concerning "Why Lesbians Became Extinct," in the year 7969, provides an amusing explanation that focuses on lesbians' notorious interest in comfort over appearance. In the skit, archaeologists have "uncovered scuffed, but perfectly intact Vibram-soled footwear, 'Doc Martens,' which still had a half-life of about a billion years." The scientists speculate that "their huge, weighted soles made it difficult for lesbians to flee from their predators" and that in some cases, particularly for the larger sized footwear, "lesbians undecided on this style looked down at their feet and actually died of fright" (Clinton, 1995, p. 6).

In summary, the lesbian romance as expressed in fiction and comedy contains many aspects of the heterosexual romance script, including an emphasis on the courtship phase; passive or reactive female roles; feminine affects; and a high value on intimate, committed relationships. In addition, less priority is given to active sexuality, physical attractiveness, and personal achievement.

Gay Male Adventure Script

A typical love script for gay men found in popular fiction closely follows the heterosexual adventure script. Independent achievement, the ability to surmount obstacles to love, the physical beauty of the loved one, and am-bivalence about intimacy are common themes. *The Front Runner* (Warren, 1974) is a prototype of the gay adventure coming-of-age script. It describes the love relationship between Harlan, a college track coach in his late 30s, and Billy Sive, a young athlete with Olympic potential. Billy's athletic prowess is used as a device to satisfy both his own and Harlan's ambitions. At the time the two meet, Harlan has been blackballed for several years from coaching at major universities due to an unfounded rumor that he had sex with one of his male students. However, he has built a reputation for himself as a coach at a small, progressive college. Billy and his two friends seek Harlan out as their coach after being thrown off a major team for being gay. Thus, the pair's love for each other satisfies their desires for both success and love.

The obstacles to love in *The Front Runner* are both internal and external. Although Harlan is the older of the two, he is less accepting of his own homosexuality. The story describes his struggle to accept his own nature. Harlan resolves his feelings when he realizes that Billy's performance is being negatively affected by the sexual tension between them: "It occurred to me then that the only way Billy Sive was going to get to Montreal [the Olympics] was through my bed" (p. 98). Once the two become lovers, external obstacles such as prejudice and discrimination from people, the media, and the Amateur Athletic Association come into play. The lovers respond by binding more strongly together, allying with their friends, and using the legal resources of the nascent gay movement.

The physical beauty of both Billy and Harlan is described in considerable detail. Harlan sizes up Billy upon meeting him in a manner closely resembling a modern personal advertisement: "My coach's eye measured his slender body at five-foot-eleven and weighed him at around 138 pounds. . . . His face . . . .was pleasantly handsome, fine-cut, with high cheekbones, a high forehead, a blunt nose, a good mouth . . . " (pp. 4-5). Harlan also remarks on Billy's beautiful, clear blue-gray eyes, light-brown curls, and racehorse legs. In turn, Harlan describes himself as "macho gay" and as physically fit as his students. His sexual attractiveness and worldliness are affirmed by the reputation he developed as a "well hung" stud when working for a time as a very high-priced hustler in New York City.

Ambivalence about intimacy also is expressed in *The Front Runner*. Harlan's internalized homophobia, combined with a realistic fear of persecution for being gay, has prevented him for 20 years from developing a love relationship. His fears are magnified the night before he and Billy make love for the first time:

> I spent the whole night . . . torturing myself with thoughts. I was going to do the wrong thing. I was going to destroy his running career, just to satisfy my selfish feelings. If we became lovers, the fury would hit us. It would obliterate us. It might even destroy our feeling for each other. I wasn't so sure that love could survive something like that. (p. 105)

Harlan's concern about the destructive power of love is well founded. They make it to the Olympics, but Billy is shot and killed during his race—presumably for being gay.

The gay male and heterosexual adventure scripts are also similar in terms of how sexuality is expressed, what affects are present, and the priority given to relationships. Literature aimed at gay men often is quite explicit. The specific postures, body parts, and organs associated with physical desire; the nuances of touch and taste; and the primitive, animalistic quality of sexual acts are eloquently, and sometimes obsessively, described. For example, the back cover of *Bayou Boy* (Eighner, 1993), published by Bad Boy Press, refers to the book as "a collection of hot, hard stories" that explore "the many ways men work up a sweat in the steamy southwest." Likewise, Johnnie Ray Rousseau, a 22-year-old gay pop singer in *Eight Days a Week* indicates to a friend that he is in love with Keith Keller, a white banker with "muscles to die for" by remarking: "It's [love] the real thing, Snooks. I can feel it in my heart. In my bones. In my anus" (Duplechan, 1985, p. 108).

Congruent with the emphasis on explicit sexuality, excitement is one of the major affects portrayed. A particular sexual ideal that is used to enhance excitement is the image of white male beefcake, that is, a young white male with a muscular, hairless torso and "washboard" abdomen (Browning, 1994). Excitement is also associated with competition (e.g., Billy's races in *The Front Runner*) and engaging with the enemy. For example, in a classic slay-the-dragon plot, the protagonist of *Lethal Silence: Mission #6*, Alex Kane, battles right-wing mercenaries whose aim it is to "squash gay men underfoot" (Preston, 1993). Fear and shame normally are channeled into anger. In *The Man: A Hero for Our Time*, a gay man whose lover was killed by a gay basher becomes *The Man*, a masked avenger who "protects the lives of the innocent" (Drake, 1995).

Finally, in the gay male adventure script, coming of age is not equated with establishing a relationship, as it is in the romance script. For example, in the gay classic, *The Best Little Boy in the World* (Reid, 1973), the protagonist's coming out/coming-of-age story ends with him concluding, "I knew I was not ready, if I ever would be, for a full-time kind of relationship" (p. 217). In those cases when a permanent relationship *is* established, personal ambition is portrayed as superseding it. For example, Harlan in *The Front Runner* explains,

> there's something we ought to agree on. For the moment, this [the relationship] has to take its place in what we're trying to do [train for the Olympics]. If it interferes, it might cause you to fail. That might spoil our feeling for each other too. (p. 113)

Comedy directed at gay men and their relationships echoes the themes found in adventure fiction. First, the emphasis many gay men are believed to place on physical attractiveness is captured in a comment by comic Steve

Moore (1995): "I'll be 40 in June. That's 130 in gay years" (p. 111). Image is clearly important in gay male culture. According to *The Unofficial Gay Manual,* "Many guys find a look that works for them and perfect it, until it becomes their persona" (Dilallo & Krumholz, 1994, p. 59). The manual then describes 13 basic gay male personas and the subliminal messages they send, including The Person-in-Black ("I'm too sexy for my shirt."), the Gym Dandy ("Look, but don't touch."), the Sugar Daddy ("Money *can* buy me love."), and the Poodle ("Only my hairdresser knows for sure.") (pp. 59-66). Readers are also informed that bad bodies, unsightly body hair, and poor taste in clothes are among the top 10 turn-offs for guys looking for love (p. 118).

Intimacy in a relationship appears to be an elusive quality for many gay men, according to other humorous advice given in *The Unofficial Gay Manual.* In a chapter titled "Someday My Prince Will Come: Dating in a World of Potential Future Ex-Lovers," the authors ask the question, "Why do so many men of steel have heels of helium?" (p. 118) and indicate that "some guys would rather be committed than find themselves in a committed relationship" (p. 140). Another stereotypic expectation is that each man will "have his own," that is, be a self-supporting peer. Actual or prospective partners who do not pull their own weight financially or in terms of status are viewed as less desirable. For example, *The Unofficial Gay Manual* suggests that it is a bad sign when a date suddenly remembers that he "forgot" his wallet when the check comes. Readers are advised, "Don't fall for it; no one *really* forgets his wallet" (p. 128).

Gay men who do manage to establish relationships are advised to be prepared for roving eyes and problems with intimacy. Couples are advised that a mortgage might prove to be a stronger bond than any marriage license:

> If you really love each other, don't be afraid of committing yourselves to some major joint investment. . . . You'll be glad to have that mortgage when your other half comes home with groceries in his arms and some hunk on his mind. (Dilallo & Krumholtz, 1994, pp. 142-143)

External solutions to relationship problems are satirized:

> If you're both feeling ambivalent toward your relationship, simple acquisitions such as Pratesi bedding, a multiple CD player or a food processor may lift you out of the doldrums. If the winter of your discontent is particularly harsh, you may need an antique or an original piece of art to relight the fire. (p. 149)

In summary, the gay male adventure script, as portrayed in fiction and comedy, incorporates many components of the heterosexual adventure script.

The courtship phase without subsequent marriage is emphasized, as are a proactive and agentic male role, an explicit sexuality, masculine affects, and a value that love relationships should not interfere with personal ambition.

Impact on Lesbian and Gay Couples

Cultural scripts are believed to act as guides for interpersonal scripts, according to script theory (Simon & Gagnon, 1986). If so, one might expect to find the romance and adventure scripts reflected in actual behavior. Self-help books are one source of information that may be used to determine what behaviors are presumed to be widespread among lesbian and gay couples. If advice books include themes similar to those identified in cultural scripts, it would suggest that couples are conforming to those scripts to some extent. A discussion of seven recent advice books for lesbian and gay couples is presented below to illustrate that the romance and adventure scripts are being reflected in how actual relationships are conducted, as predicted by script theory. Three of the advice books focus exclusively on lesbian couples (Clunis & Green, 1993; Johnson, 1990; McDaniel, 1995), two exclusively on gay male couples (Driggs & Finn, 1991; Marcus, 1992), and two on both lesbian and gay couples (Berzon, 1988; Tessina, 1989).

The courtship focus of love scripts poses an obstacle for lesbian and gay male couples, according to the self-help books examined here. Most authors included an extensive discussion of problems the couple is likely to face once the honeymoon is over. The assumption is that many lesbians and gay men have not been prepared adequately for the realities of a long-term commitment. Idealized cultural images of "wedded bliss" were singled out as creating unrealistic expectations for couples, particularly in the areas of sexual desire and marital harmony.

Actual lesbian relationships are portrayed by self-help books as operating from a romance-romance script pairing. For example, on the back jacket *Staying Power: Long-Term Lesbian Couples,* by Susan Johnson (1990), is advertised as being "the book about the one goal that most lesbians express as an ambition—the creation and nurturance of a lifetime love affair." Similarly, in *Lesbian Couples: Creating Healthy Relationships for the '90s,* authors Merilee Clunis and Dorsey Green (1993) begin with the assumption that, as women, lesbians have learned to prize couple relationships; therefore, both women in a lesbian couple will feel responsible for making the relationship work (p. 4).

Self-help books also assume that establishing intimacy is easily achieved for lesbians but that setting boundaries will be more problematic. According to Judith McDaniel (1995), in *The Lesbian Couple's Guide: Finding the*

Right Woman and Creating a Life Together, every couple she interviewed understood her when she referred to "merger madness," "the lesbian melt-down," or "the codependency tango" as being a issues in lesbian relation-ships. Tina Tessina (1989), in *Gay Relationships for Men and Women,* also indicates that "many lesbian women have a tendency to overreact about commitment, often rushing into relationships without taking the time to develop a solid foundation based on love, mutuality, and an in-depth knowl-edge of themselves and of their partners" (p. 62). Generally, difficulties are described as arising when lesbian partners "fuse," or become extensions of each other. To help avoid this problem, Clunis and Green (1993) include a chapter on "Separateness and Togetherness," in which they elaborate on the importance of maintaining one's personal boundaries when in a relationship.

Concerns about lesbian sexuality more often focus on sexual frequency, initiation, and desire than on conflicts about specific sexual practices, sexual satisfaction, or performance. Sexual excitement is portrayed as being en-hanced primarily by intimacy and affection. For instance, of the 19 tips for enhancing relationships cited by Clunis and Green (1993), only 3 focus on sexual actions and none is sexually explicit, for example, "try out some new lovemaking techniques," "cultivate some sexual fantasies," and "tell stories or fantasies to your partner while you are touching her" (pp. 74-75). In addition, topics such as celibacy, "couples for whom sex is not important" (Johnson, 1990), and "We're lovers but we're not having sex" (McDaniel, 1995) are more likely to appear in books targeting lesbians than ones aimed at both lesbians and gay men or solely at gay men.

Self-help books also provide confirmation that an adventure-adventure script pairing shapes the interpersonal scripts of gay men couples. Key prob-lems that are seen as likely to arise closely resemble elements of the adven-ture script, including those related to personal achievement, intimacy, physi-cal attractiveness, and sexual expressivity. First, intimacy is approached quite differently when the focus is on gay men. For instance, in *Intimacy Between Men,* John Driggs and Stephen Finn (1991) devote considerable attention toward persuading gay men that intimacy is a worthy goal, though it is difficult to achieve. They begin a section describing the rewards of intimacy: "At this point you may be thinking, 'This [developing intimacy] sounds like a lot of work! What's in it for me?' " (p. 16). The authors go on to explain seven benefits of emotional closeness. They also encourage gay men to learn to distinguish sexuality from intimacy. However, at this point, perhaps fearing that the very idea of intimacy may be aversive, the authors hasten to reassure the reader: "Don't worry, you will not have this calling [for inti-macy] until you are ready for it. You will not catch it from this book" (p. 90).

The significance of sexuality in gay men's relationships, as encoded in the adventure script, also appears in full relief in self-help books. Books aimed solely at gay men or jointly at lesbians and gay men all contained more explicit and specific discussions of sexuality and monogamy than the three focused exclusively on lesbians. The content usually goes beyond the obligatory mention of safer sex techniques. Included are topics such as the hazards of sexual rigidity (e.g., the desire for a specific body type or genital size) and sexual addiction (Driggs & Finn, 1991); the inhibiting effect on sexuality of the handsome, brawny, beefcake image upheld as a gay male ideal (Berzon, 1988); specific sexual games such as cross-dressing and bondage and discipline (Tessina, 1989); how to stop oneself from being sexual before getting to know a man (Marcus 1992); and very detailed descriptions of open relationship contracts (Marcus, 1992; Tessina, 1989).

Finally, the emphasis on personal achievement in the adventure script appears to be played out in gay men's relationships in terms of the importance placed on social status (including physical attractiveness), competition, and defeating one's enemies. For instance, in *Permanent Partners,* Berzon (1988) cautions gay men against getting caught up in gender roles dictating that "real" men must be self-supporting. She argues that some couples may be happier if one of the pair is a stay-at-home partner. Similarly, Driggs and Finn (1991) warn gay men that "all that glitters is not gold." Choosing a partner based on personal appearance, position, or wealth has led to disappointment in relationships for many gay men. Competition also contributes to two common dilemmas, including "Anything you can do, I can do better" and "It's my turn to be on top."

In summary, self-help books provide evidence to support the idea that the lesbian and gay love scripts described earlier have a strong impact on actual relationships. A congruence between love scripts and advice books was found along at least four dimensions, including the courtship phase and gender roles concerning intimacy, independence, and sexuality in relationships. The congruence suggests that cultural scripts provide many elements for interpersonal scripts used by lesbian and gay male couples.

Alternative Scripts

The love scripts described earlier do not represent the universe of possibilities for lesbian and gay relationship scripts. Alternative scripts can be identified within lesbian and gay culture that have developed in response to influences other than heterosexual norms, such as race, community values, and HIV/AIDS. Race brings unique elements to love scripts, including both a concern with how racism affects own-race and cross-race relationships and a celebration of cultural differences. Values that have evolved within lesbian and gay communities bring other dimensions to love scripts. One recent development has been the value shift from "perversity" to "diversity" within lesbian/gay rhetoric. Previously marginalized sexual minorities such as bisexuals, transsexuals, and sadomasochists are now being tolerated under the civil rights agenda adopted in most large communities, if not accepted. This has opened the way for more gender blending and sexual variety to occur in love scripts. Feminism is a second value that has had a profound effect on white lesbian communities, in particular, in terms of attitudes toward specific sexual practices, monogamy, physical beauty, butch-femme roles, and the value of friendship and equality in relationships. Within white gay male communities, at least two additional value systems are in operation. One focuses on achievement and its accoutrements as important elements in courtship and love, including the status, material success, and physical attractiveness of oneself or partner. Developed partly as a response to HIV, the second value system emphasizes the need to create emotional and kinship ties with partners and friends that transcend wealth and beauty.

This broad assortment of influences has resulted in several alternative love scripts, including race-relevant, gender-blended, friendship, and buddy scripts. Race-relevant scripts both incorporate a racial/cultural context and address the consequences for lesbians and gay men of color for assimilating with the white community. For example, in *Say Jesus and Come to Me,* evangelist Myrtle Black falls in love with Travis Lee, a successful singer, against a backdrop of racial and political conflicts (Shockley, 1982). The murder of two black prostitutes leads Myrtle to organize a march for equality for women of all races. Along the way, Myrtle and Travis must contend with homophobia and sexism within the black community and racism from the white community. Race-relevant scripts are more in evidence among writings of lesbians than gay men of color. Among the topics explored recently by or about lesbians of color are erotica (Lee & Silvera, 1995), interracial love relationships (Hardy, 1993), the experience of lesbians of color in general within their communities and relationships (Silvera, 1991), and experiences specifically of Latina (Ramos, 1987) and Chicana lesbians (Trujillo, 1991).

Race-relevant scripts involving gay men of color are less common and more likely to reflect white stereotypes. For instance, in pornography, gay men of color are almost always shown as submissive to white men and seldom talk to or show sexual interest in other men of color (Browning, 1994). However, gay men of color are beginning to represent themselves more frequently in popular culture. Recent African American titles include *B-Boy Blues,* a story about Mitchell Crawford and his vision of lust and love, Raheim Rivers, who is 6 feet tall and 215 pounds of mocha-chocolate muscle (Hardy, 1994), and *In the Life,* an anthology about what it means to be black and gay in America (Beam, 1986).

Gender-blended scripts combine healthy doses of romance and adventure scripts within each partner's role. Many gender-blended scripts contain an element of fantasy, particularly in terms of the adventure components. For example, one of the most popular genres among lesbians is the lesbian detective novel (e.g., Maney, 1994; Scoppettone, 1994). Although few lesbians actually appear to be employed as detectives, the appeal of the lesbian detective as heroine remains strong, perhaps because it provides a convenient way to bring intrigue and action into the plot. The romantic aspects are usually less idealized than in the traditional romance, reflecting the classic stereotype of the hard-boiled private eye, but the lesbian sleuth is never so cynical that she's unable to respond to love. Gender-blended scripts for lesbians that include explicit sexuality are also more available. For instance, *Getting Wet: Tales of Lesbian Seduction* is advertised as "sex fiction that gets under the covers and rolls them back" (Allain & Elwin, 1992).

For gay men, gender-blended scripts add elements of romance to the core adventure story. The quest for success or the ideal sexual experience, or feats of daring and revenge, are presented as being enhanced by true love. In fact, being open to love has been presented as a risk and challenge itself in newer writings about gay men's relationships, especially in light of AIDS. For example, under the heading, "be very brave," Steven Saylor (1995) explains the importance of love in response to the horrible risk imposed by HIV:

> And so the paradox: The more we love and cherish another person, the greater the rewards of the relationship and the deeper and truer the colors of the whole world become; yet at the same time, the more we love, the more vulnerable we become. . . . What I'm trying to say, I suppose, is go ahead and love, no matter how awful the risk. I gaze into the uncertain future, and I say to myself, and to you, with all the love I have: Be brave, be very brave. (pp. 104, 106)

The third alternative script, *friendship,* has long been established as a major love script for lesbians and gay men. As noted earlier, early feelings of same-sex attraction may be encoded as friendship rather than love due to the lack of available scripts modeling same-sex love relationships. Research indicates that most lesbians and gay men have a best friend relationship with their partner and, like friends, tend to be similar in interests, resources, and skills (Peplau, 1993). For some lesbians, a friendship may sustain a love relationship that does not involve sexuality. Such relationships have been labeled "Boston marriages" (Rothblum & Brehony, 1993). Boston marriages are indistinguishable from lesbian lover relationships, with the exception of the lack of sexual activity. The pair typically view themselves and are viewed by the community as a couple, engage in shared activities that are rarely done by friends (such as making out wills and buying property), and are physically affectionate with each other.

The friendship script is also sustained among gay male couples, many of whom negotiate open relationships to allow for sexual novelty, but at the same time preserve the security and intimacy of the love relationship through friendship. Gay men in open relationships usually negotiate rules that preserve the primacy of the couple emotionally, including limiting the amount of contact with outside partners to "one-night stands" or "no emotional involvement" (Hickson et al., 1992).

The fourth alternative, the *buddy* script, shifts the focus from the couple to the individual who operates within a network of "family" relationships comprising ex-lovers, friends, and some blood relatives. Love relationships generally have less priority than in the traditional scripts. The motto of the buddy script could be summed up as, "Lovers may come and go, but friends are here to stay" or, as Ethan Mordden stated it, "[M]y family is my buddies" (Mordden, 1986, p. 189). Both lesbian and gay male versions of the buddy script exist. For example, some lesbians regard friendship so highly that they are often reluctant to become lovers with friends for fear of losing the friendship if the romance does not work out. Lesbians also have a well-earned reputation for surrounding themselves with ex-lovers as friends (e.g., Becker, 1988) and for traveling in "packs." As Lea DeLaria (1995) explains, it is nearly impossible for a single dyke to get a date, because

> lesbians always travel in a group, always in a pack, because you never know when someone is going to throw a really good game of softball. With very few exceptions, everyone in this group is attached to someone else in this group and they are all EACH OTHER'S EX-LOVERS!! You want to say to them, "Hey, girls, why not let me put some new blood in this family. All the kids are gonna be retarded." (p. 57)

The buddy script as actualized by gay men incorporates personal freedom within the structure of a community household (Browning, 1994). Browning has argued that gay men have shown a unique ability to blend sex with friendship that makes sex ordinary, even recreational. More complex types of intimacy are able to occur once sex is not tied to the restrictive laws of marriage. As a result, gay men have re-formed sex into a tool for building diverse forms of comradeship. The dialectical role of friendship, sex, and attraction in gay men's lives has been further elaborated by White (quoted in Nardi, 1992):

> Friendship . . . intertwines with sexual adventure and almost always outlasts it; a casual encounter can lead to a life-long, romantic but sexless friendship.

> . . . [S]ex, love and friendship may overlap but are by no means wholly congruent. In this society, moreover, it is friendship that provides the emotional and social continuity, whereas sexuality is not more and no less than occasion for gallantry. (p. 115)

In summary, at least four alternative scripts have been identified that reflect unique influences and values within lesbian and gay communities. Overall, the alternative scripts provide definite challenges to the dominant lesbian and gay love scripts that are founded on heterosexual norms. Taken collectively, they reject white viewpoints, gender roles, and the value that a couple relationship represents the ultimate experience of intimacy. In addition, new alternative scripts continue to emerge that alter or reject the couple as the primary bond, including a lesbian or gay parenting script (e.g., Quinn, 1995) and a sister-brother script between gay men and lesbians (Nestle & Preston, 1994). The alternative scripts provide avenues for living in and with relationships that are increasingly lesbian and gay affirmative.

Conclusion

The lesbian and gay men's love scripts identified here appear to be operating at both the cultural and the interpersonal levels. The two most dominant cultural scripts, lesbian romance and gay male adventure, were found to be *institutionalized* to the extent that a considerable amount of popular fiction adheres to these two basic plots. Furthermore, the two scripts strongly parallel heterosexual love scripts by emphasizing the courtship phase and gender roles concerning intimacy, sexuality, achievement, agency, affects, and the primacy of relationships in life. An analysis of self-help books aimed at lesbian and gay male couples suggests that these cultural scripts have a strong impact on interpersonal ones, as hypothesized by script theory. Problems typically found among couples were ones likely to arise from enactment of the cultural scripts, such as lack of sexual desire in lesbian relationships and difficulties with intimacy for gay male couples. However, not all scripts available to lesbians and gay men were based on heterosexist norms. At least four alternative scripts were described that challenge or expand the dominant cultural scripts by bringing race, gender blending, friendship, and new definitions of family into the picture.

As knowledge structures, scripts serve three basic functions. They help the individual manage complex environments, operate as interpretive frameworks for evaluating events, and serve as performative structures for smooth interactions during social routines (Ginsburg, 1988). The emergence of love scripts specific to lesbian and gay relationships that has occurred in popular fiction over the past few decades suggests that new norms are beginning to operate. As new scripts proliferate, the ways lesbians and gay men organize information about relationships, evaluate them, and behave in same-sex couples are increasingly likely to be more self- and community-defined.

References

Abelson, R. P. (1981). Psychological status of the script concept. *American Psychologist, 36,* 715-729.

Allain, C., & Elwin, R. (1992). *Getting wet: Tales of lesbian seduction.* Toronto, Ontario: Women's Press.

Beam, J. (1986). *In the life: A black gay anthology.* Boston: Alyson.

Becker, C. S. (1988). *Unbroken ties: Lesbian ex-lovers.* Boston: Alyson.

Berzon, B. (1988). *Permanent partners: Building gay and lesbian relationships that last.* New York: Plume.

Browning, F. (1994). *The culture of desire: Paradox and perversity in gay lives today.* New York: Vintage.

Clinton, K. (1995). Could lesbians return? In C. Flowers (Ed.), *Out, loud, and laughing* (pp. 5-10). New York: Anchor.

Clunis, D. M., & Green, G. D. (1993). *Lesbian couples: Creating healthy relationships for the '90s.* Seattle: Seal.

Cytron, S., & Malinowitz, H. (1995). From *A dyke grows in Brooklyn* and *Take my domestic partner—please!* In C. Flowers (Ed.), *Out, loud, and laughing* (pp. 27-42). New York: Anchor.

DeLaria, L. (1995). Ms. DeLaria's dating tips for dykes. In C. Flowers (Ed.), *Out, loud, and laughing* (pp. 57-68). New York: Anchor.

Dilallo, K., & Krumholtz, J. (1994). *The unofficial gay manual.* New York: Doubleday.

Drake, R. (1995). *The man: A hero for our time. Book 1: Why?* New York: Plume.

Driggs, J. H., & Finn, S. E. (1991). *Intimacy between men.* New York: Plume.

Duplechan, L. (1985). *Eight days a week.* Boston: Alyson.

Eighner, L. (1993). *Bayou boy.* New York: Masquerade.

Foster, E. (1995). Nelson volunteers. In C. Flowers (Ed.), *Out, loud, and laughing* (pp. 69-86). New York: Anchor.

Gagnon, J. H. (1977). *Human sexualities.* Glenview, IL: Scott, Foresman.

Ginsburg, G. P. (1988). Rules, scripts and prototypes in personal relationships. In S. W. Duck (Ed.), *Handbook of personal relationships* (pp. 23-39). New York: John Wiley.

Hardy, J. (1993). *Sister/stranger: Lesbians loving across the lines.* Pittsburgh, PA: Sidewalk Revolution.

Hardy, J. M. (1994). *B-boy blues.* Boston: Alyson.

Hickson, F. C. I., Davies, P. M., Hunt, A. J., Weatherburn, P., McManus, T. J., & Coxon, A. P. M. (1992). Maintenance of open gay relationships: Some strategies for protection against HIV. *AIDS Care, 4,* 409-419.

Johnson, S. E. (1990). *Staying power: Long-term lesbian couples.* Tallahassee, FL: Naiad.

Kaplan, M. (1995). *Devotion.* Tallahassee, FL: Naiad.

Kurdek, L. A. (1994). The nature and correlates of relationship quality in gay, lesbian, and heterosexual cohabiting couples. In B. Greene & G. M. Herek (Eds.), *Psychological perspectives on lesbian and gay issues: Vol. 1. Lesbian and gay psychology: Theory, research, and clinical applications* (pp. 133-155). Thousand Oaks, CA: Sage.

Laws, J. L., & Schwarz, P. (1977). *Sexual scripts: The social construction of female sexuality.* Washington, DC: University Press of America.

Lee, C. A., & Silvera, M. (Eds.). (1995). *Pearls of passion: A treasury of lesbian erotica.* Toronto: Sister Vision.

Maney, M. (1994). *The case of the good-for-nothing girlfriend.* San Francisco: Cleis.

Marcus, E. (1992). *The gay male couple's guide* (Rev. ed.). New York: HarperCollins.

McDaniel, J. (1991). *Just say yes.* Ithaca, NY: Firebrand.

McDaniel, J. (1995). *The lesbian couple's guide.* New York: HarperCollins.

Miller, I. (1973). *Patience and Sarah.* New York: Fawcett Crest. (Original work published 1969)

Moore, S. (1995). AIDS—God, I hope I never get that again! In C. Flowers (Ed.), *Out, loud, and laughing* (pp. 111-120). New York: Anchor.

Mordden, E. (1986). *Buddies.* New York: St. Martin's.

Morgan, C. (1984). *The price of salt* (Rev. ed.). Tallahassee, FL: Naiad. (Original work published 1952)

Mosher, D. L., & MacIan, P. (1994). College men and women respond to X-rated videos intended for male or female audiences: Gender and sexual scripts. *Journal of Sex Research, 31,* 99-113.

Nardi, P. (1992). That's what friends are for: Friends as family in the gay and lesbian community. In K. Plummer (Ed.), *Modern homosexualities: Fragments of lesbian and gay experience* (pp. 108-120). London: Routledge.

Nestle, J., & Preston, J. (1994). *Sister & brother: Lesbians and gay men write about their lives together.* San Francisco: HarperCollins.

Peplau, A. L. (1993). Lesbian and gay relationships. In L. D. Garnets & D. C. Kimmell (Eds.), *Psychological perspectives on lesbian and gay male experiences* (pp. 395-419). New York: Columbia University Press.

Planet Q. (1995). Lesbian bed death. In C. Flowers (Ed.), *Out, loud, and laughing* (pp. 130-138). New York: Anchor.

Preston, J. (1993). *The mission of Alex Kane VI: Lethal silence.* New York: Masquerade.

Purnine, D. M., Carey, M. P., & Jorgensen, R. S. (1994). Gender differences regarding preferences for specific heterosexual practices. *Journal of Sex & Marital Therapy, 20,* 271-287.

Quinn, E. S. (1995). *Say uncle.* New York: Plume.

Ramos, J. (Ed.). (1987). *Compañeras: Latina lesbians.* New York: Latina Lesbian History Project.

Reid, J. (1973/1993). *The best little boy in the word.* New York: Ballantine.

Rose, S. (1985). Is romance dysfunctional? *International Journal of Women's Studies, 8,* 250-265.

Rose, S., Zand, D., & Cini, M. A. (1993). Lesbian courtship scripts. In E. D. Rothblum & K. A. Brehony (Eds.), *Boston marriages: Romantic but asexual relationships among contemporary lesbians* (pp. 70-85). Amherst: University of Massachusetts Press.

Rothblum, E. D., & Brehony, K. A. (1993). Why focus on romantic but asexual relationships among lesbians? In E. D. Rothblum & K. A. Brehony (Eds.), *Boston marriages: Romantic but asexual relationships among contemporary lesbians* (pp. 3-13). Amherst: University of Massachusetts Press.

Rule, J. (1964). *Desert of the heart.* Tallahassee, FL: Naiad.

Saylor, S. (1995). A marriage manual. In J. Preston & M. Lowenthal (Eds.), *Friends and lovers: Gay men write about the families they create* (pp. 95-106). New York: Dutton.

Sausser, G. (1990). *More lesbian etiquette.* Freedom, CA: Crossing Press.

Scoppettone, S. (1994). *My sweet untraceable you.* New York: Ballantine.

Shockley, A. A. (1982). *Say Jesus and come to me.* Tallahassee, FL: Naiad.

Silvera, M. (Ed.). (1991). *Piece of my heart.* Toronto: Sister Vision.

Lesbian and Gay Love Scripts

Simon, W., & Gagnon, J. H. (1986). Sexual scripts: Permanence and change. *Archives of Sexual Behavior, 15,* 97-120.

Snitow, A. B. (1979). Mass market romance: Pornography for women is different. *Radical History Review, 20,* 141-161.

Tessina, T. (1989). *Gay relationships for men and women.* New York: Putnam.

Toder, N. (1991). *Choices.* Boston, MA: Alyson. (Original work published 1980)

Trujillo, C. (Ed.). (1991). *Chicana lesbians: The girls our mothers warned us about.* Berkeley, CA: Third Woman.

Warren, P. N. (1974). *The front runner.* Beverly Hills, CA: Wildcat.

9

Immigrant and Refugee Lesbians

Oliva M. Espín

A large proportion of the world's immigrants and refugees are women. According to the United Nations Commission for Refugees, 80% of all refugees in the world are women and their children. One can assume that lesbians are present among these immigrants and refugees in similar proportions as in other populations of women. Demographic studies have demonstrated that the ethnic composition of the gay and lesbian population in North America is very much like the entire population (Tremble, Schneider, & Appathurai, 1989). In the United States, the current estimate is that the foreign-born population is about 20 million (Rogler, 1994). Thus, there must be about 1 million lesbians among immigrants in the United States alone and many more than that number among the refugee and immigrant population of the world. If so, the sheer numbers of lesbian migrants demand that we pay attention to this population.[1] However, except for the Cuban exodus of 1980, there is usually no open acknowledgment that a significant proportion of migrants, both men and women, might not be heterosexual.

The experiences of women in international migration has begun to draw attention from researchers, policymakers, and service providers (e.g., Andizian et al., 1983; Cole, Espín, & Rothblum, 1992; Gabaccia, 1992), but the lesbian experience is mostly absent from these studies. In fact, little is known about the experiences of either heterosexual or lesbian immigrant women in such private realms as sexuality, sexual orientation, and identity. Yet, as we know, sexuality and related issues are not entirely private, which explains why so many cultures and countries try to control and legislate them. Indeed, as one historian observed, "sexual behavior (perhaps more than religion) is the most highly symbolic activity in any society. To penetrate the symbolic system implicit in any society's sexual behavior is therefore to come closest to the heart of its uniqueness" (Trumbach, 1977, p. 24). We know that the sexual behaviors and gender roles of women serve a larger social function beyond the personal in all societies. They are used by enemies and friends alike as "proof" of either the moral fiber or the decay of social groups or nations. In most societies, women's sexual behavior and their

174

conformity to traditional gender roles signify the family's value system. Thus, in many societies, a lesbian daughter (or a heterosexual daughter, for that matter) who does not conform to traditional morality can be seen as "proof" of the lax morals of a family. This is why struggles surrounding acculturation in immigrant and refugee families frequently center on issues of daughters' sexual behaviors and women's sex roles in general. For parents and young women alike, acculturation and sexuality are closely connected; in many immigrant communities, to be Americanized is almost synonymous with being sexually promiscuous (Espín, 1984, 1987b).

Moreover, the self-appointed guardians of morality and tradition that are ever present in immigrant communities are deeply concerned with women's roles and sexual behavior. Considering that immigrant communities are more often than not besieged with rejection, racism, and scorn, those self-appointed guardians have always found fertile ground from which to control women's sexuality in the name of preserving tradition. Although young men are allowed, and encouraged, to develop new identities in the new country, girls and women are expected to continue living as if they were still in the old country. They are more often than not forced to embody cultural continuity amid cultural dislocation. Groups that are transforming their way of life through a vast and deep process of acculturation focus on preserving tradition almost exclusively through the gender roles of women. Women's roles become the bastion of traditions. The "proper" behavior of women is used to signify the difference between those who belong to the collectivity and those who do not (Yuval-Davis, 1992).

Needless to say, lesbians present unique challenges to immigrant and refugee communities while, at the same time, the expectations of their communities create enormous pressures on lesbians who are members of these families, particularly for those who come out as adolescents. As the authors of a study on Canadian lesbian and gay youth remind us,

> Every adolescent, regardless of ethnic affiliation, must resolve a number of issues as part of the coming-out process. These include: (a) deciding whether or not to disclose to the family, (b) finding a niche among gay and lesbian peers, and (c) reconciling sexual orientation with other aspects of identity. For the child of immigrant parents, the coming-out process takes place against the backdrop of ethnic traditions, values, and social networks. For some, this adds a dimension of complexity to the issues. Homosexuality, often in conflict with North American religious and cultural mores, seems even more incongruous and unacceptable in the context of conservative, Old World values. Furthermore, the rift that occurs between parent and child over sexual orientation is set in the context of an existing conflict as the child pulls away from the Old World culture to espouse the North American way of life. (Tremble et al., 1989, p. 255)

In the eyes of the parents, homosexuality is just another evil of this North American way of life.

> Paradoxically, these values [as well as the importance of family ties that appear to be so prevalent among immigrant groups] also provide the pathway to reconciliation between homosexual children and parents. When the love of children and the value of family ties are strong, nothing, including homosexuality, will permanently split the family. Ultimately, when the family system is bound by love and respect, a way is found to embrace the homosexual member. (Tremble et al., 1989, p. 257)

As an adolescent or as an adult, to be a lesbian in the midst of an immigrant community involves not only a choice about one's own life but also a choice that affects the community's perception of both itself and the family from which the lesbian comes. Coming out may jeopardize not only family ties but also the possibility of serving the community in which the talents of all members are such an important asset. Because many lesbian immigrants are single and self-supporting after adolescence and not encumbered by the demands of husband and children, frequently their educational level may be relatively higher than that of other women in the same migrant ethnic group and class. It is my impression (see, e.g., Espín, 1987a) that lesbians constitute a disproportionate number of the immigrant women who are involved in services and advocacy in their communities. At the same time, many of them feel constrained in the possibility for serving their community out of concern over being discovered and rejected by the same community they serve (Espín, 1990). All pressures on immigrant women's sexuality, however, do not come from inside their own culture. The host society also imposes its own burdens and desires through prejudices and racism.

When migrants cross borders, they also cross emotional and behavioral boundaries. Becoming a member of a new society stretches the boundaries of what is possible in several ways. It also may limit what could have been possible in the country of origin. One's life and roles change and, with them, identities change as well. The identities expected and permitted in the home culture may no longer be those expected or permitted in the host society. Boundaries are crossed when new identities and roles are incorporated into life. Most immigrants and refugees who, either eagerly or reluctantly, cross geographical borders do not fully suspect all the emotional and behavioral boundaries they are about to cross.

Migration, even when willingly chosen and eagerly sought, produces a variety of experiences with significant consequences for the individual. No matter how glad the immigrant or refugee might be to be in a new country, the transitions created by immigration often result in loneliness due to the absence of people with shared experiences; strain and fatigue from the effort to adapt and cope with cognitive overload; feelings of rejection from the new society that affect self-esteem and may lead to alienation; confusion in terms of role expectations, values, and identity; shock resulting from the differences between the two cultures; and a sense of uprootedness and impotence resulting from an inability to function competently in the new culture.

For lesbians, the crossing of borders and the subsequent crossing of boundaries take specific forms. Migration—and the acculturation process that follows—open up different possibilities (Espín, 1984, 1987a, 1987b, 1990). For example, some women become employed outside the home for the first time in their lives after the migration. Many of them encounter new opportunities for education. All of them are confronted with new alternative meanings of womanhood provided by the host society. Frequently, newly encountered sex role patterns combined with greater access to paid employment for women create possibilities to live a new lifestyle that may have been previously unavailable. One case in point is an openly lesbian life. The crossing of borders through migration may provide for many women the space and the *permission* to cross boundaries and transform their sexuality and sex roles. For lesbians, an additional border/boundary crossing takes place that relates to the coming out process. Coming out might have occurred in the home country. It might have occurred after the migration, as part of the acculturation process. Or, in some cases, it might have been the motivating force behind the migration. Many of these women have experienced discrimination because of their sexuality before the migration. After the migration, some experience discrimination based on sexual orientation combined with ethnic discrimination.

Although lesbianism is not only about sex, it is, obviously, closely connected with sexual behavior and identity. Sexuality is a universal component of human experience, yet how it is embodied and expressed is not. Sexuality, as we know, is culturally variable rather than being an immutable biological force. Even what is considered to be sexual or not in one cultural context is often strikingly different for people in different cultural environments. These cultural constructs inextricably inform the expression of all lesbian sexuality and demand learning *how to be a lesbian* in the host country regardless of previous experiences in the home country. Lesbians who have come out in their country of birth may have developed patterns of behaving and relating that might not fit the prevalent accepted codes of behavior among lesbians in the new country.

Cultural traditions, colonial and other forms of social oppression, national identity, and the vicissitudes of the historical process inform the development and perception of female sexuality and the creation of patterns of behavior among lesbians. Worldwide, definitions of what constitutes appropriate sexual behavior are strongly influenced by male sexual pleasure. Even for lesbians, these definitions carry a strong weight—even if not altogether conscious. These definitions are justified in the name of prevalent values in a given society: nationalism, religion, morality, health, science, and so forth. Worldwide, women are enculturated and socialized to embody their sexual desire or lack thereof through their particular culture's ideals of virtue. The social group's expectations are inscribed in women's individual desire and expressed through their sexuality. Not that gay men's sexuality is not subjected to conscious and unconscious controls by society; however, the expectation of conformity to society's sexual norms exercises pressures on all women's sexuality—regardless of sexual orientation.

Even though racism may be expressed subtly, the immigrant woman finds herself between the racism of the dominant society and the sexist and heterosexist expectations of her own community. The racism of the dominant society makes the retrenchment into tradition appear to be justifiable, and the rigidities of tradition appear to justify the racist/prejudicial treatment of the dominant society. Moreover, the effect of racism and sexism is not only felt as pressure from the outside but also becomes internalized, as are all forms of oppression.

Immigrant and refugee women who are lesbian develop their identity against the backdrop of these contradictions. Thus, we need to increase our knowledge and understanding of how the contradictions and interplays of sexuality/gender and racism in both the home and the host cultures are experienced and made sense of by lesbian migrants. My own research seeks to increase knowledge and understanding of sexuality and gender-related issues among immigrant and refugee women (Espín, 1987a, 1994)—specifically, by exploring the main issues and consequences entailed in crossing both geographical and psychological borders and boundaries and researching how sexuality and identity in lesbian women are affected by the migration. Both the importance of geography and place and the role of a second language are crucial in understanding the experience of immigrant lesbians.

As stated earlier, the crossing of borders through migration may provide for women the space and permission to cross other boundaries and transform their sexuality and sex roles. The notion that "identity is not one thing for any individual; rather, each individual is both located in, and opts for a number of differing and, at times, conflictual, identities, depending on the social, political, economic and ideological aspects of their situation" (Bhavnani & Phoenix, 1994, p. 9) is particularly significant when studying the experiences of lesbian migrants, because it is a central component of their psychology.

Immigrants are preoccupied with geography, with the place in which events occur (Espín, 1992). This preoccupation is connected with concerns about the possibility of events in the life course, because this possibility has been and is still being affected by the vicissitudes of place and geography. This phenomenon has two components. One is the engrossment with the vicissitudes of the country of origin that gives that place almost a sense of unreality in spite of its constant psychological presence in the life of the immigrant. The other is a fixation on *what could have been* that translates into ruminations about life's crossroads. "The migration experience creates an emergent phenomenology of incessant reference group comparisons and trade-offs between the benefits of the host society and the losses incurred in departing from the society of origin" (Rogler, 1994, p. 704). Reflections about life's possibilities, had the immigrant continued to live in the country of birth or immigrated into another country or had the immigration taken place at this or that stage of life, as well as other "what if's" are frequently present.

For immigrant and refugee lesbians, this preoccupation is tied to the process of coming out. It is inextricably linked to the process of developing a lesbian identity. Some lesbians are preoccupied with the relationship between childhood events and having become a lesbian. To this, the immigrant lesbian adds thoughts and concerns about what could have been concerning her lesbianism, concentrated in a basic question: Would I have become a lesbian if I had not emigrated? The Cuban American lesbian writer Achy Obejas (1994) illustrates these concerns in a recent story, when she ponders:

> What if we'd stayed? What if we'd never left Cuba? . . . What if we'd never left. . . . I wonder, if we'd stayed then who, if anyone . . . would have been my blond lovers, or any kind of lovers at all. . . . I try to imagine who I would have been if Fidel had never come into Havana sitting triumphantly on top of that tank, but I can't. I can only think of variations of who I am, not who I might have been. (pp. 124-125)

This preoccupation is of course connected with the process of acculturation that all migrants experience in their adaptation to their new country, and all lesbians and gay men undergo in the process of coming out. The immigrant lesbian acculturates as an immigrant and sometimes as a lesbian at the same time. As already discussed, even when she was a lesbian before the migration, she needs to learn to be a lesbian in her new cultural context. If she comes from a background other than European, she also has to acculturate as a so-called minority person.

> Identity development for persons of ethnic or racial minority groups [or immigrants] involves not only the acceptance of an external reality than can rarely be changed (e.g., being black, Puerto Rican, Jewish, or Vietnamese),

but also an intrapsychic "embracing" of that reality as a positive component of one's self. By definition, in the context of a heterosexist, racist, and sexist society, the process of identity development for [immigrant and refugee lesbians] . . . entails the embracing of "stigmatized" or "negative" identities. Coming out to self and others in the context of a sexist and heterosexist American society is compounded by coming out in the context of [what is usually] a sexist and heterosexist . . . [culture of origin, itself] immersed in racist society. (Espín, 1987a, p. 35)

I am specifically interested in discerning lesbians' comfort with descriptive terms about lesbianism in their first language. The preferential use for one language over another is deeply related to identity but also to other factors not yet studied (see, e.g., Espín, 1984, 1987b, 1992, 1994; Wierzbicka, 1994). For lesbians, the integration of the two languages when addressing sexuality may be a step toward integrating both cultural backgrounds. Conversely, the exclusive preference of one language over another may be an effort at compartmentalizing the contradictions inherent in being a lesbian and an immigrant. Through formal and informal interviews, I have explored variations in the speakers' comfort (or discomfort) when addressing sexuality in the mother tongue or in English. Even among immigrants who are fluent in English, the first language often remains the language of emotions (Espín, 1987b, 1992). Thus, speaking in a second language may distance the immigrant woman from important parts of herself. Conversely, a second language may provide a vehicle to express the inexpressible in the first language—either because the first language does not have the vocabulary or because the person censors herself from saying certain taboo things in the first language (Espín, 1984, 1987b, 1994). I contend that the language in which messages about sexuality are conveyed and encoded affects the language chosen to express sexual thoughts, feelings, and ideas and reveals important clues to one's identity process.

Two apparently contradictory patterns concerning language emerge for lesbian migrants. It is apparent that some of them could express themselves better in their first language; however, although it is easier to use their first language in terms of vocabulary, they apparently feel that it is easier to talk about lesbianism, sexuality, and related topics in their second language.

Other migrant lesbians, on the other hand, seem unable to have conversations about sexuality in their first language, because they actually do not know the vocabulary needed to talk about sexuality in their native language. These women have usually migrated at an earlier age than the first group, frequently before or during early adolescence. They have developed their knowledge of sex and, obviously, have come out while immersed in English.

Is the migrant lesbian's preference for English when discussing sexuality motivated by characteristics of English as a language, or is it that a second language offers a vehicle to express thoughts and feelings that cannot be expressed in the first language? Or does the new cultural context, in which English is spoken, allow more expression of the woman's feelings? Acquired in English, these experiences and expressions may become inextricably associated with the language (as happens with professional terminology acquired in a second language). In any case, many immigrant lesbians resort to their second language when describing their sexuality.

Aside from the obvious conclusion that both lesbian studies and migration studies are enriched by understanding the lesbian experience in an international perspective, we can derive some practical implications for primary prevention and for the practice of psychotherapy from the preceding discussion.

We can reasonably assume that the stresses of the migration, combined with the stresses of the coming out process, need to be managed before they may prove to be too much for some immigrant and refugee lesbians. Any program of prevention should take into consideration the anger and frustration, the feelings of loss, guilt, and confusion experienced by immigrant and refugee women, lesbians or not. It should also take into consideration that the new environment may be providing new openings that are exhilarating and self-enhancing and may compensate for other losses.

The service provider needs to be very aware of her own ethnic biases when working with this population and not assume automatic understanding simply because of a common lesbianism. On the other hand, the service provider should not assume automatically that lesbians are *more oppressed* in other countries. It may well be that the relationships among women in the country of origin provide a more comfortable and guiltless opportunity for relating to other lesbians (e.g., Gay, 1993). The construction of sexuality in many societies may validate variant sexual behavior for women (Blackwood, 1993). Indeed, cross-culturally, the construction of lesbianism shatters some basic assumptions about women.

As with all lesbians and with all migrants, it must be remembered that each woman's choices express something about not only who she is as an individual but also what her cultural values are. Lesbian choices, like any behavior that violates cultural norms, can represent a high personal cost to any woman. Yet, the possibility of being "true to yourself" may produce growth and be deeply satisfying for the migrant lesbian. On the other hand, any encouragement of coming out as a lesbian should be done with sensitivity to other components of the migrant woman's identity.

As with all people who come from different countries, there is as much danger in explaining individual differences away as culturally determined as there is in ignoring the impact of cultural differences on each woman's choices.

We need to learn to see lesbian migrants (and all immigrants and refugees, for that matter) "not only as victims of structural forces or as robots computing cost benefits of their moves" (Hondagneu-Sotelo, 1994, p. 6) but rather as human agents discovering themselves and creating themselves anew through their "nomadic" experiences—an apt concept developed by European feminist Rosi Braidotti (1994). In addition, there is a lot all lesbians can learn from those who have crossed many borders and boundaries in the course of their lives.

The transitions implied in the migratory process can provide additional insights into the process of coming out for all lesbians. The immigrant's acculturation into a new society is first and foremost a process of disassembling and reassembling social networks (Rogler, 1994). The process of coming out also involves a disassembling and reassembling of one's life and social networks. The immigrant's ruminations about what could have been, had she stayed in her country of birth, are paralleled by lesbians concerns about past events that are seen in a new light after the events of the present. In other words, an examination of continuities and discontinuities induced by the migration also sheds light on the continuities and discontinuities induced by the coming out process for all lesbians. It provides valuable insights into the psychological costs and benefits of refusing to live in old countries and old ways.

Notes

1. A word of clarification is needed here: I conceptualize the differences between immigrants and refugees from a psychological point of view rather than in terms of governmental decisions about who deserves one status or another. In other words, when I use the terms *immigrant* or *refugee,* I am focusing on the migrant's experience of her condition and the degree of trauma experienced, not on legal status. Usually *refugees* have experienced more traumatic events than *immigrants,* but the vicissitudes of their identity as lesbians seem to run a similar course. Thus, in this chapter I use the terms *migrant* and *immigrant* interchangeably to refer to both immigrant and refugee lesbians, and specify when I am referring only to refugees.

References

Andizian, S., Catani, M., Cicourel, A., Dittmar, N., Harper, D., Kudat, A., Morokvasic, M., Oriol, M., Parris, R. G., Streiff, J., & Setland, C. (1983). *Vivir entre dos culturas* [Living between two cultures]. Paris: Serbal/UNESCO.

Bhavnani, K-K., & Phoenix, A. (1994). Editorial introduction. Shifting identities, shifting racisms. *Feminism & Psychology, 4*(1), 5-18.

Blackwood, E. (1993). Breaking the mirror: The construction of lesbianism and the anthropological discourse on homosexuality. In D. N. Suggs & A. W. Miracle (Eds.), *Culture and human sexuality* (pp. 328-340). Belmont, CA: Wadsworth.

Braidotti, R. (1994). *Nomadic subjects.* New York: Columbia University Press.

Cole, E., Espín, O. M., & Rothblum, E. (Eds.). (1992). *Shattered societies, shattered lives: Refugee women and their mental health.* New York: Haworth.

Espín, O. M. (1984). Cultural and historical influences on sexuality in Hispanic/Latin women. In C. Vance (Ed.), *Pleasure and danger: Exploring female sexuality* (pp. 149-164). London: Routledge & Kegan Paul.

Espín, O. M. (1987a). Issues of identity in the psychology of Latina lesbians. In Boston Lesbian Psychologies Collective (Eds.), *Lesbian psychologies: Explorations and challenges* (pp. 35-55). Urbana: University of Illinois Press.

Espín, O. M. (1987b). Psychological impact of migration on Latinas: Implications for psychotherapeutic practice. *Psychology of Women Quarterly, 11*(4), 489-503.

Espín, O. M. (1990, August). *Ethnic and cultural issues in the "coming out" process among Latina lesbians.* Paper presented at the 98th Annual Convention of the American Psychological Association, Boston.

Espín, O. M. (1992). Roots uprooted: The psychological impact of historical/political dislocation. In E. Cole, O. M. Espín, & E. Rothblum (Eds.), *Refugee women and their mental health: Shattered societies, shattered lives* (pp. 9-20). New York: Haworth.

Espín, O. M. (1994, August). *Crossing borders and boundaries: The life narratives of immigrant lesbians.* Paper presented at the 102nd Convention of the American Psychological Association, Los Angeles.

Gabaccia, D. (Ed.). (1992). *Seeking common ground: Multidisciplinary studies of immigrant women in the United States.* Westport, CT: Praeger.

Gay, J. (1993). "Mummies and babies" and friends and lovers in Lesotho. In D. N. Suggs & A. W. Miracle (Eds.), *Culture and human sexuality* (pp. 341-355). Belmont, CA: Wadsworth.

Hondagneu-Sotelo, P. (1994). *Gendered transitions: Mexican experiences of immigration.* Berkeley: University of California Press.

Obejas, A. (1994). *We came all the way from Cuba so you could dress like this?* Pittsburgh, PA: Cleis.

Rogler, L. H. (1994). International migrations: A framework for directing research. *American Psychologist, 49*(8), 701-708.

Tremble, B., Schneider, M., & Appathurai, C. (1989). Growing up gay or lesbian in multicultural context. In G. Herdt (Ed.), *Gay and lesbian youth* (pp. 253-267). New York: Harrington Park.

Trumbach, R. (1977). London's sodomites. *Journal of Social History, 11*, 1-33.

Wierzbicka, A. (1994). Emotion, language, and cultural scripts. In S. Kitayama & H. R. Markus (Eds.), *Emotion and culture* (pp. 133-196). Washington, DC: American Psychological Association.

Yuval-Davis, N. (1992). Fundamentalism, multiculturalism and women in Britain. In J. Donald & A. Rattansi (Eds.), *Race, culture and difference* (pp. 278-291). London: Sage.

10

Contributions of Lesbian and Gay Parents and Their Children to the Prevention of Heterosexism

Charlotte J. Patterson

The existence of happy families in which lesbian or gay parents are raising children represents a significant challenge to longstanding, deeply held stereotypes. Even when the existence of such families is asserted only in fiction, it has proven to be extremely controversial. One well-known children's book, *Heather Has Two Mommies* (Newman, 1989), depicts the life of Heather, who is growing up as the daughter of a lesbian couple. The book explains how Mama Jane and Mama Kate wanted to have a child and found a doctor to help them, and how their daughter Heather is growing up happily among children in many different kinds of families.

This book has ignited acrimonious controversies in school districts across the country (Barbanel, 1993; Dillon, 1993). Some educators have argued that children should not be allowed to read stories like this one about children who are growing up in lesbian or gay families. Some parents have demanded that the book be removed from school libraries, and some school board members have suggested that youngsters ought to be protected even from the idea that lesbian families might exist. Indeed, the American Library Association recently listed the book as second on its list of 10 "most often challenged" books of the year (McCarthy, 1995). On the other hand, large numbers of teachers, parents, and school administrators across the country strongly support the use of books like this one (Henry, 1993).

Another book in this genre, also written for children, is *Daddy's Roommate* (Wilhoite, 1990). In this book, a boy's heterosexual parents divorce and his father begins to live with another man. The boy enjoys spending time with his father and the new roommate, but wonders about their relationship. His mother explains that what the two men feel for each other is "just one more kind of love" (Wilhoite, 1990, p. 26), and the boy is happy. This book was #1 on the American Library Association's recent list of most challenged books (McCarthy, 1995).

It is easy to understand how books like *Heather Has Two Mommies* and *Daddy's Roommate* could generate controversy. The possibility depicted by these books—that children can grow up happy and healthy in loving lesbian and gay families—is precisely the idea that heterosexist prejudice is at pains to deny. As the realities of family life shift to create more children with openly lesbian and gay parents, books like *Heather Has Two Mommies* and *Daddy's Roommate* make it easier for everyone to imagine what indeed appears to be the case—that even in the face of prejudice and discrimination, it is possible for loving lesbian and gay parents to raise competent, well-adjusted children. That contemplation of this possibility, even in fiction, is viewed by some adults as alarming or controversial illustrates clearly the need for work in this area.

If even *fiction* about lesbian mothers, gay fathers, and their children is controversial, research designed to uncover the *facts* is bound to generate heated discussion. I will describe below some research that I and others have conducted with lesbian mothers and their children and will provide an overview of the research findings to date. I will turn then to describe some implications, as yet untested, that the research may have for the prevention of heterosexism.

Mental Health of Lesbian Mothers and Their Children

Although it is not well-known by many heterosexuals, lesbian mothers and their children have been in existence for many years (Golombok, Spencer, & Rutter, 1983; Green, 1978; Hoeffer, 1981; Kirkpatrick, Smith, & Roy, 1981). Most often, women have borne children in the context of heterosexual relationships and have later come out as lesbians, generally in the context of a divorce; many such divorced women have raised their children as lesbian mothers. Despite psychological, judicial, and popular prejudices against such mothers and against their children (Falk, 1989; Hitchens, 1979/1980; Ricketts & Achtenberg, 1990), a substantial body of research has failed to identify any significant developmental differences between children of lesbian mothers and children of otherwise comparable heterosexual parents (Patterson, 1992, 1995c, 1995d). In study after study, children of divorced lesbian mothers are found to be essentially indistinguishable from children of divorced heterosexual mothers on a variety of important psychosocial outcomes (Green & Bozett, 1991; Patterson, 1992, 1995c, 1995d).

In contrast to divorced lesbian mothers, those of the so-called lesbian baby boom (Martin, 1993; Patterson, 1992; Riley, 1988; Weston, 1991) came out as lesbians first and only later had children. Relatively little research has been conducted with such families, and there are few data as yet about adjustment among the mothers or development among the children of the lesbian baby boom. Apart from my own work, and in addition to contemporary anthropological research (e.g., Lewin, 1993; Weston, 1991), a handful of studies in the published literature focus directly on the children of the lesbian baby boom (Flaks, Ficher, Masterpasqua, & Joseph, 1995; McCandlish, 1987; Steckel, 1985, 1987). The existing studies have documented healthy adjustment among both mothers and children of lesbian baby boom families, but share a number of limitations. Much remains to be learned about the lives of lesbian mothers and their children (Allen & Demo, 1995; Patterson, 1995c, 1995d).

In this context, I designed the Bay Area Families Study to contribute to the understanding of development among children born to or adopted by lesbian mothers. In the space available here, I summarize some of the aims of the study, describe its methodology, and explain some of the principal findings to date. Additional details and commentary are available elsewhere (Patterson, 1994, 1995a, 1995b; Patterson & Kosmitzki, 1995). There were no differences in the findings for boys and girls, so this variable is not mentioned further. All findings described as statistically significant reached the $p < .05$ level or better; individual research articles should be consulted for details of the statistical procedures.

For a family to be eligible to participate in the Bay Area Families Study, at least one child between 4 and 9 years of age had to be present in the home. This child had to have been born to or adopted by a lesbian mother or mothers. Finally, the family had to reside in the greater San Francisco Bay Area, where the interviews were conducted. Thirty-nine eligible families were invited to participate and 37 actually did so.

Most of the 37 participating families were headed by a lesbian couple, but others were headed by a single lesbian mother or involved a separated couple maintaining de facto joint custody arrangements that involved the child's moving back and forth between two households. The mothers were mostly white, well-educated, employed, and in their late thirties at the time of the interviews. There were almost equal numbers of boys and girls and their average age was 6 years 2 months. Most children had been conceived using donor insemination, usually with sperm from an anonymous donor.

For purposes of presentation, the biological or legal adoptive mother in each family will be referred to as the *biological mother* and the other mother, if any, will be called the *nonbiological mother.* In what follows, I describe first the assessment procedures and results for mothers and then turn to those for children.

Assessment of Maternal Self-Esteem and Adjustment

Maternal self-esteem was assessed using the Rosenberg Self-Esteem Scale (Rosenberg, 1979). This scale consists of 10 statements, with four response alternatives, indicating the respondent's degree of agreement with each statement. Results were tabulated to obtain total scores, based on the recommendations contained in Rosenberg (1979).

Maternal adjustment was assessed using the Derogatis Symptom Checklist-Revised (SCL-90-R; Derogatis, 1983), which consists of 90 items addressing a variety of psychological and somatic symptoms. Each respondent rated the extent to which she had been distressed by each symptom during the past week (0 = not at all, 4 = extremely). Nine subscales (i.e., anger/hostility, anxiety, depression, interpersonal sensitivity, obsessive/compulsiveness, paranoid ideation, phobic anxiety, psychoticism, and somatization) were scored, as was a Global Severity Index (GSI), which summarized the respondent's overall level of distress.

Results for Maternal Self-Esteem and Adjustment

Total scores on the Rosenberg Self-Esteem Scale were calculated for each mother, using the method described by Rosenberg (1979). The means for both biological and nonbiological mothers were almost identical, and both were well within the range of normal functioning. These results indicate that lesbian mothers who took part in this research reported generally positive self-esteem (Patterson & Kosmitzki, 1995).

For the Derogatis SCL-90-R, nine subscale scores and one GSI for each mother were computed, and then average scores on each measure for both biological and nonbiological mothers were calculated (Derogatis, 1983). Mean scores for biological and nonbiological mothers were virtually identical for most subscales as well as for the GSI, and they were all well within a normal range. None of the scores deviated substantially from the expected mean, indicating that lesbian mothers' reports of symptoms were no greater and no smaller than would be expected among comparable groups of heterosexual women of the same age. Thus, the results for maternal adjustment revealed that lesbian mothers who took part in this study reported few symptoms and good self-esteem (Patterson & Kosmitzki, 1995).

Assessment of Child Adjustment

To assess levels of child social competence and of child behavior problems, the Child Behavior Checklist (CBCL) (Achenbach & Edelbrock, 1983) was administered. The CBCL was selected because of its ability to discriminate children in the clinical versus normative range of functioning for both internalizing (e.g., inhibited, overcontrolled behavior) and externalizing (e.g., aggressive, antisocial, or undercontrolled behavior) problems as well as in social competence. It is designed to be completed by parents. In the present study, all participating mothers completed this instrument (Patterson, 1994).

Norms for the CBCL (Achenbach & Edelbrock, 1983) were obtained from heterogeneous normal samples of 200 children aged 4 to 5 years and 600 children aged 6 to 11 years and also from equivalent numbers of children at each age who were drawn from clinical populations (e.g., those receiving services from community mental health centers, private psychological and psychiatric clinics or practices, etc.). For purposes of the present research, mean scores reported by Achenbach and Edelbrock (1983, pp. 210-214) were averaged across 4- to 5-year and 6- to 11-year age levels to provide estimates of average scores for social competence, internalizing, externalizing, and total behavior problems among normative and clinical populations at the ages studied here. To assess the extent of their resemblance to normal and clinical populations, scores for children in the current sample were compared with these figures (Patterson, 1994).

Assessment of children's self-concepts was accomplished using five scales from Eder's Children's Self-View Questionnaire (CSVQ; Eder, 1990). These scales, designed especially to assess psychological concepts of self among children from 3 to 8 years of age, assess five different dimensions of children's views of themselves. The *Aggression scale* assessed the degree to which children saw themselves as likely to hurt or frighten others. The *Social Closeness scale* assessed the degree to which children enjoy being with people and prefer to be around others. The *Social Potency scale* assessed the degree to which children like to stand out or to be the center of attention. The *Stress Reaction scale* assessed the extent to which children said they often felt scared, upset, or angry. Finally, the *Well-Being scale* assessed the degree to which children felt joyful, content, and comfortable with themselves. The CSVQ was administered individually to participating children, by using hand puppets, and their answers were tape-recorded for later scoring (Patterson, 1994).

Children's sex role behavior preferences were assessed in a standard, open-ended interview format (Patterson, 1994), such as that employed in earlier research on children of divorced lesbian mothers (e.g., Golombok et al., 1983; Green, 1978; Green, Mandel, Hotvedt, Gray, & Smith, 1986). The interviewer explained to each child that she was interested in learning more about the friends and other children that he or she liked to play with and about his or her favorite toys and other things. She then asked each child to name the friends and other children he or she liked to play with. Following this, each child was asked to name his or her favorite toys, favorite games, and favorite characters on television, in movies, or in books. The interviewer wrote down each of the child's responses. Children's responses were also tape-recorded, and the interviewer's notes were later checked for accuracy against the audiotapes.

After testing had been completed, each child's answers for each of four topics (peer friendships, favorite toys, favorite games, and favorite characters) were coded into one of four categories with regard to their sex role relevant qualities. The four categories were *mainly same-sex* (e.g., a boy reports having mostly or entirely male friends), *mixed sexes* (e.g., an even or almost even mix of sexes in the friends mentioned by a child), *opposite sex* (e.g., a girl reports having mostly or entirely male friends), and *can't tell* (e.g., an answer was unscorable, or not clearly sex-typed—for instance, children said that playing Chutes and Ladders was one of their favorite games). Because children's play groups are known to be highly sex-segregated at this age, children were expected to give mainly same-sex answers to these questions.

Results for Children's Adjustment

As expected, social competence among children with lesbian mothers was rated as normal (Patterson, 1994). Scores for children of lesbian mothers were significantly higher than those for Achenbach and Edelbrock's (1983) clinical sample but were not different from those for the normal sample. This was true for reports given by both nonbiological and biological mothers in the lesbian mother families.

Results for behavior problems revealed the same pattern. For internalizing, externalizing, and total behavior problems, scores for children of lesbian mothers were significantly lower than those for children in the clinical sample but did not differ from those in the normal sample. This was again true of reports given by both mothers in the lesbian mother families. Overall, then, the behavior problems of lesbian mothers' children were rated as significantly smaller in magnitude than those of children in the clinical sample and as no greater than those of children in the normal sample (Patterson, 1994).

On three scales of the Eder CSVQ, there were no significant differences between the self-reports of children of lesbian as compared to those of Eder's (1990) heterosexual mothers (Patterson, 1994). Specifically, there were no significant differences between children of lesbian and heterosexual mothers on self-concepts relevant to Aggression, Social Closeness, and Social Potency. Children of lesbian mothers in the present sample did not see themselves as either more or less aggressive, sociable, or likely to enjoy being the center of attention than did children of heterosexual mothers in Eder's sample.

On two scales, however, differences did emerge between children of lesbian mothers and children of heterosexual mothers. Specifically, children of lesbian mothers reported greater reactions to stress than did children of heterosexual mothers, and they also reported a greater overall sense of well-being than did children of heterosexual mothers. In other words, children of lesbian mothers said that they more often felt angry, scared, or upset but also said that they more often felt joyful, content, and comfortable with themselves than did children of heterosexual mothers.

What is the best interpretation of this difference? One possibility is that children of lesbian mothers report greater reactivity to stress because they actually experience greater stress in their daily lives than do other children. In other words, children of lesbian mothers may actually encounter more stressful events and conditions than do children with heterosexual mothers. If so, then the results for well-being would suggest that they are coping with their experience in a successful manner.

Another possibility is that, regardless of actual stress levels, children of lesbian mothers may be more willing to report their experiences of negative emotional states. If, as some writers have suggested (Pollack & Vaughn, 1987; Rafkin, 1990), children in lesbian homes have more experience with the verbal discussion of feelings in general, then they might exhibit increased openness to the expression of negative as well as positive feelings. In this view, the greater tendency of lesbian mothers' children to admit feeling angry, upset, or scared might be attributed not so much to any differences in objective levels of stress as to a greater openness to emotional experience of all kinds.

Consistent with this latter interpretation was the finding that children of lesbian mothers reported greater feelings of joy, contentedness, and comfort with themselves than did children of heterosexual mothers in Eder's (1990) sample. Although they do not rule out the possibility that children of lesbian mothers do indeed experience greater stress, the results suggest that these children may be more willing than other children to report a variety of intense emotional experiences, whether positive or negative. Because this study was not designed to evaluate alternative interpretations of these differences, clarification of these issues must await the results of future research.

The aspect of children's sexual identity studied here was that of preferences for sex role behavior (Patterson, 1994). As expected, most children reported preferences for sex role behaviors that are considered to be normative at this age (Green, 1978). For instance, every child reported that his or her group of friends was mainly or entirely made up of same-sex children. The great majority of children also reported favorite toys and favorite characters (e.g., from books, movies, or television) that were of the same sex. In the case of favorite games, a number of children mentioned games that were not clearly sex-typed (e.g., board games such as Chutes and Ladders) and hence were not categorizable; however, the great majority mentioned games that are generally associated with their own rather than with the opposite sex. In short, preferences for sex role behavior among the children of lesbian mothers studied here appeared to be quite typical for children of these ages.

Like the findings of other studies, then, the results from the Bay Area Families Study highlight the many similarities between children growing up with lesbian versus heterosexual parents. Whether these similarities are surprising depends on one's point of view. Certainly, many people who have regular contact with lesbian mothers and their children would respond to these findings as familiar. For those who do not know many lesbian mothers, however, and who may hold negative expectations about them or about their children, the results may prove to be more of a surprise. Some possible implications of contact between heterosexual people, lesbian mothers, and their children are considered in the following section.

Social Contacts of Lesbian Mothers and Their Children

What impact does the apparently favorable mental health and adjustment of lesbian mothers and their children have on heterosexual people with whom they come into contact? Because anti-lesbian and anti-gay attitudes are widespread, many people are likely to understand lesbian and gay identities to be stigmatized. In addition, many people believe that children in the care of lesbian or gay adults may suffer a variety of difficulties and thus expect such children to be maladjusted. When such individuals come into contact with healthy, well-adjusted lesbian mothers and their children, a conflict is thus likely to be engendered by the disparity between their expectations and their observations.

Much of the existing research on attitudes of heterosexuals toward lesbian and gay people has been guided by the *contact hypothesis*. As originally put forward by Allport (1954) in the context of research on race relations, the contact hypothesis proposes that many kinds of prejudice can be reduced by equal status contact between majority and minority groups in pursuit of common goals. Considerable support for the contact hypothesis has been generated over the years in research on race relations in the United States (Stephan, 1985). More recently, and consistent with the contact hypothesis, Herek and his colleagues have reported that contact between heterosexual, lesbian, and gay individuals is related to heterosexuals' attitudes (Herek,

1991). Among heterosexuals, those who have openly lesbian or gay friends or immediate family members are more likely to hold positive attitudes toward lesbian and gay individuals (Herek, 1988, 1994; Herek & Glunt, 1993). There is also some evidence that contact with lesbian or gay friends or close relatives influences heterosexuals' attitudes in a positive direction, as expected on the basis of the contact hypothesis (Herek & Capitanio, in press).

There are, however, a number of reasons why attitude change due to contact might not occur. First, common stereotypes suggest that lesbian mothers and their children are relatively isolated in single-sex, lesbian communities and that they have little or no contact with heterosexual family members, friends, or other heterosexual members of the community. If so, then the kinds of contacts that might affect attitudes would not take place. To evaluate this possibility, I describe findings from the Bay Area Families Study about contacts of lesbian mothers and their children with members of the extended family, with adults at day care or school settings, and in the neighborhood. Far from indicating isolation, the results suggest that children of lesbian mothers take part in a rich and diverse range of contacts with heterosexual members of their families and communities.

Contact could also fail to have hypothesized effects if lesbian mothers and their children concealed information about the parents' sexual orientation from significant others. If grandparents, teachers, day care workers, and neighbors are unaware of a mother's lesbian identity, then their interactions with her or with her children will not challenge heterosexist attitudes (Casper, Schultz, & Wickens, 1992). To evaluate this issue, I describe findings from the Bay Area Families Study about the extent to which lesbian mothers were open about their sexual identities with members of the extended family, with adults at day care or school settings, and in the neighborhood. Results suggest that, in this sample, there was considerable openness; the great majority of mothers had disclosed their identities to many of the significant others of interest here.

Given these conditions, it is thus possible to ask how contacts between lesbian mothers and their children affect attitudes among members of the extended family, school or day care workers, and adults in the neighborhood. Systematic research in this area has not yet been conducted, but a number of hypotheses can be drawn from anecdotal evidence collected in the context of the Bay Area Families Study.

As will become clear below, anecdotal evidence from the Bay Area Families Study suggests that, consistent with the contact hypothesis, contacts between lesbian mothers and their children and other people sometimes result in decreases in anti-lesbian attitudes. To the extent that this is the case, it represents an effect of lesbian childbearing that was largely unanticipated but nevertheless welcomed by mothers who took part in the study. By describing results of the study, I do not intend to suggest that lesbians or gay men should consider becoming parents to reduce heterosexist attitudes on the part of people around them. Rather, my intention is to explore some possible implications of lesbian parenthood, once it has become a reality, for others in the community.

Contacts With Members of the Families of Origin

Although common stereotypes suggest that lesbian mothers and their children are rejected by and therefore isolated from extended families, the reality would appear to be quite different. As Lewin (1993) had reported in her study of lesbian mothers, I also found that most mothers in the Bay Area Families Study indicated that their children were in regular contact with relatives in their families of origin (Patterson, 1995a).

In the Bay Area Families Study, mothers were asked to indicate how often their children had contact with grandparents, aunts and uncles, and other adults who were important to their children. Results showed that most mothers reported that their children had at least monthly contact—for example, visits, letters or cards, telephone conversations—with both a grandmother and a grandfather. Similarly, the great majority of mothers also reported that their children had at least one contact per month with an aunt and at least one with an uncle. Of course, some children had much more contact and some had less. On average, though, children were described as having once-a-month or more frequent contact with at least four adult members of the mothers' extended families of origin (Patterson, 1995a).

The mothers also described themselves as very open with family members about their sexual identities. More than 90% of lesbian mothers who had living parents or siblings said that they were definitely out to them (i.e., had disclosed their lesbian identity to them). Several others described themselves as more open with some family members than with others; for example, they reported being out to one or more but not all siblings. Families in the Bay Area Families Study, then, not only had significant amounts of contact with relatives from their families of origin but were also very likely to have disclosed the mothers' lesbian identities to relatives.

Mothers in the Bay Area Families Study often reported that their family of origin's discussion about parenting in the context of lesbian identities began *before* the child's birth. Some parents responded in very positive ways to the news that their lesbian daughter was going to become a mother herself. For example, one mother recalled,

> [My partner's] mother was right away very excited. In fact, she wrote and said that she'd like to [visit our home] after [our son] was born. She knitted him an outfit, and she started shopping for him while I was pregnant.

Even within families, however, reactions often varied tremendously from person to person. For instance, the same mother also recalled that, during her pregnancy, her life partner had "turned to her sister and said she would be an aunt, and she said, 'no, I won't'. . . . But then, when [our son] was born, she was very excited." Whereas the woman's mother had welcomed the vision of herself as a grandparent, her sister initially attempted to deny the possibility of any family relationship between herself and the child to be born. This reaction was interpreted by relatives as representing negative feelings about lesbian parenting. Over time, however, the aunt-to-be's attitude shifted and she ultimately welcomed the baby as her nephew.

The responses from this family were in various ways representative of those from the rest of the sample. First, extended families generally did not respond to lesbian motherhood in a monolithic way; on the contrary, in most families, some members were initially more positive than others. Second, family members' attitudes were often described as shifting over time. Positive initial reactions were seen as having remained stable over time but negative initial responses were not. Many mothers explained that family members who had initially responded negatively had changed their views over time, often in apparent response to the arrival of a living, breathing baby.

For many family members, one of the unexpected consequences of having a lesbian mother and her child in the family was the need to consider issues surrounding possible disclosure of this fact. For example, a woman's parents might be described as having considered how to explain the arrival of a child in the life of their unmarried daughter. In effect, family members had to decide whether they wanted to disclose their own status as relatives of lesbian mothers. One woman described her partner's parents in this way:

> It was another level of coming out for them. . . . They live in a very intense extended Jewish family, and they live where they grew up. So [there are many] couples that they've been with since high school, and they had a lot of work to do in telling everyone. . . . It must have been 9 months of work for them, once I got pregnant . . . because these people had to be told. . . . And when we had [our son], every single one of their friends sent us a card or a present, and a lot of real heartfelt notes saying "we think you'll be great parents." . . . It was really nice.

For families of origin, then, the openness of lesbian mothers about their identities created many challenges. Especially when attitudes were initially negative, family members sometimes became caught up in a conflict between wanting contact with relatives and disapproving of a relative's lesbian identity. Even after this conflict was resolved in favor of continuing family relationships, family members were still left with problems about how much to disclose to others in their circle of acquaintances. Consistent with expectations based on the contact hypothesis, shifts that were described by mothers in this sample were almost uniformly in the direction of more positive attitudes over time.

Contacts With Adults and Children at School and Day Care

Another way in which families come into contact with new people is through their children's school and day care arrangements (Casper et al., 1992). The great majority of children whose families took part in the Bay Area Families Study were involved in some type of school or day care arrangement outside the home. Among the 37 families who participated in the study, 18 children attended elementary school and 17 were enrolled in some type of child care arrangement outside the home. One 4-year-old had not yet begun any regular out-of-home activities, and one family provided home schooling for their child of elementary school age. These families were the exception, however, and participation in school or day care was the rule among families in this sample.

Lesbian mothers often mentioned concerns about managing identity disclosure in the context of day care and especially school environments. Mothers who took part in the Bay Area Families Study generally handled these issues by being as open and positive as possible; all of the participating mothers described themselves as open about their lesbian identities to some or all of the personnel at the children's school or day care setting. One mother described the strategy that she and her partner used like this: "[One] issue is parent-teacher conferences. We both go. We just say, 'Hi, I'm [one mother's first name], I'm [other mother's first name], we're the parents." Another mother reported using a similar approach: "We just go in there acting like there's nothing unusual at all . . . there's just two moms."

For the most part, mothers described the receptions they received at school in positive terms. For instance, one mother said, "[Even though we live in a conservative area], we have not come across any outright discrimination. [Our son's] school knows that he has two moms, and it's never been an issue."

Based on reports like these, it would appear that schoolteachers and administrators are encountering children from these openly lesbian-parented homes without much incident. Over and above such contacts with adults, however, children of lesbian mothers who are enrolled in school or attend day care programs are also, of course, in contact with other children. The effects of such contacts on children of heterosexual parents have not yet been widely studied but may be of interest, as suggested by the following story told by one lesbian mother:

> Our straight friends who have two kids and we see all the time, their son got into a discussion at school, a little argument with the other pupils about whether same-sex partners can get married. He was like, what do you mean? They do it all the time.

Children whose classmates have lesbian or gay parents are likely to learn about their families, regardless of whether the formal school curriculum includes this topic. Attitudes are likely to be affected by such contacts, and it will be helpful to learn more about how and when such effects occur.

At school, then, children of lesbian mothers encounter a wide range of other children and adults. To the degree that they are open about mothers' sexual identities, such contacts provide educational opportunities for many heterosexual individuals whose ideas about child rearing in a lesbian or gay family may never have been put to empirical test.

Contacts With Adults and Children in the Neighborhood

Another arena in which lesbian mothers and their children may encounter new people is in the neighborhoods where the families live. Such contacts may be nourishing and supportive on the one hand, or negative and undermining on the other. Most mothers reported at least some contacts with neighbors and others living nearby. Some contacts of this kind involved adults, and some involved both adults and children. All but two mothers reported being open about their sexual identities with at least some of their neighbors, and many said that they were out to all their neighbors.

Some mothers worried about the reactions of neighbors to their lesbian identity, and especially worried about the ways in which any negative reactions might work to the detriment of their children. For instance, one mother of a 4-year-old said,

> Our next-door neighbor, he's a Baptist minister, and they have a 3½-year-old girl. They're very congenial to us. On some level, it's a problem for them, but they don't hold it against us. They just don't encourage the children to play together as much as I would.

Contacts with neighbors, although not actively negative, were nevertheless sources of concern for some families. In other families, mothers were completely open about their identities in the neighborhood, and the responses were seen as uniformly supportive. Again, one wonders how attitudes about lesbian parenting are affected among those who watch a child of lesbian parents growing up in their neighborhood.

An experience reported by a number of lesbian mothers in the Bay Area Families Study was that of having their children unexpectedly disclose information about mothers' lesbian identities to strangers. In this way, relationships with neighbors and others were often transformed in unanticipated ways. For instance, a single lesbian mother told of having hired a new babysitter. She and her daughter both liked the babysitter but they had not talked with her about the mother's lesbian identity. This mother related the following episode:

> One day, I came home, and apparently [my daughter] had announced to her that we were going to the [Gay Pride] Parade. . . . This woman was a very fundamentalist religious person, and she asked me: "I guess I have to ask you, are you gay?" And I said yes, and she told me that she couldn't work for me anymore.

This woman was distressed by the babysitter's reaction to her daughter's disclosure. From the point of view of the babysitter, though, one must note the conflict that arises when the family that she knows and likes turns out to include a lesbian mother. Even after quitting her job, this babysitter still must cope with the cognitive conflict between her attitudes on the one hand, and her personal observations of this mother and her daughter, both clearly well-adjusted, on the other. How this type of experience might affect attitudes held by the babysitter is not known.

Another mother told of suffering financial reverses and moving to a less-expensive apartment in a politically conservative neighborhood, where she worried that the neighbors might hold negative attitudes about her lesbian identity. Within weeks of moving into the new apartment, the mother overheard her daughter chatting with a new neighbor: "And I hear her telling this woman that she's new here, and she lives with her mom and her step-mom, so she has two moms, and they kiss all the time." The mother spoke of her own anxiety in being exposed in this way to a new neighbor whom she had not herself even met. Then, with a laugh, she explained her daughter's reaction, which was quite different. When her daughter came home, the mother recalled, "All she says about the conversation is, 'oh, she's new here too.' "

As adults who are concerned about how their sexual identities may affect their children, lesbian mothers may sometimes risk putting too much weight on the differences between themselves and other people. As this daughter's reaction reminded her mother, there are also many similarities between lesbian-parented and heterosexually parented families. Certainly, this is one of the central lessons of interpersonal contacts between any minority and any majority group—that although there are some areas of difference, there are also likely to be many areas of commonality on which connections can be based.

Summary and Conclusions

One lesbian mother who took part in the Bay Area Families Study explained the view she shared with many other participants about how contact between lesbian mothers, their children, and the rest of the world will affect attitudes over time. Referring to her own children and to the children of other lesbian mothers she knew, she said, "These are the kids who are going to change the world's perceptions." Through their very presence in the world and through their contacts with other people, she believed, her children and the children of her lesbian friends would serve as a counterweight against anti-gay, anti-lesbian prejudice.

The logic behind this argument is clear. Because of widespread heterosexism, negative attitudes toward lesbian mothers and their children abound, and many people believe lesbian mothers and their children to be maladjusted or otherwise disordered. According to research reported to date, however, the expectations generated by anti-lesbian prejudice appear to be incorrect. Both lesbian mothers and their children score in the normal range on assessments of mental health. Both mothers and their children also report having a wide range of contacts with members of their extended families, with people at school or day care, and with people in the neighborhood. Over time, the experiences that heterosexual individuals have with openly lesbian mothers and their children will lead to an increase in understanding and hence to declines in heterosexist attitudes.

That is a benign view that understands prejudice to stem from ignorance. In addition to sheer ignorance, however, there are a number of other reasons why people may hold negative attitudes. For example, as Herek (1991) has noted, negative attitudes toward lesbians can serve *self-expressive* functions that have nothing to do with the accuracy of beliefs underlying them. Attitudes serving a self-expressive function may relate to values of central importance to the self (e.g., denunciation of homosexuality as an expression of a religious identity) or they may involve values that are important to family members or friends (e.g., expression of negative views about lesbian or gay people in order to fit in with the perceived attitudes of family members or friends). In recent research investigating this issue (Herek, 1988, 1991, 1994), such expressive functions of negative attitudes toward homosexuality were not uncommon. Personal experience, receipt of accurate information, or both may thus be insufficient to produce attitude change among some people.

Many heterosexual parents who hold negative attitudes about homosexuality may thus be inclined to attempt to block their children's access to personal contact with and accurate information about lesbian and gay parents and their children. Such people may make efforts to remove books like *Heather Has Two Mommies* (Newman, 1989) or *Daddy's Roommate* (Wilhoite, 1990) from library shelves or, failing that, forbid their children to read them. Such steps may actually succeed, at least in the short run, in blocking many children's access to the facts as well as to fiction.

What will happen, though, when real-life Heathers and their lesbian mothers see their relatives, when they participate in neighborhood life, and when they attend school? As the fact that their relatives are lesbian or gay parents becomes known to family members, as the reality that well liked neighbors are also lesbian or gay becomes known to local residents, and as the knowledge that young people with lesbian or gay parents are among their classmates becomes evident to youngsters at school, many people will become able to make their own judgments, this time informed by personal experience. To the extent that the contact hypothesis bears out in this domain, as it has in other areas, then the relatives and neighbors of lesbian and gay parents and the classmates of their children can be expected to become less and less characterized over time by prejudice against lesbian and gay parents or against their children. Maternal reports from the Bay Area Families Study suggest that indeed this may often, though not always, be the case. One may hope that future research will evaluate these possibilities in a systematic fashion.

References

Achenbach, T. M., & Edelbrock, C. (1983). *Manual for the Child Behavior Checklist and Revised Child Behavior Profile.* Burlington, VT: University of Vermont Department of Psychiatry.

Allen, K. R., & Demo, D. H. (1995). The families of lesbians and gay men: A new frontier in family research. *Journal of Marriage and the Family, 57,* 111-127.

Allport, G. (1954). *The nature of prejudice.* New York: Addison-Wesley.

Barbanel, J. (1993, February 8). Political miscalculations threaten Fernandez's job. *New York Times,* sec. 1B, p. 2.

Casper, V., Schultz, S., & Wickens, E. (1992). Breaking the silences: Lesbian and gay parents and the schools. *Teachers College Record, 94,* 109-137.

Derogatis, L. R. (1983). *SCL-90-R administration, scoring, and procedures manual.* Towson, MD: Clinical Psychometric Research.

Dillon, S. (1993, February 11). Board removes Fernandez as New York schools chief after stormy 3-year term. *New York Times,* sec. 1A, p. 6.

Eder, R. A. (1990). Uncovering young children's psychological selves: Individual and developmental differences. *Child Development, 61,* 849-863.

Falk, P. J. (1989). Lesbian mothers: Psychosocial assumptions in family law. *American Psychologist, 44,* 941-947.

Flaks, D., Ficher, I., Masterpasqua, F., & Joseph, G. (1995). Lesbians choosing motherhood: A comparative study of lesbian and heterosexual parents and their children. *Developmental Psychology, 31,* 104-114.

Golombok, S., Spencer, A., & Rutter, M. (1983). Children in lesbian and single-parent households: Psychosexual and psychiatric appraisal. *Journal of Child Psychology and Psychiatry, 24,* 551-572.

Green, G. D., & Bozett, F. W. (1991). Lesbian mothers and gay fathers. In J. C. Gonsiorek & J. D. Weinrich (Eds.), *Homosexuality: Research implications for public policy* (pp. 197-214). Newbury Park, CA: Sage.

Green, R. (1978). Sexual identity of 37 children raised by homosexual or transsexual parents. *American Journal of Psychiatry, 135,* 692-697.

Green, R., Mandel, J. B., Hotvedt, M. E., Gray, J., & Smith, L. (1986). Lesbian mothers and their children: A comparison with solo parent heterosexual mothers and their children. *Archives of Sexual Behavior, 7,* 175-181.

Henry, T. (1993, January 12). Making gays and lesbians part of the rainbow curriculum. *USA Today,* sec. 4D, p. 1.

Herek, G. M. (1988). Heterosexuals' attitudes toward lesbians and gay men: Correlates and gender differences. *Journal of Sex Research, 25,* 451-477.

Herek, G. M. (1991). Stigma, prejudice, and violence against lesbians and gay men. In J. Gonsiorek & J. Weinrich (Eds.), *Homosexuality: Research implications for public policy* (pp. 60-80). Newbury Park, CA: Sage.

Herek, G. M. (1994). Assessing heterosexuals' attitudes toward lesbians and gay men: A review of empirical research with the ATLG scale. In B. Greene & G. Herek (Eds.), *Lesbian and gay psychology: Theory, research and clinical applications* (pp. 206-228). Thousand Oaks, CA: Sage.

Herek, G. M., & Capitanio, J. P. (in press). Some of my best friends: Intergroup contact, concealable stigma, and heterosexuals' attitudes toward gay men and lesbians. *Personality and Social Psychology Bulletin.*

Herek, G. M., & Glunt, E. K. (1993). Interpersonal contact and heterosexuals' attitudes toward gay men: Results from a national survey. *Journal of Sex Research, 30,* 239-244.

Hitchens, D. (1979/80). Social attitudes, legal standards, and personal trauma in child custody cases. *Journal of Homosexuality, 5,* 1-20, 89-95.

Hoeffer, B. (1981). Children's acquisition of sex-role behavior in lesbian-mother families. *American Journal of Orthopsychiatry, 5,* 536-544.

Kirkpatrick, M., Smith, C., & Roy, R. (1981). Lesbian mothers and their children: A comparative survey. *The American Journal of Orthopsychiatry, 51,* 545-551.

Lewin, E. (1993). *Lesbian mothers: Accounts of gender in American culture.* Ithaca, NY: Cornell University Press.

Martin, A. (1993). *The lesbian and gay parenting handbook: Creating and raising our families.* New York: HarperCollins.

McCandlish, B. (1987). Against all odds: Lesbian mother family dynamics. In F. Bozett (Ed.), *Gay and lesbian parents* (pp. 23-38). New York: Praeger.

McCarthy, S. (1995, February 8). Book banners can't keep kids down. *Newsday,* sec. A-8, p. 1.

Newman, L. (1989). *Heather has two mommies.* Boston: Alyson.

Patterson, C. J. (1992). Children of lesbian and gay parents. *Child Development, 63,* 1025-1042.

Patterson, C. J. (1994). Children of the lesbian baby boom: Behavioral adjustment, self-concepts, and sex-role identity. In B. Greene & G. Herek (Eds.), *Contemporary perspectives on lesbian and gay psychology: Theory, research, and application* (pp. 156-175). Thousand Oaks, CA: Sage.

Patterson, C. J. (1995a). *Families of the lesbian baby boom: Children's contacts with grandparents, other relatives, and adults outside the family.* Manuscript in preparation, Department of Psychology, University of Virginia.

Patterson, C. J. (1995b). Families of the lesbian baby boom: Parents' division of labor and children's adjustment. *Developmental Psychology, 31,* 115-123.

Patterson, C. J. (1995c). Lesbian and gay parenthood. In M. H. Bornstein (Ed.), *Handbook of parenting: Vol. 3. Status and social conditions of parenting* (pp. 255-274). Hillsdale, NJ: Lawrence Erlbaum.

Patterson, C. J. (1995d). Lesbian mothers, gay fathers, and their children. In A. R. D'Augelli & C. J. Patterson (Eds.), *Lesbian, gay and bisexual identities over the lifespan: Psychological perspectives* (pp. 262-290). New York: Oxford University Press.

Patterson, C. J., & Kosmitzki, C. (1995). *Families of the lesbian baby boom: Maternal mental health, household composition, and child adjustment.* Unpublished manuscript, Department of Psychology, University of Virginia.

Pollack, S., & Vaughn, J. (1987). *Politics of the heart: A lesbian parenting anthology.* Pittsburgh, PA: Cleis.

Rafkin, L. (1990). *Different mothers: Sons and daughters of lesbians talk about their lives.* Ithaca, NY: Firebrand.

Ricketts, W., & Achtenberg, R. (1990). Adoption and foster parenting for lesbians and gay men: Creating new traditions in family. In F. W. Bozett & M. B. Sussman (Eds.), *Homosexuality and family relations* (pp. 83-118). New York: Harrington Park.

Riley, C. (1988). American kinship: A lesbian account. *Feminist Issues, 8,* 75-94.

Rosenberg, S. (1979). *Conceiving the self.* New York: Basic Books.

Steckel, A. (1985). *Separation-individuation in children of lesbian and heterosexual couples.* Unpublished doctoral dissertation, Wright Institute Graduate School, Berkeley, CA.

Steckel, A. (1987). Psychosocial development of children of lesbian mothers. In F. W. Bozett (Ed.), *Gay and lesbian parents* (pp. 75-85). New York: Praeger.

Stephan, W. G. (1985). Intergroup relations. In G. Lindzey & E. Aronson (Eds.), *Handbook of social psychology* (Vol. 2, pp. 599-658). New York: Random House.

Weston, K. (1991). *Families we choose: Lesbians, gays, kinship.* New York: Columbia University Press.

Wilhoite, M. (1990). *Daddy's roommate.* Boston: Alyson.

PART III

Societal Structures and Social Change

11

Societal Reaction and Homosexuality: Culture, Acculturation, Life Events, and Social Supports as Mediators of Response to Homonegative Attitudes

Michael W. Ross

There is an important interaction between the way cultures and societies organize and structure homosexuality and the way the homosexual individual both perceives that structure and responds to it. One of the most significant, in terms of mental health, is the perception of a homonegative response and the internalization of that homonegative response. Although the term *homonegative attitude* is the more accurate one and is preferable to the term *homophobia* because there is frequently no classical phobic reaction in homonegative attitudes, there is widespread currency of the term *homophobia,* which colloquially is synonymous with *homonegative attitudes* as used in this chapter. The research described here is based on homosexual and gay men, and it is unclear how the findings may generalize to lesbians.

In this chapter, I intend to pose, and answer, four questions. First, how do cultures and societies structure and organize homosexuality? Second, what is the impact of homonegative attitudes on homosexual men? Third, what are the barriers to the negative impact of homonegative attitudes, including social supports and acculturation into gay subcultures? And fourth, how are homonegative attitudes internalized? I use societal reaction theory (Lemert, 1951, 1972) as the major base for examining homonegative attitudes and their production and imposition in Western societies.

Societal reaction theory, also known as *labeling theory,* links deviance and social control as integral parts of the same system, contrasting heterosexuality as conformity to the norm and homosexuality (among other sexual behaviors) as deviance. Lemert (1951, 1972) distinguishes between labeling and its consequences, and public labeling (such as being publicly identified through criminal prosecution or through coming out or being outed) as opposed to private labeling by the individual of one's own behaviors. This distinction is described as primary deviance (imposed labeling) as compared with control or labeling from within (secondary deviance). It is difficult to talk about actual societal reaction to homosexuality in any society, because there is inevitably a disjuncture between the official attitudes and their implementation, for example, in societies where there are criminal sanctions against homosexual behavior that are almost never enforced, or where individuals may express negative attitudes but be relatively accepting of particular homosexual persons (LaPiere, 1934). However, societal reaction theory is more concerned with the procedure of labeling rather than the consequences, so this chapter will extend this to self-labeling and the process and consequences of internalization of societal reaction to homosexuality.

Rather than distinguish social control by the agent of labeling (societal agencies or self), as Lemert does, in the present investigation it is more useful to look at the impact on the individual—that is, how the label is *accepted* rather than how it is *conferred*. Sagarin and Kelly (1975) have described this as "vulnerability"—the anticipated nature and strength of reactions. In this chapter, I will extend this to the *response* to this vulnerability and describe both the mechanisms by which the societal reaction is internalized and the mental health consequences of this internalization.

Impact of Society on Homosexual Behavior

At the level of society, one of the first questions that must be asked is whether the society within which the homosexual exists affects the way the homosexual behaves. What are the impacts of an anti-homosexual society? One hypothesis is that heterosexism affects the roles of homosexual men. If a sexual relationship is seen as valid only between a male and a female, then this norm may be imposed on other relationships, including homosexual ones. This might be expressed in the form that one partner should fill a masculine role and the other a feminine one, or the belief that if one loves another man, then one must think of oneself to some extent as feminine. There are at least two aspects of society that may contribute to such heterosexism: the sex role rigidity and conservatism of that society, and the degree of homonegative attitudes in that society. At least three bodies of work have contributed to this hypothesis. McIntosh (1968) described the "homosexual role"—a common heterosexual stereotype internalized by homosexual men of homosexual men as feminine. Gagnon and Simon (1973) suggest that homosexual men played sexual roles explicitly modeled on heterosexual ones as the only available role models; and Ross, Rogers, and McCulloch

(1978) suggest that such roles are societally imposed rather than integral to a homosexual orientation.

This hypothesis on the impact of heterosexism on homosexual men was tested by Ross (1983b), comparing Sweden, a comparatively sex role liberal and homopositive society, with Australia (and specifically two states, Victoria and Queensland, with penalties of 5 and 12 years in prison, respectively, for homosexual contact). The two countries were very similar in population size, industrialization, and, on a measure of sociopolitical similarity (Banks & Gregg, 1965), were rated as almost identical (0.918 and 0.917, respectively). Specifically, it was postulated that there would be greater opposite sex gender roles in the more anti-homosexual and conservative society, providing a societal basis for role modeling. Using the Bem Sex Role Inventory as a measure, there were no significant differences between the two countries on sex role in *heterosexual* men, but significant differences in feminine sex role in the expected direction in *homosexual* men (Australia had double the proportion of Sweden). There were significant differences for both groups in sex role conservatism, confirming the premise that Australia was more sex role conservative than Sweden. Thus, there was significantly more feminine sex role expression in gay men in Australia, the more anti-homosexual and sex role rigid society, as compared with Sweden, which is less anti-homosexual and sex role rigid. These data do indicate that heterosexism (anti-homosexual climate) and sex role rigidity subtly but clearly influence the expression of homosexual behavior, at least in terms of social sex roles, by the more salient imposition (and, by extension, internalization) of heterosexual norms of sex roles. Thus, it appears that the dominance of the heterosexual model will lead to expression of its structures and norms in homosexual men.

Marriage in Homosexual Men

A further question, which is an extension of the previous one, concerns the ultimate internalization of heterosexism and heterosexual practice, heterosexual marriage, in homosexual men. This provides an excellent paradigm for looking at the impact of heterosexism on homosexual men. What are the societal mechanisms associated with this?

Weinberg and Williams (1974) studied homosexual men in the United States, the Netherlands, and Denmark to look at the influence of homonegative societal reaction and found no significant differences in adjustment. They took this to indicate that societal reaction against homosexuality was not associated with psychopathology. Sagarin and Kelly (1975) went further and suggested that psychopathology associated with homosexuality precedes hostile societal reaction and is independent of it. However, Ross (1978, 1983a) suggested that the critical variable mediating psychological adjustment in homosexual men was not the *actual* societal reaction but the *putative* (anticipated) societal reaction. Because there is seldom a direct societal reaction in the form of criminal sanctions on a particular individual, most societal reaction is mediated through responses of others.

In a sample of homosexual men who were currently married, had previously been married but were currently divorced or separated, and a matched group who had never been married, Ross (1983a) found no differences in the actual societal reaction to homosexuality, as measured by the way others had actually reacted to the person's homosexuality, but significant differences in putative societal reaction (measured by how they thought these others would react if they found out about the respondent's homosexuality), with the currently married group expecting the worst reaction, the divorced/separated group a less negative reaction, and the never-married group the most accepting reaction. There was no significant effect of sex role conservatism. These data suggest that those anticipating the worst societal reaction stay married and that those expecting more negative reactions to homosexuality are more likely to get married. Further, in a comparison of marriage rates in homosexual men in another study (Ross, 1983a), there were significant differences between Sweden and Australia, with there being a lower rate of marriage in Sweden (7.5%) compared with Australia (13.5%), also confirming the link between societal heterosexism and heterosexual marriage in homosexual men.

Several variables distinguished between the three groups of currently, previously, and never-married homosexual men. These included a stronger belief that homosexuality was abnormal or an illness, a lower self-acceptance as homosexual, a stronger belief that people will make life difficult for someone whom they know is homosexual, trying to conceal one's homosexuality from more people, and having a lower number of homosexual friends. These data suggest that those who expect a worse reaction are more likely to hide their homosexual orientation, including in marriage, although there are a number of other reasons for heterosexual marriage (Ross, 1983a) in addition to putative societal reaction. Thus, it is the *anticipated* rather than the *actual* societal reaction to homosexuality that leads to the adoption of the heterosexist position in homosexual men.

Relationship Between Actual and Putative Societal Reaction

The question raised by the finding that putative societal reaction to homosexuality predicts heterosexual marriage in homosexual men raises the question as to what the relationship between putative and actual societal reaction might be. If actual and putative societal reactions are significantly correlated, then one might assume that they are facets of the same phenomenon—that is, that the anticipated reaction is based on the experience of the actual reaction. However, if there is no significant correlation, then it can be hypothesized that putative societal reaction is vicarious and selective and not based on actual experience or that, alternatively, people choose carefully whom they are prepared to come out to and thus control the experience. Ross (1985) looked at a list of significant and other individuals and asked homosexual men in Sweden and Australia to rate on a 7-point scale, defined at the poles by the adjectives "Accept" and "Reject," their actual reaction to the respondent's homosexuality and their anticipated reaction. For the combined Swedish and Australian samples, the correlation between actual and putative societal reaction was −0.01. However, on examining the correlations for each country separately, these were both significant but in different directions: +0.23 for Sweden, −0.33 for Australia.

Interpretation of these data adds to an understanding of the possible mechanisms of societal reaction toward homosexuality. In Sweden, more homosexual men are likely to be out about their sexual orientation (and there is more social openness and discussion of sexuality) and thus, their anticipations about reactions of others are more likely to be based on actual knowledge and experience. In Australia, however, there are three possible interpretations. First, people may have carefully chosen those they have come out to and avoided coming out to the more negative. Second, the societal reaction and personal reactions may be incongruent, with personal reactions well ahead of societal ones, and societal reaction attributed to those to whom one is not out. Third, people may have internalized the perceived societal reaction more than the actual personal reactions of others. Essentially, the difference is between the apparently experience-driven perception of societal reaction, in the sample of Swedish homosexual men, and the apparently more myth-driven or selective response of the Australian homosexual men.

Of particular importance in the applied setting, however, are the consequences of these cross-cultural differences. On several of the measures of psychological adjustment in this study, the Australian sample scored significantly below the Swedish sample, showing more depressed inadequacy, greater beliefs that homosexuals are different from heterosexuals, greater hiding of their sexual orientation, and lower self-acceptance as homosexual. It is important to note that although there were significant differences between the two samples on putative societal reaction, there were none on actual societal reaction, again confirming that it is the putative, rather than the actual, societal reaction that is associated with a lower degree of psychological adjustment. The mental health consequences of heterosexism and homonegative attitudes relate to the putative, rather than the actual, societal reaction against homosexuality, although in less heterosexist and less homophobic societies, the process appears to change qualitatively, with the putative reaction becoming based on actual experience to a much greater extent.

Life Events and Homophobia

One of the central questions regarding the development and maintenance of homonegativism is related not only to actual reactions to homosexuality but also to the role of life events more generally. Questions relate to the impact of both actual life events and vicarious life events. The great bulk of life events research has investigated actual life events. Cohen (1988) has characterized the impact of life events on psychological functioning as being based on their accumulation, with a somewhat linear relationship between numbers and functioning. One of the methodological problems with the reporting of life events relates to the "fall-off" issue (Cohen, 1988), where recent events are remembered more reliably and more consistently than past events. A second consideration, Cohen notes, relates to the impact of major versus minor life events (hassles). Recent research suggests that hassles are more predictive of distress than major life occurrences. The models of life events do, however, emphasize that they are dynamic and recursive, with life events being both the cause and the effect of psychological status. Initial adjustment may be a predictor of subsequent events as well as affecting the rating of subsequent events. Zautra, Guarnaccia, Reich, and Dohrenwend (1988) note that even after accounting for the effects of major events, hassles do contribute significantly to the prediction of psychological outcomes.

The Relative Impact of Positive and Negative Events. Cohen (1988) notes that there is overwhelming evidence that undesirable, but not desirable, events are related to psychological functioning. Measurement issues offer indirect support, and Reich and Zautra (1988) note that measures of positive and negative feeling states are generally orthogonal. Theoretically, differences between positive and negative impacts are important, because they raise the question about the impact of social supports and acculturation as buffers or as having a direct effect on homophobia. The buffer hypothesis suggests that positive events and social supports will only mitigate negative ones where negative events exist. Tennant, Bebbington, and Hurry (1981), for example, found that positive events not having a relationship to negative events had no influence on remission of neurotic symptoms. Similarly, Reich and Zautra (1988) reported that there is a significant interaction between positive and negative events, with more positive events weakening the psychological consequences of prior negative events in those who reported more prior negative events, but having little impact in those with low negative events. The direct effect hypothesis suggests that positive events will strengthen the individual to resist negative events when they occur: Reich and Zautra (1988) note that the research evidence is consistent in that positive events lead to increased positive affect. However, Barrera (1988) also notes that a factor that may influence the presence of stress-buffering effects is the match between supportive functions and the needs that are elicited by the stressful events that individuals experience. For example, homonegative events may be buffered only by homopositive support and life events. In the absence of any research looking at homophobia, it is difficult to know whether either of these models applies to such a specific situation, because homophobia is sufficiently stigmatizing to alter the presence of positive events and social supports once a person's sexual orientation becomes known, thus making it difficult to separate out the impact of previous events and postevent changes. Such global changes do, however, make it possible to look at the impact of a coming out event where it is a public one and not just to specific and selected persons.

There are a number of important questions that arise from the general research on life events and social supports, and from the specific research on homonegativity, with regard to the specific case of homonegativity. First, what role do vicarious events, as compared with actual events, play in the formation of internalized homonegativity and the impact of homonegativity on homosexual persons? Second, what is the impact of "inoculation" against adverse life events (prior exposure to stress assisting in adaptation to later stress: Eysenck, 1983). This concept would suggest that there may be an inverted U-shaped relationship between stress and psychological functioning. Third, what is the impact of the centrality of life events—for example, where an event such as being outed or coming out may be more central to a person's identity and self-concept or self-esteem than some other event, such as one related to occupation. Fourth, the issue of controllability is also important, with controllable events being likely to reduce stress. This may have important implications for research into homonegativity, with less controllable events such as being outed rather than being able to choose the time, place, and persons to whom one comes out presumably leading to greater adverse impacts. Controllability may, as Cohen (1988) has already suggested, be an important covariate in the impact of life events, although he notes that the literature for controllable versus uncontrollable events is inconsistent in its findings.

Gay Life Events

What is the evidence for gay life events (including heterosexism and homonegative attitudes) affecting psychological adjustment? First, it is important to determine what life events are important for gay men and whether they can be reliably measured. There are a number of life events inventories, but they have been developed without regard to sexual orientation—they include events such as wife-husband interactions, marriage, reproduction, and family, all of which may be inappropriate or inapplicable to homosexual people (and, by definition, heterosexist). Furthermore, events that are of significance to homosexual people—such as stigmatization, altered family relations, coming out, differences in frequency or form of relationships, and HIV/AIDS—are not represented. Consequently, Rosser and Ross (1988, 1989) developed a life events inventory for gay men, the GALES, which was initially based upon that of Tennant and Andrews (1976). However, more than 40% of the life events in Tennant and Andrews's scale were heterosexist, although some could be retained with minor changes (for example, replacing "spouse" with "lover"). Both emotional distress and life change resulting from each of the listed life events were rated on a 1 to 20 scale, where 10 was a serious illness or injury needing 1 to 2 months off work. Categories of stressors included health, bereavement, relationships, relations with friends and relatives, education, work, moving, financial and legal, sexuality, gay lifestyle, and HIV disease. The highest ratings in the two countries (Australia and New Zealand) where the GALES was tested were related to HIV disease and bereavement. The correlations between Life Change and Emotional Distress were 0.91 and 0.77 in each country, respectively, suggesting a close relationship between amount of life change required and emotional distress.

Given the development of a measure for life events that is sensitive to the gay experience and cross-nationally reliable, it was then possible to answer the question as to what the relationship between life events and mental health is in gay men. Specifically, it was now possible to test the hypothesis posed by Langner and Michael (1963) that the more socially disadvantaged the group or person, the greater the impact of life events. In a heterosexist and homonegative environment, is there a mental health impact and is this in relation to just gay-related events or to a broader spectrum of life events? It could be hypothesized that negative events lead to lowered self-esteem, which may mean that subsequent events have a greater negative impact. Ross (1990) administered the GHQ-28 (a measure of psychological functioning) and the GALES to 80 gay men and found that of the 18 events significantly associated with psychological distress, 5 were aspects of one's relationship with one's lover, 4 were related to HIV disease, and a further 4 were related to coming out issues. These data confirm that there are significant negative relationships between gay-associated lifestyle stressors and psychological functioning in gay men. Of equal significance, however, was the finding that the magnitude of the correlations between life events and psychological functioning was considerably higher than in comparable studies of hetero-sexual people. In heterosexual (or presumed heterosexual) people, these correlations were in the order of 0.15 to 0.20, whereas in the gay men, the correlations were in the order of 0.3 to 0.5. It is noteworthy that the most significant impact on psychological functioning was on the GHQ-28 scales measuring anxiety and insomnia, and somatic symptoms. These data confirm that social disadvantage (the problems caused by being homosexual in a heterosexist environment, and the impact of homonegative attitudes) does potentiate the impact of life events on homosexual people, and probably that this relationship generalizes to other disadvantaged groups. The massive im-pact of life events associated with HIV disease on psychological functioning may also need to be considered in the light of the effect of co-categorization of HIV/AIDS and homosexuality (where many homosexual men are con-sidered to have HIV disease) and the attribution of additional HIV/AIDS stigmata to homosexual men.

Social Supports

The relationship between social supports and psychological well-being is similar to that between life events and psychological well-being, with social supports playing a similar role to positive life events and being concep-tualized as having either a direct effect or a buffer effect. The stresses of homonegativity may be mitigated by social supports. Indeed, the relationship may be even closer, with homonegativity being defined as a lack of hetero-sexual social support, and homosexual social support being dependent on the availability and degree of acculturation into the gay subculture. Given the importance, noted above, of the match and specificity between the stress and the support, gay acculturation may be one of the critical variables that mediates psychological well-being and homonegativity.

The literature on social supports and stress can be summarized as concep-tualizing social support as falling into four levels. Winnubst, Buunk, and Marcelissen (1988) describe these four levels as composing structural mea-sures of social support as social integration (the number and strength of connections of individuals to significant others in their social environments). These structural measures play a role of social regulation and normative regulation by providing stable and rewarding roles, deterring the individual from ill-advised or unhealthy behavior, and maintaining stable functioning during periods of rapid social change. Social support as relationship quality emphasizes social support in terms of the subjectively experienced quality and intensity of the social relationships of the person, including their function as a psychological resource. The critical qualitative aspect of quality of social relationships may provide information that leads a person to believe he is loved and cared for (emotional support), esteemed and valued (esteem support), and part of a network of mutual obligation and communication (network support) (Cobb, 1976).

Social support as perceived helpfulness and supportiveness, according to Winnubst, Buunk, and Marcelissen (1988), is the degree to which others can be relied upon to provide advice, information, instrumental help, and empathic understanding. This understanding that others can and are willing to provide advice and support, the instrumental component of support, may lead to a perception that stresses are not particularly threatening because of this availability. Winnubst, Buunk, and Marcelissen emphasize that a distinction needs to be made between helpfulness and intimacy, because intimate others may not be able to provide needed support and information, or may provide it in an inappropriate way.

Social support as the enactment of supportive behaviors is a behavioral measure, assessing the supportive acts that occur in response to another's problems. They may be actual acts in response to a situation, or expected acts, and Winnubst, Buunk, and Marcelissen note that there are a number of taxonomies of supportive acts developed.

In the situation of homonegativity, I believe that social support in relation to specific heterosexist/homonegative contexts is the easiest way to assess social support as it may impact psychological functioning. Because general social support may come from people who are not aware of an individual's sexual orientation, and may be withdrawn or altered in response to learning of that person's sexual orientation, it is probably not a reliable measure. Furthermore, people may be prepared to offer support *in a general social context* but not in one specifically linked to sexual orientation, particularly where there is discomfort about a person's sexual orientation. For this reason, I believe that the concept of acculturation is critical to understanding social support and homonegativity. Acculturation into the gay subculture describes the context within which people develop not only the structures for social support and emotional and esteem support but also specific instrumental support relating to their sexual orientation. In the context of heterosexism, it is essentially the formation of an alternative social system to counter heterosexism.

Acculturation Into the Gay Subculture

Acculturation into racial and ethnic subcultures or into the larger society in which such subcultures are embedded has been known for some time to be associated with health and psychological consequences, both positive and negative. In the case of ethnicity, language has frequently served as a useful proxy measure; however, this is not available for the gay subculture. Instead, measures of acculturation must include measures of identification with and movement in the gay subculture. Ross, Fernández-Esquer, and Seibt (1995) have reviewed the growth of the concept of gay subculture and conclude that it has the characteristics of a separate subculture in Western nations, including in public life, gay media, gay sites, gay suburbs, gay holidays, gay tourism, gay organizations, gay clothing, gay behavior, and a gay argot; and in private life, gay social gatherings, social networks, gay professional relationships, and, of course, a gay identity that may be public or private. Involvement in the gay subculture, however, may be transient or episodic as well as relatively permanent. Measures of these may be useful indicators of the degree to which a person is acculturated into the gay subculture and the extent to which that person has gay social supports available. These social supports are, I believe, a specific buffer to heterosexism and to homonegative attitudes—the mechanism being not only the provision of all the significant sectors of social support (connections to significant others, relationship quality, perceived help and support, and enactment of supportive behaviors) but also the provision of a set of alternative norms and a sense of community. This may go further: Weston (1991) notes that families of choice have both coexisted with and, in many cases, replaced biological families for many gay people as a result of both geographical isolation and familial disapproval of the sexual orientation of a family member. Ross et al. (1995) also describe the development of gay subcultures and the development of formal communities from informal ones, suggesting that acculturation will be more possible in more formally developed gay communities. The significance of acculturation in the sexual safety of gay men has already been demonstrated as important by Seibt et al. (1995), with the more acculturated gay men engaging in less risky sex, thus suggesting that acculturation and health are associated in the gay community as in migrant communities.

Internalized Homophobia

Internalized homonegative attitudes are hypothesized to be the result of the internalization of heterosexist and homonegative norms and to be responsible for psychological dysfunction. Such internalized attitudes are also probably closely related to negative putative societal reaction to homosexuality—if they are not identical, they are probably facets of the same dimension, with internalized homonegative attitudes being the expression of negative and internalized putative societal reaction to homosexuality. However, theorizing about internalized homonegative attitudes has been restricted by the lack of clarity about what actually constitute internalized homonegative attitudes. Ross and Rosser (1996) examined the dimensions of homonegative attitudes in gay men in the United States and found that they formed four clusters: public identification as being gay, perception of stigma associated with a homosexual orientation, social comfort with other gay men, and beliefs about the moral and religious acceptability of being gay. Each of these dimensions refers either to identifying oneself as a member of a stigmatized minority or to acceptance of the heterosexist and homonegative beliefs of a society. They bring the theorizing about the processes of control and labeling of homosexual orientation full circle, to explain not only the process but also the product of societal reaction. They also provide a validation of the findings of the previously noted studies on putative societal reaction to homosexuality and a reliable measure of internalized homophobia.

Conclusions

This chapter began with the theoretical approaches (societal reaction and labeling theory) to the impact of homonegative attitudes on gay men and has refined societal reaction by noting the possible mechanisms involved in influencing the stereotyping and expression of sex roles in gay men and the importance of putative societal reaction as an explanatory variable. It has looked at heterosexual marriage in homosexual men as an expression of heterosexism, and the individual and societal variables mediating this, as well as the way societal attitudes toward sex roles and homosexuality modify the impact of heterosexism and homonegative attitudes. The measurement and impact of gay life events on psychological functioning have been described, as have the potentiating effects of stigma and minority status on the emotional distress and life change impact of life events. The role of both homosexually specific and general social supports as buffers for the negative influence of heterosexism and homonegative attitudes has been reviewed in terms of both theory and empirical data, with gay acculturation being identified as a major potential source of social support. Similarly, the development of alternative families of choice as well as alternative and homopositive norms have been postulated as buffers to heterosexist and homonegative attitudes and beliefs. Finally, the structure of internalized homonegative attitudes in gay men has been identified and its strong similarity to, and probable derivation from, negative putative societal reaction to homosexuality has been discussed. It is apparent that the phenomena associated with heterosexism and homonegative attitudes are complex, associated both with societal and individual mechanisms and with psychological adjustment. Some of the links between society, attitudes and beliefs, and behaviors and mental health in gay men have been explored, but it is apparent that there is still enormous scope for elaborating the theoretical and practical details of the links between societal control and psychological adjustment in stigmatized minorities such as gay men and lesbians, and of the roles of community and social support in providing alternative norms that are homopositive rather than heterosexist.

References

Banks, A. S., & Gregg, P. M. (1965). Grouping political systems: Q-factor analysis of a cross-polity survey. *American Behavioral Scientist, 9,* 3-6.

Barrera M. (1988). Models of social support and life stress. In L. H. Cohen (Ed.), *Life events and psychological functioning* (pp. 211-236). Newbury Park, CA: Sage.

Cobb, S. (1976). Social support as a moderator of life stress. *Psychosomatic Medicine, 38,* 300-314.

Cohen, L. H. (1988). Measurement of life events. In L. H. Cohen (Ed.), *Life events and psychological functioning* (pp. 11-30). Newbury Park, CA: Sage.

Eysenck, H. J. (1983). Stress, disease and personality: The "inoculation" effect. In C. Cooper (Ed.), *Stress research* (pp. 121-146). New York: John Wiley.

Gagnon, J. H., & Simon, W. (1973). *Sexual conduct: The social sources of human sexuality.* London: Hutchinson.

Langner, T. S., & Michael, S. T. (1963). *Life stress and mental illness: The Midtown Manhattan Study.* New York: Macmillan.

LaPiere, R. T. (1934). Attitudes vs. action. *Social Forces, 13,* 230-237.

Lemert, E. M. (1951). *Social pathology.* New York: McGraw-Hill.

Lemert, E. M. (1972). *Social problems and the sociology of deviance.* Englewood Cliffs, NJ: Prentice Hall.

McIntosh, M. (1968). The homosexual role. *Social Problems, 16,* 182-192.

Reich, J. W., & Zautra, A. J. (1988). Direct and stress-moderating effects of positive life experiences. In L. H. Cohen (Ed.), *Life events and psychological functioning* (pp. 149-180). Newbury Park, CA: Sage.

Ross, M. W. (1978). The relationship of perceived societal hostility, conformity and psychological adjustment in homosexual males. *Journal of Homosexuality, 4,* 157-168.

Ross, M. W. (1983a). *The married homosexual man: A psychological study.* London: Routledge & Kegan Paul.

Ross, M. W. (1983b). Societal relationships and gender role in homosexuals: A cross-cultural comparison. *Journal of Sex Research, 19,* 273-288.

Ross, M. W. (1985). Actual and anticipated societal reaction to homosexuality and adjustment in two societies. *Journal of Sex Research, 21,* 40-55.

Ross, M. W. (1990). The relationship between life events and mental health in homosexual men. *Journal of Clinical Psychology, 46,* 402-411.

Ross, M. W., Fernández-Esquer, M. E., & Seibt, A. (1995). Understanding across the sexual orientation gap: Sexuality as culture. In D. Landis & R. Bhagat (Eds.), *Handbook of intercultural training* (2nd ed., pp. 414-430). Thousand Oaks, CA: Sage.

Ross, M. W., Rogers, L. J., & McCulloch, H. (1978). Stigma, sex and society: A new look at gender differentiation and sexual variation. *Journal of Homosexuality, 3,* 315-330.

Ross, M. W., & Rosser, B. R. S. (1996). Measurement and correlates of internalized homophobia: A factor analytic study. *Journal of Clinical Psychology, 52,* 15-21.

Rosser, B. R. S., & Ross, M. W. (1988). Perceived emotional and life change impact of AIDS on homosexual men in two countries. *Psychology and Health, 2,* 301-317.

Rosser, B. R. S., & Ross, M. W. (1989). A gay life events scale for homosexual men. *Journal of Gay and Lesbian Psychotherapy, 1,* 87-101.

Sagarin, E., & Kelly, R. J. (1975). Sexual deviance and labeling perspectives. In W. R. Gove (Ed.), *The labeling of deviance: Evaluating a perspective* (pp. 347-379). Beverly Hills, CA: Sage.

Seibt, A. C., Ross, M. W., Freeman, A., Krepcho, M., Hedrich, A., McAlister, A., & Fernández-Esquer, M. E. (1995). Relationship between safe sex and acculturation into the gay subculture. *AIDS Care, 7*(Suppl. 1), S85-S88.

Tennant, C., & Andrews, G. (1976). A scale to measure the stress of life events. *Australian and New Zealand Journal of Psychiatry, 10,* 27-32.

Tennant, C., Bebbington, P., & Hurry, J. (1981). The short-term outcome of neurotic disorders in the community: The relation of remission to clinical factors and "neutralizing" life events. *British Journal of Psychiatry, 139,* 213-220.

Weinberg, M. S., & Williams, C. J. (1974). *Male homosexuals: Their problems and adaptations.* New York: Oxford University Press.

Weston, K. (1991). *Families we choose: Lesbians, gays, kinship.* New York: Columbia University Press.

Winnubst, J. A. M., Buunk, B. P., & Marcelissen, F. H. G. (1988). Social support and stress: Perspectives and processes. In S. Fisher & J. Reason (Eds.), *Handbook of life stress, cognition and health* (pp. 511-528). New York: John Wiley.

Zautra, A. J., Guarnaccia, C. A., Reich, J. W., & Dohrenwend, B. P. (1988). The contribution of small events to stress and distress. In L. H. Cohen (Ed.), *Life events and psychological functioning* (pp. 123-148). Newbury Park, CA: Sage.

12

The Prevention of Anti-Lesbian/Gay Hate Crimes Through Social Change and Empowerment

Jeanine C. Cogan

Violence against individual lesbians and gay men is a fact of life in the United States that threatens and intimidates all those who identify as lesbian, gay, or bisexual. The relative lack of attention to this topic from social scientists, lawmakers, politicians, and the general public reflects a heterosexist cultural milieu that both allows and further perpetuates such violence. Preventing hate crimes based on sexual orientation is imperative and requires a dynamic framework that includes both social change and individual empowerment.

The Existence of Violence Against Lesbians and Gay Men

Violent persecution of lesbians and gay men has occurred throughout history and, as some researchers suggest, may have increased over the past few decades (Dean, Wu, & Martin, 1992; Herek, 1989; National Gay and Lesbian Task Force, 1991). As the gay liberation movement has succeeded in increasing visibility and social power for lesbians and gay men, the dominant (heterosexual) group has responded through increased opposition and violent resistance.

When anti-lesbian/gay hate crimes began to receive increasing attention in the 1980s, they were not a priority for social scientists. Therefore, initial documentation of their existence comes mainly from grassroots community groups and organizations. Summarizing much of this research, Kevin Berrill (1992a) found the following median rates of lesbian/gay harassment across

AUTHOR'S NOTE: The research presented in this chapter was supported by a grant to Gregory M. Herek from the National Institute of Mental Health. I would like to acknowledge my colleagues, Gregory M. Herek and J. R. Gillis, and friend, Joanie Erickson, who provided feedback regarding this manuscript.

219

24 different studies: 9% of those surveyed experienced assault with a weapon; 17% simple physical assault; 19% vandalism and property crimes; 44% had been threatened with violence; 33% had been chased or followed; 25% had objects thrown at them; 13% had been spat upon; and 80% had been verbally harassed.

This research played a central role in the recognition of violence against lesbians and gay men as a serious social issue; however, the quality of these surveys varied widely (Berrill, 1992a). Prevalence data from studies that met more systematic methodological standards were called for. As rigorous studies by social scientists have been completed, similar rates of lesbian/gay victimization have emerged. In a pilot study of adults from Sacramento, California, my colleagues, Gregory Herek, Roy Gillis, and Eric Glunt, and I found that 11% had experienced an assault with a weapon, based on their sexual orientation, since age 16; 14% had experienced an assault without a weapon; 17% a vandalism; 45% had been threatened with violence; 32% had been chased or followed; 33% had had objects thrown at them; and the overwhelming majority (82%) had been verbally harassed (see Herek, Gillis, Cogan, & Glunt, 1995, for complete description). These findings are strikingly similar to the medians reported by Berrill (1992a) and reveal a disturbing amount of anti-lesbian/gay victimization that warrants further attention.

Anti-Lesbian/Gay Victimization
and Psychological Distress

According to Garnets, Herek, and Levy (1990) anti-lesbian/gay hate crimes may result in more psychological distress than other crimes with more long-term implications. In addition to coping with the distress caused by a victimization, victims of anti-lesbian/gay hate crimes experience an attack on their lesbian/gay identity that may cause its own set of consequences. One such consequence may be an increased sense of vulnerability associated with one's sexual identity so that being lesbian or gay becomes a source of conflict and danger rather than joy and intimacy (Norris & Kaniasty, 1991).

These potential psychological consequences of hate crimes have only recently been examined. Hershberger and D'Augelli (1995) observed moderate correlations (ranging from .21 to .28) between three different measures of victimization and general psychological distress among a sample of 165 gay youths. The authors found that victimization had a negative impact on mental health.

In a second study, with 147 adults from the Sacramento area, conducted by my colleagues and me, those lesbians, gay men, and bisexuals who experienced victimization based on their sexual orientation reported higher levels of psychological distress than others. Compared to individuals who had not been the target of a crime based on sexual orientation, those who were victims of an anti-lesbian/gay hate crime against their person (physical and sexual assault) consistently scored higher on psychological distress as measured by the Center for Epidemiologic Studies Depression scale, or CES-D (Radloff, 1977); the crime-related Post Traumatic Stress Disorder scale (PTSD; Kilpatrick et al., 1989); and the short version of Spielberger's State Anger and State Anxiety scales (Spielberger, Jacobs, Russel, & Crane, 1983).

In addition, we found evidence of respondents' beliefs about the benevolence of the impersonal world and people, personal safety, and self-worth to be negatively affected by an anti-lesbian/gay physical or sexual assault. Whereas many of the differences were of small magnitude, individuals who experienced bias-related person crimes were more fearful of future crimes and perceived themselves as more vulnerable than others. They also displayed less willingness to believe in the benevolence of people and the world. These data support the theory, proposed by Garnets and colleagues, that violence against lesbians and gay men may result in greater psychological distress than other crimes.

Hate Crimes in Context: Heterosexism

To understand the existence and consequences of anti-lesbian/gay hate crimes and to propose prevention strategies, this topic must be discussed within an appropriate context. Anti-lesbian/gay violence is an extreme and painful extension of heterosexist ideology. Heterosexism, as defined by my colleague Greg Herek (1994), is "the ideological system that denies, denigrates, and stigmatizes any non-heterosexual form of behavior, identity, relationship or community" (p. 91). Heterosexuality is designated the only acceptable sexual orientation, as is reflected through societal customs and institutions (also referred to as *cultural heterosexism*) and individual attitudes and behavior (also referred to as *psychological heterosexism*) (Herek, 1992b, 1994).

Certainly, for lesbians and gay men, everyday life serves as testimony to the existence of heterosexism. Consider the following typical examples:

1. The daily hassles of consistently and incessantly being approached with heterosexual assumptions (e.g., "Are you married?"). In addition, deciding when to challenge and if an overt challenge to these assumptions is safe (e.g., When a coworker assumes you are heterosexual, you need to weigh the costs and benefits of speaking the truth).

2. The ongoing psychological energy it takes to be out and proud in a culture that still condemns homosexuality through its institutional policies

and practices (e.g., policy on gays in the military, no right to legally marry, lack of civil rights protection).

3. The absence of cultural or social validation of lesbian/gay relationships (e.g., lack of support for a significant relationship ending, inaccurate or stereotypical depictions of lesbian/gay relationships in the media, lack of formal rituals recognizing lesbian/gay commitment).

4. The devaluation of lesbian/gay research, which is often viewed as too narrow in focus or irrelevant (which harks back to my days in graduate school, when I received the same messages about focusing on research issues important to women).

In addition to individual testimony, research with convenience samples and national survey data by social scientists document an overall disapproving and hostile attitude toward lesbians and gay men. Research with convenience samples has generally found that lesbians and gay men are consistently treated more negatively than heterosexual counterparts. More specifically, college students are more likely to decline an opportunity to meet someone when that person's sexual orientation is revealed as lesbian or gay (Kite, 1992); more likely to label a gay man as less masculine than a straight man (Karr, 1978); less likely to assist a person needing help if he or she is wearing a pro-gay T-shirt (Gray, Russell, & Blockley, 1991); more likely to rate same-sex couples as less satisfied in their relationships than heterosexual couples (Testa, Kinder, & Ironson, 1987); and more likely to blame and be less empathetic toward homosexuals with HIV than heterosexuals with HIV (Fish & Rye, 1991; Weiner, 1988, 1993). In addition, survey data with national population samples have found that the majority of respondents feel sex between two people of the same gender is wrong, disgusting, and not a natural expression of sexuality (Herek & Capitanio, in press; Herek & Glunt, 1993).

The Prevention of Hate Crimes: Creating an Agenda

Borrowing from the wisdom of the public health field, the goal of primary prevention efforts in mental health is to decrease the number of newly occurring cases of people experiencing psychological distress. Preventionists acknowledge the complex and often interacting factors that cause psychological distress, yet their fundamental emphasis is placed upon the role of environmental and social conditions (e.g., Albee, 1986; Cowen, 1991). Certainly, there is a whole literature highlighting the role of stress, as a social condition, in the cause of both physical and mental problems (e.g., Albee,

1986). Further, preventionists recognize that the individual is vulnerable to psychological distress when she or he does not have the qualities and skills to cope adequately with difficult conditions (Albee, 1986; Cowen, 1991).

Albee (e.g., 1984) proposed a prevention equation that accounts for both social conditions and the individual as a dynamic social agent.[1] The following equation, adapted from Albee's, proposes that emotional disturbance results when stress caused by exploitation overpowers the individual's ego strength.[2]

$$\text{Incidence} = \frac{\text{stress caused by exploitation}}{\text{ego strength}}$$

I had the honor of working with George Albee, who has been considered by some the father of primary prevention, while I was in graduate school at the University of Vermont. Therefore, much of my conceptualization of prevention has been greatly influenced by Albee's work. *Ego strength* is a term Albee (1984) used to encompass four critical correlates to positive mental health: competence, social support, self-esteem, and coping skills, which will be discussed in more detail later. According to this model, the goal of preventing negative mental health is to decrease stress caused by exploitation while simultaneously increasing individual ego strength. This model offers a useful conceptual framework for the prevention of anti-lesbian/gay hate crimes. First, we will discuss the top half of this model, the numerator (stress caused by heterosexism), and possible strategies for change. Second, we will discuss the denominator (increasing ego strength) of Albee's model for all individuals (as the ultimate prevention tool) and for the victims of anti-lesbian/gay violence.

Defining the Stressor: Exploitation

As is reflected in Albee's prevention model, exploitation is often a central cause of psychological distress. He has written extensively on the role of social conditions, such as involuntary unemployment, poverty, the experience of sexism, racism, and the like, in creating adult psychopathology (Albee, 1979, 1981, 1986, 1992; Albee, Joffe, & Dusenbury, 1988). Considering the importance of context, oppression, and social conditions in the etiology of psychological distress is not unique to preventionists, however. Other entire subfields, such as feminist psychology, have critiqued traditional paradigms that focus almost exclusively on individualistic explanations to psychological distress. Feminist psychologists opened up this discourse decades ago, marked by such critical works as *Women & Madness,* by Phylis Chesler, published in 1972. Chesler challenged both social conditioning and psychological theorizing that served to isolate and exploit women as a group. Her work provided an impetus for volumes of feminist analyses of traditional psychological theories and practices (see, e.g., Brown & Ballou, 1992; Kaplan, 1983; Kitzinger & Perkins, 1993).

Learning From Feminist Theorists: The Social Construction of Mental Illness. Laura Brown (1992) has suggested that a critical question in the etiology of adult psychopathology is whether behavior called abnormal may actually be a normal, and at times creative, response to difficult personal and social histories that are greatly determined by one's experience with oppression(s). People cope with confusing and destructive conditions the best they can; thus, certain seemingly odd behaviors that might be classified as symptoms of mental illness may instead be considered an effective form of survival. She offers an alternative to narrowly identifying pathology as originating within the individual, through her diagnosis "Abuse/Oppression Artifact Disorder" (p. 226). Rather than viewing the individual separately from her past history and context, in this conceptualization "repeated exposures to the noxious and dangerous manifestations of sexism, racism, or other forms of cultural oppression" are identified as important stressors that must be considered before applying a label of deviance (p. 221).

Along these lines, Maria Root (1992) has argued for the classification of the chronic experience of racism, sexism, heterosexism, and other "isms" as a form of *insidious trauma* that needs to be taken into account when assessing psychological well-being. The cumulative effect of being devalued and treated differently due to characteristics intrinsic to one's identity, such as gender, race, and sexual orientation, may be a form of trauma that can lead to mental health problems (Root, 1992). Root suggests that because the experience of trauma wounds deeply in a way that challenges the meaning of life, insidious trauma may lead to various forms of symptomatology such as anxiety, depression, paranoia, and substance abuse.

Clearly, the findings from the study my colleagues and I conducted, discussed earlier, lend some support to this theory. Individuals who experienced an assault based on their identity as a lesbian or gay person showed higher levels of depression and PTSD symptoms. These findings point to an increased psychological vulnerability of belonging to a marginalized group that experiences consistent and violent discrimination.

Eliminating Heterosexism Through Social Change

To eliminate stress caused by exploitation, the most logical goal would be to remove the stressor. This involves the elimination of not only hate crimes but also the entire oppressive system of heterosexism. The first step toward directly confronting heterosexism, which is all-pervasive and has infiltrated every social structure of our society (and many others), is to envision a world free of heterosexism (see Livingston, Chapter 14, this volume). Second, forming coalitions with other marginalized groups, with the goal of eradicating all oppressions, is critical. Third, specific societal institutions such as the law and the educational system may be utilized to challenge heterosexism. Finally, interpersonal contact between heterosexuals and lesbians and gay men can be a powerful agent to social change.

Dare to Vision—Dare to Act. Preventionists advocating social change are a threat to not only traditional psychology but also the societal power structure that defines deviance, failure, and pathology in strictly individualistic terms. Any suggestions implying social change are discounted as lofty and unattainable. Consequently, for decades preventionists have struggled for credibility both in terms of recognition and in funding resources (see Kessler & Goldston, 1986). Certainly, other areas of psychology, such as feminist psychology and lesbian/gay psychology, have been limited and discredited in a similar fashion. To suggest the current societal organization is painfully flawed is to directly challenge the existing systems of oppression. Thus, suggesting social change is viewed as moving from *science* to *politics,* which certainly is not perceived as the role of social scientists. Earlier writings of preventionists reveal the tension between attaining credibility and maintaining the goals of social change; many pages were dedicated to proving the efficacy of prevention ideals through empirical data of successful prevention programs (see the entire volume of Kessler & Goldston, 1986).

All people, however, including social scientists, are critical and necessary agents in the political world. Politics involves judgments and decisions about public matters that concern us all. The traditional narrow definition of politics as certain roles and activities (e.g., senator voting on bills) formulates it as a specialized endeavor of concern to only a few. This prevents many people from viewing politics as personally and socially relevant.

In addition, science is value-laden. Social scientists cannot remain neutral. In fact, psychology, with its tendency to focus on the individual in a vacuum, devoid of social context, contributes to heterosexism and other exploitative social conditions (see Kitzinger & Perkins, 1993, for a critical evaluation of how psychology upholds the status quo; Kitzinger, Chapter 1, this volume; and Perkins, Chapter 5, this volume). To become agents of change, psychologists must dare to act by challenging the systems of oppression that create psychological distress.

This indeed calls for the ability to envision a world without oppression, which psychologists may find especially challenging, given their focus on those who are damaged and on negative mental health. With a vision, however, we may see clear goals necessary for eradicating heterosexism. Below I offer some experiences (which heterosexuals currently take for granted) that may characterize the lives of lesbians and gay men in a society free of heterosexism.

In relationships, lesbians and gay men would be able to

1. talk freely about intimate relationships and not have to consider carefully what pronoun to use when describing lovers or partners within every interaction (i.e., is this person safe to disclose my sexual orientation to?) and openly express affection toward partners as well as pain and grief if a relationship ends;
2. receive support for relationships from families of origin, religious institutions, and society at large, as reflected through social, public, and legal recognition;
3. see their love portrayed as beautiful, thriving, and enduring on the movie screen, in romantic novels, and in song lyrics.

On the job, lesbians and gay men would be able to

1. socialize without inhibition with colleagues rather than fear being found out. This socializing increases opportunities for collaborative work, getting a promotion, further training, and other career enhancing benefits;
2. live with job security rather than the fear of job loss due to the myth that being lesbian/gay makes one lack the proper qualifications (as is currently the case for gay teachers, health care professionals, or child care providers, for example).

As parents, lesbians and gay men would be able to

1. raise children without the fear of losing custody. Although research has found that children of lesbian and gay parents are just as psychologically healthy as children of heterosexual parents (Patterson, Chapter 10, this volume) the courts continually consider sexual orientation in determining the "best interest of the child."

Implicit in this vision are specific steps toward change. For example, to gain institutional recognition of lesbian/gay relationships, employees can organize for partner benefits in the workplace. For a more thorough and eloquent discussion of how a vision can frame prevention efforts, I refer the reader to Joy Livingston's chapter in this volume (see also Fahy, 1995, and Pharr, 1988).

Seeing the Big Picture. In a disturbing social and political climate where splintering of groups is becoming so pronounced and often results in competition between marginalized groups, recognizing the interdependence of political struggles is imperative. Whereas the political tactic of divide-and-conquer has been used by the dominating class throughout history (e.g., Zinn, 1980), current political leaders have employed this strategy with renewed vigor. Perhaps due to increased social power and visibility of certain marginalized groups (e.g., lesbians and gay men), ethnic, class, gender, and sexual orientation divisions have been used by politicians both to hinder continued advancement and to curb resistance.

A number of recent legislative and political moves in the state of California, in which I live, undoubtedly illustrate this point. In 1994, politicians introduced and won support for Proposition 187, a bill that restricted services to illegal immigrants. This bill was packaged to voters as a "Save the State" initiative, preying on middle-class economic insecurity created by both a long, though often denied, recession and racial mythology. Historically, solutions to economically difficult times have included a crackdown on immigrants, often resulting in increased discrimination toward specific minority groups. For example, in response to more than 1 million Mexicans legally immigrating to the United States between 1971 and 1986, plus many more arriving in the United States without legal work permits, Congress passed the Immigration Reform and Control Act of 1986 (in Amott & Matthaei, 1991). This law granted legal status to legal immigrants while simultaneously imposing fines for employers who hired undocumented workers. Rather than decreasing the number of illegal immigrants, as the law was designed to do, a government report released in 1990 found that this law resulted in widespread harassment of and discrimination toward Latino and Latina workers by employers insisting on proof of citizenship upon demand (Amott & Matthaei, 1991). Despite this kind of governmental evidence, the newer similar legislation, Proposition 187, was not only introduced by politicians but also passed into law. This suggests that the political motive of Proposition 187 supporters is to create a climate of racial divisiveness by enhancing feelings of "us"—read as hardworking white men who deserve to reap the subsequent benefits—and "them"—read as those who get a free ride.

Another recent political move that has contributed to this climate of "us" versus "them" is lead by presidential hopeful Pete Wilson: the attack on Affirmative Action. Using inaccurate claims, as reflected in this newspaper headline, "Swatting Away Those Pesky Facts on Affirmative Action: Wilson's Attack on UC Policy Seemed to Key on Politics, not Good Data," Wilson repeatedly argued that white males were gravely affected by affirmative action, and women and people of color no longer needed this type of "special treatment." At a Board of Regents meeting in July 1995, Wilson made an unusual appearance (though himself a regent, he did not attend most meetings) advocating, and as some board members admitted, pressuring them to vote to dismantle Affirmative Action on all the University of

California campuses. Although every president, chancellor, student body, and most other organized university groups of all the University of California campuses unanimously supported the goals of affirmative action, the Board of Regents voted against it. The key political strategy in this movement to abolish affirmative action is to pit groups against each other under the rhetoric of changing from a system of preferential treatment (the benefiting group being people of color and women) to one of justice and merit (as defined by and benefiting white men).

Social Psychological Dynamics of Scapegoating. Masked ever so carefully as serving some greater good, such as saving California or saving America (thus, we hear loaded names like the "Contract for America"), the real objective of passing Proposition 187 and dismantling affirmative action is to place the economic and political power more firmly into the hands of white, middle- to upper-class, heterosexual men who need to blame the current economic climate on an unsuspecting group. This inaccurate attribution is classic during difficult economic times and is the crux of the social psychological phenomenon of *displaced aggression,* or the *scapegoat theory.* According to this theory, when the cause of frustration is too intimidating or vague, people tend to focus their hostility outward onto a scapegoat. The scapegoat then is held responsible for causing the current frustration and often becomes the target of violence. A notable example of such scapegoating occurred between 1882 and 1930, a time of great economic frustration. Statistics show that lynching of black people in the U.S. South was higher during this period, when very low cotton prices resulted in economic hardship (Hovland & Sears, 1940).

The current economic difficulties, though largely due to the growing disparity between a small percentage of those who are very rich and the rest of society, is being blamed on marginalized groups that are most likely targets of scapegoating. Whereas American productivity increased by more than 30% between 1977 and 1992, the average wage of those workers fell by 13%. Compare this to the wages of corporate executives, which increased by 220% during this same time period (Erwin, 1995a). Instead of recognizing this as an important factor in our economic plight, we "blame the ghetto, barrio, working mothers, a poor work ethic and the loss of family values" (Erwin, 1995a, p. A2). This explains the scapegoating of welfare recipients as responsible for our skyrocketing national deficit despite the fact that monies designated for Aid to Families of Dependent Children account for only 1% of our federal budget (Erwin, 1995b).

Scapegoating results in an "us" versus "them" distinction. This distinction creates *in* and *out* groups, in which people immediately favor their own group even when the distinction between groups is inconsequential (Tajfel, 1982; Tajfel & Billig, 1974). This also leads people to exaggerate the differences between groups. In fact, once people are categorized into different groups, the characteristics that make one group different from another become more salient than the characteristics that make the groups similar (Krueger & Rothbart, 1988). Stereotypes of various marginalized groups frequently reflect cultural values about outsiders in general, where out-group members are viewed as inferior to the dominant in-group (Herek, 1995). Common stereotypes of lesbians and gay men, blacks, and Jews have emerged within our U.S. history. Each of these groups characterized as the outsider has been categorized, at one time or another, as animalistic, hypersexual, overvisible, heretical, and conspiratorial (Herek, 1995).

Clearly, this is a fragile common thread that connects people from these various marginalized groups; each is easily targeted as a scapegoat. This interdependence of economic exploitation, sexism, racism, and heterosexism has been further established by many psychologists and activists (e.g., see Albee, 1992, for an excellent discussion; Livingston, Chapter 14, this volume; Pharr, 1988, for the link between sexism and heterosexism; West, 1993). We must acknowledge the connection of political movements while simultaneously combating divisive politics. The urgency for marginalized groups to work together through communication, a shared vision, mutual support, and pooled resources is great. Gay men of European descent need to recognize the negative effect of dismantling Affirmative Action and join this movement. This could be accomplished through writing letters to elected state officials and congressional representatives, working with other people and organizations staging protests, and providing accurate information about the number of women and people of color in higher level positions. Heterosexual people of color need to join the lesbian/gay movement to help increase visibility and to challenge inaccurate but damaging myths and stereotypes. The premise is that one movement or one cause ultimately will not be effective in successfully challenging the power structure.

Forming Coalitions for the Prevention of Hate Crimes. Hate crimes are not unique to lesbians and gay men. They have been a reality of life for most minority groups (Herek, 1994). The purpose of hate crimes is to intimidate an entire group of people for their specific group identification, for example, ethnic minorities, religious minorities, lesbians and gay men. In addition to being attacks on an one's physical self, hate crimes are attacks on one's identity and community (in Herek, 1994). As a powerful form of terrorism, hate crimes serve the same purpose regardless of which marginalized group is the target of the crime. In addition, people who direct hate toward one group are likely also to direct it toward other minority groups.

An example of coalition building around hate crimes occurred in the community in which I live. In Sacramento, there was a series of firebombings in 1993, motivated by hate toward various minority groups. Firebombings occurred at a feminist women's health center, a Jewish synagogue, the office of the Japanese American Citizens League, the State Office of Human Rights and Fair Housing Commission, the local headquarters of the National Association for the Advancement of Colored People, and at the house of an Asian American City Councilmember. In response to these crimes, people from all the communities that were attacked, as well as other communities such as lesbians and gay men, joined together and organized open forums, press conferences, and a monetary reward for information regarding the perpetrators. This collaboration created an environment in which any further hate crimes would not be tolerated. Although this response began as a reaction to appalling incidents, the collaborative spirit persisted with such solutions as establishing a hate crimes hot line and a recognition that forming coalitions makes each group more powerful.

Law and Politics as Agents of Change. Earlier, I discussed ways in which the law has been manipulated to uphold specific political interests. In a review of the law and heterosexism, we see a history of legislation punishing homosexual behavior and instituting violence against lesbians and gay men (see Herek, 1994, for review). Today, discrimination against lesbians and gay men remains legal in employment, housing, and services (Herek, 1994). Although the law can be utilized as a tool of oppression, it can also be a tool for eliminating heterosexism. Legislating morality or empathy has been the subject of lively debate. Social psychological research suggests that engaging in (or in this case, legislating) certain behaviors does result in attitude change. In fact, the critical decision by the Supreme Court to desegregate schools was based on the belief that a legislative effort would decrease racial prejudice. The evidence suggested that substantial attitude change did directly follow this legislative act of desegregation (Amir, 1969; Pettigrew, 1969).

Following this same rationale, lesbians and gay men must actively organize for federal and local civil protection. Conservative groups such as the Oregon Citizen's Alliance (OCA) have successfully recognized the law as a vehicle for promoting their political agenda. These groups have advocated legislation that institutionalizes homosexuality as abnormal and unworthy of any legal protection (Biaggio, Hisey, & O'Donnell, 1993). Though the OCA effort failed, a similar movement succeeded in Colorado. These movements use divide-and-conquer tactics described earlier, preying on the social mood of insecurity. Proponents within these movements used very effective catch phrases, such as "no special rights," to suggest that lesbians and gay men were to be treated as a privileged group, worthy of that to which no other group would be entitled. Such terms blurred the real intent of the effort for lesbians and gay men to receive the same civil rights protection as blacks and Hispanics, for example. Clearly, these strategies that spread misinformation and breed "us" versus "them" dichotomies must be challenged.

Social scientists play a critical role in framing public policy by conducting research that reveals these psychological dynamics. Research that dispels commonly held stereotypes that justify current discrimination must be introduced into the political arena. An excellent recent example of the role of research in shaping public policy was the reinstatement of Colonel Margarethe Cammermeyer into the military. Social scientist Gregory Herek submitted an affidavit presenting research relevant to the U.S. military's policy on sexual orientation (see Herek, 1995, for complete affidavit; also Herek, 1993). These data were directly cited in Judge Zilly's ruling to reinstate Colonel Cammermeyer:

> No data exist to indicate that lesbians and gay men are less capable than heterosexuals of controlling their sexual or romantic urges, refraining from the abuse of power, or exercising good judgement in handling authority . . . justifications for the policy are based on heterosexual members' fear and dislike of homosexuals. ("Outcomes," 1994, p. 3)

Educational Institutions as Agents of Social Change. Although many colleges and universities still have policies and practices that uphold heterosexist attitudes and behavior (see Berrill, 1992b), they also offer hope for the possibilities of significant change. Many have been in the forefront of creating an environment intolerant of heterosexism. Universities have taken such proactive measures as extending spousal benefits to lesbian/gay partners, establishing offices that address the needs of lesbians and gay men, offering lesbian/gay courses, and establishing institutional committees that focus on lesbian/gay issues on campus (Berrill, 1992b). As an example, the University of California at Davis (UC Davis), where I work, publishes an anti-discrimination statement in their student handbook clearly articulating that heterosexism, along with other discrimination, is prohibited. In congruence with this statement, UC Davis has a recognized committee that receives funding and serves to inform the chancellor on lesbian, gay, and bisexual issues. Through this committee, an official speaker's bureau has been in existence and has conducted more than 250 panels within the past 5 years. Though there is no available outcome data on the efficacy of such programming, the feedback forms from participants are overwhelmingly positive, and the high visibility and recognition of the speaker's bureau help to create an atmosphere of mutual respect in which heterosexism will not be tolerated.

Coming Out as a Strategy for Change: The Contact Hypothesis Revisited. Developed by Gordon Allport in 1954, the *contact hypothesis* proposed that many forms of prejudice could be reduced by equal status contact between majority and minority groups in the pursuit of common goals. Researchers have found that interpersonal contact between different racial groups is one of the most productive ways to reduce negative stereotyping, feelings of prejudice, and discriminatory behavior (Amir, 1969; Stephan, 1987).

Indeed, applying this theory to relations between heterosexuals and lesbians and gay men generates similar results. Heterosexuals reporting interpersonal contact with lesbians or gay men express more positive attitudes toward them (Ellis & Brent, 1993; Hansen, 1982; Herek & Capitanio, in press; Herek & Glunt, 1993).

Herek and Capitanio (in press) further determined specific conditions within intergroup contact that resulted in more positive attitudes toward lesbians and gay men. From a national telephone survey of 538 English-speaking heterosexual adults, the following conditions were associated with more positive attitudes: having more interpersonal contact with lesbians and gay men, having contact with more than one lesbian or gay individual, having contact with a lesbian or gay person who is a close friend or relative (rather than a distant family member or acquaintance), and learning that that person is lesbian or gay through direct rather than indirect disclosure. The obvious implication of this research is that lesbians and gay men can have a pronounced influence on heterosexuals' attitudes by coming out directly to friends and family and, perhaps, to a lesser degree to acquaintances.

Building Resistance Through Empowerment: Increasing Ego Strength

This last section of the chapter focuses on strengthening the individual so that she or he may be both resilient to stress, such as that caused by anti-lesbian/gay violence, and also an active agent with influence and power over the environment. As mentioned earlier, ego strength is a term used by Albee to identity four major correlates to psychological well-being: sense of competence, high self-esteem, having social support, and adequate coping skills. Another way of conceptualizing these correlates is under the umbrella term *empowerment*. Empowerment is defined by Cohen (1989) as the critical human need to feel effective and a sense of agency in the world. Empowerment focuses on the process that enhances people's strengths and their abilities to control their own lives and situations within a social environment (Rappaport, 1981). A diversion from traditional mental health models that centralize deviance and pathology, the empowerment-centered philosophy for promoting positive mental health emphasizes that everyone has the ability to shape events within their lives rather than be powerless and helpless (Cohen, 1989; Hatfield, 1987).

Preventing Future Perpetrators by Increasing Ego Strength of All People

A striking empowerment-centered suggestion for developing strong ego strength in all individuals was offered by Albee (1992), in a chapter titled "Saving Children Means Social Revolution." As a member of the Commission on the Prevention of Mental/Emotional Disabilities of the National Mental Health Association, Albee discussed how the members asked themselves, "If we had just one prevention program we could put in place, and knew it would succeed, which one would that be?" (p. 313). After many hours of discussion and debate, they came to the consensus of offering a program that

> would ensure [that] every born baby anywhere in the world would be a healthy full-term infant weighing at least eight pounds and welcomed into the world by economically secure parents who had wanted the child and planned jointly for her or his conception and birth. (p. 313)

Certainly, such a program underscores the importance of early development, which is why so much of prevention is geared toward children (e.g., see entire volume of Albee, Bond, & Monsey, 1992). In addition, this proposal highlights the interdependence of social conditions and the development of individual ego strength. Positive environmental variables that allow ego strength, or, as Emery Cowen (1991) refers to it, "wellness," in individuals to flourish. Children would develop competence if they were able to concentrate on learning rather than poverty, hunger, or neglect; had sufficient and appropriate educational programs, supplies, and funding; and had teachers who were well paid and respected. Children would develop high self-esteem if each were valued, and no social hierarchies labeled and limited their potential; if they were pushed to succeed rather than expected to fail; and if parents were emotionally available and nurturing. Children would develop strong friendship networks if they learned how to love and respect one another and view each other as equals rather than enemies. Finally, children would develop coping skills through learning such values as negotiation, cooperation, and communication. Such dynamic interaction between the environment and the person would foster robust ego strength that would deter heterosexism as a whole and violence against lesbians and gay men in particular, because individuals with high self-esteem, a sense of belonging to a community, and feelings of competence would not be likely candidates for perpetrating discrimination and violence.

Increasing Ego Strength of Hate Crime Victims

The reality is that until hate crimes are completely obliterated from the lives of lesbians and gay men, dealing effectively with their aftermath is critical. The Community United Against Violence (CUAV) is an example of a grassroots organization committed to responding to hate crime violence with intelligence and compassion. This San Francisco-based organization is referred to by Gregory Herek (1992a) as "one of the oldest and most successful community organizations for responding to violence against lesbians and gay men" (p. 241). Although CUAV focuses on prevention as well, this discussion will highlight the organization's role of responsiveness. As a client advocate, CUAV helps victims of violence deal with its aftermath by providing crisis intervention services or short-term counseling. The focus of these services is to offer and explore options for the clients to access available resources, including, for example, self-defense training (which may increase one's sense of competence and lessen feelings of vulnerability), legal resources (which increase one's options to pursue justice), and support groups (which prevent feelings of isolation, "I am the only one"). Among the primary objectives of counselors is enhancing choice—facilitating a sense of personal agency within the individual—a critical component of the empowerment philosophy.

CUAV, now a dynamic and complex resource for victims of anti-lesbian/gay violence, began as merely an answering machine on someone's telephone. Implementing something seemingly so minor achieved the fundamental yet critical step of documenting violence against lesbians and gay men. Such measures eventually led to funding for crisis intervention, community outreach, and in-service training, which is another critical response to victims of anti-lesbian/gay violence. Educating our communities and the public at large about the prevalence of anti-lesbian/gay victimization and the aftermath must be a priority.

Conclusion

As an extension of heterosexism, violence against lesbians and gay men is associated with a range of psychological stressors. Eliminating the violence against lesbians and gay men, as well as the social milieu that upholds and perpetuates such violence, must be a common goal of social scientists, policymakers, and activists. I submit three calls for action.

1. We must transform the social conditions that lead to exploitation and increased psychological distress.

2. We must acknowledge and appreciate the connections between political movements and must form coalitions, both of which are necessary for challenging the current power structure and changing social conditions.

3. As social scientists, we must recognize that we are significant agents of change and, through framing meaningful research questions and receiving funding, we can influence policy and societal attitudes.

Participating in the political process, whether it be through imparting positive values to growing children, conducting research that dispels damaging stereotypes, or organizing for legislation that guarantees lesbians and gay men civil rights protection, each of us can and does make a difference. Each member of society must accept individual responsibility for securing a world free of exploitation.

Notes

1. Albee's model has changed in detail and description over the years, so this model will vary depending upon the specific reference the reader identifies.

2. For the purposes of this chapter, certain of the details of the full equation have not been included (e.g., a discussion of organic factors). The reader is referred to Albee (1984) for additional detail.

References

Albee, G. W. (1979). Politics, power, prevention, and social change. *Clinical Psychologist, 33,* 12-13.

Albee, G. W. (1981). The prevention of sexism. *Professional Psychology, 12,* 20-28.

Albee, G. W. (1984). A competency model must replace the defect model. In J. M. Joffe, G. W. Albee, & L. D. Kelly (Eds.), *Readings in primary prevention of psychopathology* (pp. 228-245). London: University Press.

Albee, G. W. (1986). Toward a just society: Lessons from observations on the primary prevention of psychopathology. *American Psychologist, 41,* 891-898.

Albee, G. W. (1992). Saving children means social revolution. In G. W. Albee, L. A. Bond, & T. V. Monsey (Eds.), *Improving children's lives: Global perspectives on prevention* (pp. 311-329). Newbury Park, CA: Sage.

Albee, G. W., Bond, L. A., & Monsey, T. V. (Eds.). (1992). *Improving children's lives: Global perspectives on prevention.* Newbury Park, CA: Sage.

Albee, G. W., Joffe, J. M., & Dusenbury, L. A. (Eds.). (1988). *Prevention, powerlessness, and politics: Readings on social change.* Newbury Park, CA: Sage.

Allport, G. (1954). *The nature of prejudice.* Cambridge, MA: Addison-Wesley.

Amir, Y. (1969). Contact-hypothesis in ethnic relations. *Psychological Bulletin, 71,* 319-342.

Amott, T. L., & Matthaei, J. A. (1991). *Race, gender & work: A multicultural economic history of women in the United States.* Boston: South End.

Berrill, K. T. (1992a). Antigay violence and victimization in the United States: An overview. In G. M. Herek & K. T. Berrill (Eds.), *Hate crimes: Confronting violence against lesbians and gay men* (pp. 19-45). Newbury Park, CA: Sage.

Berrill, K. T. (1992b). Organizing against hate on campus: Strategies for activists. In G. M. Herek & K. T. Berrill (Eds.), *Hate crimes: Confronting violence against lesbians and gay men* (pp. 259-269). Newbury Park, CA: Sage.

Biaggio, M., Hisey, K., & O'Donnell, J. (1993). *The antihomosexual referendum in Oregon: A case study in bigotry.* Paper presented at the meeting of the Association for Women in Psychology, Atlanta.

Brown, L. S. (1992). A feminist critique of the personality disorders. In L. S. Brown & M. Ballou (Eds.), *Personality and psychopathology: Feminist reappraisals* (pp. 206-228). New York: Guilford.

Brown, L. S., & Ballou, M. (Eds.) (1992). *Personality and psychopathology: Feminist reappraisals.* New York: Guilford.

Chesler, P. (1972). *Women & madness.* New York: Doubleday.

Cohen, M. B. (1989). Social work practice with homeless mentally ill people: Engaging the client. *Social Work, 34,* 505-509.

Cowen, E. L. (1991). In pursuit of wellness. *American Psychologist, 46,* 404-408.

Dean, L., Wu, S., & Martin, J. L. (1992). Trends in violence and discrimination against gay men in New York City: 1984 to 1990. In G. M. Herek & K. T. Berrill (Eds.), *Hate crimes: Confronting violence against lesbians and gay men* (pp. 46-64). Newbury Park, CA: Sage.

Ellis, A. L., & Brent, V. R. (1993). Prior interpersonal contact with and attitudes towards gays and lesbians in an interviewing context. *Journal of Homosexuality, 25*(4), 31-45.

Erwin, D. G. (1995a, June 4). Bias debate drives wedge deep and fast. *Sacramento Bee,* p. A2.

Erwin, D. G. (1995b, February 7). No easy answers beyond the facts of welfare. *Sacramento Bee,* p. A2.

Fahy, U. (1995). *How to make the world a better place for gays and lesbians.* New York: Warner Books.

Fish, T. A., & Rye, B. J. (1991). Attitudes toward a homosexual or heterosexual person with AIDS. *Journal of Applied Social Psychology, 21,* 651-667.

Garnets, L., Herek, G. M., & Levy, B. (1990). Violence and victimization of lesbians and gay men: Mental health consequences. *Journal of Interpersonal Violence, 5,* 366-383.

Gray, C., Russell, P., & Blockley, S. (1991). The effects of helping behaviour of wearing pro-gay identification. *British Journal of Social Psychology, 30,* 171-178.

Hansen, G. L. (1982). Measuring prejudice against homosexuality (homosexism) among college students: A new scale. *Journal of Social Psychology, 117,* 233-236.

Hatfield, A. B. (1987). Consumer issues in mental health. *New Directions for Mental Health Services, 34,* 35-51.

Herek, G. M. (1989). Hate crimes against lesbians and gay men: Issues for research and policy. *American Psychologist, 44,* 948-955.

Herek, G. M. (1992a). The community response to violence in San Francisco: An interview with Wenny Kusuma, Lester Olmstead-Rose, and Jill Tregor. In G. M. Herek, & K. T. Berrill (Eds.), *Hate crimes: Confronting violence against lesbians and gay men* (pp. 241-258). Newbury Park, CA: Sage.

Herek, G. M. (1992b). The social context of hate crimes: Notes on cultural heterosexism. In G. M. Herek & K. T. Berrill (Eds.), *Hate crimes: Confronting violence against lesbians and gay men* (pp. 89-104). Newbury Park, CA: Sage.

Herek, G. M. (1993). Sexual orientation and military service: A social science perspective. *American Psychologist, 48,* 538-549.

Herek, G. M. (1994). Heterosexism, hate crimes, and the law. In M. Costanzo & O. Oskamp (Eds.), *Violence and the law* (pp. 89-112). London: Sage.

Herek, G. M. (1995). On prejudice toward gay people and gays as security risks. In M. Wolinsky & K. Sherrill (Eds.), *Gays and the military* (pp. 121-140). Princeton: Princeton University Press.

Herek, G. M., & Capitanio, J. P. (in press). "Some of my best friends": Intergroup contact, concealable stigma, and heterosexuals' attitudes toward gay men and lesbians. *Personality and Social Psychology Bulletin.*

Herek, G. M., Gillis, J. R., Cogan, J. C., & Glunt, E. (1995). *Psychological correlates of hate crime victimization: A preliminary study of lesbians, gay men, and bisexuals.* Manuscript submitted for publication.

Herek, G. M., & Glunt, E. K. (1993). Interpersonal contact and heterosexuals' attitudes toward gay men: Results from a national survey. *Journal of Sex Research, 30,* 239-244.

Hershberger, S. L., & D'Augelli, A. R. (1995). The impact of victimization on the mental health and suicidality of lesbian, gay, and bisexual youth. *Developmental Psychology, 31,* 65-74.

Hovland, C. I., & Sears, R. (1940). Minor studies of aggression: Correlation of lynchings with economic indices. *Journal of Psychology, 9,* 301-310.

Kaplan, M. (1983). A woman's view of the DSM-III. *American Psychologist, 38,* 786-792.

Karr, R. G. (1978). Homosexual labeling and the male role. *Journal of Social Issues, 34,* 73-83.

Kessler, M., & Goldston, S. E. (Eds.). (1986). *A decade of progress in primary prevention: Primary prevention of psychopathology.* Hanover, NH: University Press of New England.

Kilpatrick, D. G., Saunders, B. E., Amick-McMullan, A., Best, C. L., Veronen, L. J., & Resnick, H. S. (1989). Victim and crime factors associated with the development of crime-related post-traumatic stress disorder. *Behavior Therapy, 20,* 199-214.

Kite, M. E. (1992). Individual differences in males' reactions to gay males and lesbians. *Journal of Applied Social Psychology, 22,* 1222-1239.

Kitzinger, C., & Perkins, R. (1993). *Changing our minds: Lesbian feminism and psychology.* New York: New York University Press.

Krueger, J., & Rothbart, M. (1988). Use of categorical and individuating information in making inferences about personality. *Journal of Personality and Social Psychology, 55,* 187-195.

National Gay & Lesbian Task Force. (1991). *Anti-gay/lesbian violence, victimization & defamation in 1990.* Washington, DC: Author.

Norris, F. H., & Kaniasty, K. (1991). The psychological experience of crime: A test of the mediating role of beliefs in explaining the distress of victims. *Journal of Social and Clinical Psychology, 10,* 239-261.

Outcomes: A social science newsletter for the Sacramento area lesbian/gay/bisexual/transgender communities. (1994, Summer). *Copy Editor,* pp. 1, 3.

Pettigrew, T. F. (1969). Racially separate or together? *Journal of Social Issues, 2,* 43-69.

Pharr, S. (1988). *Homophobia: A weapon of sexism.* Little Rock, AR: Chardon.

Radloff, L. (1977). The CES-D scale: A self-report depression scale for research in the general population. *Applied Psychological Measurement, 1,* 385-401.

Rappaport, J. (1981). In praise of paradox: A social policy of empowerment over prevention. *American Journal of Community Psychology, 9,* 1-25.

Root, M. P. (1992). Reconstructing the impact of trauma on personality. In L. S. Brown & M. Ballou (Eds.), *Personality and psychopathology: Feminist reappraisals* (pp. 229-266). New York: Guilford.

Spielberger, C. D., Jacobs, G., Russel, S., & Crane, R. S. (1983). Assessment of anger: The state-trait anger scale. In J. N. Butcher & C. D. Spielberger (Eds.), *Advances in personality assessment* (Vol. 2, pp. 161-189). Hillsdale, NJ: Lawrence Erlbaum.

Stephan, W. G. (1987). The contact hypothesis in intergroup relations. In C. Hendrick (Ed.), *Group processes and intergroup relations.* Newbury Park, CA: Sage.

Tajfel, H. (1982). Social psychology of intergroup relations. *Annual Review of Psychology, 33,* 1-39.

Tajfel, H., & Billig, M. (1974). Familiarity and categorization in intergroup behavior. *Journal of Experimental Social Psychology, 10,* 159-170.

Testa, R. J., Kinder, B. N., & Ironson, G. (1987). Conceptions of masculinity and femininity as a basis for stereotypes of male and female homosexuals. *Journal of Sex Research, 23,* 163-172.

Weiner, B. (1988). An attributional analysis of changing reactions to persons with AIDS. In R. A. Berk (Ed.), *The social impact of AIDS in the U.S.* (pp. 123-132). Cambridge, MA: ABT.

Weiner, B. (1993). AIDS from an attributional perspective. In J. B. Pryor & G. D. Reeder (Eds.), *The social psychology of HIV infection* (pp. 287-302). Hillsdale, NJ: Lawrence Erlbaum.

West, C. (1993). *Race matters.* Boston: Beacon.

Zinn, H. (1980). *A people's history of the United States: 1492—present.* New York: Harper.

13

Homo-Phobia, Homo-Ignorance, Homo-Hate: Heterosexism and AIDS

Lynda J. Ames

[AIDS education should reaffirm] the heterosexual ethic which is the foundation of our civilization.

William E. Dannemeyer (quoted in Bayer, 1989, p. 216)

This is heterosexism.

Congressman Dannemeyer assumes and then asserts as fact that only heterosexuals are involved in the positive forces of civilization, only heterosexuality is recognized as civilized. Other sexualities are, by definition, transgressive and not worthy of the term *civilization*. Dannemeyer has been perhaps more brazen and more clear in his prejudice than most, but he is hardly alone in his thinking.

This common heterosexism has, of course, consequences. It has had an enormous impact on the way a disease, AIDS (Acquired Immune Deficiency Syndrome), has been socially understood, scientifically researched, and medically treated. Heterosexism, though, is not uniformly expressed; there are critical differences between simple ignorance and ignorant hatefulness. Clearly, hatred and ignorance and fear of gay sexuality all have had a negative and deadly influence on public policy and individual responses to this very much equal opportunity disease.

The various manifestations of heterosexism interact with the other social prejudices of our time and culture, notably misogyny, racism, and classism. In those intersections, the effect of heterosexism has been the death of

239

many people, increased displays of hatred, and the social acceptability of hate.

In this chapter, I will survey specific instances of heterosexism as they have occurred around the specter of AIDS, taking note of those different expressions—fear, ignorance, and hate—and of their intersections with other isms. I will draw on the now voluminous literature on the history and social consequences of AIDS and on my own research and personal experiences in conducting that research. For 2.5 years, I was employed on a grant from the U.S. Centers for Disease Control (CDC), documenting and analyzing the responses of small-city gay men to the epidemic. Housed in a large state department of health, I could observe how public health bureaucrats and policymakers understood the disease and understood—or did not, would not, understand—the victims of AIDS and the gay community in general.

AIDS: A Brief History

In the early 1980s, public health officials became aware of a strange outbreak of rare infections, infections that often proved fatal even if the specific bug was not usually so.[1] Eventually, the outbreak was attributed to an immune disorder and it seemed to be occurring primarily, if not exclusively, among gay men. The disease was soon labeled GRID—Gay-Related Immune Disorder. Newspapers reported this phenomenon as a "gay plague." Thus, the idea of the disease as a problem of gays was firmly implanted and would never quite be excised.

A few public health officials were appropriately alarmed and fought diligently to track down the cause of this disorder. For many years, though, the alarm was not generally shared. Resources for epidemiology and basic research were few and inadequate. In those years, many, many people died and many, many more became infected and would die later.

It is widely believed that the relative inaction of the official world during the early years of the epidemic was due to hatred and fear of gays. Larry Kramer (1991) has termed the public health policies of the Reagan presidency *genocide*. As long as the disease was seen to afflict gays and not the general public, it was seen to pose no *real* problem.

As the few alarmed public health officials continued their work, though, it became increasingly obvious that AIDS was not limited to any population or to any single transmission route. Nevertheless, the disease has never quite shaken its "contamination" with gay sexuality. That continues to have consequences for the national response to AIDS and for gay people and communities.

Homo-Ignorance

It is not at all surprising that our society is ignorant about gay sexuality. We are ignorant about sexuality in general, despite the culture's seeming obsession with sex. When the epidemic broke, information about gay sexuality was primarily found in the Kinsey reports of the 1940s and 1950s. Little in the way of systematic work had been done since (Curran quoted in Treichler, 1988; Turner, Miller, & Moses, 1989).

From the beginning, straight researchers, the media, and the public shared the idea of gay men's sex as weird, gross, promiscuous—and irresponsible (Adam, 1992; Albert, 1986; Treichler, 1988; Watney, 1988). There was revulsion in even discussing the specific acts that facilitated transmission of the virus. Indeed, many of the acts were actually criminal offenses in 24 states and the District of Columbia (Bayer, 1989).

Heterosexist assumptions were clear in the ignorant early assumption that anal intercourse *was* sex for gay men, sort of a gay missionary position, so to speak. Insertion of a penis into an orifice was seen to be necessary before an act was labeled *sex* (Bersani, 1988). This became an obsession for public health officials and the media (Callen, quoted in Navarre, 1988). At the time, though, no one knew what practices were typical.

Learning took time. Gay men engage in a variety of sexual acts, some quite dangerous in terms of potential HIV[2] transmission, others not so dangerous. It became clear, too, that the riskier practices were not uniformly distributed. For example, in our research with a small-city sample, we found that many men did not even like anal sex (Ames, Atchinson, & Rose, 1995). The delay in learning cost lives.

There is still ignorance about the context of gay men's sex. It comes as a surprise to some that gay men use sex just as straight people use sex: to exhibit love, to establish families, to satisfy lust. Public health campaigns and many researchers often simply ignore love and commitment. For instance, men are urged not to have anal sex, period, and at least to wear a condom if they must engage in that practice. But unprotected anal sex can be safe, in the context of a mutually monogamous, virus-free relationship. In studies of "relapse," though, men in such relationships who engage in anal intercourse are deemed to have relapsed away from safe sex (see, e.g., the discussion on relapse in Miller, Turner, & Moses [1990].

Thus, ignorance still informs pubic health policies. Nonetheless, there has arguably been some decrease in ignorance among the public. So-called mainstream movies like *Philadelphia* and *Long Time Companion,* which portray gay men in loving relationships, in pain over dead friends and lovers—as perfectly normal people—have helped ease ignorance and increase compassion, at least among some segments of society. A doctor quoted by Koenig and Cooke (1989) makes the same point, that treating and working with gay men reduces stereotypes of " 'fast-lane types and limp-wrists' " (p. 77).

Ignorance is curable.

Lesbians. One of the places homo-ignorance shows up most strongly is in the social treatment of lesbians vis-à-vis AIDS. There are two weirdly co-occuring phenomena here. First, there has been complete ignorance among public health officials and the public about the differences between gay men and lesbians, even that there *are* differences. Second, there is the misogynist denial that lesbians contract HIV. In other words, lesbians are just like gay men; lesbians don't get AIDS. Both cannot be true; neither is.

It seems that lesbians don't exist; if lesbians do exist, they don't have sex; if they do have sex, it isn't risky sex. Furthermore, it is assumed that lesbians do not have male sex partners (either before or after coming out) or inject drugs. Mostly, lesbians are invisible in discussions of AIDS prevention (Banzhaf et al., 1990; Hollibaugh, 1995; Patton, 1993; Stoller, 1995).

Early CDC publications did not mention lesbians, except possibly as appropriate blood donors (Maslanka, 1993). This lack of concern about lesbians and AIDS did not go away. The multisite project I worked on began designing a random survey of residents of high-risk neighborhoods. The questions were very sexually explicit and the instrument was quite long. When I suggested including two additional questions for women who had sex with women, the team refused. Lesbians were assumed not to be a risk group; there was no interest whatsoever in testing that assumption or even in gathering no-cost data on the frequency of lesbian sex.

At the same time, the words *gay* and *AIDS* are seen as synonymous, and the sex of the gay person seems not to matter very much. Gay magazines, marches, and movies often include, as a matter of course, discussions of AIDS. Other media and the public also may not distinguish between gay men and lesbians vis-à-vis AIDS (Squire, 1993). In places, lesbians have actually been urged to defer giving blood (Grover, 1988). AIDS is queer; queers get AIDS; queers are queers. This is not so very different from assumptions that medical studies on men and aspirin, for example, are generalizable to women. There is little official understanding of how the sexual practices of lesbians differ from those of gay men (or of heterosexuals, for that matter— "what do you *do* in bed, anyway?"); or of how the disease progresses differently for women than for men; or of how communities of lesbians differ from communities of gay men.

Consequently, there are now very few AIDS prevention or awareness programs focused on lesbians (Banzhaf et al., 1990). First, public health officials assume lesbians do not need programs, because they are not susceptible to AIDS. It is true that lesbians' risk for AIDS involves shared needles, sex with men, or the transfer of blood (such as in some S/M sex), leaving many, if not most, lesbians having safe sex. However, many lesbians *are* at risk from these unsafe practices. Second, lesbians are assumed not to need programs different from those for gay men. This is one intersection of heterosexism and misogyny.

The (One and Only) Gay Community. Not only have lesbians and gay men been assumed to be part of the same community, but there has also been little recognition of differences even among gay male communities, differences generated by class and race and by geography (Adam, 1992; Grover, 1988). *The* gay community is assumed white and affluent and urban. This community, thus, is able to do for its own. It has resources of talent and money and leisure. "They" not only can do for their own, they should.

In fact, gay communities *have* marshaled their resources and have made significant differences in the course of the epidemic (Kayal, 1993). Gay male communities wrote and delivered AIDS-prevention educational programs long before official public health agencies did; they formed caregiving networks and advocacy groups; they donated money to basic research. According to Cindy Patton (cited in Crimp, 1988), gay people *invented* safer sex. These efforts were and still are effective in reducing high-risk behaviors and the rates of infection (Miller et al., 1990).

However, not all gay men are affluent; not all gay men even have access to an identifiable community of gay men. In small towns, we have learned, the resources for education and support are quite different from those in large cities (Ames & Beeker, 1990a, 1990b; Kelly, St. Lawrence, Hood, & Brasfield, 1989). Poor gay men cannot rely on savings to support them during periods of illness. Gay men of color have community issues quite different from those of gay white men.

Ironically—I should rather say, tragically—because portions of the gay men's community *did* respond with so many resources, there is often a perception that they (gay men) are taking care of themselves. Thus, the rest of society does not have to worry about them; public health officials can concentrate instead on the general population.

So, gay communities in small towns, communities of poor gay men, and communities of color are left to marshal their own, often inadequate, resources. In many ways, the more affluent communities of gay men have learned to stretch the boundaries of their communities to encompass other communities more fully (Kayal, 1993). Nevertheless, assumptions of the uniformity of gay community have meant fewer programs and supports targeted to nonstereotypical gay men, and more infection than would otherwise have occurred (Miller et al., 1990).

These classist and racist assumptions are operative in other spheres of our society, notably in terms of the content of public education and of popular culture, where images of poor people and people of color are rare and often one-dimensional. In AIDS education, there are programs aimed at poor people and programs aimed at so-called minorities (Banzhaf et al., 1990; Sosnowitz, 1995). Often, these programs assume injecting drug use—problematic in itself. But there is often little understanding that many of the poor, many people of color, many injecting drug users (IDUs) are *also* gay. Thus, education programs, support programs, medical programs do not address the whole of a life and cannot be wholly effective.

Homo-Fear

If there is considerable ignorance about the lives of gay men and lesbians, there is also outright fear. Public health officials have been notably fearful of explicit talk about gay men's sex and ignorant about the subject. For instance, many public health messages use clinical terms rather than "street" terms (Adam, 1992). We hear *anal intercourse* rather than *ass fuck* or just *fuck*. Clinical usage sterilizes a distasteful topic. Further, the use of explicit terms is feared by some to condone gay sexuality (Crimp, 1988; Grover, 1988). However, insofar as educational programs do not use the language and concepts used by the target group, the programs cannot be effective.

In the project I worked on, we also were urged to use clinical terms. In one bizarre instance, a review board asked us not to use the spelling *cum*. We had used, arbitrarily to be sure, *cum* as a noun (ejaculated semen) and *come* as a verb (to ejaculate). We were asked to change all spellings to *come*. (We refused.) When we wrote papers quoting gay men, we were asked not to use the names of celebrities. That is, when gay men talked about their fantasies, for instance, and we quoted them exactly, the powers-that-be were fearful of being sued. (We would not make the changes.) It was assumed that gay sexuality was so discrediting that the celebrities would take steps to prevent their names from being used even in dusty, scholarly journals. I suspect that some of those powers themselves were fearful of being thought gay because they did AIDS work, and projected these fears onto celebrities. Such fear is not uncommon.

Some of the fear people have is arguably related to the deadly disease itself. There remains a great deal of public ignorance about transmission routes. However, a number of studies conclude that discrimination against gay people by health care workers and the public is more rooted in homophobia than in the fear of AIDS itself (Adam, 1992; Jackson & Hunter, 1992).

The fear sometimes expressed is that the government has colluded with powerful gay leaders to suppress information about AIDS, to prevent appropriate public health controls such as mandatory testing or quarantine (Bersani, 1988; Crimp, 1988). Such fear seems ludicrous—alas, there are no "powerful" gay leaders with anywhere near that much influence. Yet, this fear drives considerable public discourse, which necessarily only increases fear.

There is a widely held belief that gay men's sex is irresponsible and, in itself, deadly. Anal intercourse has been identified as deadly, irrespective of the presence of HIV (Patton, 1993). Indeed, arguments have been made that much public health education has been aimed at reducing gay sex, period (Crimp, 1988; Kayal, 1993). Insofar as that is true, it reflects great fear of gay sexuality.

Fear also surfaces in the clear demarcations made between so-called innocent victims on the one hand (hemophiliacs and other transfusion recipients, babies) and gay men and intravenous drug users (IDUs) on the other. High pre-AIDS levels of blood donation among gay men have been blamed for the contamination of the blood supply and the infection of many "innocent" people. Not widely blamed, though, are the various organizations controlling the blood supply. These organizations could have taken steps very much earlier to make the supply safe but did not, resulting in many, many "innocent" infections (Bayer, 1989; Shilts, 1987). Instead, it is gay men and their "deviant" sexual practices that are blamed.

Ongoing fear, fanned by politicians and media, has helped cause a withdrawal of compassion. The epidemic has gone on for a decade and a half without a cure. Fear that there will never be a cure and that "irresponsible" sexual behavior will spread the disease far and wide may overwhelm any newfound understanding and empathy.

Among Gay Men. Fear has also made an appearance in gay communities. In fact, there are two fears: fear of AIDS and death, linked with internalized homophobia; and fear of increased heterosexism. Gay men especially must fear infection—they still constitute a majority of persons with AIDS. In some ways the epidemic has pulled the community together, in shared grief and in the sense that we as gay people must take care of ourselves. However, the fear can also create divisions in the community. The data from our study indicated that many men were much more wary of their fellows, much less trusting, even while other men had grown closer (Ames, Atchinson, & Rose, 1994). Hollibaugh (1995) reports similar divisions among lesbians. Such distrust is due, in part, to public health messages demonizing gay sex. Men become fearful of their own sexuality (Bersani, 1988).

In the early days of the epidemic, there was a raging, angry, divisive debate about the baths (Bayer, 1989; Crimp, 1988; Moss, 1989; Shilts, 1987) and it has recently revived (Miles, 1995). Some public health officials and some in the gay community were and still are desperate to close the bathhouses, where anonymous sex with multiple partners occurred. There was significant indication early in the epidemic that the new disease was sexually transmitted. However, for gay people, sexuality had long since become political. Among many in the communities, there was strong resistance to letting the government have any say in the way gay men practiced their sexuality. Existing heterosexism contributed to a strong fear among gay people that the government would seize the flimsiest of excuses to shut down gay life. Closing the baths was often seen to be just that beginning, that excuse (Bayer, 1989; Bersani, 1988; Miles, 1995).

Although the public health consequences of closing the baths are still argued, the debate could have and should focus on public health. Instead, fear of both gay men's sexuality and gay men's reasonable reaction to that heterosexism distracted the argument, perhaps costing many lives.

Between Lesbians and Gay Men. The fear of both AIDS and the heterosexism surrounding AIDS has had interesting effects on the community between lesbians and gay men. In the first place, there have been, from the beginning, many lesbians involved in the fight against AIDS (Hollibaugh, 1995; Squire, 1993; Stoller, 1995). Many lesbians felt that the national response to the outbreak of the epidemic demonstrated how little straight society cared for gays. Thus, the response was to take care of our own. Lesbians have also been a driving force in the fight to have the particular needs of women addressed in public health programs and in the definition and treatment of the disease itself.

Yet, there has also developed a schism between lesbians and gay men (Stoller, 1995). This schism is due partly to misogyny among men in general, including gay men, and partly to the heterosexist assumption that lesbians and gay men are alike. As an illustration of these issues, let me tell a quick story. I was at a party and was asked by another woman what I did for a living. I said I was working on a research project of gay men and AIDS. She began to lecture me on why lesbians should not help gay men on the issue of AIDS. Lesbians did not get AIDS, after all, and gay men would certainly not help us if the tables were turned. Furthermore, she said, she was tired of everyone assuming she, as a lesbian, was automatically interested in AIDS issues and at risk for contracting HIV.

I think it is safe to say that feminism is no more prevalent among gay men than among straight men (Banzhaf et al., 1990). The woman might have been right that gay men would not have put themselves out for a disease striking lesbians; she also might have been wrong. In any case, such beliefs are not uncommon among lesbians. Hall et al. (cited in Squire, 1993) call lesbians doing AIDS work " 'wives to the gay men's movement' " and mean it as a derogatory remark. Clearly, AIDS via heterosexism and misogyny has also increased divisions among lesbians and heightened tensions between lesbians and gay men (Crimp, 1988).

Capitalism, Heterosexism, and AIDS. In our capitalist society, people with catastrophic diseases are dependent on either expensive, privately financed health care or an inadequate, stigmatizing, government-funded system. Again, class is significant here. People who are poor, even people who are not poor but are underinsured, who get AIDS simply do not receive the kind of preventive and long-term ameliorative care they need (Crystal & Jackson, 1992; Shacknai, 1992). Public hospitals are understaffed to begin with, and the underpaid, often undertrained staff has frequently been too fearful to treat AIDS patients (Hollibaugh, 1995; Jackson & Hunter, 1992; Krieger & Appleman, 1994).

However, even having adequate insurance is not always enough and not always possible. There have been many incidents of HIV-infected people being summarily cut off, *dis*-insured, by the companies they had been paying to insure them (Carrick, 1989; NHeLP, 1991). The excuse has been the costly nature of AIDS treatment—if the insurance company pays the costs, the rates of healthy, "innocent" people will go up. This dis-insuring does not occur, though, for other catastrophic illnesses, even ones caused by irresponsible habits: For example, smoking leads to lung cancer, which is expensive to treat.

Further, private insurance companies have begun redlining gay districts (Jackson, 1992). As lending agencies used to refuse to lend to inner-city and other areas where poor people lived, drawing a red line around such areas, insurance companies refuse to sell insurance in districts presumed to be colonized by gay men.

It is perhaps the zenith of heterosexism that gay couples cannot marry and are then refused family health benefits because they are not married. There is widespread ignorance, as I noted earlier, about the fact that gay sex serves the same purposes as straight sex, notably in family formation, so there is the presumption that gay couples are not family. And there is fear that if gay couples are recognized officially in any way, by marriage, by family health benefits, that gay sexuality will thereby be encouraged and will increase.

So, gay people with HIV may not utilize their partners' health benefits and are dependent on having their own. This is a problem for self-employed people and the many, many in this country whose jobs do not come with good health coverage.

Homo-Hate

It is not always easy to distinguish hate from fear from ignorance. These aspects of heterosexism are intertwined and often, even typically, coexist. However, I think it is especially important to distinguish hateful behavior as much as possible. Ignorance is curable. Even fear can be mollified. Hate requires a very different response.

Although it has been suggested that the public attention to gay people has decreased ignorance and possibly increased empathy, a Gallup Poll in 1987 found that 42% of respondents agreed that AIDS is a divine punishment for sinful behavior (Kahn, 1993). This, of course, demonstrates an ignorance about the disease and who its victims are. It clearly demonstrates hate.

Since the advent of the epidemic and its identification with gay men, there has been an increase in incidents of gay bashing—against both lesbians and gay men. McKenzie (1991) reports a fourfold increase since AIDS; Kahn (1993) cites the New York City Gay and Lesbian Anti-Violence Committee's finding that homophobic assaults increased by 35% from 1987 to 1988. The National Research Council also notes a general increase in anti-gay violence (Miller et al., 1990). According to the National Gay and Lesbian Task Force (Krieger & Appleman, 1994), there is also a rise in anti-gay behavior by *organized* hate groups and by individuals. This is outright, undeniable hate.

We encounter hate even in places it should not have a chance to exist. A hospital patient diagnosed with AIDS had a pamphlet left at his bedside that described homosexuality as a sinful practice (NHeLP, 1991).

A gay male colleague of mine, working in the state health department charged with combating AIDS, was chatting in a shared-use area about some of the responses on our survey. A standard recommendation to gay men engaging in anal sex is to use condoms with the spermicide non-oxynol-9. (The spermicide kills the virus.) A standard recommendation for IDUs is to clean syringes and needles with bleach. One of our respondents was slightly mixed up, referring to non-oxy*dol*-9—Oxydol is brand-name laundry detergent.

On overhearing the comment, a straight, male, senior staff member of this public health agency remarked, "Yeah, you guys *should* use bleach on your condoms." This, too, is hate.

Hate is regularly spewed by politicians. Senator Jesse Helms's name comes up often: " 'We have got to call a spade a spade and a perverted human being a perverted human being' " (Crimp, 1988 p. 261). Pat Buchanan, Reagan's speechwriter, and perennial candidate for president, is another favorite: " 'The poor homosexuals, they have declared war upon nature, and now nature is exacting an awful retribution' " (Krieger & Appleman, 1994, p. 17). I began this chapter with a quote from Congressman Dannemeyer. A "Republican candidate for mayor of Houston, Texas, 'joked' that one of his plans for combating AIDS was to 'shoot the queers' " (Krieger & Appleman, 1994, p. 29).

Homo-hate did not start with AIDS. In many ways, though, both the fear of AIDS and ignorance of gay life have let the hate go unchallenged. Hate-filled people feel much freer, apparently, to act on their hate and to encourage others to hateful acts. Hate is not so easily cured.

Conclusion

I have surveyed many of the ways that hate, ignorance, and fear have cost and continue to cost time—and lives—in combating AIDS; there are many more I did not have space to mention. Heterosexism's intersections and overlaps with misogyny, racism, and classism have increased the number of lives lost and ruined.

At the same time, though, publicity and activity around AIDS have promoted some decrease in ignorance and some decrease in fear in places. Both ignorance and fear are curable, and progress has arguably been made. Progress notwithstanding, the fear and ignorance around AIDS have become an acceptable warrant for hate and hateful behavior. We must conclude that the net effect is devastatingly negative.

This chapter was drafted for conference presentation. I was fortunate to discuss these ideas at the conference workshop with other women working on AIDS issues, as either researchers or practitioners.[3] It was our sense that people are growing tired of hearing about AIDS, of caring about people with the disease. After 15 years, people seem to be angry that there is no cure or vaccine. We fear that people have reached their limit of sympathy. Perhaps we can expect no more decreases in general ignorance but only increases in fear instead. We discussed the possibility that people have begun anew to blame gay men, perhaps lesbians too, for infecting the general population. If so, we may expect even greater increases in hate and hateful acts.

We remained, at the end of our discussion, overwhelmed with the consequences of heterosexism on AIDS and AIDS on heterosexism. We remained without a recommendation for preventing hate.

Notes

1. For this section, I rely primarily on Bayer (1989), Shilts (1987), and Treichler (1988).
2. Human Immuno-Deficiency Virus, the putative cause of AIDS.
3. My thanks to Laura Solomon, Beth Farner, and Jacqueline Weinstock.

References

Adam, B. D. (1992). Sociology and people living with AIDS. In J. Huber & B. Schneider (Eds.), *The social context of AIDS* (pp. 3-18). Newbury Park, CA: Sage.

Albert, E. (1986). Illness and deviance: The response of the press to AIDS. In D. Feldman & T. Johnson (Eds.), *The social dimensions of AIDS: Method and theory* (pp. 163-178). New York: Praeger.

Ames, L. J., Atchinson, A. B., & Rose, D. T. (1994, August). *Community and politics among gay men: Empowerment through AIDS?* Paper presented at the annual meetings of the American Sociological Association, Los Angeles.

Ames, L. J., Atchinson, A. B., & Rose, D. T. (1995). Love, lust, fear: Sexual decision-making among gay men. *Journal of Homosexuality, 30*(1), 53-73.

Ames, L. J., & Beeker, C. (1990a, June). *Gay men in small cities: How risky are they?* Presentation at the Sixth International Conference on AIDS, San Francisco.

Ames, L. J., & Beeker, C. (1990b, October). *What the other guys do: Peer support and AIDS risk reduction.* Paper presented at the annual meetings of the American Public Health Association, New York City.

Banzhaf, M., Chris, C., Christensen, K., Donzig, A., Deneberg, R., Leonard, Z., Levine, D., Lurie, R., Pearl, M., Saalfield, C., Thistlethwaite, P., Walker, J., & Weil, B. (1990). *Women, AIDS, and activism.* Boston: South End.

Bayer, R. (1989). *Private acts, social consequences: AIDS and the politics of public health.* New York: Free Press.

Bersani, L. (1988). Is the rectum a grave? In D. Crimp (Ed.), *AIDS: Cultural analysis, cultural activism* (pp. 197-222). Cambridge: MIT Press.

Carrick, P. (1989). AIDS: Ethical, legal, and public policy implications. In E. Juengst & B. Koenig (Eds.), *The meaning of AIDS: Implications for medical science, clinical practice, and public health policy* (pp. 163-173). New York: Praeger.

Crimp, D. (1988). How to have promiscuity in an epidemic. In D. Crimp (Ed.), *AIDS: Cultural analysis, cultural activism* (pp. 257-270). Cambridge: MIT Press.

Crystal, S., & Jackson, M. (1992). Health care and the social construction of AIDS: The impact of disease definitions. In J. Huber & B. Schneider (Eds.), *The social context of AIDS* (pp. 163-180). Newbury Park, CA: Sage.

Grover, J. Z. (1988). AIDS: Keywords. In D. Crimp (Ed.), *AIDS: Cultural analysis, cultural activism* (pp. 17-30). Cambridge: MIT Press.

Hollibaugh, A. (1995). Lesbian denial and lesbian leadership in the AIDS epidemic: Bravery and fear in the construction of a lesbian geography of risk. In B. Schneider & N. Stoller (Eds.), *Women resisting AIDS: Feminist strategies of empowerment* (pp. 219-230). Philadelphia, PA: Temple University Press.

Jackson, M. H. (1992). Health insurance: The battle over limits on coverage. In N. Hunter & W. Rubenstein (Eds.), *AIDS agenda: Emerging issues in civil rights* (pp. 147-179). New York: New Press.

Jackson, M. H., & Hunter, N. D. (1992). "The very fabric of health care": The duty of health care providers to treat people infected by HIV. In N. Hunter & W. Rubenstein (Eds.), *AIDS agenda: Emerging issues in civil rights* (pp. 123-146). New York: New Press.

Kahn, A. D. (1993). *AIDS, the winter war.* Philadelphia, PA: Temple University Press.

Kayal, P. M. (1993). *Bearing witness: Gay men's health crisis and the politics of AIDS.* Boulder, CO: Westview.

Kelly, J. A., St. Lawrence, J. S., Hood, H. V., & Brasfield, T. L. (1989). Behavioral intervention to reduce AIDS risk activities. *Journal of Consulting and Clinical Psychology, 57,* 60-67.

Koenig, B. A., & Cooke, M. (1989). Physician response to a new, lethal, and presumably infectious disease: Medical residents and the AIDS epidemic in San Francisco. In E. Juengst & B. Koenig (Eds.), *The meaning of AIDS: Implications for medical science, clinical practice, and public health policy* (pp. 72-85). New York: Praeger.

Kramer, L. (1991). The plague years. In N. F. McKenzie (Ed.), *The AIDS reader: Social, political, and ethical issues* (pp. 113-121). New York: Meridian.

Krieger, N., & Appleman, R. (1994). The politics of AIDS. In N. Krieger & G. Margo (Eds.), *AIDS: The politics of survival* (pp. 3-52). Amityville, NY: Baywood.

McKenzie, N. F. (1991). Introduction: The demands of the HIV epidemic. In N. F. McKenzie (Ed.), *The AIDS reader: Social, political, and ethical issues* (pp. 1-16). New York: Meridian.

Maslanka, H. (1993). Women volunteers at GMHC. In C. Squire (Ed.), *Women and AIDS: Psychological perspectives* (pp. 110-125). Newbury Park, CA: Sage.

Miles, S. (1995, July/August). And the bathhouse played on. *OUT, 24,* 86-91, 128-134, 137-138.

Miller, H. G., Turner, C. F., & Moses, L. E. (Eds.). (1990). *AIDS: The second decade.* Washington, DC: National Academy Press.

Moss, A. R. (1989). Coercive and voluntary policies in the AIDS epidemic. In E. Juengst & B. Koenig (Eds.), *The meaning of AIDS: Implications for medical science, clinical practice, and public health policy* (pp. 174-183). New York: Praeger.

Navarre, M. (1988). Fighting the victim label: PWA coalition portfolio. In D. Crimp (Ed.), *AIDS: Cultural analysis, cultural activism* (pp. 143-168). Cambridge: MIT Press.

NHeLP (National Health Law Program). (1991). Health benefits: How the system is responding to AIDS. In N. F. McKenzie (Ed.), *The AIDS reader: Social, political, and ethical issues* (pp. 247-272). New York: Meridian.

Patton, C. (1993). "With champagne and roses": Women at risk from/in AIDS discourse. In C. Squire (Ed.), *Women and AIDS: Psychological perspectives* (pp. 165-187). Newbury Park, CA: Sage.

Shacknai, D. (1992). Wealth = health: The public financing of AIDS care. In N. Hunter & W. Rubenstein (Eds.), *AIDS agenda: Emerging issues in civil rights* (pp. 181-201). New York: New Press.

Shilts, R. (1987). *And the band played on: Politics, people, and the AIDS epidemic.* New York: Penguin.

Sosnowitz, B. G. (1995). AIDS prevention, minority women, and gender assertiveness. In B. Schneider & N. Stoller (Eds.), *Women resisting AIDS: Feminist strategies of empowerment* (pp. 139-161). Philadelphia, PA: Temple University Press.

Squire, C. (1993). Introduction. In C. Squire (Ed.), *Women and AIDS: Psychological perspectives* (pp. 1-15). Newbury Park, CA: Sage.

Stoller, N. E. (1995). Lesbian involvement in the AIDS epidemic: Changing roles and generational differences. In B. Schneider & N. Stoller (Eds.), *Women resisting AIDS: Feminist strategies of empowerment* (pp. 270-285). Philadelphia, PA: Temple University Press.

Treichler, P. (1988). AIDS, homophobia, and biomedical discourse: An epidemic of signification. In D. Crimp (Ed.), *AIDS: Cultural analysis, cultural activism* (pp. 31-71). Cambridge: MIT Press.

Turner, C. F., Miller, H. G., & Moses, L. E. (Eds.). (1989). *AIDS: Sexual behavior and intravenous drug use*. Washington, DC: National Academy Press.

Watney, S. (1988). The spectacle of AIDS. In D. Crimp (Ed.), *AIDS: Cultural analysis, cultural activism* (pp. 71-86). Cambridge: MIT Press.

14

Individual Action and Political Strategies: Creating a Future Free of Heterosexism

Joy A. Livingston

Heterosexism is the system of institutions that supports heterosexuality as the norm and treats any other sexual identity as either nonexistent or abnormal. Heterosexism is intimately linked with sexism—they are two systems of oppression that rely on one another.

Sexism is the belief system that supports patriarchy: the rule of men over women. Sexism asserts that men are more valuable and more important than women and, therefore, men should rule over women. Included in and crucial to men's right to rule over women is control of women's sexuality. Indeed, patriarchy depends on compulsory heterosexuality to ensure that men maintain power over women.

The Future Without Heterosexism

What would the future look like without heterosexism? My attempt to imagine a future free of heterosexism began with thinking of a world without the daily annoyances:

- I would not wake to read in the morning paper that the U.S. President's security guards wore rubber gloves when gay and lesbian elected officials came to call.
- My sweetheart and I would dance together at my nephew's bar mitzvah without a second thought. It would not be an act of defiance.
- My friends who teach young children would not hide their faces from the cameras when we gathered as an obvious group of blatant lesbians.

253

- A local library would not have to fight over making the book *Daddy's Room-mate* available to children. Letters to the editor about this struggle would not refer to me and my kind as "mankind's perversities."

Still, my future vision was not well formed. Of course, it would be wonderful to be free of all the daily reminders that I am not entitled to full rights of citizenship. But I wanted more; I wanted to imagine a future worth fighting for, a future that could be described by what it had, not what it lacked.

I began by thinking about relationships. In the future free of heterosexism I imagined, people would live in all types of families. We would be judged on whether there is love in our hearts, not on the gender of the persons we love. Some of us would live with a single partner, others would live alone, still others would live with multiple partners. Some families would have children, others would not. Social, economic, and political institutions would not require any one type of configuration or sexual identity.

In this future free of heterosexism I imagined, gender would not determine who one could be or what one could do, any more than would race or ethnicity. Our sexual identity, our gender, our race, our ethnicity, and other important characteristics would remain important but would not determine our opportunities in either the public or the private world. In this future, it would still be important to me that I am Jewish and lesbian and female. I would maintain a sense of these identities by ritual and separatist gatherings. I would be part of a culturally rich community that celebrated diversity, not by eliminating but by nurturing differences.

As I began to imagine this future (with the aid of my favorite reading material, feminist science fiction), the picture went far beyond identity and relationships.

Were we to achieve a world free of heterosexism, there would also be no hunger. Everyone would have a decent place to live, with plenty of sunshine and quiet spaces. We would all have meaningful, satisfying work that did not require sacrificing time with ourselves and loved ones. We would all have clean air to breath, good water to drink, and plenty of healthy soil. Our food would be grown locally, without chemicals. We would prosper in harmony with all the other creatures of the earth. Indeed, the earth would be healthy and well loved in this future free of heterosexism.

Children would grow up in safety, with plenty of opportunity to explore and create. Women would live in safety without restrictions on our mobility. Sexuality would be celebrated as beautiful and life affirming.

In this future free of heterosexism, love, compassion, and pleasure would be primary values, rather than power, control, and profit. Dominant power would be obsolete.

This future is not just the stuff of feminist science fiction. It is the vision I work toward. To get to a future free of heterosexism, we must begin with a clear vision. Then we have to figure out how to get from here to there.

Systems of Oppression

To get from our present heterosexism to a future free of heterosexism, we have to understand fully the barriers in our way. We need to understand heteropatriarchy and heterosexism. This complex system has been in place for some 3,000 to 4,000 years. One tool that has kept it in place these many years is the belief that heteropatriarchy is the one and only way we can organize human society. First, we must remember that heterosexism has not and will not always exist. As long as we think heterosexist patriarchy is inevitable, we are limited to reform rather than real change. It is imperative that we know it is not inevitable; it is a social, economic, and political system of enormous power, but it is not the will of God. With enormous effort, it can be defeated.

Fundamentally, heterosexism is about power. Of course, so too are all systems of oppression. They are all about one group (the oppressors) having and maintaining power over another group (the oppressed). Having power can be very rewarding for the oppressors; it provides economic advantage, psychological benefits, and other rewards. As Jean Baker Miller (1978) has so clearly pointed out, those in power see it as a just and right system and often do not acknowledge the power they hold. The system is justified by rationalizing that it is normal and right for those in power to have that power. For example, heterosexuality is named normal, homosexuality a perversion. Men are defined as more rational and therefore better equipped to be in charge. White people are said to be better able to govern themselves than people of color. And so on.

Heterosexism is about dominant power. All dominant power systems and their resultant oppressions are interconnected. I will address three of these issues in relation to heterosexism: sex, race, and class.

Sex

Sexism relies on heterosexism. The clearest explanation of this link is found in Adrienne Rich's work on compulsory heterosexuality. In essence, Rich (1980) argues that compulsory heterosexuality is at the root of women's oppression, because it keeps women dependent on men and maintains "male right of physical, economical, and emotional access."

Several factors make heterosexuality compulsory. First is the set of myths that assert it is "only natural." Note that in systems of oppression, those in power are seen as the normal and superior persons. All our institutions argue that heterosexuality is "inevitable"; all normal women will want sexual relations with men, and then marriage (which, of course, is key to patriarchy). These institutions say women *need* men for psychic completion, for "normal" sexuality (read vaginal penetration). And, of course, only "sick" women do not want men. If the myths are not enough, then lesbian existence is distorted or erased to ensure it is either an invisible or an unattractive option.

Although patriarchy has plenty of material conditions that ensure its survival, it also makes certain to capture women psychologically. Compulsory heterosexuality is part of both material and psychological oppression. It maintains the belief that men are central to women's happiness and survival—that women *need* men.

The false notion that women need men has many consequences. It encourages horizontal hostility among women (i.e., competition, distrust, dislike). It makes it possible for women to betray their sisters in favor of men. It undermines women's autonomous organizations and makes many women wonder "what about the men?"

When women are self-defined, men are not needed; they are, in fact, irrelevant, which is treason to patriarchy. Therefore, self-defined women are treated like traitors—nonwomen. Regardless of their self-definition, they are named lesbian, which is to say, not real women. All independent women, women who speak out for women, who value women, are so labeled. Gloria Steinem (1986, p. 7) once said, "I had rejected the idea of patriarchy and the power of men to define and restrict women—therefore I must be a lesbian. What else could a non-male defined woman possibly be?"

Race

Racism also supports the heteropatriarchal structure. It, too, identifies the superior and inferior people, those with power and those without power. As many women of color have so clearly articulated, we cannot understand sexism without understanding racism.

Consider the following example. We often identify reproductive rights and the right to choose as central to women's control of our lives and bodies. Indeed, the same patriarchal powers that seek to control women's lives through control of our reproduction seek to control all women's lives through control of their sexuality. But many of us often forget that Margaret Sanger's early efforts to make birth control accessible to women were actually focused on decreasing pregnancies among women of color and immigrant women. Sanger was part of the movement to improve the breeding stock, which was defined as increasing the number of white children. Today, we see the same value of white babies over babies of color when enormous resources are invested in white women conceiving babies, using artificial insemination and other technologies, but women of color are sterilized and compelled to use contraceptives. Both lesbians and heterosexual women who are choosing to have children must address these issues.

Not only do racism and heterosexism link throughout social, political, and economic structures, but heterosexism also operates in communities of color as it does in white communities. Lesbians and gay men of color, like their white sisters and brothers, face heterosexism in their own communities. I cannot speak directly to the experience of gays and lesbians of color, but I can speak as a Jewish lesbian (and I believe we share some similar dynamics of oppression). Each year at our Seder, we tell the story of Puah and how there came to be a bit of *humitz* (unleavened bread) on the Seder plate. To make a long story short, Puah asked the rabbi what place there was for a lesbian in Judaism. He was beside himself with rage and answered that there was as much place for a lesbian in Judaism as for *humitz* on the Seder plate. After much mourning at this terrible loss, Puah solved the problem. She placed a bit of bread (*humitz*) on the Seder plate, and all rejoiced that she had found a place in Judaism.

We understand that a place in our communities is more than something that makes us feel good; it is essential to our survival. As a Jewish lesbian, I need my Jewish community as much as my lesbian community.

Another example of the link between oppressions is AIDS. Significantly more people of color have died of this so-called gay disease than have gay men. It is only heterosexual white people who are called "innocent victims" of this horrific virus.

Class

Perhaps it all boils down to economics. Certainly, we can understand much of the heteropatriarchal structure if we look for the profit makers. Oppressors do not oppress only because it makes them feel superior and righteous; they also make money. There are many discussions that outline the ways in which sexism supports capitalism through women's low wages, unpaid labor, and so on (e.g., Enloe, 1989; hooks, 1984; Waring, 1988). Here I will focus on understanding the links between heterosexism and economic structures.

The most obvious link is that lesbians are women. To the extent that women earn lower wages, have access to a more limited number of occupations, and generally fare more poorly than men do economically, so too do lesbians. When lesbians live with partners, their dual incomes are lower than that of heterosexual couples, because they do not have a male wage earner. Lesbians are among the single mothers receiving public benefits (welfare) to support themselves and their children. When public officials and angry white men charge into their war on the poor, lesbians too suffer.

The capitalist system needs heteropatriarchy. It provides the rationale for low-paid women workers and the fodder for factories essential to profits. It is no wonder the same structure maintains heterosexism as part of maintaining patriarchy. Gay men and lesbians who have not been hired or have lost jobs because of their sexual identity are well aware of this link.

Of course, we see the link when gay and lesbian employees do not receive equal pay for equal work. This occurs primarily in terms of employee benefits, especially health care insurance. But when we talk about health care insurance, we begin to touch on the complexities of interconnected systems of oppression. At present, only those with health care insurance can afford good quality health care. That insurance coverage is linked to certain types of employment (permanent, full-time). Although I believe in equal pay for equal work and therefore support extending health care coverage to the families and partners of gay and lesbian employees, I think it is essential to recognize this does not address the problem of access to health care for all citizens.

Understanding the links and interconnections among all types of oppression is vital to understanding how heterosexism works. Radical right wing Christian fundamentalist groups understand these links very well. These groups denigrate people of color, Jews, queers, and feminists alike. They understand that all movements to end oppression seek to topple the patriarchal structure, the power of some people to dominate others.

Fighting Against Systems of Oppression

Before we examine specific individual actions and political strategies for fighting oppression and systemic injustice, it is useful to outline the ways in which oppressors respond to change efforts.

When oppressed people rise up and protest the system's injustice, the oppressors squash the protest and maintain the status quo. If the oppressors want to instill fear, they use violence. Dissidents are jailed, tortured, and murdered. We are regularly reminded of these tactics in repressive regimes throughout the world, but they are also used here at home. Gay and lesbian youths are institutionalized to cure them of their evil ways; ACT UP is closely followed by the FBI; poor women are forced to use contraceptives or are involuntarily sterilized. In the United States, the tactics are more subtle but still designed to repress revolt.

In the United States, however, more often the oppressors either discount and trivialize the protest or attribute nonexistent power to the oppressed. This strategy allows the oppressors to maintain the fallacy that the system is operating in a just and right way and that the protests of injustice are ill-founded and misguided. Increasingly, right-wing Christian fundamentalist groups have taken on this work for those in power and, of course, the media have always been key players. The following are some examples of this tactic:

- Feminists are trivialized and called "libbers" or demonized and called "feminazis." Either we are a silly bunch of girls who want to use boys' bathrooms or we are tyrants requiring all men to sacrifice their genitals to the alter of feminine power.

- People of color who protest racism are labeled angry and unreasonable, often reported as creating a problem where none exists, because race does not matter in our color-blind society. Or people of color are accused of practicing reverse discrimination and either taking away white people's economic opportunities or making white people feel uncomfortable.

- Gays and lesbians who fight for their rights are portrayed as making a big deal about nothing; who cares who you sleep with anyway? Or they are portrayed as wielding incredible power to "impose" their morals and lifestyle on unsuspecting youths and adults.

- According to many angry white men, women on welfare have consolidated enough power to have caused the current national economic crisis. If a welfare mother protests the injustice of federal funds supporting wealthy defense contractors rather than feeding her children, she is ungrateful and lazy. When low- and middle-income earners protest tax breaks for the wealthy, they are creating class warfare.

Whatever the protest, when oppressors trivialize or shift blame, they effectively divert attention from the system of oppression. When the protests grow too numerous and widespread to resist with discounting tactics, oppressors often resort to appeasement that is carefully designed to keep the system intact while reducing resistance from the oppressed.

For example, Roosevelt's New Deal was really about maintaining capitalism in the face of rising working-class power. Adding two white women to the Supreme Court and a few women to the Congress is about pretending women can achieve whatever they want. Allowing gay men and lesbians in the military as long as they "don't tell" was a failed attempt to appease.

Although appeasement is often reform in the right direction, it does not change the system of oppression. Reform does not shift the balance of power. It allows the oppressors to maintain their power without fundamentally altering social, economic, or political structures.

Systems of oppression are carefully maintained by those in power, in part by ensuring that there is not a careful analysis of social, economic, and political structures. Those in power use many tactics to ensure that we do not understand who benefits at whose expense. Those in power make sure we do not name the oppressors. Oppressors are very careful to describe the system as agentless; somehow there is this system that is a bit unfair now and then, but there are no specific actors who are responsible for or benefit from the system of oppression. To create a future free of heterosexism, we must name the oppressors.

Individual Actions

Individually, each of us can act toward creating a future free of heterosexism. We need to understand that if we limit ourselves to individual action alone, we are only chipping away at a system and will not likely create a significant change. Nevertheless, we can make individual contributions while also participating in collective political strategies.

In all our actions, we must operate from an understanding that all oppressions are linked. We cannot fight for our rights as gays and lesbians without also resisting racism and anti-Semitism. We must understand that the war on the poor is a gay and lesbian issue.

We each must take personal responsibility to educate ourselves so that we understand these links. There are many sorts of opportunities to read books, attend conferences, and participate in workshops both within and outside of academic circles.

It is the responsibility of each of us to educate ourselves rather than rely only on those facing oppression to be our teachers or serve as the experts. At any one time, I might feel like talking about lesbian experience or anti-Semitism—or I might not. Don't impose on me your story of your uncle's anti-Semitic or homophobic remark; determine whether I want to talk about it with you first. If I do not, remember that is my right; you are not entitled to my time and energy. Again, it is the responsibility of each of us to learn about oppression and the links between systems of oppression.

We must understand that fighting against heterosexism will not be popular with the power holders. As I have outlined, oppressors battle against attempts to change systems of oppression by repressing, discounting, and appeasing protesters. Understand those responses, rely on your creativity, and realize that fighting oppression will not make you popular.

I often hear myself and others talk of trying to be effective. *Effective* means speaking in words that people can hear and taking action that will make a difference. I've come to believe we cannot be effective, as we've defined it, for several reasons.

First, no matter what words I use, someone who does not want to hear me will not; actually, I can thank my father for teaching me this lesson. Someone who does not want to hear will come up with any number of excuses for not hearing: Your approach is alienating; your sample size is too small and not representative; you are not being objective.

Second, taking reasonable action that has results assumes that there is a just system that we can change if only we play by some set of rules; we just have to figure out what the rules are. The system is not just and though there are rules, they are designed to prevent us from creating any meaningful changes.

Finally, being effective generally is code for playing by the rules—and that means keeping quiet. It means controlling our rage and harnessing whatever power we might have so that we behave properly. I have found that I reach many more people if I speak from my passion and rage. We have to identify the oppressors and not worry about sparing feelings. This is an issue of power and exploitation—it is not about manners.

Individually, we must be willing to take risks. As so many people have pointed out, struggling against oppression is not always fun and easy. It means being willing to make mistakes and to hear from others that we have said or done something offensive. It means making a commitment to action and facing our fears. We cannot take action without taking risks.

Audre Lorde (1988) urged us to use our privilege in the service of the things we say we believe in. It was the best advice I've heard on how to take individual action toward fighting oppression.

To me, her advice means speaking out against oppression that does not necessarily focus directly on you as the oppressed. If you are heterosexual, it means speaking out when you hear an anti-gay joke or standing up to publicly protest a heterosexist policy in your institution. If you are a white woman, it means speaking out every time someone around you makes a racist remark, whether with family members, coworkers, or students.

Use your privilege in the service of the things you say you believe in. Don't wait for an outraged graduate student to challenge sexist, racist, or heterosexist policies in your institution. If you are a tenured faculty member, use your position to take a stand, regardless of what labels this will earn you from your colleagues.

Use your resources and communication skills to resist oppression. Write letters, call congressional representatives, donate money, and attend political rallies. These are not acts of altruism; you will feel powerful every time you do them.

Use your privilege in the service of the things you say you believe in. Connect with community groups and share your resources. Include among your committee responsibilities a private nonprofit board in your community working on women's safety, workers' rights, AIDS, or other issues of oppression. Commit time outside your professional institution; you have incredible skills to share and you have access to resources. Share your copier, fax, Internet connection. Talk to people outside the institution and ask them what kind of research would help their efforts. Make yourself useful.

If you are heterosexual, become aware of the way you use your privilege every day. Try to go an entire week without revealing the gender of your spouse (this includes references to in-laws). Each time you meet a new person, do not assume you know his or her sexual orientation. Think about the questions you ask and the choices you are asking people to make. For example, a few years ago I took a course with 20 other women. The introductory question to break the ice and get us talking concerned our families. As we went around the circle, each woman talked about her children and husband, boyfriend, or ex. When it came time for me to speak, I had to decide whether to come out in this first introduction. As all gays and lesbians know how to do, I talked about my life and my partner without revealing her gender. But of course, the fact that I was the only person to avoid identifying gender marked me just as well.

If you are not heterosexual, come out. Visibility is essential. Ask yourself if you really do need to stay silent: What will happen if you come out? Obviously, there are times when silence will allow you to keep your children, your job, your home, and perhaps even your life. But there are many times when we choose silence without that level of risk. We need to take risks and by so doing make coming out less and less risky.

Political Strategy

Political strategy must be based on a clear analysis and the goal of eliminating heteropatriarchy if we are to eliminate heterosexism. I am very concerned to see much of recent political strategy based on the notion that lesbians and gay men are just like heterosexuals. The only difference between us is our choice of sexual partners, and that is actually not even a choice but something over which we have no control. This position does nothing to challenge heteropatriarchy nor does it accurately represent our lives as lesbians and gay men.

Gay, lesbian, and bisexual people are not just like heterosexuals. Our sexual identity is far more than our sexual partners. I was a lesbian long before I slept with a woman and I will continue to be a lesbian if I lose my partner. I love women, I prefer the company of women, my sense of myself and my social life are very much organized around my lesbianism. Any lesbian or gay man, and probably any heterosexual, could tell you immediately whether they just walked into a gay, lesbian, or straight crowd. The energy is absolutely different.

Our difference as lesbians and gay men is part of our challenge to heteropatriarchy. We must not discount that difference. We must organize as lesbians and gay men for our human and equal rights, not because we are the same as heterosexuals but because we are different. A future free of heterosexism must include us as full citizens, regardless of our differences.

Moreover, we are about equal rights, not because we cannot help but be queer but because we are human beings. The only reason people have ever wanted to know why I turned out to be a lesbian was so they could figure out what went wrong and how they could fix me. The question of why we are queer is completely irrelevant. Do we oppose anti-Semitism only if it is directed against Jews born into Judaism and not if it is directed against those who are Jews by choice? Our rights cannot be based on the origins of our sexual identity. If so, we support heteropatriarchy by allowing the system to determine who is deserving and who is not.

Politically, we must recognize the difference between reform and revolution. I was quite involved in the effort to extend health benefits to the lesbian and gay partners of my state university's faculty and staff. It was a matter of equal pay for equal work. But this was merely a reform effort. We won, but we did not really change any systems. We did not make any progress toward extending decent health care to all citizens as a right rather than a privilege of certain selective employment. We did not change institutional support of marriage except that now, with the prescribed certification and criteria, gays and lesbians can fit.

Many of our political goals are, in fact, reforms rather than revolutionary change. The best example of this is the recent attempt to legalize gay and lesbian marriages. Such an effort merely extends heteropatriarchy into the gay and lesbian community. Now we, too, can join the state-sanctioned institution designed to oppress women. Marriage is about men's ownership and power over women. Rather than seek to join this oppressive institution, we must work to change systems so that we do not need state recognition to have access to health care, the right to participate in decisions about our partners' lives, and other legal benefits that accrue to married heterosexuals. Cultural and familial recognition for our lives and loves will not be granted through state-recognized marriage. That is an ongoing struggle, regardless of our right to marry.

We must organize politically with full understanding of the social, economic, and political power structure that maintains heteropatriarchy. We must distinguish between politics and community. Certainly, there are gay men and lesbians with conservative political views. I have heard gay men and lesbians talk about inclusiveness and making room for all political perspectives. Indeed, in our social gatherings and community building, we might concern ourselves with inclusiveness of all political views but not in political organizing. Politically, we must operate from an analysis that clearly identifies the structures of power and the agents of oppression. We have to understand that eliminating heterosexism and homophobia *requires* the elimination of sexism, racism, and class oppression. Politically, we cannot allow elected officials to buy our votes by supporting gay rights bills but defeating minimum wage increases, welfare benefits, environmental protections, and so on. Make no mistake about it, the Contract on America will not help us create a future free of heterosexism. Conservative politics, whether espoused by Republicans or Democrats, supports heteropatriarchy.

We must remember we are talking about overthrowing power structures. We are fighting power, not attitudes. Our political strategies cannot rely on education and attempts to change attitudes alone. Oppressors will not stop oppressing just because it is the right thing to do.

Liberal reformers understood this in the 19th century. They moved from trying to convince people that reform was the right thing to do into organizing. Women won the vote because of very powerful organizing; it was not given to us. We marched and tore up golf courses, we had hunger strikes while in jail, and we made it impossible for key elected officials to move without hearing about votes for women.

We must organize, organize, organize. Organizing is the only way social progress has ever been made. It is because gays and lesbians have been organizing since Stonewall that we can assemble and publish a volume such as this one or conduct the conference from which it arose. Mental health professionals did not decide to make homosexuality sane because they saw the light; they could not resist the political tide.

As we organize, we must remember that all oppressions are linked. We will not win this fight on one issue alone. Coalitions are essential. We must work against racism and class oppression as well as sexism and the myriad other oppressions if we are to create a future free of heterosexism. Coalition work requires a commitment to address a wide range of issues; it means making certain gay and lesbian rights organizations take a stand on the war on the poor. It also means holding our allies responsible for remembering our issues. I work for abortion rights and I expect my heterosexual sisters to work for the Employment Non-Discrimination Act.

In these times of hate and meanness, remember that fighting to create a future free of heterosexism is fighting *for* love and compassion. In the reign of the Contract on America, we mostly find ourselves fighting against and resisting virulent forms of heterosexism, sexism, racism, and class oppression. I think the heteropatriarchal system works to keep us focused on these daily battles for survival; it ensures that we merely plod along, often burned out and depressed.

It is a revolutionary act to continue envisioning a future free of heterosexism and to continue believing we can make it happen. I believe we can make it happen. We can use our resources to act individually and collectively, based on a clear political strategy that understands that all oppressions are linked. We must remind ourselves and others that we are not fighting for a world of restrictions. We are fighting for a world that celebrates love and compassion, a world in which each person truly lives in freedom.

References

Enloe, C. (1989). *Bananas, beaches, and bases: Making feminist sense of international politics.* Berkeley: University of California Press.

hooks, b. (1984). *Feminist theory: From margin to center.* Boston: South End.

Lorde, A. (1988, June). Panel discussion at the annual meeting of the National Women's Studies Association, University of Minnesota, Minneapolis.

Miller, J. B. (1978). *Toward a new psychology of women.* Boston: Beacon.

Rich, A. (1980). Compulsory heterosexuality and lesbian existence. *Signs: Journal of Women in Culture and Society, 5*(4), 631-660.

Steinem, G. (1986) The politics of supporting lesbianism. *Newsletter of the Boston Bisexual Women's Network, 4*(5), pp. 1, 7-9.

Waring, M. (1988). *If women counted: A new feminist economics.* San Francisco: Harper & Row.

Index

About the Contributors

Lynda J. Ames, Ph.D., is Assistant Professor of Sociology at the State University of New York, Plattsburgh. She has conducted research on the responses of gay men to the AIDS crisis for the New York State Department of Health, AIDS Institute. She also conducts research on gender equity in pay-setting systems and has written a book on the empowerment of women in poverty (forthcoming).

Lynne A. Bond, Ph.D., is Professor of Psychology at the University of Vermont. Her research, publications, and teaching have focused on strategies for optimizing human development, with emphasis on social and cognitive development of women and children, gender development, and primary prevention approaches. She is president of the Vermont Conferences on the Primary Prevention of Psychopathology, Inc., and has edited seven volumes in its publication series.

Laura S. Brown, Ph.D., is a clinical forensic psychologist in private practice and Clinical Professor of Psychology at the University of Washington. She has published and taught extensively on the topics of feminist therapy, theory, ethics, and practice, and on psychotherapy with lesbians. In 1995, she received an award for distinguished professional contributions from the American Psychological Association.

Connie S. Chan, Ph.D., is Associate Professor of Human Services at the College of Public and Community Service at the University of Massachusetts Boston, where she is also co-director of the Institute for Asian American Studies, an institute that conducts research, policy, and curriculum development on Asian American issues. Her research and publications focus upon the intersection of gender, culture, and sexuality issues in Asian American women.

Jeanine C. Cogan, Ph.D., is conducting postdoctoral research at the University of California, Davis on the mental health consequences of anti-gay/anti-lesbian hate crimes. Most of her professional work has focused on experiences of marginalized and stigmatized groups. Her interests are diverse

279

and include the consequences of the social construction of beauty, the experiences of women with a chronic mental illness, the interdependence of feminism and sexual identity, AIDS-related stigma as an obstacle to prevention strategies, and cross-cultural research.

Anthony R. D'Augelli, Ph.D., is Professor of Human Development at the Pennsylvania State University. A community/clinical psychologist, his extensive research and writing focus on helping processes in community settings. Most recently, he has studied lesbian, gay, and bisexual youths. Along with Charlotte J. Patterson, he is the coeditor of *Lesbian, Gay, and Bisexual Identities Over the Lifespan: Psychological Perspectives.*

Oliva M. Espín, Ph.D., is Professor of Women's Studies at San Diego State University and part-time core faculty member at the California School of Professional Psychology. She has published on psychotherapy with Latinas, immigrant and refugee women, women's sexuality, and other topics. She has recently coedited *Refugee Women and Their Mental Health: Shattered Societies, Shattered Lives.* Her book, *Power, Culture, and Tradition: The Lives of Immigrant Latina Healers,* is forthcoming. She is past president of the Society for the Psychological Study of Lesbian and Gay Issues.

Beverly Greene, Ph.D., is Professor of Psychology at St. John's University and a clinical psychologist in private practice in New York City. In addition, she is coeditor of *Women of Color: Integrating Ethnic and Gender Identities in Psychotherapy.* She is coeditor of the American Psychological Association Division 44 series of annual publications, *Psychological Perspectives on Lesbian and Gay Issues.* She is also a contributor to professional books and journals and the recipient of national awards for professional contributions.

Celia Kitzinger, Ph.D., is Director of Women's Studies at Loughborough University, United Kingdom. In addition to numerous articles on lesbian and feminist issues, she authored *The Social Construction of Lesbianism,* which won a Distinguished Publication Award from the Association for Women in Psychology. She is coauthor (with Rachel Perkins) of *Changing Our Minds: Lesbian Feminism and Psychology,* and with Sue Wilkinson is coeditor of *Heterosexuality: A "Feminism & Psychology" Reader.*

Joy A. Livingston, Ph.D., is a consultant, providing needs assessment and evaluation research, project management, and group facilitation to a variety of human service organizations on such issues as HIV/AIDS, children's mental health, women's economic status, and disability rights. As a lesbian feminist activist, she has worked on a number of issues, including implementation of the University of Vermont's nondiscrimination policy regarding health care benefits for lesbian and gay employees.

Charlotte J. Patterson, Ph.D., is Associate Professor of Psychology at the University of Virginia. Her Bay Area Families Study is an ongoing examination of psychosocial development among children who were born to or adopted by lesbian mothers. She coedited (with Anthony R. D'Augelli) the book titled *Lesbian, Gay, and Bisexual Identities Over the Lifespan: Psychological Perspectives.* She was guest editor for the January 1995 special issue of *Developmental Psychology,* devoted to research on sexual orientation and human development.

Rachel E. Perkins, Ph.D., is Clinical Director of Services for people with serious ongoing mental health problems, with Pathfinder NHS Trust, London. She was formerly a lecturer in clinical psychology at the Institute of Psychiatry, University of London. She has written widely on topics relating to serious long-term mental health problems, with a specific focus on women and lesbians with such difficulties. With Celia Kitzinger, she wrote *Changing Our Minds: Lesbian Feminism and Psychology.*

Suzanna Rose, Ph.D., is Associate Professor of Psychology and Women's Studies at the University of Missouri-St. Louis. Her research focuses primarily on how gender, sexual orientation, and race affect romantic relationships, sexuality, and friendship. She founded the St. Louis Lesbian and Gay Research Project and is Director of the St. Louis Lesbian and Gay Anti-Violence Project, which provides help for survivors of hate crimes.

Michael W. Ross, Ph.D., M.P.H., M.H.P.E.D., is Professor of Public Health in the Center for Health Promotion Research and Development at the University of Texas at Houston. He is the author of numerous scientific papers, book chapters, and books on STDs, HIV, sexuality, psychology, drug use and minorities, and HIV/AIDS-related burnout. He served as head of the AIDS Program for the South Australian Health Commission and later was director of the National Center in HIV Social Research Unit at the University of New South Wales.

Esther D. Rothblum, Ph.D., is Professor of Pyschology at the University of Vermont. Her research and writing have focused on lesbian mental health and other mental health issues of particular relevance to women. Her journal and book publications include the edited volumes *Loving Boldly: Issues Facing Lesbians,* and *Boston Marriages: Romantic But Asexual Relationships Among Contemporary Lesbians.* Since 1984, she has been coeditor of the journal *Women and Therapy,* and she is editor of the new *Journal of Lesbian Studies.*

Paula C. Rust, Ph.D., is Associate Professor of Sociology at Hamilton College in Clinton, New York, where she teaches lesbian, bisexual, gay, and transgender studies. Her research focuses on the formation of sexual identities, communities, and politics, and on the internal politics of sexual and gender minority communities. She is the author of the book *Bisexuality and the Challenge to Lesbian Politics: Sex, Loyalty, and Revolution,* and a 1993 article in *Gender & Society* challenging linear developmental models of sexual identity formation. She is studying the process by which bisexual people construct bisexual identities and use these identities as the foundation for bisexual communities and politics.